THE LOCAL GOVERNANCE OF CRIME:
APPEALS TO COMMUNITY AND PARTNERSHIPS

CLARENDON STUDIES IN CRIMINOLOGY

Published under the auspices of the Institute of Criminology, University of Cambridge, the Mannheim Centre, London School of Economics, and the Centre for Criminological Research, University of Oxford

GENERAL EDITOR: ROGER HOOD (University of Oxford)

EDITORS: ANTHONY BOTTOMS and TREVOR BENNETT
(University of Cambridge)

DAVID DOWNES and PAUL ROCK
(London School of Economics)

LUCIA ZEDNER and RICHARD YOUNG
(University of Oxford)

Recent titles in this series:

Prisons and the Problem of Order
SPARKS, BOTTOMS, and HAY

Law in Policing: Legal Regulation and Police Practices
DIXON

Policing the Risk Society
ERICSON and HAGGERTY

Crime in Ireland 1945–95: Here be Dragons
BREWER, LOCKHART, and RODGERS

Sexed Work: Gender, Race and Resistance in a Brooklyn Drug Market
MAHER

Reconstructing a Women's Prison
PAUL ROCK

Forthcoming titles:

Victims of White Collar Crime: The Social and Media Construction of Business Fraud
LEVI and PITHOUSE

Procedural Fairness at the Police Station
CHOONGH

THE LOCAL GOVERNANCE OF CRIME:

Appeals to Community and Partnerships

Adam Crawford

CLARENDON PRESS · OXFORD
1997

Oxford University Press, Great Clarendon Street, Oxford ox2 6DP
Oxford New York
Athens Auckland Bangkok Bogota Bombay
Buenos Aires Calcutta Cape Town Dar es Salaam
Delhi Florence Hong Kong Istanbul Karachi
Kuala Lumpur Madras Madrid Melbourne
Mexico City Nairobi Paris Singapore
Taipei Tokyo Toronto
and associated companies in
Berlin Ibadan

Oxford is a trade mark of Oxford University Press

Published in the United States
by Oxford University Press Inc., New York

British Library Cataloguing in Publication Data
Data available

Library of Congress Cataloging in Publication Data
Crawford, Adam.
The local governance of crime : appeals to community and
partnerships / Thomas Adam Michael Crawford.
p. cm.—(Clarendon studies in criminology)
Includes bibliographical references and index.
1. Crime prevention—Great Britain—Citizen participation.
2. Criminal justice, Administration of—Great Britain—Citizen
participation. I. Title. II. Series.
HV9960.G7C69 1997
364.4´0941—dc21
97–5572
ISBN 0–19–826253–1

1 3 5 7 9 10 8 6 4 2

Typeset by Theresa M. Murphy and Vera A. Keep, Cheltenham
Printed in Great Britain
on acid-free paper by
Bookcraft Ltd., Midsomer Norton, Somerset

Dedication

For Sheilagh, Susan, and Alexandra, three generations of strong women.

General Editor's Introduction

Clarendon Studies in Criminology, the successor to *Cambridge Studies in Criminology*, which was founded by Leon Radzinowicz and J. W. C. Turner more than fifty years ago, aims to provide a forum for outstanding work in criminology, criminal justice, penology and the wider field of deviant behaviour. It is edited under the auspices of three criminological centres: the Cambridge Institute of Criminology, the Mannheim Centre for Criminology and Criminal Justice at the London School of Economics, and the Oxford Centre for Criminological Research.

Adam Crawford's stimulating articles on the theme of this book, captured in it sub-title—*Appeals to Community and Partnerships*—will have whetted the appetite of many readers. In this wide-ranging and readable work on *The Local Governance of Crime* he has reflected on and elaborated his thesis: that the movement towards systems of crime control based on local community involvement—'*together* we can crack crime'—raises important political, social, organisational and legal issues which have yet to be fully appreciated.

By welding together the findings of his empirical research into crime prevention and victim-offender mediation 'partnerships' with a wide-ranging analysis of socio-political and criminological theories, the author has laid bare a number of themes of critical importance. Of particular significance is his analysis of the way in which the concept of 'community' has been deployed and manipulated in order to mobilize public participation in crime control. He describes the realities behind the rhetoric of 'partnerships' and discusses the issues of representation, legitimacy and democratic accountability to which they give rise. He points to the possible consequences of a crime control philosophy and organisational model which places its prime emphasis on the needs of the community, which, as he astutely points out, could in certain circumstances result not in communal harmony but in the exclusion and ghettoisation of deviants. What is presented as a constructive model of local justice, based on a communality of interests, may, by ignoring the need to resolve conflicts between different approaches and values, turn out to be 'parochial, intolerant, oppressive and unjust'. Thus, Adam Crawford draws our attention to the fact that the movement of 'the sites of power' in crime control towards local crime prevention initiatives is far from being unproblematic.

It is impossible within the space of a short introduction to do justice to the richness of the observations and analysis contained in this impressive book. It deserves to be read not only by theoretically minded criminologists, political scientists and sociologists, but also by anyone who has responsibility for devising or implementing criminal policy. It should certainly be a required text for all concerned in the 'crime partnership business'.

The editors are delighted that this important work has been published in the *Clarendon Series*.

Roger Hood
Oxford, March 1997

Preface

In the prolonged gestation of, and initial reflection upon, this book some parts were first published in a different form elsewhere. Consequently, I have drawn from the following articles:

'The Partnership Approach: Corporatism at the Local Level?' (1994) *Social and Legal Studies*, 3, 497–519;

'Social Values and Managerial Goals: Police and Probation Officers' Experiences and Views of Inter-Agency Co-operation' (1994) *Policing and Society*, 4, 323–39;

'Appeals to Community and Crime Prevention' (1995) *Crime, Law and Social Change*, 22, 97–126;

'Inter-Agency Co-operation and Community-Based Crime Prevention: Some Reflections on the Work of Pearson and Colleagues' (1995) *British Journal of Criminology*, 35, 17–33 (written with Matthew Jones).
I would like to thank the editors and publishers concerned for their permission to use the material.

I would like to acknowledge the invaluable contribution of Matthew Jones for his research assistance on the first part of the initial research project, for his input into the articles that we co-authored and for the many discussions in the preparation of this book. Matthew's interview skills were apparent throughout, and crucial to the success of, the research. Ruth Goatly and Judy Heather were instrumental in getting this project off the ground and in assisting with its direction and support in the early years. The University of Hertfordshire generously funded the first phase of the research. For a 'new university' to invest in the research of a young and relatively unknown academic was a bold step, for which I am grateful. It gave me the space to develop my own ideas and carry out empirical enquiry without being beholden to the stringencies of contract research and without requiring the production of quick fix policy solutions. I only hope that the trust and confidence that they showed has borne the fruit of some reward. This indulgence was precious and was enhanced by the University of Leeds which funded the second phase of the research and allowed me the space and time in which to write this book. Thanks go to John Bell as Head of

Department for granting me suitable study leave. The Centre for Criminal Justice Studies, in the Faculty of Law at the University of Leeds has proved to be a very convivial and stimulating atmosphere in which to work. I am grateful to the administrative and library staff for their assistance and for keeping me sane on my infrequent descents from the 'attic'.

Most particularly, I would like to thank Clive Walker, Ian Brownlee, David Wall, Phil Mizen, Pat O'Malley, Les Johnston, George Pavlich and Susan Flint for their many helpful comments and criticisms on all or parts of the final manuscript, as well as for their collegial support and for their encouragement throughout. Clifford Shearing, Nicola Lacey, Mike Nellis, Roger Matthews, Kevin Stenson, Lucia Zedner, Reece Walters, and John Pratt have all commented at different times upon incarnations of this work, from which I have learnt and for which I am grateful. A number of other people have helped shape my ideas, both directly and indirectly. I owe so much to my parents that it is unfathomable. I have had the pleasure of being the student of, teaching and working with, Carol Smart from which I have benefited greatly. Working with John Young gave me some important insights, a shame 'the book' never happened! Kieran, Ian, Mark, and Julie have all been willing to 'listen', and even to probe with perceptive insights, when wine and the time should have told them that they should have known better! Finally, and above all, thanks to Susan for the pleasures of companionship, sharing, and love, and to Alex for reminding me that each day has new challenges.

Contents

List of Figures and Tables

1
Introduction

In a recent review of the state of English language criminology, John Braithwaite came to the somewhat pessimistic conclusion that:

> The present state of criminology is one of abject failure in its own terms. We cannot say anything convincing to the community about the causes of crime; we cannot prescribe policies that will work to reduce crime; we cannot in all honesty say that societies spending more on criminological research get better criminal justice policies than those that spend little or nothing on criminology. Certainly we can say some important things about justice, but philosophers and jurisprudes were making a good fist of those points before ever a criminological research establishment was created.
>
> (Braithwaite 1989a: 133)

One problem, upon which this 'abject failure' has been founded, is that criminology has increasingly drawn its own terms of reference in a highly restrictive and narrow fashion. It is often as a result of the quest to produce research findings which have an impact upon immediate (short-term) policy debates that criminologists have ignored the larger canvas upon which are inscribed more enduring processes of change. Criminology, too often, has become disconnected from social and political trends, their implications and the theoretical debates aimed at their explanation. This narrow focus of criminology, for some, may mark the maturing of the discipline but, for others, it constitutes its capture by a discourse of administration, whereby criminologists increasingly respond to the desire to find more efficient means of control. In the consequent battle over 'what works', wider arguments have become lost. Consequently, the cumulative effects of creeping or piecemeal change often appear to pass by unnoticed.

A second problem, alluded to in Braithwaite's comments, is that empirical and normative debates have tended to be segregated and intellectually compartmentalized. Whilst Braithwaite is right to suggest that philosophers and jurists have long been concerned with issues of justice, nevertheless, they have steered clear of engagement with empirical debates, often leaving them open to accusations of utopianism and idealism. Criminologists and sociologists, on the other hand, have immersed themselves in highly specified empirical arguments with scant regard for normative and philosophical issues. As a result there is little criminological engagement with public debate on issues of the direction and morality of society and public policy. Attempts to answer the highly problematic and contingent question, 'does the latest policy initiative work?', whilst not themselves irrelevant, tend to obscure the questions: what ought to be our standards of behaviour as a society? and what social institutions should we be building? In this light, crime is too often seen as a technical problem requiring an administrative solution. This is an aspect of what Pat O'Malley (1994a) has referred to as the 'demoralization of justice'. There is a pressing need for criminology to reconnect the 'empirical' with the 'normative'.

Consequently, key elements of the criminological enterprise ought to be concerned with holding up a mirror to the deleterious effects of strategies of crime control, posing difficult questions about their impact upon our social formation and cultural sensibilities (Garland 1990), and simultaneously raising the issue of what constitutes appropriate notions of justice. It is towards these agendas that this book seeks to make a modest contribution. So, at the heart of this book lies a central normative question: what kinds of social formations do we want to foster and encourage through, and around, strategies of crime control? This raises the subissues of: first, where society may be presently heading, either by default or by design, under the influence of the emerging forms of governance of crime, and secondly, what alternative avenues are, or may be, available?

To return to Braithwaite's analysis, it would be wrong to undermine or diminish the impact of criminological knowledge (in its broadest sense) upon the ways in which crime is regulated. It is a contention of this book that criminological knowledge circulates within lay and professional discourses. In doing so, it enters and affects the day-to-day governance of crime but does so neither in straightforward nor necessarily predictable ways. This understanding of the reflexivity of criminological knowledge is one that Giddens has emphasized, for some time, in relation to sociology:

The development of sociological knowledge is parasitical upon lay agents' concepts; on the other hand, notions coined in the meta-languages of the social sciences routinely reenter the universe of actions they were initially formulated to describe or account for. But it does not lead in a direct way to a transparent social world. *Sociological knowledge spirals in and out of the universe of social life, reconstructing both itself and that universe as an integral part of that process.*

(Giddens 1990: 15–16, emphasis in original)

Examples of this reflexivity include the ways in which insurance has appropriated and utilized victimological notions of risk (Simon 1987); the growing role of the police as 'information brokers' of 'expert' knowledge between various organizations and the public (Ericson 1994), and debates about crime displacement. Thus, a further task for criminology, I contend, must be to monitor this reflexive process and to highlight its implications.

This book is an excavation and analysis of current criminal justice discourses and practices which coalesce around appeals to 'community', 'prevention', and 'partnerships': the conceptual trilogy which lies at the heart of this book's concerns. Through my reference to 'appeals', I seek deliberately to highlight the fact that the essential subject matters of this book are *governmental strategies*, which originate both from within and outside of the state. These strategies have uncertain and contested outcomes, as they embody their own contradictory logics and confront countervailing tactics. Hence, a major focus will be fixed upon the complex ways in which these are translated into everyday practices. The use of the term 'governance' itself, in part, reflects both this and the extent to which the recent socio-political landscape has been transformed in relation to crime control and prevention, as well as other areas of public policy.[1] Rhodes sets out a useful definition, in which:

governance signifies a change in the meaning of government, referring to a *new* process of governing; or a *changed* condition of ordered rule; or the *new* method by which society is governed.

(1995: 1–2, emphasis in original)

---

[1] Some commentators have sought to relate the emergence of new patterns of local governance, a political dynamic, with the transition from Fordism to post-Fordism, an economic dynamic (see the discussion in Hay 1995; and Jessop 1995). In order to avoid the economic determinism, reductionism, and functionalism of many such contentions, no such association is present (either implicitly or explicitly) in the arguments that follow.

In addition, the term 'governance' highlights a major shift in political analysis. It is, simultaneously, a new way of looking at things, as
well as a new set of things to look at. It seeks to problematize, rather
than reject out of hand, the 'conceptual trinity of market-state-
civil society' which has dominated the analysis of modern social
formations (Jessop 1995: 310). It is precisely the shifting and
interpenetrating relations between this 'conceptual trinity', the subsequent implications for crime control, and problems of conceptualization that this produces, which constitutes the core concerns of
this book.

In the pages that follow, I will attempt to advance an explanation
for the emergence of these strategies and the socio-political context
which has given birth to them. Furthermore, I will consider the
discourses and administrative arrangements to which they give rise,
their significance, and implications for the future of crime control. I
will argue that we are witnessing a profound restructuring of the
mechanisms and technologies governing the regulation of crime.
Criminologists, like many sociologists and political scientists, have
failed sufficiently to recognize the shape of the new political and
administrative edifice which slowly is being constructed. Yet, this is
not a monolith but a dispersed and fragmented web of networks and
'partnerships', in which the interests of the central state collide with
local power élites, established agencies, charitable bodies, private
businesses, and representatives of other organized groups. The proliferation of these 'neo-corporatist grey areas' (Habermas 1989b:
61) pose fundamental questions about the pursuit of social values as
we turn to face the twenty-first century. This book seeks to understand better these shifts, their practices and contradictions within
the field of crime control, without ever suggesting that they represent either the inevitable outcome of unfolding processes of rationalization or the unidirectional product of class power relations and
antagonisms. Whilst both elements are part of the analysis that
follows, there will be a deliberate attempt to identify the sites of
ambiguity and contestation.

Insights from Theory

To date, much has been written about 'community policing' (Greene
and Mastrofski 1988; Friedmann 1992; Rosenbaum 1994; Fielding
1995), specifically its ideals, characteristics, programmes, and

practices. Yet much of this literature has remained trapped in the aforementioned constraining intellectual embrace. It has tended to consider moves towards the 'community' (be it decentralization or community involvement and participation) from within internal police institutional parameters. Accounts of 'community policing' have tended to amount to little more than stories of organizational rearrangement and rearticulation, without connecting these to wider socio-political developments. Furthermore, they have tended to be ahistoric, with little connection to longer-term patterns of social change. That is not to suggest that such approaches are irrelevant, but rather to recognize that they only ever constitute a partial account. For this reason the theoretical debates and empirical research in this book transcend the organizational strait-jacket of specific criminal justice agencies and seek to connect simultaneous developments across different organizations.

Thus, in the ensuing analysis of the appeal to 'community' and 'partnerships', the focus is upon 'crime control' and 'security' rather than 'policing' *tout court*. As I argue in Chapter 2, our current conception of crime control and criminal justice practice, since the late eighteenth century, has become detached from a broader concern with political economy and notions of the rational governance of the population. Hence, the concept of 'governance' is used deliberately to (re)capture and signify this breadth: to encompass street level strategies and informal arrangements, as well as those embodied in policy guidelines, formal professional criteria, and legislation. I also use the term to underscore the extent to which the recent socio-political vista is being reconstituted in relation to crime control and other areas of public policy, as well as to signal a simultaneous shift in political analysis.

The recognition by contemporary social theorists of the twin processes of globalization and localization in 'high modernity' (Giddens 1990), represents an important backcloth for social commentary. And yet, it has been insufficiently recognized and developed within the field of criminology. This book will seek to address this absence in considering the problematic future of policing and crime control in the face of the perceived transformation of the nation state against a background in which increasing significance is accorded, simultaneously, to local experience and global change, as well as their interconnectedness. The principal concern of this book, however, is with the importance of the 'local'

and growing appeals to 'community' (on the implications of globalization for policing and crime control, see Anderson 1989; Fijnaut
1993; Walker 1993; South 1994; Sheptycki 1995). This is not to
suggest that the two processes can be neatly separated. On the
contrary, these two seemingly opposing trends are both complementary and interpenetrative, the global is to be found within the
local and simultaneously, the local is to be found within the global
(Robertson 1995).

In order to make sense of some of the seemingly disparate
developments in criminal justice we need to locate them within this
wider lens. Such an endeavour has been facilitated, recently, by the
development of a number of concepts in social and political theory
which seek to describe and map a series of processes and relations
which appear to be unfolding across diverse areas of social life as we
move towards the end of the twentieth century. These include,
'governing without government' (Rhodes 1995: 3), the 'death of the
social' (Rose 1996), the 'hollowing out of the national state' (Jessop
1993: 10), the emergence of the 'risk society' (Beck 1992), and 'less
government, but more governance' (Osborne and Gaebler 1992:
34). All these concepts—or perhaps more appropriately, metaphors
—are used, in different ways and with differing emphases, to
describe a pattern of shifting relations which involve: the fusion of,
and changing relations between, the state, the market, and civil
society; a move from 'the social' to 'community'; greater individual
and group responsibility for the management of local risks and
security; and the emergence of new forms of management of public
services and structures for policy formation and implementation.

This book seeks to engage with these theoretical debates and to·
import some of their insights into the field of criminology, in order
to try to make sense of recent trends and developments in the local
governance of crime and personal security. These trends are to be
found with differing emphases and inflexions across diverse areas of
social life. They also resonate with similar developments in different
societies throughout Western Europe, North America, and Australasia. It is the central contention of this book that these shifts give
rise to new patterns of local governance which evoke key questions
about the legitimate responsibilities of individuals, organizations,
and the state; the regulation of social conflicts; the nature of
organizational and democratic accountability; and notions of social
justice.

At the heart of these shifts, I will argue, lie invocations to 'community', the very woolliness of which nourishes and sustains its appeal. Consequently, this book will seek to examine the growing appeals to 'community' and 'partnerships' in criminal justice policy, and the involvement of actual communities and partnerships in criminal justice practices. In the chapters that follow I will attempt to make sense of a perceived shift away from *formal* criminal justice institutions towards a new found emphasis upon *informal* community institutions as modes of crime control. In so doing, I will evaluate the inadequacies of existing conceptualizations of the place and role of 'community' in crime control.

The Empirical Research: Aims and Methods

The theoretical discussions will be supported by the findings of two empirical research projects conducted over recent years. The collective aims of the two projects, in different ways, were: first, to consider the ways in which a variety of criminal justice agencies come together in 'partnerships' around given strategies of crime control and the nature of their interrelations and conflict management; secondly, to examine novel crime control developments in which appeals to 'community' constitute an explicit (or implicit) element of their attraction; and thirdly, to evaluate the extent to which divergent strategies of local governance, which emerge around the edges of the criminal justice system, constitute practices of social inclusion through strategies of reintegration or result in the social exclusion of given members of society.

The two research projects include a two year research study of a number of community-based crime prevention initiatives in the South East of England, supplemented by a study of a number of similar projects in the North of England; and a study of community mediation and victim/offender reparation schemes in the North of England. Central to both these spheres of crime control are: appeals to 'community', 'partnerships', an emphasis on informal modes of conflict resolution, and claims to crime reduction. All of these themes and issues are central to the arguments in this book.

Both projects draw upon qualitative and quantitative data in ways that complement each other. However, an emphasis will be given to the qualitative, interview based research which allows a deeper exploration of the complexities of the issues under consideration.

To this end both projects deliberately embody comparative elements, and yet require sufficient sensitivity to be accorded to the local contexts in which the projects were situated. A brief description of the research case studies is to be found in Appendix A. It is important to note that the empirical data will be used illustratively. Hence, the aim is not to claim that the findings are generalizable to all parts of the UK, nor that the experiences are replicated wherever similar initiatives occur. Rather, it is to suggest that the empirical findings can be used to support and highlight the thrust of theoretical arguments as to tendencies and trends within the structures and practices of crime control and prevention.

Project One—Community and Partnerships in Crime Prevention

The choice of community crime prevention as the focus of this research project lies first in its explicit appeal to 'community' as a means of delivering crime prevention; secondly, in its aim for proactive informal intervention rather than reactive professional intervention upon which the criminal justice system has largely been founded; and thirdly, in the dramatic expansion of community crime prevention and a multi-agency approach over the past decade (see Chapter 2). Further, the rise of managerialism and its effects, which will form a key element of the analysis that follows (Chapter 3), in part explains the relevance and direct connection of this empirical research work with the theoretical debates. For, at the heart of the managerial model of criminal justice are two central administrative techniques: first, situational crime prevention—the management of opportunity structures through manipulations in the physical environment—and secondly, the co-ordination of the interactions and interdependency of criminal justice as a 'system'. Thus the development of community-based inter-agency crime prevention holds a particularly prominent and symbolic place in a managerialist approach to neighbourhood crime control.

The fieldwork was conducted in two stages. The first stage occurred over a two year period, between 1991 and 1993. This research was focused on nine 'core' crime prevention initiatives in, and around, the Greater London area, stretching from deprived inner-city neighbourhoods to small town initiatives in the commuter belt. This was supplemented by a second stage of research involving two community crime prevention projects in the North of England, conducted between 1994 and 1995. Collectively, the research data includes:

1 over 170 hours of recorded in-depth interviews with front-line agency personnel and community representatives;
2 more than 120 hours of inter-agency forum meeting observations together with frequent visits to projects; and,
3 a survey of over 240 randomly selected rank and file police and probation officers in one of the areas, in the South of England research, in which a number of the initiatives was situated. Questions related to the officers' attitudes and experiences of community crime prevention and the multi-agency approach.

This multiple research strategy of survey, observation, and interview affords specific insights into the policy formation and implementation processes particularly relevant to inter-organizational contexts. It enables the assessment of the disjuncture between what people advocate—what they say they do—and what they actually do in practice. For, as Rutherford has noted, the 'institutional dissonance between words and deeds' is particularly acute within the field of criminal justice (Rutherford 1993: 160). A multiple strategy allows for an exploration of different understandings and levels of meaning regarding what has occurred or been resolved at an observed meeting. It also facilitates the evaluation of the interaction between formal and informal representations, forms of communication, and conflict.

Project Two—Community and Partnerships in Victim/ Offender Mediation and Reparation

The choice of victim/offender mediation as the focus of the second research project, may seem odd at first sight. Victim/offender mediation holds a marginal place on the criminal justice agenda, relatively few cases pass through mediation as compared with the courts and penal institutions. And yet, this in part explains its relevance to the concerns of this book. Victim/offender mediation and reparation carries significant symbolic weight beyond its relatively small numerical importance in terms of case referrals. The practice of mediation and reparation brings into sharp relief issues and debates with much wider ramifications which inform and transcend the whole of the criminal justice process. This is particularly evident given three interrelated factors. First, the conceptual location of victim/offender mediation is simultaneously both inside and yet outside of criminal justice systems. This dual position of being in two places at the same time is alluded to by Lucia Zedner (1994: 234) in her assessment of mediation and reparation schemes as being a 'conceptual cuckoo' in the criminal justice nest. Secondly, like community crime prevention, its organizational location or bureaucratic positioning connects with, is influenced by, and seeks to influence, a wide variety of criminal justice agencies. Finally, the diverse interests, with often conflicting motivations, from which mediation and reparation draws support provide another medium upon which wider debates are etched.

Further, mediation and reparation connects with a number of discursive appeals around which a host of normative and moral, as well as administrative and managerial, concerns coalesce. First it connects with a critique of existing criminal justice institutions: that they cost too much; they operate to slowly, they fail to achieve their objectives of reducing crime and the fear of crime, and they inadequately meet the interests and needs of the parties. Secondly, and more importantly for the purpose of this book, appeals to informal justice and mediation embody a quest to revive some notion of 'community', in which informal social institutions act to regulate conflict by means of social control processes.

The research into victim/offender mediation was conducted between 1993 and 1996. The data includes:

1 a survey of annual reports of community mediation and victim/ offender reparation schemes operating around the UK in early 1994; and
2 in-depth interviews with key agency personnel, scheme co- ordinators, and mediators associated with two victim/offender mediation and reparation schemes in the North of England. The interviews were again supplemented by some observational re- search work.

The Organization of the Book

Throughout, the book will seek to answer a number of inter-related questions: Why do appeals to 'community' and 'partnerships' in criminal justice policy appear to be on the increase? How do we make sense of this? What are the implications of the actual involve- ment of communities and the establishment of partnerships in crime control initiatives? Is crime control the appropriate vehicle around which to organize communities and partnerships? And if so, what sort of communities will we be generating through such a focus?

In order to address the question 'why'? which was posed in the preceding paragraph, we need to begin by considering how it is that we have come to where we are today, and the exact nature of the shifts unfolding around us. Chapter 2, therefore, begins by charting important changes and developments in crime control and the regulation of order in the eighteenth and nineteenth centuries. The focus then moves to consider the more recent genesis of appeals to 'partnerships', 'community', and 'prevention' within contemporary British crime control policy and practice. This overview includes a brief historical account of the growth of an elaborate division of labour in which specialized agencies have carved up the tasks of criminological work. The manner in which agencies and professional groups have pursued their own claims to specialist expertise and tried to influence criminal justice policy accordingly is considered. This theme is continued in Chapter 3, which seeks to address the question, 'why now'? In doing so, a number of dominant explanations for the recent changes outlined in Chapter 2 which are associated with appeals to 'community' and 'partnerships' will be advanced. It will be argued that in order to make sense of these shifts we need to connect them to wider social trends and transformations in the politics of local governance. In particular, Chapter 3 focuses upon the growth of privatization (in all its diverse guises), the increasing managerialism and the influence of the 'new public management', and the emergence of what has been called the 'risk society' (Beck 1992; Ericson 1996). This chapter concludes with a discussion of explanations for the shifts heralded by the conceptual trilogy at the heart of this book's concerns, and advances an explanation which focuses upon issues of legitimacy and responsibility. It is argued that appeals to community and partnerships in crime control make up an important element in the recalibration of what constitute the legitimate responsibilities of individuals, groups, and the state.

Chapters 4 and 5 introduce the bulk of the empirical data. Chapter 4 evaluates the nature of inter-organizational relations between key criminal justice agencies. It draws upon the findings of the survey of police and probation officers in order to explore the experiences and attitudes of rank and file officers to the process of inter-agency work. The different understandings of key concepts like 'prevention' among officers is discussed and their implications regarding differential power relations considered. The contrasting ideologies, interests, and practices which arise from differing structural traditions, socialization processes, and role expectations of police and probation officers are also illustrated. The nature of inter-organizational conflicts and the manner in which conflicts are managed in practice is considered through an examination of the research case studies. Chapter 5 develops upon an understanding of these tensions by considering the nature of 'community' to which appeals are made in criminal justice discourses and policies, or phrased as a question, what is meant by 'community'? And thus, whose 'community'? Here some of the empirical data from both research projects is examined in order to illustrate the various ends and interests which the concept of 'community' serves. This involves an evaluation of the role of 'community' in the discourses and practices of crime prevention partnerships and mediation and reparation schemes. This discussion raises important issues concerning representation and participation, and the correspondence between community representatives and the communities they purport to represent through their involvement at an institutional level. Further, the chapter goes on to examine the contribution of 'community' to the practices of social order and crime prevention. In other words, what is it that 'community' has to offer crime control?

Chapter 6 seeks to evaluate and critique existing theoretical explanations for the nature of 'partnerships' as constituting new forms of local governance. It seeks to advance a critical overview and synthesis of three bodies of theoretical literature which address issues pertinent to the shifting governance of crime: 'policy networks', 'governmentality', and 'neo-corporatist' theory. Two central questions are considered: first, does this process of 'government at a distance' that 'partnerships' herald, represent a fragmentation and weakening of the capacity of the central state or its strengthening? and secondly, at the level of these new structures of governance, who is steering policy formation? which interests are dominant? In so considering, particular attention is given to the processes of inclusion into, and exclusion from, the policy making processes and the impact of differential power relations within partnerships. In Chapter 7, the ramifications of partnerships for organizational and democratic accountability are considered. The chapter goes on to examine recent changes in financial and informational accountability and their relationship to the democratic process. The chapter then considers how partnerships might be rendered more account-able, first, through an exploration of key democratic principles that ought to underpin 'partnerships', and secondly, by way of a review and assessment of some of the recent contributions to how one might begin to build such institutions, their limitations, and pos-sibilities.

Chapter 8 takes a particularly jaundiced look at some of the possible implications of shifts in responsibility for governance. In particular, it examines the implications for social justice of localiza-tion through community partnerships. Particular regard is given to the spatial and social distribution of crime as well as concerns over 'spirals of ghettoization'. It is argued that we need to address spatial and social polarization, and develop forms of social cohesion which both foster social solidarities, and yet preserve a cosmopolitan acceptance of cultural difference. The appropriate conditions for forging co-operation across boundaries of difference, it is argued, require interventions to address political and economic inequality and asymmetries of power. The chapter concludes with a discussion of the conditions under which such a public purpose should seek to go beyond 'localism'.

By way of conclusion Chapter 9 pulls together the arguments advanced throughout within a framework which seeks to prioritize issues for further consideration. It sketches out a research agenda which begins to conceptualize the salient contours of 'community' and 'partnerships', and points towards topics requiring further investigation. The chapter advances the case for a more open and constructive management of inter-organizational and intra-communal conflicts which fosters appropriate conditions for forging co-operation across boundaries of identity, community, and differ-ence. In response to the new and difficult social questions raised by the foregoing, the book concludes with a consideration of their implications for criminology and the politics of crime control. It is argued that a politics of crime control which fails to acknowledge and address the fact that the sites of power are shifting and that the contemporary conversations and communications that matter are occurring in novel and non-traditional settings, will always be partial and limited. This, it is suggested, presents a challenge to academics, policy makers, and citizens to think more politically and normatively than hitherto about the principles which should underpin the nature and form of 'partnerships' between communities and organizations, be they 'private', 'public', or 'hybrid'.

2

The Genesis of the 'Partnership' Approach and Appeals to 'Community' in Crime Control

In this chapter I will seek to outline the genesis of the 'partnership' approach and the recent rebirth of appeals to 'community' and 'prevention' within contemporary British crime control policy and practice. In order to trace and explain why 'partnerships' and 'community' have emerged as pre-eminent elements in contemporary criminal justice discourse at the end of the twentieth century, we must consider a number of historical strands. Therefore, this chapter begins with a brief historical account of earlier forms of local governance in crime control and some of the transformations in policing and criminal justice which have occurred over the past two hundred years. In particular there is a review of the changes heralded by the arrival of the 'new police' and the construction of a penal complex against the background of industrialization and mass urbanization. The understanding of, and responses to, crime which emerged between the mid eighteenth and mid twentieth centuries crystallized many of the currently held, taken for granted institutional and intellectual assumptions about crime and its control. This limited historical account will focus upon the impact of the growth of an elaborate institutional division of labour and the construction of a complex administrative apparatus. In so doing, special attention will be accorded to the related processes of bureaucratization and professionalization and their impact on criminal justice. The chapter will then go on to examine the recent interest in 'prevention', 'community', and 'partnerships' within crime control policy. Each of these concepts will be considered in turn, outlining the most important policy developments, academic debates, and practical initiatives. The ways in which and the extent to which these notions have impacted upon different criminal justice agencies and their work will be examined. Throughout the analysis will focus upon the recurring critical relationships between, on the one hand, formal and professionalized systems of crime control and, on the other hand, the attraction of informal or community-based models.

A Brief Historical Excursion

There are inevitably certain pitfalls in the kind of brief historical review that follows. In seeking to tease out salient strands within often complex, uneven, and sometimes contingent historical developments, there are clear dangers of oversimplification. By reducing history to neat dichotomies, lines of development or 'master' tendencies, there is an inclination to highlight and caricature historical difference and change at the expense of identifying significant continuities (Ignatieff 1981; Cohen 1985; 1989). There are also hazards in conflating diffuse, fragmented patterns and variable regional developments. This is particularly apparent in the field of crime control where geographical disparities evidence institutional, cultural, and socio-economic variations (Hobbs 1988). Whilst what follows by necessity stands guilty before the accusation of reductionism, I intend it to be a form of *strategic reductionism*, which is illustrative by its very accentuation upon differences and transformations. It is my argument that this kind of historical insight allows us to identify more readily the patterns in the sands shifting under our own feet. In a similar vein to the instructive examination of history in order to identify continuities (see Pearson 1983), it is also enlightening to seek in history the nature of salient departures and change. And yet, it is my intention to use historical insights neither to suggest that we are returning to previous ways (a circular theory of history) nor to advance an understanding of social change which is unidirectional (an inevitable evolutionary theory of history). Rather, as Garland (1995: 19) has shown, if we are to understand criminology's key conceptions and frames of reference, as well as their relations to institutional practices, we need to ask 'genealogical questions' about their constitution and examine the historical processes which led to their emergence.

Earlier Forms of 'Government at a Distance'

Crime control and the law are intimately bound up with political power. The birth of the modern British police in the nineteenth century, after a long and protracted gestation and in the face of widespread opposition, transformed the relations of governance. As the embodiment of the state's legitimate monopolization of force, policing has come to lie at the heart of the British legal and political order. The history of the modern police and the criminal justice complex is closely associated with the idea of the sovereign nation state. However, our current conception of 'police' is very different from the notion of 'policing' or 'police science' as used in the late eighteenth century by the likes of Jeremy Bentham, Adam Smith, and Patrick Colquhoun (Steedman 1984: 8; Reiner 1992a: 762). For them, 'police' and 'policing' were seen as broader aspects of political economy and good governance. 'Police' in this broader conception was understood to embody 'a triangle of sovereignty-discipline-government', focused upon the general population and with 'the apparatus of security' as its essential mechanism (Foucault 1991: 102). The study of crime and criminal justice practices was thus part of a much larger concern with what Foucault termed 'governmentality' (Foucault 1991; Burchell et al. 1991). With the ensuing bureaucratization and professionalization of policing in the late nineteenth century and throughout the twentieth century, the definition of *policing* has taken on a modified and very much narrower meaning. Policing has come to be synonymous with what 'the police', in their symbolic blue uniforms and strange hats, actually do.[1] In this lies an important modern cultural linkage between, on the one hand, the 'police' and 'policing', and on the other, 'connotations of government control and governmental authority' (Shearing et al. 1980: 17). However, broader conceptions of 'crime prevention' and 'local community governance' have a longer history.

Prior to the 'new police' and Peel's reforms, public safety, policing, and crime control had been subject to forms of 'government at a distance'. For example, the tything system, which Critchley traces back to the reign of King Alfred, involved a principle of social obligation. It constituted a form of genuine 'community responsibility' (Critchley 1978: 2). Through its mutual pledging, it required

---

[1] Melville Lee wonderfully described the symbolic importance of the new police uniform and helmet in 1829, given public hostility, as being 'just homely enough to save the situation' (cited in Critchley 1978: 51).

communities to keep the King's Peace. Within its origins in Saxon law, the system required all male citizens over the age of twelve (unless excused through high social position) to form a collective group of about ten neighbourhood families. This constituted the administrative unit known as a tything. Within this unit there existed a collective responsibility upon the community to keep good order and to produce for trial any member of the group who committed a crime. Each tything was also committed to ensure payment of the King's taxes and to maintain game laws. Groups of tythings were formed into a 'hundred', the members of which were responsible to a 'hundredman' or 'royal reeve'. The 'reeve' enforced judicial and administrative power under the King.

The aim of collective security which underlies the tything system was supported by community penalties, paid in advance: the tythe. Morris defined it as 'a system of compulsory collective bail fixed for individuals, not after their arrest for crime, but as a safeguard in anticipation of it' (cited in Critchley 1978: 3). Thus severe fines could be imposed on all the members if the 'reeve' failed to perform his tasks properly. After the Norman conquest, tything was modified and systematized into the 'frankpledge' system, which became the most important police institution of the Middle Ages. This signalled a moderate yet significant shift towards centralization. Fines went into the King's Treasury and the system was supervised by royal officials rather than local nobility.

The Statute of Winchester of 1285 consolidated and reaffirmed the principle of local responsibility for policing. It continued to require people to be members of communities with certain responsibilities for public security. Central to this was the recognition, by the Act, of the role of the parish constable. Constables were unpaid, annually elected local community leaders under specific obligation to conduct arrests and to bring offenders before the local court. The Act introduced a system of 'watch and ward', whereby town watchmen supplemented the work of constables (Critchley 1978: 6–7). Furthermore, it revived the practice of 'hue and cry' which imposed an obligation upon the local public to drop their work and pursue a fugitive upon a 'hue and cry' being raised. Failure to respond was regarded as siding with the fugitive for which there were due punishments.

It would be wrong to imply that these early examples of community responsibility for crime control were always consensual, conciliatory or even egalitarian. More often than not they were highly discretionary, were savagely brutal and reinforced social hierarchies and class relations (see Hay *et al.* 1975; Brewer and Styles 1980). Behind the façade of apparently self-imposed communal obligations lay coercion, contestation, and resistance. Community responsibility for crime control produced deep tensions and conflicts. There was also widespread corruption. Nevertheless, by the eighteenth century, control still remained largely exercised through informal, communal, and often face to face relations (Gatrell 1996: 385).

However, the system lost much of its local legitimacy under centralizing pressures as élite interests became more associated with the emerging central state in London (Brogden *et al.* 1988: 53–4). Traditional allegiances and local ties increasingly were shattered under the pressures of conflicting economic interests. The corrupt and arbitrary nature of much that passed for local justice, arose out of the ambiguities within the roles of major actors, such as those of the constables. They were caught within the tensions of being both a member of the community and an agent for policing that community's social and moral values. Those who could afford to do so bought themselves out of their local obligations, often employing the services of a surrogate to perform their duties. Consequently, an informal economy of crime control began to develop, supplemented by the use of informers and thief catchers, particularly in more urban areas (McMullan 1987: 133–4). Ultimately, the transformations in social relations and growing class tensions wrought by the advent of industrialization, posed fundamental questions about the nature of the emerging social order, the role and effectiveness of the parish constable and the local justice system therein.

The 'New Police' and the Peelian Legacy

The turbulent changes of the early nineteenth century shaped a fundamentally different conception of 'the crime problem'. Crime became the object of an explosion of statistical data which it was claimed served to reveal the moral decline of the nation, most notably in its cities. There was, and remains, much debate as to whether the crime rate actually was increasing or whether it was a reflection of the greater ease of prosecution or heightened official reaction (Philips 1980: 178–80). Nevertheless, crime came to be, and has remained, a cipher for much wider concerns and anxieties about social order and change. The Victorian city, in particular, became interwoven in popular imagination with notions of dangerousness, degradation, and squalor. Crime became a metaphor for class antagonisms and fears about property, disease, contagion, and alienness. The new language of crime was, therefore, an essentially cultural product, a mirror of the times in which it emerged (Weiner 1990).

It was against this background that, after a protracted struggle, the 'new police' were born in 1829, as a 'bureaucracy of official morality' (Storch 1975: 61). The primary responsibility of the 'new police' was to be the 'prevention of crime'. This was made clear in the Metropolitan Police's first instruction book published in 1829. It stated that:

It should be understood at the outset that the principal object to be obtained is the prevention of crime. To this great end every effort of the police is to be directed. The security of person and property, the preservation of public tranquillity and all other objects of a police establishment will thus be better effected than by the detection and punishment of the offender after he has succeeded in committing the crime. This should constantly be kept in mind by every member of the police force, as the guide for his own conduct. Officers and police constables should endeavour to distinguish themselves by such vigilance and activity as may render it impossible for any one to commit a crime within that portion of the town under their charge.

(Cited in Emsley 1983: 66)

Hence, the initial Peelian approach to modern policing had at its heart a philosophy of crime prevention, with an emphasis on visible uniform patrolling of the streets. Through such crime prevention, the role of the police was conceived as a symbolic representation of social order and respectability. In Storch's (1976) evocative phrase the police were 'domestic missionaries'. This model of policing, first introduced into London, was adopted and adapted within forces throughout England and Wales by the late nineteenth century.

However, the priority given to crime prevention and 'service work' more generally, probably derived more from concerns over, and the quest for, legitimation of the 'new police'—given the protracted hostility of both the urban working class and the rural landed gentry—rather than anything to do with police efficiency or effectiveness. Under organizational pressures, however, crime prevention soon became redefined in increasingly narrow terms and was subsequently pushed to the margins of institutional public policing. It promptly became clear that short of a restricted visible presence in neighbourhoods, as little more than local 'scarecrows', there was limited import placed within police work on prevention. First, there was always the danger that crime prevention could become synonymous with the more intrusive forms of surveillance which were associated in the minds of many with the spectre of centralized French policing. Surveillance carried connotations of government spies and secret police. Secondly, there was little to show for the success of crime prevention, as the police could not easily measure a 'non crime'. The First Report of the Select Committee on Police soon came to the conclusion that 'you cannot apprehend a man that is going to commit a burglary' (cited in Emsley 1991: 56). Further, this became increasingly a problem within an institution whose developing culture and organizational practice placed ever more store by a culturally celebrated 'action-orientation' and an emphasis on visible outcomes. This was exacerbated by the growing emphasis upon statistics as a premise for the government of populations. In this context foot patrols were both unglamorous and unlikely to produce 'results'. Consequently, crime fighting became glorified as the central pillar of modern policing.

Moreover, the Peelian legacy embodied a contradictory logic. Whilst its philosophy lay in notions of prevention, it sought simultaneously the specialization, bureaucratization, and professionalization of the police. These all had negative institutional implications for the meaning and extent of crime prevention within the police, as well as for relations between the police and public. As a consequence, law enforcement and order maintenance soon became established as the core activities of police officers, despite an enduring breadth of 'service' functions, around which the police increasingly defined themselves and sought external legitimacy. An important aspect of the legitimacy of the 'new police' lay in a particular relationship between police and the public. The new legitimacy was to be 'legalistic', professional, and bureaucratic.[2] Fairness and equity—in contradistinction to the arbitrariness and corrupt practices of feudal authority—were to be founded upon legal principles. Universal rules applied by impersonal professionals became the standard totems of modern criminal justice. Thus the

---

[2] 'Due process' based upon 'formally rational' legal rules, as Weber (1966) suggested, gives rise to its own forms of legitimacy, which ideally are not subject to the vagaries of personal characteristics or social position.

managers of the 'new police' sought to establish forms of physical, social, psychological, and symbolic distance between the police and the community they policed. For example, recruits were often brought in from outside the geographical communities that they were to police. Furthermore, the qualifications for entry into the police were raised by Rowan and Mayne the first Metropolitan Police Commissioners, and disciplinary codes strictly applied.[3] Despite the myth of the police as 'citizens in uniform', increasingly 'real' citizens were expected to support and assist the police and criminal justice agencies but not to be, or do, like them.

The Processes of Bureaucratization and Professionalization: From the Late Nineteenth Century to the Post Second World War Period

Since the late nineteenth century we have witnessed the slow growth of an elaborate and complex division of labour in relation to the tasks of crime control, in which specialized organizations and groups have appropriated aspects of criminological work. The resultant proliferation of criminal justice agencies and practices has been driven by claims of 'expertise' concerning either the institutional problem of governing crime and criminals or the 'scientific goal' of 'knowing' the criminal and crime's causes (Garland 1994). This 'expertise' was a component part of the twin processes of bureaucratization and professionalization in criminal justice. However, in Britain it was not until the twentieth century that the beginnings of a clear system based upon 'specialization' and 'classification', could be said truly to have taken hold (Garland 1985: 21). Just as policing increasingly became the preserve of experts so too did the process of prosecution and the tasks within and around the courtroom (Emsley 1995: 167). Similarly, the expansion in the repertoire of penal sanctions was accompanied by a proliferation of new agencies and personnel such as psychiatrists, psychologists, social workers, probation, and prison officers. Differentiation produced new and expanding fields of knowledge, technologies, and practices. These were often in conflict with each other. New organizational groups, in their quest to further their claim to professionalism, engaged in 'turf wars', competing over the soul and body of the criminal and the

---

[3] Consequently, in the early years of the Metropolitan police there was a high turnover of recruits, with large numbers dismissed through breach of discipline (Emsley 19983: 63). This served to underline a new professionalism and a departure from the earlier reliance on amateur volunteers.

ensuing administrative process, as the objects of their 'expertise'. The resultant complex web of institutions employed a considerable army of human agents, consumed a wealth of material resources, and produced a range of technical knowledge and administrative arrangements.

The subsequent history of crime control has been one in which established criminal justice agencies and professional groups have pursued their own organizational interests through their claims to specialist expertise (Cohen 1985: chapter 5). In accordance with these claims they have tried to influence criminal justice policy. In so doing, they have drawn upon divergent sources to support and validate their social function and control over the markets for their services. Legitimacy for many institutions within this criminal justice complex, therefore, was defined often in terms of their administrative and utilitarian aims (Garland 1990: 182). Foucault's (1979) perceptive analysis of punishment has highlighted the manner in which, as a consequence of an extensive process of rationalization, the act of punishment has become stripped of its moral dramatization and ritualized practices, and has been transformed into an increasingly routinized, professionalized, and bureaucratic instrumental process, with little space for emotion and spectacle. More recently, Garland (1990) has drawn out the Weberian themes within Foucault's analysis, in stressing the range of 'rationalization processes' which have transformed the way we think about and utilize punishment. Within the burgeoning penal complex, Garland identifies tendencies towards centralization together with the establishment of hierarchical chains of command, and a measure of uniformity which had not existed in previous disparate establishments. He goes on to show how, under the logic of rationalization, the cultural significance of punishment has become transformed (Garland 1990: 183). The dehumanized, passionless, and matter-of-fact way in which bureaucratic organizations operate has recast the social meaning and practices of criminal justice and punishment. The hold that professions have come to exert over punishment has left it increasingly technical and 'scientific', whilst the moral content has been simultaneously de-emphasized and direct public participation and involvement removed (Garland 1990: 185). A similar analysis can be shed upon the criminal justice system more generally, including policing (Spitzer 1983). Whilst the police have never succeeded in realizing fully their quest for professionalization (at least not to the same degree as other occupational groups) it has remained a central explanatory logic in twentieth century developments in policing (Reiner 1992b: 63). Similarly, the significant impact of standardization, bureaucratization, and centralization have been noted by police commentators (Emsley 1991; Brogden *et al.* 1988; Wall 1994).

Whilst it is not being suggested that there was a radical or sudden rupture with previous practices, there are clearly identifiable elements of discontinuity and change which have become crystallized during the late nineteenth and twentieth centuries. We can summarize these crudely as follows. First and crucially, the role of the community and public was transformed. The responsibility for policing was firmly located in the state. Its paid agents alone were to be ultimately responsible for the nature and form of policing/crime control (Philips 1989: 114). This is not to say that the private provision of policing and security services disappeared, but rather that they came to assume a less significant and more subordinate role (South 1988; Johnston 1992). Communities and the public were defined as recipients of a service. This conception has remained dominant, and was supported and extended by the establishment of the welfare state in the twentieth century.

Secondly, the relationship between criminal justice agencies (notably the police) and the public was transmuted. The 'new police' sought to differentiate themselves from the public. As Shearing notes: 'The new police were not the public and the public were not the police' (1996: 84). The 'citizen in uniform', as an ideal representation, may have sought to reassure the public of the limited powers and force of the 'new police', but symbolically and figuratively the police sought separation from the citizenry.

Thirdly, there was a general move away from local communal justice towards centralized state administered public justice. The role of local involvement within criminal justice policy making and implementation processes, where it existed, withered throughout this period, although in many areas of criminal justice—such as the police and the courts—it was not until the 1950s and 1960s that this centralization process really took off. Consequently, the scope for voluntarism declined.

Fourthly, there was a greater focus upon the detection, apprehension, and sentencing of offenders, as against the increasingly peripheral role accorded to crime prevention. Despite the intentions of Peel and others to establish a police force committed to an holistic approach to crime prevention, this goal soon became eclipsed by internal organizational demands.

Fifthly, the amateurism of pre-nineteenth-century justice came to be replaced by a growing emphasis upon professionalism. Criminological work became increasingly specialized around distinct professional and occupational groups, with their own internal organizational coherence and claims to expertise.

Sixthly, the relations between criminal justice agencies became increasingly ones of competition and conflict. Competition arose both in the struggle for scarce Treasury resources and in the battle of organizational ideologies over aetiology and legitimacy. Conflict, on the other hand, was founded upon the complex division of labour and the increasing importance of the differing organizational systems of recruitment, processes of socialization, traditions, and practices. This differentiation often produced inter-organizational mistrust. Furthermore, conflict was also structural. In so far as the criminal justice complex adhered to an adversarial model of 'due process' with inter-organizational checks and balances, conflict was institutionalized. Hence, organizational autonomy and independence became important hallmarks of bureaucratized justice.

In conclusion and at the danger of oversimplification, we can summarize that the institutions of crime control collectively became increasingly centralized, professionalized, specialized, and bureaucratic. We should be careful, however, not to over-emphasize the extent, rather than the existence, of this shift. Important irrationalities, anomalies, and historically contingent institutions have persisted, and even today have an abiding presence.[4]

---

[4] Even Weber noted that England did not neatly fit his ideal type of 'formally rational' legality, with its associated professionalization and bureaucratization (1966: 202). Most notable characteristics were the enduring reliance upon an important 'lay element' within the criminal justice process, from the role of the magistracy to that of juries, the quasi-charismatic status and authority of the judge, and the discretionary and localized nature of court law finding and decision making which Weber likened to characteristics of 'khadi justice' (Weber 1966: 317).

The Emergence of New Discourses and Practices

In the past two decades we have seen a growing rejection of what Manning (1977) refers to as the 'impossible mandate' of central government responsibility for social order. Where once the state was expected to hand down an authoritative answer for the problems and needs of society, now we are increasingly witnessing a situation in which those same problems and needs are rebounding back on society, so that society has become implicated in the task of resolving them (Donzelot 1991: 178). In contemporary appeals to 'community' and 'partnerships', crime control is no longer conceived of as the sole duty of the professional police officer or other criminal justice agents. Rather, it is becoming more fragmented and dispersed throughout state institutions, private organizations, and the public. Responsibility for the crime problem, according to current governmental strategies, is now everyone's. It is shared property.

Marching hand in hand with this has been an appeal to greater 'lay' consultation and citizen involvement in the processes of policy formation and service delivery. At the heart of the current political and management revolution, it is argued, lies a proclaimed shift from the hierarchical decision making of bureaucrats and professionals towards 'consumer power'. A language of 'partnerships' has been borne. In contrast to a reliance upon rigid, autonomous bureaucracies, networks of diverse group interests have become the dominant ethic. They have been accompanied by a greater emphasis upon the desirability of a more holistic, rather than specialist, approach to social problems, such as crime. Simultaneously, there is a new found emphasis on informal mechanisms of social control rather than the formal systems of processing offenders. Loss prevention and security management have been moved to centre stage of the crime control agenda. In sum, there appears to be a move towards a much broader conception of security and policing, which transcends the capacities and competencies of singular 'modern' institutions.

At the heart of this 'major shift in paradigm' (Tuck 1988), lie three concepts around which governmental strategies coalesce and have been constructed: 'prevention', 'community', and 'partnerships'. All three terms share a considerable degree of ill definition and vacuity. And yet, this has not stopped political parties, organizations, commercial interests, pressure groups, academics, and the public using them to pursue particular agendas or to justify and legitimate certain policies and demands. It is not my intention authoritatively to define these terms, but rather to consider the ways in which those who have sought to influence policy have used them and the ends which they have served. As I hope to show, these three concepts are not discrete terms but overlapping ones, sharing elements of a common history. In examining these concepts in turn, therefore, I will be imposing a certain degree of false rigidity upon each of them, but I do so in order to try to trace their individual as well as their inter-connected recent histories and lines of development. Furthermore, whilst the stories which follow focus upon the British experience, they are by no means unique to Britain, but share parallels with developments across North America, Europe, and Australasia, albeit with their own cultural and socio-political inflexions (see Willemse 1994; Neill 1994; National Crime Prevention Council 1994; O'Malley and Sutton 1996).

Crime Prevention

The Police

Outside of the rhetorical claims that crime prevention constitutes a central aim of policing and periodic restatements of intention by the police, prevention has remained a peripheral activity of the police (Weatheritt 1986: 49). The early policy shifts towards reviving 'prevention' as a core aspect of crime control can be traced back to the late 1950s. However, it was not until 1963 that the Home Office established a National Crime Prevention Centre in Stafford. The Home Office also set up the Cornish Committee on the Prevention and Detection of Crime which reported in 1965. The Report arrived at a number of recommendations (Home Office 1965). First, it proposed the training of specialized officers in crime prevention who would become the identified 'experts' in preventive technologies. Additionally, in one of the earliest declarations of a 'partnership approach', the Committee suggested that a concerted effort should be placed upon endeavours to network and liaise with other organizations outside the police, in order for those agencies to take on some responsibility for crime prevention. To this end, it recommended the setting up of 'crime prevention panels' to elicit wider support and contacts. Panels were formed in the ensuing years in a patchwork and *ad hoc* fashion, but never acquired an official or formal status. Often chaired by police officers, they became a means of disseminating information about crime prevention and publicizing campaigns within given localities. Further, the Cornish Report recommended the establishment of a Home Office Standing Committee on Crime Prevention, incorporating the Association of Chief Police Officers (ACPO) amongst its essential membership. Finally, it advocated a policing strategy based on a more sophisticated and professional approach to be adopted, regarding publicity and advice material used by the police for crime prevention.

In many respects the Cornish Committee did not depart from the established organizational ethos of specialization, professionalization, and bureaucratization, although it sought to extend this to the somewhat novel context of breathing life back into crime prevention. The Report gave a glimpse into an emerging recognition of tensions within the historic organizational mission of policing which were causing dilemmas for crime prevention. It warned of the potential dangers that specialization may result in the organizational marginalization of crime prevention. The Report, therefore, was clear to state that the specialism should not be taken to imply any reduction in the responsibility of other officers in respect of general crime prevention. Many of its recommendations were to echo, and resonate with, the findings of the Home Office's Morgan Report some twenty six years later (Morgan 1991). It was, however, a report before its time, largely out of step with the policing of the day. The Cornish Committee Report, as Heal correctly identifies, appeared to be flying in the face of popular opinion:

which still saw reaction as the most effective answer to crime. It was the period of fast developing technology and information systems and, for many, these wonders seemed to be the answer to rising crime.

(Heal 1988: 9)

Nevertheless, the 1960s and 1970s did see the development of specialist crime prevention departments. They also saw the beginnings of a slightly wider conception of crime prevention within policing, through an amplified emphasis upon the proactive collection and co-ordination of 'low level' information. Consequently, for example, school liaison schemes were set up in many forces.

The quiet warnings of the Cornish Committee largely went

unheeded, whilst its fears soon became realized. Crime prevention as a police specialism soon resulted in its ghettoization. By the mid 1980s crime prevention officers comprised on average 0.5 per cent of force strength (Weatheritt 1986). By the end of the 1980s this figure was still typically under 1 per cent (Harvey *et al.* 1989: 85). Harvey *et al.* use a football analogy to conjure up the essential contradiction of this approach. They suggest that calling a unit within the police service a 'Crime Prevention Department' is like calling a goalkeeper the 'goal prevention officer', thus absolving his or her team-mates from the task of preventing goals (Harvey *et al.* 1989: 83). With the evolution of crime prevention as a specialism and the increased use of undercover and plain-clothes officers, the Peelian vision of overt crime prevention as an holistic and general feature of police work, appeared to have been truly buried.

More recently, there have been some small-scale attempts to reintegrate crime prevention as a specialism within mainstream policing. This process has involved redefining the line command structure for all crime management matters, and encouraging a greater awareness of crime prevention amongst rank and file officers through training (Johnston *et al.* 1993). However, it is to be doubted that minor organizational and managerial readjustments (with re-source implications of their own) alone can overcome deeply embedded cultural oppositions, role expectations, structural dilem-mas, and intra-organizational demands which historically have downplayed the place for, and role of, crime prevention within the police.

The Contribution of Criminological Research

Outside the police a new-found interest in crime prevention emerged in the early 1980s, constructed and focused around in-formal institutions of control. At one level this was the product of an essential pessimism. With the collapse of the 'rehabilitative ideal' in the 'nothing works' era of the 1970s, most Anglo-American influenced societies seemed to be experiencing what one commen-tator has called, a 'crisis of penological modernism' (Garland 1990: 7). The criminal justice complex, which had emerged over the previous two hundred years, appeared to have failed in its own terms, had lost direction, and had become an increasingly crippling financial burden. Research findings began to converge around a consensus that the formal processes of criminal justice—through the

detection, apprehension, prosecution, and sentencing of offenders—
have only a limited effect in controlling crime (Broady 1976; Clarke
and Hough 1984). Further, the findings of the first British Crime
Survey (and its successors) revealed the extensive non-reporting of
crime, thus highlighting the fact that for most offenders and victims
the formal criminal justice system is largely irrelevant (Hough and
Mayhew 1983). Meanwhile, official crime rates continued to soar
and the prison population mushroomed.

On a more optimistic note, academics and policy makers began to
look to the importance of mechanisms of informal social control in
the fight against crime (Shapland and Vagg 1988). Three landmark
contributions (all by American criminologists) to the development
of intellectual thought in the field of informal processes of social
control in crime prevention, have continued to exert a lasting
impact. The first is the influential work of Oscar Newman (1972)
who, drawing upon the earlier pioneering work of Jacobs (1961),
elaborated the concept of 'defensible space'. He argued that the
nature of certain built environments (notably large public sector
housing estates constructed in the 1950s and 1960s) can have a
suffocating impact upon important 'natural' social processes which
prevent or lessen the likelihood of crime. He argued that through
design modifications 'defensible spaces' can be reconstructed and,
consequently, processes of informal control revived. Appropriate
modifications should seek to eliminate 'confused' and 'anonymous'
areas which belong to, and are cared for by, no one and over which
no one has direct control. At the same time they should seek to
emphasize the importance of 'territoriality', 'surveillance', 'image',
and 'environment'. Subsequently, Newman's work has been developed and extended in the British context by Alice Coleman (1985),
who concluded that poor physical design causes social breakdown
due to the dual processes of destroying 'community' and letting in
outsiders at will. Her work was widely recognized by, and has had
considerable influence upon, British government thinking which
enabled her to access the resources to engage in large scale experimental research.

The second significant contribution was that of Wilson and
Kelling's 'broken window' thesis, in which they argued that a breakdown of informal social control, due to high levels of incivilities and
signs of disorder, produces further crime and 'cycles of urban decline' (Wilson and Kelling 1982). Crudely put, their thesis runs as

follows: incivilities and signs of disorder (from unrepaired broken windows and graffiti to drunks and groups of youths hanging around on the streets) create a sense that 'no one cares', which leads to a heightened feeling of insecurity and fear, which, in turn, results in social withdrawal or flight from the area, thus decreasing the power of informal social control, which increases crime, and so on. For Wilson and Kelling, therefore, securing and propping up informal control mechanisms, through the aggressive policing of disorder and incivilities, constitutes the central means of reversing the spirals of neighbourhood breakdown and disorder. It is only then that communities and families can begin to exert informal control which prevents future crime, echoing the thoughts of Chicago School sociologists of the 1930s.

The third and final major contribution to criminological debate was that of opportunity theory and situational crime prevention advanced by Ron Clarke and colleagues (see Mayhew *et al.* 1976). Although American, he did most of his pioneering work whilst Director of the Home Office Research and Planning Unit in London, and from that position significantly influenced subsequent Home Office policy (Clarke and Mayhew 1980; Clarke 1980a; 1980b; Heal and Laycock 1986). Clarke and colleagues have argued that most crime is opportunistic. Therefore, it is believed, most criminals can be deterred from committing a particular crime, at a given time and in a particular way, by altering the management or design of the immediate environment so as to reduce the opportunities for crime. Opportunity reduction can take two broad forms, either by reducing the attractiveness of the object of crime (increasing the risk of detection through surveillance or decreasing its value on an illicit market, for example, through property marking) or by reducing the physical opportunities for crime, by making it harder to commit. Therefore, it is argued, that through simple modifications to situational characteristics in the physical environment—like replacing coin-operated public telephone boxes with magnetic stripe cards, removing coin-operated gas meters, introducing surveillance cameras or even 'sleeping policemen' (bumps in the road)—crime can be prevented.

These three inter-connected criminological developments produced a considerable degree of interest and research activity around the role of informal processes of regulation. They all manifest a 'common-sense' appeal, which has proved particularly attractive to politicians and policy makers alike. And yet, all three are powerfully driven by an ideological antagonism to the idea of crime being determined by predispositional socio-economic factors expressed in individuals. They also all represent a reorientation of the criminological gaze away from offenders and criminals towards offences and crimes (particularly their location and interaction with the local environment). In so doing, they appear to abandon any possibilities of, or interest in, offender rehabilitation. However, even those most critical of, and hostile to, these contributions, have been forced to take on board and recognize the importance of proactive intervention at an informal level (Lea and Young 1984; Young 1992).

Central Government

These developing ideas also found resonance in the Gladstone Report of the Home Office Working Group on 'Co-ordinating Crime Prevention Efforts' published in 1980. It sketched out a methodology for crime prevention which was both problem-oriented and project-focused (Gladstone 1980). It involves four stages: first, a thorough analysis of the crime problem, 'high crime' area, or situation in which the offence occurs, in order to establish the conditions that need to be met for the offence(s) to be committed; secondly, the identification of measures which would make it more difficult or impossible to fulfil these conditions; thirdly, the assessment of the practicability, likely effectiveness, and cost of each measure; and fourthly, the selection of the most promising measures. This methodology embodied an implicit situational—offence focused—orientation. Two further stages to this methodology have been added subsequently, an implementation process, and the subsequent monitoring and evaluation of the initiatives undertaken. This collective method was put into practice in high profile Home Office projects and has largely set the agenda ever since (Hope 1985; Hope and Murphy 1983).

Spurred on by the findings and methodology of the Gladstone Report, the Home Office recognized the increased importance accorded to crime prevention when it participated in an influential seminar held on crime prevention at the Police Staff College in September 1982, which led to the publication of the booklet 'Crime Prevention: A Co-ordinated Approach'. In the following year, the Home Office set up its own Crime Prevention Unit. At this stage in policy discourse, crime prevention became intrinsically interwoven with the promotion of a 'partnership' approach (to which I will return in more detail later in this chapter). It was argued that crime prevention by its very nature requires the involvement of, on the one hand, ordinary people in communities and, on the other hand, organizations and groups with services or competencies which may in some way impact upon crime. Essentially, this was the message that began to emerge more loudly from the Home Office following the establishment (within central government) of the inter-departmental working group on crime reduction and the subsequent Home Office circular 8/1984. The circular opened with the declaration that:

A primary objective of the police has always been the prevention of crime. However, since some of the factors affecting crime lie outside the control or direct influence of the police, crime prevention can not be left to them alone. Every individual citizen and all those agencies whose policies and practices can influence the extent of crime should make their contribution. Preventing crime is a task for the whole community

(Home Office 1984a).

This message has been vigorously reiterated in the ensuing years. The Home Office followed up circular 8/1984 with the establishment of the Home Office Standing Conference on Crime Prevention in January 1985 and subsequently with the introduction of a centrally organized medium for delivering the new message. Initially, this took the form of the experimental Five Towns Initiative set up in 1985. This was succeeded in 1988 by the more extensive and enduring Safer Cities Projects. As the flagship of central government thinking on crime prevention, the Safer Cities Projects combine the focus on crime prevention with a partnership approach. They provide 'pump-priming' resources over a three year period, for a local co-ordinator plus limited administrative assistance, and supported by an inter-agency steering committee, to run grant funds to assist local crime prevention 'partnerships' in designated areas (Ekblom 1992; Tilley 1993). The stated aims of the Safer Cities Programme are 'to reduce crime', 'to lessen the fear of crime', and 'to create safer cities where economic enterprise and community life can flourish'. Since its establishment, the Safer Cities Programme has gone through two 'phases', the first supported twenty Safer Cities projects between 1988 and 1995, by the end of which it was claimed to have initiated in excess of 3,600 crime prevention and community safety schemes at a cost of £22 million, plus £8 million in administration. Originally, the Safer Cities programme provided Home Office funding to the sum of £250,000 per project each year, although, by contrast the second phase projects receive on average £100,000 per annum. It was hoped that this money would act to 'lever' in other local funds (Tilley 1992: 2).

The 'second phase' was announced in 1992 although the projects did not begin to be set up until 1994. At the same time the funding was transferred from the Home Office to the Department of the Environment. The current programme is destined to run until 1998 and has been extended to cover a further thirty-two towns and cities around the country.[5] Whilst funded by central government they are externally managed by non-profit making organizations, including the National Association for the Care and Resettlement of Offenders (NACRO), Crime Concern, and the Society of Voluntary Associates (SOVA). Central government, however, maintains a considerable degree of control over the process.

The Safer Cities programme represents a classic 'trickle down' process whereby central government has sought to implant a particular model of policy formation and implementation, and to stimulate its spread through 'seed corn' funding. Despite its problematic structure and short-term project orientation (see Crawford forthcoming), it has impacted on grass roots projects, as well as voluntary and statutory organizations and business, raising the profile of crime prevention and inter-agency partnerships. Further, it has caused projects, agencies, and groups to establish procedures which continue to endure beyond the funding period and to reconsider intra-organizational working patterns which had been taken for granted.

In order to complement the Safer Cities approach the government has nourished similar activities in other social fields. In line with its commitment to incorporate the business sector into the provision, and resourcing, of crime prevention the government established Crime Concern in 1988. Crime Concern was given the task of encouraging the private sector to examine its own crime problems and actively to enlist corporate support for crime prevention and community safety initiatives. It is a national organization which, as a registered charity, raises funds and provides assistance on a

---

[5] The 1992 Conservative Party manifesto originally promised 40 new 'second phase' projects, but the Department of the Environment has stopped at 32, after which all new funding is to be directed through the general Single Regeneration Budget.

consultancy basis to local 'partnerships'. As well as the money it raises itself to pay for its activities and staff, the Home Office provides an annual grant of £0.5 million. Its aim is to act as an 'independent' catalyst to local activity and to disseminate 'good practice' in the field of crime prevention. In addition, Crime Concern currently manages fourteen Safer Cities Projects and supports a number of other city or borough-wide crime reduction programmes. In the intervening years since its establishment, Crime Concern has firmly marked itself as a major player in the spread of community-based and inter-agency crime prevention.

Despite some forms of social crime prevention work that agencies like NACRO (see below) were pioneering in the 1980s, in Britain the crime prevention juggernaut was being driven almost exclusively by opportunity reduction and situational approaches, the fuel for which was continually being injected by central government and its newly established administrative structures. A recent illustration is the Department of Environment's circular (5/1994) sent out to local authority chief executives on 'planning out crime' (Department of the Environment 1994). The circular is concerned almost exclusively with what one commentator calls 'locks, lights and landscapes' (*The Guardian*, 28 February 1994). By the 1990s the message had become a familiar one: crime prevention is an important responsibility of all institutions (be they public or private), associations, communities, and individuals. This message has become an element of the cultural furniture, reinforced through advertising and media campaigns which seek to encourage individuals to play their part in contributing to crime prevention. Foremost amongst these have been the Home Office's (1991) booklet 'Practical Ways to Crack Crime' and the car crime prevention television campaigns. I will pick up the threads of these developments, below, under the heading of 'partnerships'. First let us turn our gaze beyond central government and the police to consider the recent role and activity of other organizations and agencies implicated or involved in crime prevention.

Local Government

In the early 1980s there was little acceptance in local government of any responsibility for crime prevention. However, the mid 1980s saw a number of mainly Labour controlled councils entering the crime prevention arena, albeit under the revised title of 'community safety'. A confluence of various diverse factors brought this about and led to the establishment of Community Safety Departments in many councils in larger cities. The first was the increasing politicization of crime and the fear of crime, together with a realization—reiterated in the findings of pioneering local victimization surveys (Kinsey 1985; Jones *et al.* 1986; Crawford *et al.* 1990)—that criminal victimization is predominantly intra-class as well as intra-racial, and that it disproportionately affects those already most socially disadvantaged. Secondly, some Labour councils became keen to distance themselves from the media inspired 'anti-police' label that many had attracted in the late 1970s and early 1980s. Others sought involvement in crime prevention in order to monitor and to influence local policing as a form of 'second tier' police accountability (Jefferson *et al.* 1988). By the end of the 1980s more and more councils, encouraged (some might say, cajoled) by central government, were beginning to see crime prevention as a legitimate concern of theirs. In 1990 the Association of Metropolitan Authorities (AMA) published an important framework document on crime prevention (AMA 1990). In this they called for local authorities to be given statutory responsibility for crime prevention, so as to encourage them to continue and extend the work in which they were already engaged. Their argument was that at a local level local government is the only body which has the necessary long-term commitment, ability, and resources to take the lead in bringing together the various agencies and the general public (AMA 1990: 22). In the context of reduced local government finances, it was argued that local authorities could only guarantee funding and long-term commitment to those duties which carry statutory responsibility.

Some local authorities have been, and continue to be, at the centre of many of the most innovative developments in the field of crime prevention and community safety (Local Government Management Board 1996). However, most of their work has focused upon 'high crime' estates under local authority control. In this, many local authorities have worked closely with the voluntary sector, particularly NACRO who had by the mid 1980s already developed a track record of pioneering work in the field. In 1979 NACRO set up its Crime Prevention Unit and a year later launched its influential Safe Neighbourhoods Unit (SNU). Their estate-based work, in conjunction with local councils and the police, often involved local residents in elements of decentralized management, overseen by a multi-agency steering committee. Usually, initiatives embraced a multi-focus approach combining situational and social interventions. On the basis of its work, SNU came to advocate good, localized, and locally accountable management as the key to community safety (Bright 1991: 76–7). In this it echoed the experience of the Priority Estates Projects (PEP) which initially had been set up in 1979 with funding from the Department of Environment as a sticking plaster over some of the most unpopular, marginal, and run down council estates (Power 1984; Foster and Hope 1993; Power and Tunstall 1995).

One field in which local authorities now work closely with the police and in which crime prevention officers' 'expertise' has been extended, is that of architectural design. Drawing upon criminological findings pioneered and inspired by the work of Newman, Coleman, and others, many police forces now have a designated Police Architectural Liaison Officer (or Crime Prevention Design Advisor, as they prefer to be called in the Metropolitan police force). Their role is to liaise with local authorities and developers over design measures to reduce crime. The National Crime Prevention Centre produced a Manual of Guidance in order to standardize and encourage the spread of 'best practice'. In addition, local police forces throughout the country promote the 'Secured by Design' scheme. This scheme covers new housing, the rehabilitation of existing housing and commercial developments. It is a free service for architects, builders, and local authorities which provides guidance, information, and advice. In this relationship between the police and local authority or developers, the police adopt the role of 'information brokers' of up-to-date technological knowledge. In so doing, they have been quick to add 'environmental design' to their tool kit of specialist crime prevention expertise.

The Probation Service

In the past decade the government also has strongly encouraged the contribution of the probation service to crime prevention. In many regards the debate over the appropriate role and involvement, if any, of the probation service in crime prevention has become enmeshed in political arguments concerning the future role of the service, more generally (May 1991). This debate has been fuelled by the government's desire to reorientate the probation service away from its traditional social work basis and individual offender focus towards a more disciplinary correctionalist agency with a wider focus, incorporating victims' perspectives and public safety issues (Nellis 1995a). This desire culminated in the 1991 Criminal Justice Act. The Act sought to move the probation service to the 'centre stage' of the criminal justice system, through its emphasis upon 'punishments in the community' for what it called 'less serious offenders'. This new 'centre stage' role met with the qualified support of many probation managers (Stratham and Whitehead 1992). However, with it came the government's agenda to remove the last vestiges of 'rehabilitation', officer discretion, and the prized 'social work identity'. In their place, the government has sought to prioritize containment, surveillance, and control within probation work.

Circular 8/1984 had urged the probation service to join the new co-ordinated approach to crime prevention. This was followed up in 1984 by the Home Office's 'Statement of National Objectives and Priorities' for the probation service which encouraged the service to contribute beyond individual work with offenders (Home Office 1984). This message was broadly welcomed both by the Association of Chief Probation Officers (ACOP) and the Central Council of Probation Committees (CCPC) (ACOP 1985; 1988; CCPC 1987). However, the National Association of Probation Officers (NAPO), the voice of rank and file probation officers, adopted a more cautious, bordering on hostile, approach (NAPO 1984). What was at stake were a number of loosely connected and politically sensitive questions: what is meant by crime prevention? what does the probation service have to offer, or benefit from, it? and in what ways will contributing to crime prevention affect the service's traditional work with offenders?

By and large, probation managers embraced the rhetorical shift towards crime prevention because it appeared to offer a source of new found legitimacy at a time when the service was the subject of ongoing government threats over resources and its future role. For some probation managers crime prevention represents 'a major opportunity to present some traditional probation service objectives in a way which commands widespread public support' (Bryant 1989: 15). For others it is thought that involvement in initiatives which address the impact of crime on victims and the fear of crime for ordinary people, could be used as a more secure premise from which to articulate a distinct probation identity for the future, in contrast to the government's attempts at a 'coercive tilt' to the service (Nellis 1995a: 33–5). And yet, for many the probation service's willingness to embrace crime prevention was conducted simply in the name of the 'goal of organizational self-preservation' (Gilling 1996: 227). Many main grade officers saw crime prevention and community safety as a smoke screen for a much more fundamental, politically motivated assault upon the social work basis and client orientation of the service. NAPO was neither ready for a philosophical reassessment of a future probation vision nor did it accept the pragmatic line of management thinking. It saw any contribution of the probation service as being limited to the field of social crime prevention based upon probation officers' existing work with offenders. The implication was that the work should be limited to what Brantingham and Faust (1976) have called *tertiary* prevention—i.e. activity related to known offenders—rather than either *primary* prevention, i.e. work with the general population and interventions into the social and physical environment, or *secondary* prevention, i.e. work with 'at risk' groups of potential offenders. Moreover the bulk of the probation service's crime prevention work is of a tertiary kind, as Geraghty's review for the Home Office concluded (Geraghty 1991: 5). However, the distinctive part that the service might play in wider prevention was never made explicitly clear by the Home Office. Much of the dominant government thinking on crime prevention, with its greater focus on the offence rather than the offender, appeared to many to bypass the service.

Nevertheless, since the mid 1980s, considerable effort has gone into trying to persuade probation officers of the legitimate place of both primary and secondary prevention within probation work, and the essential role of probation officers in the development of new initiatives (Laycock and Pease 1985; Geraghty 1991). The principal thrust of the argument centres around the notion of 'partnership', for the probation service was not being asked to take on prevention alone, or to set up a small number of specialist crime prevention officers within its ranks, but rather to use its information and experience in working with offenders in the development of crime prevention with other agencies. By the time of the Home Office's 'Three Year Plan for the Probation Service, 1993–96' the aim of 'reducing and preventing crime and the fear of crime by working in partnership with others' had been accorded the special place of the first operational goal (Home Office 1992a: 12). Nevertheless, today the contribution and commitment of the service to crime prevention remains regionally variable and the subject of ongoing debate at the level of main grade officers, even if it has been accepted amongst managers.

National Developments in the 1990s

By the beginning of the 1990s there was an emergent consensus amongst academics and some policy makers that in theory, if not in practice, the ideal approach to prevention is one which combines interventions that address both 'precipitating factors' (the 'situational' criminal opportunities for crime) and 'predisposing influences' (wider social, psychological, and economic needs which encourage individuals to exploit opportunities) (Bottoms 1990; AMA 1990: 22–3; Heal 1992: 265; SNU 1993). The Home Office reinforced the initial message of circular 8/1984 by issuing circular 44/1990 'Crime Prevention—The Success of the Partnership Approach'. It was accompanied by a good practice booklet which was sent out to local authority chief executives, chief police and probation officers, and other relevant agencies (Home Office 1990a; 1990b). The Home Office then charged the Standing Conference on Crime Prevention chaired by James Morgan with the responsibility for reviewing the development of crime prevention since the 1984 circular and making recommendations for the future. The 1990 circular had called upon all those involved in crime prevention and community safety to review their activities and requested them to submit documentation as to the nature and extent of local crime prevention work in which they were engaged, to the Standing Committee. The Standing Conference's subsequent report represents an important milestone in the British development of crime prevention through a 'partnership' approach and acted to stimulate further activity (Morgan 1991). In the Report's recommendations the committee supported the AMA's view that local authorities should be given statutory responsibility. This they justified by arguing that

the absence of elected members from crime prevention structures may have the effect of marginalising crime prevention from local political issues. Any meaningful local structure for crime prevention must relate to the local democratic structure.

(Morgan 1991: 20)

The Report also recommended that a code of practice for local authorities be established in order to encourage the spread of crime prevention partnerships. However, these sentiments did not accord with government ideology, which was set against local authority ownership of crime prevention and which instead sought to 'leap-frog' established local government administrative structures. Consequently, the government's curt response to the Report was to disband the Standing Conference, replacing it with a National Board for Crime Prevention, and to ignore many of their central conclusions (Home Office 1992c; 1993a).

At this stage, it is necessary to address the question that a critic undoubtedly will raise, that, since 1993 (particularly under the stewardship of Michael Howard as Home Secretary) the criminal justice policy agenda in Britain appears to have swung back to an emphasis upon the formal processes of crime control and most notably the role of the courts and prisons. What has been the impact of this upon crime prevention? Has the latter not waned under the pressure of the prevailing populist politics of 'catch 'em, lock 'em up, and give society a break'? Clearly, the unsettled and ambiguous punitive turn in government rhetoric post-1993, towards a tougher 'prison works' ideology, including the abandonment of certain key elements of the Criminal Justice Act 1991,[6] appears on the surface to have little to do with 'community punishments' or even crime prevention. Nevertheless, this must be qualified at three different levels.

First, at an empirical level, crime prevention continues to remain a central element within present crime control strategies. For example, in September 1994 the Home Secretary launched the 'partners against crime' initiative, combining an attempt to increase the number of neighbourhood watch schemes by 50 per cent, with the inauguration of 'street watch' and the extension of Neighbourhood Constables and Special Constables. Furthermore, on 22 November 1995 the Home Secretary announced the launch of an

---

[6] Within six months of the implementation of the 1991 Act, which came into force in October 1992, the government committed itself to a dramatic U-turn involving the repeal of the sections in the Act which introduce both 'unfit fines' and the restrictions upon judges and magistrates to take previous convictions into consideration when sentencing. In doing so, through the Criminal Justice Act 1993, it blamed the influence of liberal minded academics, penal reformers, and civil servants for the unceremonious *volte face* (see Brownlee 1994). More recently, the government's 1996 criminal justice white paper continues this approach (Home Office 1996).

additional government initiative in crime prevention with the establishment of the national Crime Prevention Agency. Its task is to focus and co-ordinate the national agenda and disseminate good practice. Based at Easingwold, North Yorkshire, alongside the new police crime prevention training centre, the Agency replaces the National Board for Crime Prevention. It brings together the Home Office, the Police, Crime Concern, and a number of individuals from business, the media, and academia (*The Guardian*, 23 November 1995). The end of 1995 also saw the government announce the establishment of a special fund through the Home Office, known as the 'CCTV Challenge Competition', to support bids to resource the installation of CCTV cameras in public places as a crime prevention measure. As part of this programme £15 million is to be made available in the financial year 1996/7, the aim being to help provide up to 10,000 more CCTV cameras in high streets and other places over the ensuing three years (Home Office 1995a). In addition, crime prevention has begun to invade the normal operation of aspects of economic and urban policy, and the governing criteria for the award of central funding in diverse areas of traditional social policy, such as the Single Regeneration Budget Challenge Fund.

It would be wrong to see crime prevention as in an inverse or hydraulic relationship with the formal system of the police, the courts, and the prison, whereby more of one results in less of the other. They are not mutually exclusive but should be seen as potentially complementary. Prevention does not represent an alternative development to the formal system but part of a broader extension of it. As Cohen has shown these processes are not 'alternatives' but rather developments and patterns which are part of a much larger framework of social control that may supplement and assist the established formal criminal justice system (Cohen 1985).

Secondly, there has been an essential tension within Conservative Party 'law and order' policy over the past seventeen years, which has expressed itself in the various policy twists and U-turns. The 'free economy and the strong state' dualism, at the centre of the Thatcherite project, can no longer be seen as comfortable bedfellows. The cost of the strong 'law and order' state, introduced by the Thatcher government in the early 1980s—more police, punitive criminal laws, and prisons—together with the (associated) rising crime rates, has increasingly produced a legacy of fiscal crisis on top of failure to meet its stated objective, the reduction of crime. The demands of the

Treasury, and of the 'marketising impulse' of government policy, have produced fissures and reverberations running throughout the strong state. Overlaying and accentuating these tensions in the New Right idiom of the 'free market and the strong state', is a much deeper and more enduring conflict of ideas around crime control. Garland has identified this as follows:

there are two contrasting visions at work in contemporary criminal justice —the passionate, morally toned desire to punish and the administrative, rationalistic, normalizing concern to manage. These visions clash in many important respects, but both are deeply embedded within the social process of punishing. It is in the conflict and tension between them that we find one of the key determinants of contemporary penal [and more broadly crime control] practice.

(Garland 1990: 180)

It is this tension which we see expressed in some of the more contradictory elements of criminal justice policy rhetoric and mood swings in political populism, as well as in some of the institutions to which they give rise. As a consequence, official criminology is increasingly dualistic and polarized. Garland calls these two voices within official criminology; a 'criminology of the self' and a 'criminology of the other'. He suggests that:

One is invoked to routinize crime, allay disproportionate fears and promote preventive action. The other is concerned to demonize the criminal, to excite popular fears and hostilities, and to promote support for state punishment.

(Garland 1995: 461)

Hence, the post-1993 'punitive counter-tendency', whilst reflecting an important element within the more enduring policy frame, by no means represents its totality.

Thirdly, as I hope to show in Chapter 3, the forces driving the current shifts, of which crime prevention is a part, are not reducible merely to party politics or government through the 'state'. Whilst they *do* connect with broader political ideologies and governmental strategies they do not do so in any uncomplicated fashion. They are more enduring than the vagaries of political rhetoric. We should be wary of taking too seriously the declarations of politicians, in spite of their sometimes very real and damaging effects. Therefore, it is my contention that the more recent backlash marks an intensification of the contradictions within established government policies and governmental strategies, rather than a departure from them. It also marks a growing schism within government rhetoric, which is in large part dependent upon the audience to which it is addressed. The dominant message loudly proclaimed to the public is increasingly out of step with the quieter tone relayed to those charged with the task of managing the criminal justice system. Whilst the former stresses the traditional punitive rhetoric of the 'party of law and order', with its accent on formal procedures for the detection, prosecution, sentencing, and imprisonment of offenders, the latter is more concerned with cost efficiencies, prevention, and appeasing the Treasury. This new climate, whilst significant, particularly in its effect upon existing tensions, should not be read as a simple rejection of the significant developments which took place in the run up to 1993.

Hence, by the mid 1990s the definition of, and responsibility for, crime prevention in government policy and public discourse have fundamentally altered from that of twenty years ago. The concept of crime prevention has become much broader and more extensive in its meaning. It has come to encompass the work of agencies which hitherto had not seen crime as a legitimate concern of theirs. Beyond the employees of those organizations already discussed, social workers, health service workers, teachers, architects, town planners, business people, and a plethora of voluntary group workers and local associations have been drawn into the work of crime prevention. Crime prevention has become simultaneously 'common sense' and 'the task of everyone'. The police remain the 'experts' in crime prevention and the government clearly sees them as having a leadership role in partnerships, yet crime prevention has become predominantly reconstructed as a non-expert function, something which intrinsically relies upon the public and which the police can pass on with little training. This was clearly recognized in the police's own training manual, which declared that: 'the overwhelming majority of crime prevention advice is commonsense, based on existing professional police knowledge, and can be given immediately' (Home Office 1988a: 1). The police role in crime prevention, therefore, has been transmuted, far beyond the Peelian vision, into that of an 'information broker' and advisor to other institutions, groups, and individuals. But more than this, they have become the energizers and facilitators of those 'others' in their new-found obligations. As a future-orientated doctrine, crime prevention now speaks to all of us, as it asks us to consider the avoidance and prevention of 'risks' or 'risky situations' in our working and everyday lives. The task of prevention, no longer solely deposited in the blue uniforms of the police, has become dispersed throughout the social fabric, a shift in responsibility that some institutions, for diverse and complex reasons, have been willing to embrace.

This growing interest in crime prevention dovetails the two other central concepts underlying the current shift in focus: appeals to 'community' and 'partnerships'. They are interconnected in a variety of ways. At one level, the conjunction of both 'prevention' and 'community' arises because the 'community' constitutes a pre-eminent institution of informal (preventative) social control (Skogan 1990a). At a second level, it represents a suitable location for mobilizing individuals, a way of reaching ordinary people and encouraging them to adopt preventative measures (Hope and Shaw 1988b: 8). Similarly, the relationship between 'prevention' and 'partnerships' can be explained in part by the fact that crime prevention has tended to exist as a peripheral concern of numerous agencies, and yet a core activity of none. In addition, crime prevention appears to transcend the competence and organizational capacity of any established criminal justice agency. Therefore, the promotion of prevention would appear to need to tap into and harness the workings of those wider diverse organizations already in existence. Consequently, the field of crime prevention has been, for some time, at the forefront of criminological developments of both 'community' involvement and the elaboration of a 'partnership' approach. I will begin by considering the recent experience and development of a 'community' orientation, before going on to examine inter-agency 'partnerships'.

Appeals to Community

Across diverse fields of public and social policy, appeals to 'community' have become commonplace. From 'community medicine' through 'community architecture' to 'care in the community', government programmes (and opposition parties' proposals) have been launched to political acclaim (Butcher *et al.* 1993). 'Community' has become a policy buzz word. In the field of crime and criminal justice this emphasis upon 'community' has been particularly acute, as witnessed by the various initiatives in 'community policing', 'community-based crime prevention', 'community mediation', and 'punishments in the community'. The attraction of the notion of 'community' unites and transcends the established British political parties. On the political Right, conservative commentators like John Gray (1993; 1995) and David Willetts (1992) draw heavily upon the concept of 'community', as do those on the Left, particularly within the 'New' Labour Party (Blair 1996). For the more radical Left 'community' is seen as the home of grass roots activism and the space in which to challenge structures of gender, race, and class inequalities, as well as to support mutuality and self-empowerment. The diverse interests, ideologies, and symbolic referents embodied in appeals to 'community' are the subjects of detailed discussions in Chapters 3 and 5, for the moment I will concentrate upon a brief outline of the growing policy discourse referencing appeals to 'community' and some of the recent governmental strategies to which they have given rise.

Community Policing

The interest and fascination with 'community policing' is probably the most obvious and well documented expression of this appeal to 'community' in the field of criminal justice. A multitude of experiments and initiatives within police organizations around the world have been initiated in the name of 'community policing' (Friedmann 1992). Often there is little that these programmes share beyond a label of unfathomable plasticity. However, a common aspiration of many initiatives is to reconfigure the Peelian legacy in order, somehow, to reconstitute physical and psychological relations between the police and public, to build trust, and to encourage greater public assistance in policing.

In Britain, according to established accounts of recent police developments, the 1960s and in particular the introduction of Unit Beat Policing and panda cars, was the era in which it all went wrong (Holdaway 1983; Weatheritt 1986). However, the seeds of the problem had been sown long before, and lay in the historic police quest for greater professionalism, specialism, and technological sophistication. The decade in which the 'white heat of technology' burnt bright brought concerns about police–public relations to a head. The intention of the Unit Beat reorganization, introduced by a Home Office circular in 1967, may have been to offer a closer service between police and public. However, it had the unintended consequence, in part due to poor resourcing and police culture, of removing officers from the streets and transferring them into panda cars. This was coupled with the increased use of telephones, computers, and other forms of technology to which the police had turned in their quest for greater efficiency. This period also marked the proliferation of specialist tactical squads and reconfirmation of criminal investigation as the most prestigious arm of policing. The police portrayed themselves, and came to be represented in the media, as 'crime fighters' in the style of reactive 'fire brigade' policing (Sparks 1992a; Reiner 1992b: 76). Consequently, whilst communication between one officer and another improved, as did the ability of patrol officers to speed from one incident to the next, commentators became aware of a growing lack of opportunity for face to face contact, short of conflictual arrest situations, between police and policed. The notion of the 'professional' separation of the police from the public appeared to have become a chasm.

The modern notion of 'community policing' was thus directly born out of a critique of a traditional model of police professionalism. Consequently, it has become not a single concept but a catch-all phrase for a variety of organizational strategies aimed at improving the quality of service provision within the police (Weatheritt 1983: 4–5). In Britain the clamours for a change to the dominant reactive 'fire brigade' style of policing became more acute against the background of corruption scandals, rising crime rates, and falling clear-up rates, urban disorders and a perceived growing lack of public confidence of the late 1970s and early 1980s. Added to this were the findings of official Home Office research which questioned the effectiveness of policing (Clarke and Hough 1984). The new concern became articulated in the notion of 'community policing', particularly as espoused by John Alderson the former Chief Constable of Devon and Cornwall. His belief was that as police forces have grown in size and complexity they have become remote from the people they serve. Consequently, the contact that the police have with the public tends to be reactive and conflict ridden, leaving a relationship which has little space for consent. In its place he argued for the pressing need to build 'consensus policing' around a much closer relationship between police and public in which contact is proactive and non-conflictual (Alderson 1979). This sentiment was endorsed by Lord Scarman (1981) in his report into the Brixton disorders of April 1981.

This argument was given greater poignancy by Left Realist criminologists who added concerns about political accountability into
the community policing debate. In an incisive critique of the drift
towards 'military' policing, Kinsey *et al.* (1986: chapter 2) argue
that local accountability constitutes a central element of effective
policing. They declare that the aggressive policing of certain communities and the consequential alienation from the police of members of that community, has led to a declining flow of information
to the police from the public. This they argue, sets in train a vicious
circle in which the police become more reliant upon aggressive,
proactive fishing expeditions into the community, like Operation
Swamp 81 which sparked the Brixton disorders. At the heart of their
thesis is the contention that policing cannot hope to be effective
without good public co-operation, which should include forms of
consultation and democratic accountability (Kinsey *et al.* 1986:
chapter 8). For it is only if the public, and particularly those most
likely to have information of value to the police, feel confidence in
the police that the crucial flow of information, upon which policing
depends, will be restored. They rely upon locally based survey
evidence to show that those people with the greatest level of contact
with the police are most likely to be distrustful of the police. In
order to restore policing by consent, they argue, these groups need
to be brought back into processes of consultation and trust building,
in order to restimulate the vital flow of information. Along with
other critical criminologists, Kinsey *et al.* (1986) propose increasing
the responsibility and responsiveness of the police to their local
communities, combined with a corresponding public participation
in directing policing strategy at the local level (Taylor 1981; Lea and
Young 1984; Spencer 1985a).

'Community policing' came to be seen, therefore, as the collective
answer to abuses of power, lack of effectiveness, poor public confidence, and concerns about legitimacy. Weatheritt identifies three
defining characteristics in much that passes for 'community policing'; the greater use of foot patrols and the posting of officers to
geographic areas for which they have continuing responsibility; the
development of partnerships in crime prevention; and the establishment of structures and processes for consulting local communities
about their policing priorities and problems (1993a: 126). I have
already discussed the growth of partnerships in crime prevention, so
now I will consider, briefly, the development of the other two

defining characteristics, beat patrols and 'community' consultation arrangements.

First, foot patrols as a means of delivering a high level of police visibility and non-conflictual police–public contact had been a cornerstone of the Peelian legacy. Thus, for many police officers an important element of the appeal of community policing lies in its sense of continuity with aspects of traditional policing. For many chief constables it is a case of 'old wine in new bottles' (Reiner 1991: 110). Further, it appears to connect with a real public demand. Surveys of the public have repeatedly reinforced the message for community policing through the finding that the public wants to see more officers on the beat (Wilmott 1987). As Weatheritt notes, this policy of returning officers to the beat was not just good for public relations, it also made economic sense in the late 1970s, as many forces had been required to introduce vehicle mileage restrictions due to the increases in petrol price (1993a: 127). It also connected with research findings which showed that a high percentage of police work, somewhere in the region of 80 to 90 per cent, is generated by calls from the public for a variety of incidents that require police assistance, mostly of a non-criminal nature.

The debate about the best use of patrol officers also connected with important research findings on police effectiveness. Two Home Office research studies concluded that the capacity of police patrols to prevent crime was severely limited, and that most crime was detected, not by the Sherlock Holmes image of the lone detective (or his latter-day counterpart, Inspector Morse) unassisted by the public, but on the basis of co-operation and information from the public (Morris and Heal 1981; Clarke and Hough 1984). Home Office researchers concluded that, by their estimation, on average a patrol officer in London could expect to pass within one hundred yards of a burglary in progress once every eight years and even then they would probably not even know that a crime was being committed. These findings seemed to play into the hands of the advocates of community policing and to focus concern around the most efficient use of patrols in stimulating information and public co-operation. Spurred on by the government's quest for 'value for money', particularly given the amount of police time and personnel that patrolling absorbs, a considerable degree of subsequent effort has gone into developing forms of 'focused', 'geographical', 'sector', and 'problem-oriented' patrols (Goldstein 1990; Bennett 1991; Bennett and Kemp 1995; Dixon and Stanko 1995).

Secondly, the growth of community consultation procedures needs to be set against the background of debates about police accountability. The declining role of police authorities became particularly acute after the 1964 Police Act and the realization of the legal limitations of their powers during the bitter policing of the 1984/5 miners' strike (Spencer 1985b). More recently, this trend has continued with the Police and Magistrates' Courts Act 1994 which further limited the democratic input into formal accountability structures of police authorities.[7] Lord Scarman's Report (1981) had called for the establishment of local community consultation arrangements. This led to the enactment of section 106 of the Police and Criminal Evidence Act 1984. The Act did not state what form consultation should take but Home Officer circular 2/1985 recommended the setting up of formal police consultative committees (PCCs) (Home Office 1985). Largely, this advice has been followed, so that by the end of 1991 well over 500 groups had been set up throughout the country (Weatheritt 1993a: 134). Their principal aim is public participation through a number of objectives: the improved articulation of the community's viewpoint; the improved education of the community about policing; the resolution of any conflict between police and any particular community group; and encouraging practical 'self-help' community crime prevention initiatives (Morgan 1989: 221). However, the available research suggests that PCCs are highly dependent upon the police for information and support. Furthermore, police knowledge and expertise is largely unchallenged in the face of committee members who are relatively ignorant of policing (Morgan 1989; Stratta 1990: 3). As a consequence, meetings frequently take the form of the police 'educating' the community representatives about policing and the limitations of the police service.

---

[7] As a consequence of the Police and Magistrates' Court Act 1994, just under half of the members of the new police authorities will be selected by nomination rather than election, whereas previously two thirds of their membership had been drawn from elected local authority councillors and one third local magistrates. Of a total membership of seventeen, only nine will be elected. Three of the remaining eight will be nominated magistrates and five will be jointly nominated by the police authority and the Home Secretary, in keeping with the government's desire to bring outsiders, particularly business people, into the running of the police.

Neighbourhood Watch

The expansion of neighbourhood watch is often held up as the icon of successful community policing. In some senses it brings together elements of all three of Weatheritt's defining characteristics, although primarily concerned with crime prevention partnerships. Neighbourhood watch, therefore, combines both the crime prevention impulse and the 'community' ethic. Neighbourhood watch seeks to generate community-based activity in two inter-related ways. First, it represents a means of encouraging individuals and families to become more security conscious, both in terms of their own responsibility for personal crime prevention and for community security through surveillance. Secondly, it seeks to build upon and promote a shared concern about matters of crime and security in the hope that this will produce new patterns of informal social interaction amongst people living within a locality, thereby creating forms of internal community control and regulation along the lines advocated by Wilson and Kelling's 'broken window' thesis (1982).

The first neighbourhood watch schemes were set up in 1982 and by December 1993 there were over five million households in England and Wales covered by a total of 130,000 schemes (Central Statistics Office 1995: 168). They were heavily promoted by senior police officers, most notably Sir Kenneth Newman the Metropolitan Commissioner of Police in the early and mid 1980s. Between the years 1988 and 1992 the proportion of households where a scheme had been established rose from 18 per cent to 28 per cent (Home Office 1994b). However, we should be careful not to over-interpret the significance of such impressive figures, as membership of a scheme can include diverse levels of activism or participation from, at one extreme, placing a sticker in the window, to the highly energetic scheme co-ordinator at the other extreme. Nevertheless, this expansion created a crucial problem for the police. They increasingly became aware that a considerable amount of police time and resources were needed in order to set up, maintain, and sustain active neighbourhood watch schemes. It could be argued that by the 1990s neighbourhood watch was floundering on the rocks of its own perceived numerical success. This caused some commentators to describe some situation as characterized by 'low take up rates, weak community penetration and limping, dormant or still-born schemes' (McConville and Shepard 1992: 115). Further, the evaluation research shows that neighbourhood watch has had little or no success in achieving a reduction of crime, although it may have some effect in addressing communal fear of crime and producing greater levels of trust and confidence in relations between public and police (Bennett 1990; 1991; Rosenbaum 1988a). Simultaneously, neighbourhood watch has been easiest to establish in more affluent, suburban areas with low crime rates, rather than in inner-city, crime prone public sector housing estates with heterogeneous populations (Hussain 1988; McConville and Shepard 1992).

In order to reinvigorate the neighbourhood watch movement the Home Secretary, Michael Howard announced in September 1994 that neighbourhood watch schemes were to be encouraged to include patrols of active citizens, who would 'walk with a purpose' in their local areas. This is the kind of 'voluntary collective action' which the Home Secretary, in his earlier Disraeli lecture of February 1994, had declared to be the mainstay of civil society, the provision of public goods and collective wants by communities as opposed to state intervention (Howard 1994). However, this proposal received a mixed response, particularly from the police themselves. Subsequently, it had to be toned down by excising any reference to 'patrols' to avoid the idea that what was being suggested amounted to 'policing on the cheap'. A further concern raised was the spectre of vigilantism. This episode exposes crucial tensions and ambiguities in how far the process of devolving responsibility for crime control can be legitimately taken. Nevertheless, 'community policing' in all its diverse guises and neighbourhood watch have now become part of the accepted, dominant philosophy expressed not only by all mainstream political parties but also most chief constables (Reiner 1991: 125).

Community Punishments and Sanctions

Similarly, appeals to community have found resonance in other fields of criminal justice. One notable example concerns policies advocating 'punishments in the community'. The British experience has largely been driven by the heavy burden to the Treasury of the cost of imprisonment. This has resulted in the introduction of a variety of new sentences, which somehow fall short of actual penal incarceration, and yet are often deliberately 'tougher' (i.e. more like the existing prison) than their predecessors. Hence, in this context 'in the community' is translated into anything which is not 'in prison'.[8] This was particularly evident in the policy debates preceding the 1991 Criminal Justice Act (Home Office 1988d; 1990d). The Act embodied a notion of 'twin tracking' or 'bifurcation', by which the purpose of the criminal justice system should be seen as separating 'less serious offenders' to be dealt with 'in the community', from more serious offenders who constitute a potential danger to the public (Bottoms 1995). The Act introduced a sentencing regime which allows for a 'combination order' which combines probation and community service and which permits any community sentence to be combined with a fine or compensation. In doing so, the Act sought to make community service orders, which had been statutory sentences since the early 1970s, more attractive to the magistracy and judiciary. It also leaves statutory space for home curfews, or electronic tagging, which despite the unsuccessful original Home Office pilot studies (Mair and Nee 1990) remain on the policy agenda. The probation service in its new 'centre stage' role has been handed the responsibility for managing punishments in the community. The resultant effects and unintended consequences of the introduction of 'community punishments' upon the penal complex and those who pass through it, has been the subject of much debate which need not detain us here, it will suffice to note that commentators have identified the complex yet crucial processes of 'net widening' (in which new populations are dragged into the criminal justice net), 'mesh thinning' (in which the degree of interference in the lives of those involved is increased) 'penal inflation' (in which the degree of punitiveness of interventions is increased), 'institutional blurring' (by which the boundaries between 'inside' and 'outside' the system are confused), and 'transcarceration' (by which those incarcerated move from one institution of incarceration to another) (see Cohen 1979; 1985; Nelken 1985; Hudson 1993).[9]

Finally, at the fringes of policy debates, more genuinely community based sanctioning processes have been experimented with recently in Britain, notably in the form of community mediation, both victim/offender mediation and reparation and neighbourhood

---

[8] This negative understanding of 'community' is reminiscent of the experiences of community care for mentally ill patients in the 1980s. 'Community' became synonymous with closing down mental health institutions rather than the provision of alternative 'care in the community'.

[9] The most notable example of transcarceration has been the transfer of individuals from mental health institutions to prison, via 'the community', with the closing down of the former.

mediation.[10] Mediation, in this context, is a process of third party facilitation of communication between conflicting parties (either 'face to face' or through the mediator as a 'go between') in which, in theory, the parties reach their own solutions to their problems. The mediator acts as an intermediary—a conduit in communication—but has no authority to make a decision or force a settlement. Nevertheless, the mediator has a powerfully influential role in the process. Ideally, it is consent based, participatory and forward looking in which the parties arrive at mutually agreed settlements as to reparation. Within the concept of mediation, however, the questions of who initiates the process and its relationship with the existing formal criminal court, remain deliberately open-ended (Davis *et al.* 1987: 5). Consequently, different schemes operate at different points within the process and with differing relations to established agencies (see Crawford 1996b). Similarly, the development of community mediation in Britain has been piecemeal, fragmented, and highly localized.

Despite the fact that the Home Office's interest in victim/offender mediation waned after it funded four pilot projects in 1985, elsewhere there has been a growing interest in mediation. Senior judges, policy makers, police officers, and other criminal justice practitioners have voiced their support for the wider use of mediation. In addition, the Labour Party (1995b) is committed to extending the use of mediation at least in the resolution of neighbourhood disputes. Furthermore, despite the lack of direct central funding both victim/offender and community mediation schemes continue to survive and operate largely on local sources of funding. Collectively they have constituted themselves under a national umbrella organization, namely Mediation UK.

Further, important new developments in Community (or Family Group) Conferencing, borrowing from the experiences of New Zealand and Australia (Morris *et al.* 1993; Alder and Wundersitz 1994), are beginning to be experimented with in Britain, through NACRO, Mediation UK and some police forces, notably Thames Valley (Mediation UK 1995: 8–9). They are attracting widespread interest among policy makers as well as academics. They involve a

---

[10] The essential difference between victim/offender and community mediation schemes is that the latter tend to deal with disputes which have not been defined as crimes by any formal agency. Often these disputes involve existing interpersonal relations, particularly between neighbours.

process which takes court or police referrals to a 'conference' at which victims, offenders, their families, supporters, and relevant agency personnel attempt to come to terms with what has occurred and how it can best be resolved. This process draws more explicitly upon community as an agent of control—through ceremonies of shame and reintegration—by drawing in more participants within the mediation process (Braithwaite and Mugford 1994). I will return to consider the workings and significance of mediation schemes in greater detail later in this book (see Chapter 5).

Policy makers have not been impervious to the insights provided by such initiatives and research findings, albeit that the implications that they have drawn from them are often fundamentally different. For example, the notion that informal family and communal relations can act as more important deterrents to crime than formal court sanctions (see Braithwaite 1989b: chapter 5, for a summary of research) has been eagerly picked up by politicians and policy makers alike. The established political parties have recently been vying to compete with each other over new policies that seek to 'name and shame' offenders particularly young people, increase parental responsibility for the crimes of their children, and criminalize the anti-social activities of neighbours. These and other initiatives have moved the 'punishment in the community' debate further forward, as they seek to activate, facilitate, and utilize existing informal control for the purposes of the formal penal system. Furthermore, they do so in ways which resonate with earlier, pre-industrial forms of punishment.

As this brief sketch illustrates, the criminal justice policies which appeal to the notion of 'community', in some form or other, are diverse in their nature and orientation (see Bottoms 1995). Yet they all embody to some degree a perceived need to connect the formal criminal justice process with informal control mechanisms and to involve ordinary people in its working. However the assumptions upon which the resultant policies are premised, their intended purpose, the interest they serve, and their implications all raise vexed issues to which I will return in order to explain their appeal (Chapter 3) and to consider their implications in the light of my own empirical research findings (Chapter 5).

Inter-Agency Partnerships

The development of the partnership approach, as I have already implied, is intrinsically bound up with the growth of both 'crime prevention' and 'appeals to community'. In many senses inter-agency partnerships are merely the extension of the concept of 'community' to organizations. In the past decade these organizational communities' have become an important and growing part of the map of British government, generally, and the criminal justice landscape, in particular. Central government initiatives including the Urban Programme, City Challenge, the recent Single Regeneration Budget, and the establishment of English Partnerships, have all acted as stimuli to a 'partnership' approach across areas of social policy and urban regeneration.[11]

Consequently, we have seen the proliferation of a diversity of structures designed to bring together representatives of relevant statutory bodies, private corporations, voluntary organizations, and sometimes representatives of 'the community'. These new systems of local governance comprise what some commentators have referred to as 'issue networks' or 'policy communities' (Marsh and Rhodes 1992: 249–51). The expansion of partnerships has come to constitute a 'quiet revolution' in the nature and shape of the administrative structures of British governance. It has been so extensive that it recently caused the managing director of the business strategy group of Business in the Community[12] to state that:

The opportunity now as we approach the millennium is to become the leader amongst industrialised nations in combining international

[11] City Challenge created a series of competitions, as a result of which 31 local areas have been selected to spend £37.5 million on innovative ways of responding to urban decline. The process required the establishment of new administrative mechanisms which combine public, private, and voluntary sectors in order to implement five year programmes. The government allocated no new money for City Challenge, which is not an independent programme as such, but a new process for allocating funds that are top-sliced from the budgets of other programmes that run alongside it in every area. In 1994 the government developed upon the Challenge model on a wider regional basis with the Single Regeneration Budget and its integrated regional offices.

[12] Business in the Community is an organization which aims to encourage 'partnerships' in key areas of concern such as education and the environment. It also seeks to promote good practice in corporate community involvement and to provide information and advice to the business community. It has a membership of 450 UK companies, and seeks to promote an ideology of corporate community investment in the UK along the lines of the United Ways initiative in the USA.

competitiveness and social cohesiveness through the active engagement in
partnership of business, public and not-for-profit sectors.

(Grayson 1994: 50)

However, the 'partnership' approach and variants of it are to be
found not only in Britain but also blossoming across Europe and
North America (Blumstein 1986; Steenhuis 1986; van Dijk 1995). It
has even acquired an international status with the recognition of the
unanimous resolution of the United Nations Congress on the Prevention of Crime and the Treatment of Offenders, in August 1990.
The resolution reiterates the now familiar declaration that crime
prevention is not simply a matter for police but must:

bring together those with responsibility for planning and development,
for family, health, employment and training, housing and social services,
leisure activities, schools, the police, and the justice system in order to deal
with the conditions that generate crime.

(United Nations 1991)

In British criminal justice policy a growing body of opinion both
in academic and government circles has endorsed the need for
greater multi-agency 'co-operation' primarily at a local level, as
providing the most effective means of policy formation and service
delivery. The essential argument for a multi-agency approach lies in
what Young (1992: 45) has referred to as the 'realities of crime and
social control'. Social control in modern industrial societies, it is
argued, is by its very nature multi-agency. Different agencies have a
different 'purchase on a given crime problem' due to their particular
expertise (Young 1991). The problem, however, is that this response
is not co-ordinated, but disparate, with no overall rationale. It lacks
'systematization'. Agencies are more often in conflict with each
other than mutually supportive. The result is what Raine and Willson refer to as 'a Byzantine soap opera of organisational complexity
and politics' (1993: 166). Further, it is argued that the work of one
agency impacts upon the work of the next, in terms of its capacity to
intervene, the forms of intervention available, its resources, and so
on. Different agencies interact in divergent ways in relation to
specific crime problems. Criminal justice agencies, therefore, are
both inter-connected and mutually dependent. As a consequence of
the logic of this argument, failings in criminal justice have come to
be defined as arising out of the lack of co-ordination. It has become
fashionable to talk about criminal justice as a 'non-system' to stress
this dysfunctionality (Moxon 1985). In its place practitioners have

been, and continue to be, urged to form *horizontal* 'partnerships' which cut across *vertical* bureaucratic imperatives. These 'partnerships' in the field of crime prevention have been defined in a British government publication as the:

co-ordinated action by a variety of relevant local agencies: bringing together in each location the police, local authorities, the probation service, representatives from local business and industry, and voluntary and community groups to consider the particular crime problems faced by the local community and to use the collective expertise and resources available to devise measures to tackle those problems.

(Home Office 1990a: 23)

As we have already seen, circulars 8/1984 and 44/1990 sought to reinforce and extend the centrality of 'inter-agency co-operation' to contemporary criminal justice policy, supported by subsequent initiatives. Together these developments have helped establish the new government orthodoxy that: 'the police service alone cannot tackle the problem of crime' (Home Office 1993b: 1). This vogue for 'partnerships against crime' is not restricted to the rhetoric of the political Right of recent Conservative governments. For some years, the Labour Party's official policy has been that 'our aim is to make us all partners against crime' (Labour Party 1987; 1994; Blair 1996); and see also the policy of the Liberal Democrats (1996).

However, it is not only within the field of crime prevention that partnerships have been promulgated as a panacea to the ills of criminal justice inefficiencies and ineffectiveness. Other early developments occurred in the field of child abuse. The extensive enquiry into the Cleveland child abuse cases in 1987 came to a central conclusion that much that had gone wrong in the handling of the cases arose out of poor relations and channels of communication between the essential bodies involved, particularly the police and social services. Elizabeth Butler-Sloss (1988: 248–51) in the Report's recommendations identified the need for improved inter-agency co-ordination in dealing with child abuse cases in the future. In the light of the recommendations changes to practice have been made and new procedures introduced to implement them. Likewise, Lord Justice Woolf's report into the prison disturbances at Strangeways and elsewhere in the country in 1990, recommended 'closer co-operation between different parts of the criminal justice system' (Woolf and Tumin 1991: 433; Bottoms 1995). In the field of juvenile justice important decisions about cautioning policy for some time now have been in the hands of multi-agency panels. Encouraged by Home Office circulars 14/1985 and 59/1990, juvenile justice workers in conjunction with the police and in liaison with other relevant organizations have formed diversionary panels (Pratt 1989; Davis *et al.* 1989).

The probation service, despite its track record of working with voluntary bodies, also became the subject of central government's 'partnership' mania (Smith *et al.* 1993). With the probation service's move to the 'centre stage' of criminal justice through its delivery of community punishments, partnerships were advocated as a key means of providing that service. The role envisaged for the service was originally articulated in the Home Office's (1990e) discussion document 'Partnership in Dealing with Offenders in the Community'. It stresses the importance of a partnership approach both to traditional areas of probation work, i.e. supervising offenders in the community, work with prisoners before and after release and to more novel areas of work, such as community-based crime prevention. This was followed up, some two years later, by a 'decision document' of the same title, which declared that, 'the probation service should take the lead in developing local partnership arrangements and should make financial provision for resourcing this work' (Home Office 1992b: 1). To this end the document first sought to describe a formalized agreement between the probation service and what it referred to as the 'independent sector': an amalgam of voluntary organizations, community associations, and private companies. Secondly, it was suggested that 'around 5 per cent' of the revenue budget of each probation service should be allocated to partnership schemes.

The notion of 'partnership' alluded to in this context appears to have a more specific meaning than elsewhere, in part because of the tradition of 'informal' partnerships with voluntary agencies in the provision of certain services. In the probation context there is a greater concern with, first, the formal—almost contractual—nature of arrangements, and secondly, the structured purchaser/provider relations between the parties. The 'partnerships' envisioned within the government's proposal for the probation service appear to involve more the competitive contracting out of services whereby the probation service purchases voluntary sector provision, than a creative mutual negotiation over the service to be provided with all the parties contributing equally. The underlying philosophy seems to be about the construction of a 'mixed economy' in the provision of criminal justice services rather than anything else, a theme I return to in the next chapter (Nellis 1995b).

In other diverse fields of criminal justice, including racial harassment and domestic violence, the importance of 'multi-agency' work has been repeatedly stressed. To reinforce this message at a national level, a Criminal Justice Consultative Council, consisting of representatives of senior management from all the relevant agencies, was set up in 1991. Its aim is to secure a 'peak' level framework for maximum co-operation in the management throughout the criminal justice process. More locally, this is supplemented by Area Criminal Justice Liaison Committees which provide co-ordination across court services.

This recent growth and extensive reception of the 'partnership' approach across policy fields in such a short period of time is exceptional. This is particularly so in the field of criminal justice, given the competing interests that justice seeks to serve and balance, as well as the structural conflicts and diverse organizational bodies with divergent cultural traditions to which this complexity has given rise. It is as if collectively we have suddenly awoken from a two hundred year reverie to find that we have been preoccupied with playing a game according to the wrong set of rules. And yet, the new rules do not seem to fit the structure of the game, the terrain it is played on, or the traditional relations between the players, let alone between them and the spectators, now called upon to join the game. The image of the 'client'—the passive recipient of a service—has been replaced by a new contractual image of co-operation in which individuals are called upon in an active and responsible capacity. In place of a rhetorical model of professional 'expertise' is one which emphasizes shared information, stressing the importance of diverse knowledgeable organizations and the knowledgeable public. And yet, as I shall seek to demonstrate in Chapter 4, rather than being rejected, expertise is being recalibrated, restructured, and redefined. Partnerships may be becoming the conduits of 'expert' local knowledge about crime from the public to diverse agencies. Simultaneously, those partnerships are seeking to impart 'expert' advice to local people upon how best to prevent crime themselves. In this there is a structured form of discursive duplicity or what O'Malley has termed a series of 'subterranean translation processes' (1996: 323) in operation.

Hence, the ethos and practice of 'partnerships' embody deep structural antagonisms and unresolved tensions. Partnerships, in all their guises place a high premium upon consensus, communication, mutuality, and the sharing of knowledge. And yet, the reality of competition, conflict, and organizational autonomy remain essential characteristics of criminal justice. For if, as Rock notes, it is the 'independent interdependence' between organizations which constitutes 'the weak force which binds the criminal justice system together' (Rock 1990: 39), then what impact will a leap to embrace partnerships entail? 'Independence' and 'partnership' stand in a highly ambiguous relation to each other. What shock waves might such a dramatic change in rhetoric send through the taken for granted pillars—and 'weak force'—of the criminological enterprise? In the rush to 'partnerships' little thought has been given to such questions or their implications.

Conclusions

In this chapter I have traced a number of historic developments and changes in crime control discourses and practices, in order to highlight the significance of the recent appeals to 'prevention', 'community', and 'partnerships'. The preceding discussion has not sought to constitute a comprehensive or exhaustive overview of recent developments and changes, but has endeavoured to highlight some of the more salient policy interventions, organizational initiatives, and debates which have occurred in recent years in Britain. It has been suggested that around these inter-connected terms a coalescence of strategies is being formed which needs to be understood for all its nuances. That is not to suggest that the shifts outlined in this chapter have a unitary logic or essential trajectory. Rather, I have tried to show how many of the developments have occurred in the pursuit of diverse interests and for different organizational imperatives. Similarly, they cannot all be reduced to a simple singular objective of a coherent governing party political ideology. The trends are more deeply rooted and intricate than that.

It has been argued that a particular vision of crime control constructed from the mid eighteenth century to the mid twentieth century implicitly, and often explicitly, has been called into question by these recent trends in policy. The complex division of criminal justice labour, produced under the weight of processes of professionalization, bureaucratization, and specialization, appears to be under attack, at least at a discursive level. There are important continuities with past developments, and yet, these are now being forced to co-exist alongside fundamental shifts in rhetoric. The central, unifying symbol of the blue-uniformed police officer as the repository of social order has become fragmented as that task is increasingly dispersed throughout the body politic. Institutions which previously perceived crime control as outside their legitimate concerns have joined, for different and sometimes contradictory reasons, the 'corporate fight against crime'. Where once the public was perceived to be the recipient of an 'expert' service, the injunction now is that only *together* we will crack crime'. The public along with diverse organizations, associations, and private business has become implicated in the task of crime control.

It has been suggested that the cumulative weight of the trilogy of 'prevention', 'community', and 'partnerships', has significantly altered the shape of criminal justice policy. This rhetorical shift embodies a powerful critique of the established criminal justice institutional framework upon which the promise of crime control had come to be founded over the past two hundred years or so. And yet, this critique has not been realized in the developments to which policy has given rise. For while it appears to call into question the very processes of professionalization, specialization, centralization, and bureaucratization, as well as the established division of criminal justice labour, none of these has been displaced as a core element of the criminological enterprise. They have become fused and confused within the new discourses. Thus, whilst in essence the shift to crime prevention and community involvement implies a critique of 'expertise', in practice expertise remains an essential element in contemporary criminal justice communications. We are left with a complex interplay between the logics of new discourses and the practices of old institutions, so that the former are transformed and mutated beyond their surface logic, immediate appearance or intended outcomes. Consequently, appeals to 'community', 'prevention', and 'partnership' can neither be understood as having fully transformed the shape of criminal justice according to their own self-proclaimed image, nor can they be said to constitute a smoke screen behind which the same old practices are occurring. To identify the real shifts that this trilogy of concepts heralds, we need to connect them to wider social and political trends and currents.

Further, we need to question why this potentially fundamental reassessment of the criminal justice complex should be occurring at this particular historic junction. These are the tasks of the next chapter.

3

The Shifting Social and Political Context: Questions of Legitimacy and Responsibility

Having outlined the recent growth and inter-connected histories of 'crime prevention', appeals to 'community' and 'partnerships', two related questions present themselves as in need of being addressed: why should this conceptual shift to 'community', 'prevention', and 'partnerships' have taken place? and why at this particular historic juncture? This chapter will attempt to explore and answer these questions.

I begin by reviewing and critically assessing some of the contemporary explanations advanced for the emergence of 'community partnerships' in the late twentieth century. This will involve the examination of policy and academic justifications for the current trends in criminal justice discourse. I will then go on to advance an alternative analysis. This perspective will focus upon issues of legitimacy and responsibility. It will be argued that appeals to 'community' and 'partnerships' make up an important element in the recalibration of what constitutes the legitimate responsibilities of individuals, groups, and the state. In order to comprehend fully the nature and significance of the developments set out in the previous chapter we need to locate them within, and connect them to, more extensive social and political changes. Therefore, I will sketch out and accent a number of broad political trends and shifts which simultaneously are unfolding across a variety of areas of social life. This wider canvas, it will be argued, allows us to trace and evaluate the ideologies and governmental strategies which underpin these developments, and against which we can better understand changes in patterns of governance of which appeals to 'community' and 'partnerships' are a part.

How can we explain this major trend in criminal policy rhetoric? Implicitly, if not explicitly, the cumulative weight of the major shifts in paradigm outlined in Chapter 2, raises fundamental questions about the modern criminological enterprise. These shifts call into question whether the social processes and implications of crime can be contained within specialist institutions constructed for that purpose. They problematize the role of 'expertise' and 'specialization' within bureaucracies. Further, they call into question the idea that criminal justice, as a hitherto understood project, is a fundamental organizing institution in the construction of a better society. Consequently, they raise doubts as to whether the project of 'modernity', of using knowledge and technology to control and improve social conditions on behalf of the whole population, is itself a desirable or attainable end. The holistic, community-based rhetoric of current policy discourse speaks to, and echoes, a pre-modern age, of tradition, informality, homogeneity, and mutuality.

Dominant Explanations for the Shifts in Rhetoric

A frequent explanation given by criminal justice practitioners is epitomized by a comment from one police officer involved in a community-based crime prevention project in the course of my research. He suggested that, 'we've just got to do something new. The crime rate is getting out of control and we don't know what else to do.' However, in the quest to excavate deeper understandings, we need to look beyond such surface level explanations of rising crime and the naïve fumbling for new remedies. For the purpose of the analysis that follows, we can identify three broad, dominant explanations for the recent policy shifts encapsulated by the combined appeals to 'prevention', 'community', and 'partnerships'. These I will consider in turn under the headings of 'system failures', 'state overload', and the 'dispersal of discipline' theses.

'System Failures' Thesis

One dominant explanation for the rise of the 'partnership approach' and appeals to 'community' is premised upon the assumption that deficiencies in criminal justice are 'system failures': that along with other local services, criminal justice lacks 'co-ordination', 'fit', and 'systematization'. This is explained, by some, as the product of modernity and the associated dual processes of first, the growing specialization of institutions and division of labour along organizational lines and secondly, the historic quest of professions to control a market for their services and 'expertise'. From this perspective these historic developments are seen as conflicting with contemporary social needs of administrative rationalization and the efficient management of crime control. Thus, 'professionalization' and 'specialization' as rationalizing enterprises have produced, over time, their own irrationalities and incongruencies.

John Mudd (1984), an American commentator, provides one such explanation which constitutes a useful entry point into the issues at the heart of the debate. He highlights the existence, in advanced capitalist societies in the late twentieth century, of what he refers to as a number of 'institutionalised gaps'. He suggests that these 'gaps' take two broad forms. First, gaps exist among the increasingly specialized but inter-related administrative agencies, what he terms the 'co-ordination problem'. Secondly, gaps exist between the actions of these agencies and the preferences of those served, or what he calls the 'responsiveness problem' (Mudd 1984: 2). These gaps, Mudd argues, are the product of historic developments which have prioritized specialization and institutional autonomy. They represent the basic flaws in contemporary neighbourhood services.

Mudd cogently illustrates the implications of the first system failure, the 'co-ordination' problem, for contemporary society by reference to what he describes as the 'rat problem'. He outlines his analogy, in relation to neighbourhood services more generally, as follows:

If a rat is found in an apartment, it is a housing inspection responsibility; if it runs into a restaurant, the health department has jurisdiction; if it goes outside and dies in an alley, public works takes over. More complex undertakings compound the confusion.

(Mudd 1984: 8)

The same analogy is easily applied to the criminal justice context. Wilson and Kelling, developing upon Mudd's analogy, conclude that:

a police officer who takes public complaints about rats seriously will go crazy trying to figure out what agency in the city has responsibility for rat control and then inducing it to kill the rats (1989: 52).

The solutions to these 'system failures' are essentially managerial ones. They involve the removal of gaps and the limitation of friction and conflict for the smooth running of the system as a whole. On the basis of his experience in New York City government in the early 1980s, Mudd's own remedy is the establishment of neighbourhood level 'district cabinets'. These should bring together supervisors of each relevant agency to meet regularly and address common concerns. These 'district cabinets' represent an ideal type 'partnerships'. In the field of policing, and crime control in Britain, this kind of analysis is echoed throughout the pages of Home Office research reports as well as official inquiry reports such as Butler-Sloss's Report into the Cleveland child abuse cases in the late 1980s. Researchers at the Home Office have made various attempts at modelling the criminal justice system in order to emphasize its interdependence and 'system quality' (Morgan 1985; Moxon 1985). The implicit assumption is that criminal justice is a set of interdependent subsystems which need to be better managed in order to reduce waste, limit duplication, and friction. 'Coherence, co-ordination, and integration' constitute the rallying cries of this perspective (Blumstein 1986). The emerging model is one that has many parallels with the 'rational organization of an industrial enterprise' in which the various departments work together in a well co-ordinated fashion towards the same corporate goal (Peters 1986: 32).

Recently, the concept of 'coproduction' has entered the criminological vocabulary, as a way of understanding and addressing Mudd's second 'system failure', the 'responsiveness problem': the lack of correspondence between agencies and the public. In relation to the public responsiveness of agencies in the field of crime control, not surprisingly, it is with regard to the police that most effort has been devoted. Friedmann (1992: 14), in an important contribution to the debate worth considering in some detail, suggests that there are five logical possibilities to the relation between the 'police' and the wider 'community' (including public and private organizations). The first sees the two concepts as 'mutually exclusive entities'. This he regards as unsatisfactory, echoing Banton's earlier critique that such a model is 'as if no one could belong to both at the same time' (Banton 1974: 164). Police officers live in, and are members of, communities. They also share some common experiences and background as the community members that they police, even if they are simultaneously members of a reasonably exclusive, highly cohesive, culturally defensive, and socially isolated community of police officers (Reiner 1992b; chapter 3). And yet, it is this ideal separation which constituted an important aspect of early police legitimacy through the quest for professionalism and the adherence to the ideal of impersonal rule enforcement.

The second way of looking at the police–community relation, envisages the two as 'completely overlapping entities'. Friedmann suggests that this is only a limited possibility in the short period and narrow confines of the police training academy, where there is no community other than the police (1992: 16). Nevertheless the academy serves only as a training vehicle to get the police officers out on to the streets where they then confront a wider community. However, this notion of overlap brings us on to Friedmann's next two conceptual models. The third possibility lies in the notion of the 'police as all-encompassing the community'. Police states in which citizens as informers act, or are compelled into acting, as an arm of the state, is the closest that reality has come to approximate this vision of police–community relations. Here lies the Orwellian nightmare of the all-seeing and all-knowing Big Brother which co-opts the community through fear, terror, or anxiety into the tasks of policing. This Friedmann suggests, while possible, is neither practical nor desirable. The fourth option is its opposite: a 'community that all encompasses its police'. In this situation, the community polices itself through informal social control without the need for uniformed officers. The examples that Friedmann points to include the Israeli kibbutzim and religious orthodox communities such as some Hasidic movements. Anthropological and historical examples can also be found to support such a vision of the regulation of norm infractions (see Merry 1988). Such communities are likely to have a strongly defined sense of internal cohesion and self-containment. In contemporary society, however, they are always likely only to be 'relatively autonomous', subject to external intrusion by some regulatory authority (Moore 1973: 720). This, as Friedmann notes, is pertinent particularly in the increasingly 'global village' of the internationalized community in which we live (1992: 17). In such a context, he argues, this vision is impractical, particularly in 'larger communities, cities, and states'.

This brings us to the fifth logical possibility, that of the police and community as 'partially overlapping', the extent of which is dependent upon the special or particular circumstances arrived at by political democratic consensus (Friedmann 1992: 17). The police are by no means the only force of social control in society. What is important is that the 'police accept a limited role that is prescribed by society, and both police and community admit their mutual interdependence' (Friedmann 1992: 18). 'Coproduction', he goes on to argue, produces the conditions under which mutual understanding, responsiveness, and support can flourish alongside a joint interest of police and community in developing a set of activities together to produce security and public safety. This, he suggests, is the desirable future of police–public relations in which both citizens and appropriate agencies, such as social services, are drawn together systematically in a web of coproduction. Friedmann draws upon the earlier work of Whitaker (1980) to identify the three components of 'coproduction': first, 'where citizens request assistance from public agents', in which case the agency depends on service requests; second, 'where individual citizens provide assistance to public agents', here citizens initiate or are expected to help an agency perform its tasks; and third, 'where citizens and agents interact to adjust each other's expectations and actions', in which agents and citizens reciprocate to establish a 'common understanding of citizens' problems and possible solutions' (Friedmann 1992: 22). All three are essential elements of coproduction, but it is in the third that 'the promise of community change lies'. This type of analysis resonates with the Scarman Report on the Brixton Disorders of the early 1980s (Scarman 1981) and John Alderson's (1979) vision of 'community policing'.

Although Friedmann produces a highly idealized schema, he conveniently encapsulates the intellectual and philosophical justifications for the recent turns in policy rhetoric, although in a somewhat different language. Implicit in this analysis is the assumption that, in the quest for police–community separation, which marks out many of the developments in criminal justice over the past two hundred years, we have gone down the wrong road. In the process we have forgotten the vital importance of informal control mechanisms, to which we need to look to resecure the proper vision of 'partial overlap', mutual interdependence, and coproduction. This approach does not necessarily embody a critique of the role of public authorities, but rather suggests a need to reorder the nature of relationships among public authorities and between them and the public.

An essential problem with Friedmann's analysis lies in its very premise. Banton (1974: 164), in his earlier critique of the phrase 'police–community relations', touches on the fact that it assumes, or at least it tends towards assuming, a representation of the two categories as undifferentiated and homogeneous. As we will consider in further detail in Chapters 4 and 5, two empirical issues arise. First, the police and the function of policing, in its broadest sense, are institutionally (both within and outside 'the police') fragmented; and secondly, communities (particularly geographic ones) are rarely homogeneous. This approach assumes an unproblematic consensus within and between both the local state and communities. Further, there is a tendency to contrast formal with informal control (often shorthand terms for 'state' and 'civil society'), as if they were somehow distinct rather than both constituted by, and constitutive of, each other, as well as being 'homologous': sharing the same mythic constructs (Fitzpatrick 1992). Finally, while identifying real historical tensions, this perspective represents only a partial account of the growth of 'partnership' relations. It embodies a weak pluralist understanding of social power, in which power is the product of competition between interests which are freely represented, both at the level of community and between agencies. As such, it discounts any notion of structural differences in power and marginalizes political and ideological factors.

'State Overload' Thesis

A second dominant explanation develops upon some of the insights of the 'system failures' thesis but gives them a distinctive twist. Here the central argument is that the contemporary bureaucratic state—including the police and other statutory criminal justice agencies—has become 'overloaded' and can no longer fulfil the expectations placed upon it. The financial burden on the state requires a reassessment of public expectations and the responsibilities of a 'minimal state'. Markets are to replace state planning as regulators of economic activity. 'Partnerships' are a vehicle through which the decision making processes of social government are 'marketized'. In addition, 'partnerships' are a means by which the recalibration of public expectations is sought and the conditions for 'responsible citizenry' created.

In a more radical neo-liberal version, the interventionist 'welfare' state is viewed as a malignant monolith (Gamble 1986; Levitas

1986a). Such a perspective warns that governments have become arrogant in their attempts, through programmes of social engineering, to overreach what is both possible and desirable (Hayek 1944). In that the 'welfare' state depends upon bureaucracies, it is subject to constant pressures from those within them to expand their own empires, thus fuelling the cost of inefficient public services. In the long shadows cast by the 'welfare' state, it is argued, the conditions for the exercise of responsibility do not exist. Welfarism, so the argument continues, saps initiative and enterprise (Keat and Abercrombie 1991). The state creates a morally damaging 'culture of dependency' which undermines the exercise of genuine responsibility (Murray 1990). It produces a 'client mentality' to the provision of goods and services. It also destroys older forms of social support such as voluntary associations, charities, churches, communities, and even families (Murray 1994; 1995; Dennis and Erdos 1992). The solution, for neo-liberal commentators, lies in the abandonment of overarching social and welfare programmes, the transfer of greater individual and collective responsibility for services, traditionally provided by the state, and the freeing of market forces in order to allow individuals and groups to exercise their responsibility (Friedman 1962). Hence, for the New Right 'community' has become a metaphor for 'rolling back' the state and 'freeing up' collective voluntarism and entrepreneurship (Herrnstein and Murry 1994: 536–40). Furthermore, 'community' represents the 'last great Eldorado of unexploited altruism' to be mined and used (Pinker 1995: 86), and particularly attractive to governments with tight budgets. And yet, unlike the managerialist account of 'system failures' there is a clear moral message here. It is argued that in order to address the problems of crime the values of dependency, passivity, and irresponsibility—which the welfare state has perpetuated—must be overthrown and displaced from all spheres of policy and life. What is called for, therefore, is a 'remoralisation of society' (Davies 1987). As social undertakings are opened up to markets and forms of 'enterprise', so 'autonomy', 'self-help', and 'choice' re-enter the spaces vacated by the state. With them, it is suggested come new forms of 'responsibility' (van den Haag 1985; Tame 1991).

Criminal justice, for a considerable time, was shielded from the logic of this type of thinking. This was largely due to the perceived necessity of a 'strong state' to contain any social fall-out associated with the upheaval wrought by the advent of post-welfarism. However, the extreme implications for some commentators of the acknowledgement that the formal criminal justice system is almost irrelevant to controlling crime, is that it is little more than 'an expensive formal charade which should be run as cheaply as possible' (Tuck 1991). Through appeals to 'community', 'prevention', and 'partnerships', programmes for action have been conceived as part of a process of negotiating and facilitating the reassessment of public expectations and the responsibilities of groups and individuals. 'Partnerships' constructed around a new language in which individuals are 'consumers', relations are 'businesslike' and communities are called upon to provide services once expected of the state, are the new rationalities of government 'beyond the state'. These are what Garland (1996) refers to as 'responsibilization strategies'. Theories of state 'overload', as we shall see, have found their voice among the rhetorics and strategies which have come to dominate much contemporary British government analysis. Here they collide and sometimes fuse with more managerial understandings of 'system failures'.

The 'Dispersal of Discipline' Thesis

The previous two explanations both adopt a positive, justificatory account of policy restructuring. By contrast, the third perspective is highly critical of recent trends. Cohen (1979), developing upon the work of Foucault (1979), argues that appeals to 'community' represent the consolidation of the 'disciplinary society'. They herald a move from the concentration to the dispersal of disciplinary forms of control. This occurs through what Foucault identified as a 'carceral archipelago' of intermediary institutions, processes, and technologies, which transport disciplinary techniques developed in the nineteenth century 'to the entire social body' (1979: 298). This, Cohen argues, represents the fulfilment of the nineteenth century disciplinary project, rather than a reaction against it. Developments begun a century ago are being extended through a 'continuous' and 'subtle gradation of institutions' (Cohen 1979: 360). As a result, it becomes increasingly difficult to identify the boundaries between the official system of crime control and those of the 'family' and the 'community', where they begin and end (Mathieson 1983). Consequently, Cohen (1979) argues, we may end up inhabiting the 'punitive city'. Here, we have a glimpse into Friedmann's earlier noted notion of the 'police as all-encompassing the community'.

Multi-agency and community partnerships, according to this perspective, are seen as both the site of, and a set of social processes which facilitate, the expansion of disciplinary social control into new areas of social life (Scraton 1985). Through 'partnerships', social welfare and non-criminal justice agencies as well as community groups are co-opted into the disciplinary process (Gordon 1987; Brake and Hale 1992: 75–6). This is seen largely as a uni-directional project in which control moves outwards from the police and criminal justice complex into the social body. In this process the former invades and colonizes the latter.

Bottoms (1983) has criticized this analysis for its failure to acknowledge neglected features of contemporary criminal justice systems which are non-disciplinary, such as the fine. He is critical of the overarching use of the notion of 'discipline', particularly in Foucault's sense of the word, whereby individuals are the subjects of intentional knowledge and 'correctional training' (Bottoms 1983: 175–8). As we saw in the previous chapter, much of the focus of the new-found interest in prevention is concerned *not* with 'knowing' individual offenders 'as a whole person', nor with using that knowledge to correct them through 'normalising judgement'. Rather, it lies in the manipulation of spatial characteristics and the construction of abstract populations, more indirect forms of control. The shift from offender to offence as the site of knowledge and correction means that social control is increasingly concerned with the regulation of whole groups and categories of people, not individuals as was the promise of nineteenth-century penal reforms (Simon 1988).

Nevertheless, Cohen and others highlight important and real dangers consequent upon the blurring of institutional and functional boundaries. First, they raise important issues concerning the dissemination of ideologies of conduct, and the way in which groups may be co-opted onto certain agendas by more powerful agencies. As a consequence, the 'net' of control may be extended, unintentionally or not, into new fields with potentially unforeseen consequences. Therefore, unlike the previous two accounts the issue of power and the differential ability of groups, organizations, and communities to effect change is central. In this it marks an important advance. Secondly, it raises the fundamentally important issues of the state as a problematic concept, both in its potential to expand and in its blurring boundaries. However, in relation to the role of the state there is a tendency to prioritize the former insight at the expense of the latter. In a misreading of Foucault, too many critical criminologists have tended to conflate disciplinary social control and the state. Net widening, too frequently, is viewed as synonymous with an expanding state (McMahon 1990). This runs counter to Foucault's more general project to decentre critical social theory's preoccupation with the state as the locus of power (Foucault 1977; 1979; and see Poulantzas 1978). This point has been recognized by Cohen (1989: 351) in a subsequent review of the social control literature. As he notes, despite the important recognition of the phenomenon of 'boundary blurring', including the fusion of the public and private spheres, the state often remains an essentialist and unitary construct in the literature. Consequently, there is insufficient attention given to non-statist 'private' control mechanisms, beyond seeing them as the subjects of capture, co-option by the state, dependence upon the state, or—particularly in relation to private business and market-driven initiatives (Spitzer 1987: 55–6)—taking over gaps vacated by the state. They are rarely seen as agents or the engines of change.

However, there is a further danger implicit in the 'dispersal of discipline' thesis, that it amounts to little more than a critique by inversion. Where the 'system failures' thesis assumes a logical and rational unfolding of change determined by a dominating factor of social need, in this instance efficiency and effectiveness, the 'dispersal of discipline' thesis sees an inexorable unfolding of *more* social control. Where the former searches for utilitarian aspects of efficient control and coherence within multi-agency arrangements, the latter seeks to uncover their function for the dispersal of discipline and their hidden utility for state power. What one viewpoint sees through rose-tinted glasses the other sees through jaundiced eyes. The 'dispersal of discipline' thesis is in essence a 'conspiratorial' perspective (Sampson *et al.* 1988). Emphasis is given to the coercive nature of the local state as it seeks to highlight a sinister and malign interpretation of the 'partnership' approach. From within this viewpoint multi-agency and community partnerships are essentially and always a 'bad thing'. Intervention is seen as an unwanted and unwarranted encroachment into private life. There is little recognition that 'formal control is often *less* intrusive than the unrelenting surveillance of informal controls' (Matthews 1987: 45 emphasis in original). There is a tendency to universalize experience, by reference to 'master tendencies' and logics which leave little space for contradictions, ironies, and failures. In seeking the sinister, what Cohen (1989: 350) later recognizes as the 'hermeneutics of suspicion', there is a refusal to analyse discourses in their own context. Instead, motivation is implied, usually in pejorative terms.

Finally, the 'dispersal of discipline' literature rejects, rather than engages with, the language of responsibility, so prevalent in the 'state overload' thesis (O'Malley 1994b: 23). It is unable to challenge neo-liberal assertions about responsibility because it is unwilling to confront the consideration of the conditions under which responsibility can be exercised, maximized, and rendered accountable. In this, as in related areas, it is influenced by a pessimism and 'impossibilism' of the 'nothing works' era, which leaves little sense of the role for progressive reforms (Matthews 1987: 51; McMahon 1990: 143–5). In sum, whilst shedding an important critical light on developments, otherwise all too often embraced as a virtue, this approach fails to constitute a sufficiently nuanced explanation of unfolding trends and countervailing forces. In addition, it lacks adequate ground upon which to construct an alternative understanding which engages with some of the more important (political and theoretical) insights advanced by the other two dominant accounts.

Questions of Legitimacy and Responsibility

There is a need to look beyond the above partial accounts. However, any alternative explanation must engage with the important insights and contentions provided by the foregoing analyses. It must connect with, and draw upon, accounts of political economy and address the political and ideological assumptions which underlie governmental strategies of action which coalesce around appeals to 'community', 'prevention', and 'partnerships'. In particular, as I will argue throughout, we need to understand these appeals in the context of problems of legitimacy and responsibility for the local governance of crime. For, as I note in Chapter 2, the history of policing and crime control, its nature and shape, largely has been constrained by, and moulded around, quests for legitimacy. So, for example, some of the particularities of British policing can only be explained in terms of pragmatic historic compromises in the quest for legitimacy (Reiner 1992). This legitimacy was structured around the competing interests of social hierarchies and class formations, as it is today, albeit in different forms. Similarly, we saw in the last chapter the historic importance of shifts in responsibility for both the form and substance of strategies of crime control.

What is clear is that we appear to be knee-deep in a *fin de siècle* malaise in which the role and efficacy of social institutions have been called into question in fundamental ways. New uncertainties (both global and ecological) appear to present themselves as unfathomable. Crime, as a symbol of an old uncertainty—social disorder—strikes even deeper to the core of this malaise. It feeds an unquenched thirst for security, identity, and moral order. Eric Hobsbawm (1995) in his review of the 'short twentieth century', the 'Age of Extremes', has summarized this sense of crisis. He suggests that our present plight reveals that human collective institutions have 'lost control over the collective consequences of human action' (1995: 565). Indeed, whether they ever had such control is itself a moot point. However, he goes on to suggest that 'one of the intellectual attractions which helps to explain the brief vogue for the neo-liberal utopia was precisely that it purported to by-pass collective human decisions' (Hobsbawm 1995: 565). Explaining this sense of anxiety and despondency and the importance of crime control within it, therefore, is an important prerequisite for the construction of a socially just response to it.

Mudd's earlier analysis provides a useful starting point in discussions of legitimacy. The combination and culmination of the two 'flaws' that he highlights, implicitly focus upon the dual problems of *state performance* and *incompatible steering objectives*. Together these serve to undermine public authority in the nature of government. The range and complexity of the tasks required, the level of expectation, and demand for services are seen to be out of step with the state's capacity to fulfil them. Together, these 'problems' strike at the very heart of questions concerning state legitimacy. They infer what Beetham calls 'legitimacy deficits' (1991: 17–18). These he defines as arising where there is either 'the absence of shared beliefs' or a 'discrepancy between rules and supporting beliefs' (Beetham 1991: 20). This crisis of legitimacy in criminal justice has been most clearly reflected in a crisis of confidence among the public in policing. For example, Skogan concludes his analysis of the 1988 British Crime Survey's findings as to public attitudes towards policing by commenting that:

Almost a decade ago, the Scarman report called for better relations between police and the public; however, surveys of public opinion suggest that since then the gulf between them has grown wider rather than narrower.

(Skogan 1990b: 51)

However, legitimacy problems also lie at the heart of the 'state overload' thesis. In order to construct an alternative account which engages with this approach, I suggest, we need to turn to an alternative body of political theory literature on 'legitimation crisis' (Habermas 1976). According to this perspective, fundamental contradictions within capitalist societies have resulted in the contemporary state being unable to fulfil its tasks in relation to the economy without encountering acute legitimation problems of its own (Offe 1984). The instability of the political economy—particularly evident in the 1970s—has resulted in the extension of state regulation into fields of civil society (welfare functions and economic intervention). This interventionism has led to the politicization of ever greater spheres of life and to demands on the state's competence. Therefore, these legitimacy deficits are seen as arising as a consequence of inherent tensions within a capitalist political economy which the state sought unsuccessfully to resolve, rather than as a consequence of that intervention as neo-liberal commentators would have it. Resultant legitimacy deficits conform to two broad kinds. The first involves winning the support and the co-operation of groups and individuals who are asked to sacrifice some of their interests in favour of what is defined as the 'general interest'. The second involves the presentation of a consistent image of the jurisdiction and role of legitimate state intervention, in other words, what the boundaries of the modern state ought to be.

Attempts by the state to manage the crisis, along the 'overload thesis' lines, have involved New Right administrations in rolling back the state in the economic sphere and the provision of social welfare and strengthening it in limited 'market supporting activities', most notably for our purposes, the maintenance of order and the provision of security for property. This is the ideology of the 'free market and the strong state' (Gamble 1979). This form of crisis management, it is suggested, did not resolve the legitimacy deficits of the state but rather displaced them into new arenas—most notably the apparatuses of policing, crime control, and punishment—thereby politicizing those spheres and opening them up to greater public concern and attention (see Sparks 1994). The politicization of policing and crime control in Britain so evident since the late

1970s and early 1980s, was indicative for some commentators of a shift towards a 'law and order' society (Hall 1979). However, it also marked the emergence of new legitimacy problems for government and the criminal justice agencies themselves. Thus, weaknesses in the 'strong state' have increasingly been exposed. Legitimacy deficits have revealed themselves as crises of efficiency, effectiveness, and economy in the contemporary language of current government discourse.

In the light of legitimacy deficits, neo-liberal governments have sought to recalibrate that which constitutes the legitimate expectations of the public and the responsibilities of individuals, families, groups, and the state in diverse areas of social life, including crime control. Garland's (1996) conceptualization of recent policy trends in crime control as embodying 'responsibilization strategies' is useful here. It alerts us to the recurring new governmental message that the state alone cannot, and should not, wholly be responsible for the prevention and detection of crime and personal security. The burden increasingly falls to private individuals, groups, and associations to take responsibility for the prevention, policing, and control of their own problems. O'Malley (1992: 257) terms this a process of 'prudentialism', whereby the private calculus of risk and insurance is incorporated into the responsibilities of the individual and family as potential victims. To be fully 'responsible', people are increasingly required to purchase 'appropriate'—on the basis of risk assessment criteria and market mechanisms—forms of security against all types of personal and familial harm, loss or suffering. As we saw in the last chapter, where once government and the police claimed that the task of policing should be appropriately left to the 'professionals', now they pronounce: 'policing cannot be left to the police alone' (Home Office 1993b).[1] The community, in various different ways, has been called upon to join in the 'fight against crime'. And yet, as I shall seek to show, these new interventions have not resolved

[1] In an interesting twist to debates about the history of responsibility for crime control, an English chief constable has recently argued that the new 'more "corporate" approach to criminal justice would imply a reversal of the trends of the past 150 years whereby the system has abdicated responsibility for law enforcement and peacekeeping to the police' (Pollard 1996: 161). In the 'Alice Through the Looking-Glass' world of policing, where things are the inverse of what they appear to be, according to this account it would seem that the police historically have never been the masters of their own destiny but rather the servants of society. Responsibility, with the ownership, control, and power that accompanied it, now appears as an unwanted and unwarranted burden.

legitimacy deficits but have produced their own legitimacy problems, which in turn have been displaced deeper into the social fabric.

Neo-liberal ideology connects and overlaps with the conceptual trilogy of 'prevention', 'community', and 'partnerships'. 'Community' and 'partnerships' are largely the medium through which responsibilities are recalibrated and legitimacy for the new regime sought. Prevention is primarily the message. Situational crime prevention, in particular, embodies neo-liberal assumptions about crime causation and human behaviour (King 1989; O'Malley 1992; 1994a). Offenders are viewed as 'rational choice' actors who weigh up the potential gains, risks, and cost before committing an offence: the abstract and universal 'abiographical' individual (O'Malley 1992: 264). Thus, crime is seen as the product of rational, utilitarian decision making. Conceptually, situational crime prevention ushers in the marketization of crime. Criminal behaviour is assumed to be like other transactions in the market place. Van den Haag, a prominent neo-conservative exponent of the economic model of crime, makes this point abundantly clear:

> Changes in the rates of particular types of crime do not depend much on changes in the criminal inclinations of individuals and on whatever causes them. Such inclination, and their causes are likely to be fairly constant. Changes in the frequency of any given crime more often depend on changes in the opportunity to commit the crime (at a risk acceptable to the criminal) and on variations of the benefit derived from it . . . This attitude depends on the likelihood and size of punishments.
>
> (van den Haag 1975: 77)

The offender in situational crime prevention like the economic model is abstracted from his or her social or structural context. The offenders represent the *homo economicus* of classical economics translated into neo-conservative thinking about crime. What is assumed to differentiate the 'criminal' from law-abiding members of society is his or her evaluation of benefits and costs regardless of their social situation or other crimogenic factors. Consequently, situational crime prevention emphasizes the fundamental moral responsibility of the offender, whilst deflecting attention away from the social causes of crime, or what Cornish and Clarke (1986) prefer to call an offender's 'pre-disposition to offend'. Through the manipulation of situational factors causal theories of crime are banished.

However, not only are offenders stripped of their social characteristics but so too are the victims, or more importantly the potential victims, of crime. Victims, are also perceived as 'rational choice' actors. The structural dimensions of crime victimization are ignored. The potential victim is seen as 'free' to make choices about whether or not to install target hardening measures, like secure windows and doors, and to manage their personal safety. Choice carries with it responsibility. Within situational crime prevention discourse, victims have become responsible for their own safety and security. As will be argued in the ensuing chapters, it is against this background that 'community' has become identified as the principal site around which legitimization is being sought for a new relationship between state and the public. And yet, as in earlier periods of history, this is a site of contestation.

The Wider Socio-political Landscape

In order to grasp fully the political context in which this combined quest for legitimacy and shifts in responsibility are unfolding, we need to connect the developments outlined so far to wider forces of change. This broader socio-political landscape embodies trends which simultaneously are driven by, but also sometimes serve to undermine and problematize, the neo-liberal agenda. Alongside appeals to 'community', the increased resort to crime prevention initiatives and the proliferation of 'partnerships', we can identify a further three pre-eminent characteristics of the shifting patterns of governance. They comprise the following trends in criminal justice policy and practice: the growth of privatization (in all its forms); the management of risk through insurance; and the expanding influence of 'new public management'. These are inter-related aspects of recent and unfolding governmental strategies. Importantly they connect, and are fuelled by, neo-liberal ideology. However, they also go beyond its confines and raise problematic tensions within the New Right political project. They have their origins both within and beyond the state. Let us consider these in turn.

Privatization

Privatization in the UK has been relatively late in coming to criminal justice by comparison with other public services. Nevertheless, it is currently exercising a considerable hold over criminal justice policy. However, we need to specify exactly what 'privatization' is taken to mean, as it expresses itself in a number of diverse transformations to the scope and form of a public civic polity, public intervention, and service delivery. These we can conceptually differentiate under the following broad social processes and policy developments.

The Use of Markets and Quasi-markets as Means of Delivering Services

Under the influence of increasingly dominant neo-liberal ideology and encouraged by right-wing pressure groups such as the Institute for Economic Affairs and the Adam Smith Institute, competition and markets have come to be seen as key ingredients for more efficient and better quality services (Adam Smith Institute 1984; Young 1987; Pyle 1995). This takes the form of contracting out services, the privatization of public bodies, the use of special purpose bodies (i.e. quangos), and the marketizing of public service delivery. In the UK the privatization of prisons (Matthews 1989; Ryan and Ward 1989; Farrell 1989; Logan 1990) and the contracting out of policing functions (South 1988; 1995; Johnston 1992; 1994a) constitute important elements of recent and current central government policy (Home Affairs Committee 1987; Home Office 1988b; 1993; 1994a; 1995b; Sheehy 1993). This has resulted in private enterprises taking over certain public functions, thus constituting 'government at a distance'. What has been transferred is the provision of services and goods, from public government to private corporations. However, in the process the boundaries between 'public' and 'private', direction and delivery, have become blurred. A hybrid or 'grey' sphere in the administration and delivery of key public goods has begun to emerge (Hoogenboom 1991).

A particularly stark example of this blurring of public and private spheres is illustrated by the recent developments in Sedgefield, County Durham, where in late 1993 the District Council set up its own uniformed 'Community Force' to patrol the streets on a 24-hour basis (at an initial cost of £180,000). Although similar to a commercial security patrol, the force is a department of the council, not a commercial company. It has its own control room and ten patrol officers, using mobile telephones, two-way radios, and marked patrol cars (Southgate *et al.* 1995: 38). Developments along these lines are likely to increase as more neighbourhoods turn to the private security sector in search of 'community safety' through patrols. For example, in a recent paper published by the Institute for

Economic Affairs, the author called upon government to provide tax incentives to encourage individuals to improve the security of their own property and to purchase private policing (Pyle 1995: 61).

Similar developments in privatization are to be found throughout many industrialized societies, most notably Australia and the USA (Shearing 1992; McDonald 1994). Whilst nobody knows the exact extent of the private security industry in Britain (Jones and Newburn 1995: 223–4), the number of people it employs is estimated to have outgrown the number of public police officers. The best recent 'guestimate' is that at the end of 1994 some 7,850 firms were employing more than 162,000 people, compared with 142,000 police (cited in Gallagher 1995: 23). The annual turnover of the private security industry increased from £400 million in the early 1980s to over £1.2 billion in 1990 and £2.8 billion by 1994, according to the British Security Industry Association (cited in McCrystal 1995: 15–17; Jones and Newburn 1995: 226).

The 'Civilianization' and 'Voluntarization' of Public Services

Many services within criminal justice traditionally provided by 'experts' and 'professionals' are increasingly becoming subject to the processes of civilianization and voluntarization (Gill and Mawby 1990a). These twin governmental strategies embody efforts to draw non-professional lay people into public service provision and to transfer to groups and individuals responsibility for their own welfare and security (Marx 1989; Johnston 1992). In Britain, civilianization has been a key aspect of recent and proposed changes to the delivery of policing services, so defined in public policy discourse as 'ancillary tasks' (Home Office 1994a; 1995b). The recent pursuit of civilianization in the police can be traced back to the Home Office circular 114/1983, which informed chief police officers that new bids for increased establishments would not normally be approved if existing police officers remained in posts which could be filled more economically by civilians. A second circular, issued some five years later, entitled 'Civilian Staff in the Police' (105/1988), identified twenty-five categories of work suitable for civilianization. Her Majesty's Inspectorate of Police have been charged with the responsibility for reviewing the success of the process of replacing police officers with civilians doing traditional elements of 'ancillary' police work.

The increased use of the special constabulary represents a further illustration of these developments which simultaneously blurs the boundaries, and draws out the interconnections, between voluntarization and civilianization (Gill and Mawby 1990b; Leon 1989). In November 1990, the government launched a recruitment drive to expand dramatically the number of special constables (Southgate *et al.* 1995). The government's current aim is to double the 1990 figure of 15,000 to 30,000. To this end the Home Office has recently established a working party to consider all aspects of the special constabulary, including ways of achieving its expansion. At the end of 1993 there were 20,566 specials in England and Wales (Barclay 1995: 6).

The reliance upon volunteers for the provision of services throughout the various diverse criminal justice agencies is becoming more extensive. In some areas, however, such as the provision of services for victims, voluntarism has a longer and more established history (Maguire and Corbett 1987). At its most general (and most vocal) level, voluntarization and civilianization have taken the form of appeals to the active 'private' citizen. Recently, the government announced a drive to make Britain a more 'neighbourly society' by increasing the number of volunteers throughout social life. To do this, a new organization entitled the Voluntary Partnership is to be established, to advise ministers on how to promote voluntary work. In launching the scheme the Home Secretary quoted figures which suggested that the number of volunteers had already grown by 15 per cent to 23 million between 1981 and 1991.[2] The government's intention is that, as the role of the state is withdrawn (or redrawn) in relation to the provision of public services, the scope for voluntary action is expanded and advanced (Howard 1994). Thus, the residual role of central government increasingly is being identified with activating and facilitating (steering) individuals in their performance of the duties of citizenship.

[2] In addition, the government is committing itself to setting up twenty local agencies each with a budget of £60,000 for two years, a further £1.5 million for fifty innovative projects involving young and elderly people and a publicity campaign. To do so the government plans to spend £6 million over three years on a strategy that will include offering everyone aged 15–25 the opportunity to do voluntary work (*The Guardian*, 7 June 1995). It is worth noting that both the Liberal and Labour parties also have their own proposals to increase voluntary work within the population, principally by means of a full-time, voluntary corps.

The Growth of Zones of Private Governance

Increasingly, we have seen the emergence of zones of private governance or what Macaulay refers to as spheres of 'private government' (Macaulay 1986: 446). However, first a note of caution needs to be sounded. We should be aware of the fact that 'private government' as such is not itself new, as the history of policing demonstrates. Rather, these concepts represent simultaneously, the emergence of social developments as well as the development of emergent ways of understanding things. Thus the maturing of 'legal pluralist' ideas within the sociology and anthropology of law literature—from Eugene Ehrlich's (1936) writings in the first half of the century to today—frames an important intellectual questioning of the often taken for granted relationship between law, modes of governance and the state (see Merry 1988; Macaulay 1986; Hunt and Wickham 1994).

That which has been 'privatized', under the growth of zones of private governance, is both the delivery and direction of security management and policing. However, it would be incorrect to suggest that this form of privatization has come about merely at the deliberate instigation or even tacit approval of government. In many senses private corporations have intentionally appropriated this role (Shearing 1992). These zones of private governance often take a physical form, whereby private property is the defining criteria of entrance and exit. They constitute privately owned and publicly used spaces. The growth of 'mass private property' as the locus of much (and increasingly in the case of the UK) social activity, like shopping, entertainment and leisure, has increasingly undermined the congruence between private property and 'private space' (Shearing and Stenning 1987). Ever greater amounts of 'public places' are located on private property and policed by private security companies. Thus, the already ambiguous relation between public and private spheres in the context of policing (Johnston 1992) has become further blurred.

The expansion of 'mass private property' has provided private corporations with the legal space and economic incentive to do their own policing. This has transformed the nature of modes of regulation therein (Shearing and Stenning 1983). Subsequently, the advent of 'mass private property' has not only brought about a change in the 'hands of policing' but also in its style and nature: 'Policing changed as its location changed' (Shearing 1992: 423). As Shearing and Stenning (1987) have shown, the strategies of private policing are derived more directly from the profit motive than notions of social cohesion and so are more instrumental than moral. They are more concerned with the prevention of loss than with the detection and conviction of crimes and criminals (Shearing and Stenning 1981).

In addition, zones of private governance may take on non-physical forms, whereby one becomes the member of a particular association, network or organization in order to gain access to certain services and facilities, be it Visa card, a home shopping club, or so on. In both configurations, entry or membership carry with them the (implicit) acceptance of the 'rules of the game': the modes of governance. Many of these 'zones' involve forms of self and/or co-regulation (Shearing and Stenning 1983). They are often referred to, or perceived, as 'consensual' forms of control, in that individuals may not realize—in a formal or conflictual way—that they are the subjects of regulation. If the law is invoked it is more likely to be contract law, not criminal law. The power of removal, dismissal or termination to which such contracts may give rise are potent administrative instruments. Thus, these 'zones' embody the normalization of surveillance, to be found in shopping malls, airports, sports stadia, and entertainment events like Disney World (Shearing and Stenning 1984). Increasingly, the social world is being transformed into, and perceived as, a series of private realms with their own membership criteria and modes of internal rules and regulation to which membership implies acceptance and accords legitimacy. Consequently, we appear to slip seamlessly, and often unknowingly, from one 'corporate bubble of governance' (Shearing 1995) to the next. What is crucially important about the expansion of these privately defined orders is that they are 'in some cases inconsistent with, or even in conflict with, the public order proclaimed by the state' (Shearing and Stenning 1987: 14).

The Decline of the Public Sphere

Associated with the above developments is a decline in the nature, use, and extent of public spaces, and in the public sphere more generally. This expresses itself in a number of inter-related ways. First, through a growth in what Lasch refers to as 'privatism' (1980: 25). This he identifies as an introspective preoccupation with the care and development of the self, resulting in forms of both social and spatial withdrawal. What is interesting is that, if we accept this argument, any withdrawal would appear to run counter to the spirit of voluntarism upon which much government policy is premised. Evidence from the latest British Social Attitudes Survey suggests that people are still strongly attached to the idea that government should continue to do the things for which the welfare state accepted responsibility and should not transfer more functions onto individual citizens (Taylor-Gooby 1994). What is clear, however, is that the present ability and/or willingness of people to take on responsibilities is more complex than neo-liberal ideology would have it.

Both the privatization of life and anxieties about life in public appear to march hand in hand (Taylor 1995b; 1995c). Certainly, surveys suggest that the fear of crime itself constitutes a major factor in explaining why some groups of the population are increasingly withdrawing into the perceived safety of their own homes at certain times of the day (Crawford *et al.* 1990: chapter 3). In many senses, the whole debate about 'fear of crime', which has spawned a mini-industry of its own, is a trope for the decline and impoverishment of public spaces. The unease and anxieties of which respondents of 'fear of crime' surveys speak focus on dimly lit and litter strewn local streets, run-down public transport, decaying housing estates, city centre underpasses, and ill-kept parks (Taylor *et al.* 1996). These public spaces have become *residual* areas both in their nature and in terms of their use. For those who continue to inhabit public spaces, particularly young people, their use has taken on a form of 'street level politics', in which battles over territory are played out (Webster 1994). This territorialism merely serves to reinforce a sense of topophobia (fear of place) in 'others'. Further, traditional modes of governance of such public spaces, through intermediaries like park keepers and bus conductors, have all but disappeared (Matthews 1992a: 39). Consequently, many of these public spaces have become fearful places to be avoided: 'no man's lands' within and around British cities. Finally, there is a related decline and disappearance of many traditional channels of political and social participation within the public sphere of which Habermas (1989a) has written, like churches, political parties, trade unions, and so on. Together these trends constitute a significant transformation in the notion of a public sphere and people's experiences of it.

The Management of Risk: Enter the Risk Society?

The recent paradigmatic shift from the formal apparatus of detecting, apprehending, and sentencing offenders to proactive and informal crime prevention is symptomatic of a wider growth of risk management and its association with what Feeley and Simon have described as 'actuarial justice' (1994). The assessment of risk forms the basis of preventative strategies like selective incapacitation, criminal profiling, risk of custody scales, preventative intervention with 'at risk' groups, and community-based initiatives. It also informs insurance policy decision making concerning the granting and conditions of cover, i.e. the known level of crime within a geographical area, the type of housing, the lifestyle of the occupants, the presence (or absence) of certain security hardware, and so on. Similarly, insurance has fuelled the dramatic expansion of CCTV cameras by cutting the premiums where they are in operation (Davies 1996). Insurance has become central to the 'rationalization of risk' on the basis of 'probabilistic calculations' and 'statistical distributions'. It has been suggested that through risk assessments attempts are made to manage and:

manipulate the public as a demographic mass or aggregate, bypassing the res cognitans of individuals altogether ... the new practices radically reframe the issues, and target something very different, that is, the crime rate, understood as the distribution of behaviours in the population as a whole.

(Feeley and Simon 1994: 175–8)

In this emerging 'new penology', membership of risk categories or populations is increasingly becoming a defining criterion in configurations of social organization (Simon 1987; Feeley and Simon 1992). This form of risk assessment, particularly as a means of managing crime, is informed by a neo-classical understanding of human behaviour and connects with neo-liberal notions of individual responsibility and choice. Interestingly, the associated emphasis upon loss prevention and risk management rather than on crime fighting and chasing criminals transcends and unifies the governance of security and crime control along the public–private continuum, so that functional aspects of 'public policing' come closer to resemble those of 'private security'.

The proliferation of risk assessment, insurance, and prevention represents the hallmark of what some social commentators have called the wider 'risk society' (Beck 1992; Beck *et al.* 1994; Giddens 1990). The 'risk society', according to Ericson (1994; 1996), has four principal logics with implications for the governance of crime. The first, as we have already seen, is that of insurance: 'risk is the neologism for insurance' (Ericson 1996). The second characteristic is what Ericson refers to as the 'logic of the norm'. Risk categories constitute population groups, and yet, measurement is inexact. Calculation of future risks—be they criminal victimization, ill health, accident or unemployment—and the resultant risk groups which people are forced to inhabit, can never be an exact science. Consequently, deviation from the mean is the norm. The third logic of the risk society is of 'the future market'. The preoccupation with risk causes us to look constantly to the future. The final logic is a negative one, there is 'no guarantee against risk'. It is here that trust steps in to fill the void. 'Trust and risk intertwine . . . What is seen as "acceptable" risk—the minimisation of danger—varies in different contexts, but is usually central in sustaining trust' (Giddens 1990: 35). Trust in technologies, institutions, and people becomes an increasingly important, yet fragile element of the risk society. Ericson has summarized the current shifts, encapsulated in the concept of the 'risk society' as a movement from 'deviance-control-order' to 'knowledge-risk-security' as the totems of criminological concern and policing philosophy (Ericson 1994: 167–8). In this new era, the role of the police is transformed:

in practice community policing has allowed the police, in important ways, to become knowledge brokers, expert advisors and security managers to the public and other institutions.

(Ericson 1994: 164)

In this, 'prevention', 'partnerships', and 'community' come to solidify around the management of risk and security through information, surveillance, and knowledge.

Managerialism and the New Public Management

The influence of 'new public management' upon criminal justice may have been relatively late in arriving—compared with other public services—but its impact, although largely neglected by criminological commentators, is nevertheless extensive.

The Three Es and Criminal Justice

The 'new public management' refers to the introduction of private sector managerial methods to the public sector. Its canons are the three Es of *efficiency*, *effectiveness*, and *economy*. 'New public management' focuses upon 'management by objectives' and a results-orientation. Simultaneously, it promises 'closeness to customers', by flattening bureaucracies and transferring power away from hierarchical organizations and professional cartels directly to the consumer. An early precursor of developments was the Rayner Efficiency Unit set up in 1979 to generate improved efficiency in Whitehall. It set in train a shift from the hierarchical decision making of bureaucrats and professionals towards 'consumer power'. The practice of 'social auditing' promised to end the 'producers' cartel'. It also promised to open up to scrutiny the previously closed world of professional and bureaucratic decision making.

The early developments in the field of criminal justice can be traced back to the introduction of the Financial Management Initiative (see Stewart and Walsh 1992). Home Office circular 114/1983 addressed to all chief constables and police authorities declared that as a result of 'constraints on public expenditure', future increases in resources would be made conditional upon improvements in efficiency and effectiveness in the achievement of objectives. Circular 114/1983 heralded a new outlook on resource management in policing, prioritizing 'the dreaded three Es' (Reiner and Cross 1991a: 6). This shift in policy in relation to policing was further extended by a successor circular 106/1988 (Home Office 1988c). Together the recommendations of the 'Inquiry into Police Responsibilities and Rewards' chaired by Sir Patrick Sheehy (1993) and the government's White Paper, 'Police Reform' (Home Office 1993b), both published in June 1993, sharpened the managerialist agenda for policing (McLaughlin and Murji 1995). They recommended the removal of internal barriers to effective managerial control, the flattening of the internal organizational structure and the introduction of greater flexibility of working patterns. As a consequence, there has been considerable upheaval, change, and resistance within the police. Similar reorganizations have been imposed upon the probation service (McWilliams 1992; Humphrey 1993).

In addition, 'management by objectives' and outcomes has taken a firm grip on criminal justice agencies. In the late 1980s the Conservative government subjected the criminal justice system to a barrage of investigations by the Audit Commission, the National Audit Office and the Public Accounts Office (Davies 1990; Jones 1993). Recommendations as to 'internal flexibilities', 'efficiency savings', 'performance indicators', and organizational restructuring have resulted in the imposition of 'new public management' ideas across the diverse agencies of criminal justice. They have met with mixed degrees of success in the police (Reiner 1992c), the probation service (Nellis 1995a: 22–3), the penal establishment, and the courts (McLaughlin and Muncie 1994).

More recently, the use of citizens' charters, such as the Courts Charter and the Victim's Charter, have become a further aspect of the government's managerialist policy agenda in criminal justice, as elsewhere. They are part of the 'closeness to the customer' rhetoric of managerialism which has also found expression in the government's legislative programme (Lacey 1994). Charters aim to appeal directly over the heads of bureaucrats and public servants to individual consumers. They are designed to establish good practice and to identify quality service to which organizations should be committed and held responsible by individual citizens. To this end, some charters create procedures of complaint or redress for individuals where the equality of the service is found to be out of accord with the standards required by the charter. However, despite the language of 'rights' they create few (if any) legally supportable obligations. The Victim's Charter is a case in point here. It claims to wear the clothes of victims' rights, yet sets down no grievance procedure or mode of redress. Instead, it deals in 'unenforceable entitlements' (Fenwick 1995: 852). Nevertheless, it creates a powerful managerialist rhetorical device in which 'consumer sovereignty' is hailed as paramount.

Charters highlight a further element of managerialism, the importance placed upon the 'administration of policy' (Crawford 1994a: 511), through informal processes such as circulars, charters, internal guidelines, policy objectives, mission statements, and so on. This *policy* schema is premised upon a quasi-legal or non-legal basis rather than founded upon formal notions of legality. Peters has perceptively noted that in the philosophy of social control which managerialism heralds, 'purpose is no longer contained within the meaning of the law but it has come to be determined as part of extra-legal policy and it has come to govern the law's meaning itself' (1986: 32).

Administrative Criminology and 'Smooth Management'

In the field of criminal justice, 'new public management' has been accompanied and promoted by a large body of 'administrative criminology', saturated with a lack of interest in aetiological debates, a 'nothing (much) works' pessimism, and a greater concern with managing the system, than with any expectation of significantly reducing crime rates (Young 1986). From within this body of research literature there has been a preoccupation with evaluating technologically driven situational crime prevention measures, identifying perceived (in)efficiencies in the formal criminal justice process and its 'smooth management', as opposed to any real concern with criminality itself. Drawing upon the 'system failures' thesis, there is a growing emphasis within administrative criminology on the efficient and cost effective management of criminal justice which places greater import on its *system-like* qualities. Criminal justice is increasingly viewed as requiring 'smoothing' through the elimination of 'friction', 'duplication', and 'bottlenecks' (Moxon 1985), all of which is in accordance with the increased use of crime prevention, inter-agency networks, pretrial diversion, 'fast-track' prosecution, and early case assessment to weed out 'junk cases'. These developments are not unique to England but are to be found across Europe and North America (van Dijk *et al.* 1986; Christie 1993). As Feeley and Simon suggest the new iconography of criminal justice is 'the flow chart of systems analysis' (Feeley and Simon 1994: 188). Consequently, we appear to be witnessing what one commentator has referred to as the growth of an 'essentially bureaucratic-administrative law-enforcement system' (Bottoms 1983: 186), in which institutionally derived managerial goals rather than normatively or socially derived ones, have become dominant (Peters 1986; Garland 1980: 184). This aspect of managerialism is in potential tension and ambiguous relation to the morally toned, punitive 'law and order' rhetoric of traditional Conservatism.

Enter 'Quangoland'

'New public management' has radically altered the shape of government and the civil service, in addition to its direct impact upon criminal justice. Most prominent has been the recent proliferation of 'quangos' (quasi-autonomous-non-governmental organizations). Quangos were primarily introduced by the government, particularly in the 1980s, in order to generate a mix of public and private service delivery and a separation of purchase from provision (Pliatzky 1992). In doing so, quangos contract either with central or local government. It has been estimated in a recent study by Democratic Audit, that in 1993 there were already over 5,500 such quangos, although the government list (which excludes NHS Trusts amongst others) put the figure at only 1,389 (Mulgan 1993: 2). And yet, even these numbers represent merely best 'guestimates', as the real figure is almost immeasurable and subject to contested definition. The unifying concept of a 'quango' belies a diverse patchwork of different organizations with variable objectives. A substantial number of people are involved in the running of quangos. According to one estimate, by the end of 1992 there were over 17,000 members of appointed bodies compared with about 25,000 councillors (Skelcher and Stewart 1993). In many ways these people represent the 'new magistracy', a non-elected elite.

A notable example of the use of quangos has been the establishment of the ninety or so Next Steps Agencies across diverse public policy areas, including criminal justice. They have replaced traditional relations between ministers and civil servants. The purpose of the Agencies is to hive off operational and administrative issues whilst leaving ministers solely responsible for policy matters. The Next Step Agencies, like quangos more generally, represent an explicit attempt to create new forms of 'government at a distance'. Further, they aspire to separate more clearly the functions of policy decisions—the *steering* process—from service delivery—the *rowing process* (Osborne and Gaebler 1992: 35). This was clearly the strategy behind the establishment of Next Step Agencies such as the Prison Service Agency. However, the sacking of Derrick Lewis, the head of the Prison Service Agency by the Home Secretary in October 1995, has shown such a separation to be neither straightforward nor free of complex political ramifications. While the Home Secretary complained of management failures for the state of the Prison Service, Mr Lewis complained of regular interference by the Home Secretary in the day-to-day running of the administration, to such an extent that he felt unable exert autonomous control (Travis 1995). He saw policy failings and political interference as the cause of problems within the Prison Service (Lewis 1996). The case demonstrates that the introduction of new intermediate bodies may serve to conflate and confuse both policy formation and policy implementation. This raises central questions about the possibility and effectivity of such a separation. The case is also illustrative of the manner in which legitimacy deficits are displaced and dispersed into new domains, not resolved, through such structural reorganizations.

Conclusions

The interconnected developments outlined above, are more advanced and visible in other fields of social life and policy outside the governance of crime (Rose and Miller 1992). In many senses criminal justice is not at the leading edge of change, but is retracing emergent trends first established elsewhere, whilst leaving its own distinctive footprints. Consequently, to date little theoretical attention has been paid within criminology to mapping the collective connections and contours of these shifts or to speculating as to their future implications. Despite notable examples (O'Malley 1992; Bottoms and Wiles 1995; Garland 1996), much of the recent commentary has tended to take a largely uncritical reading of these trends outside highly specified fields of enquiry. These trends constitute salient constituent parts of unfolding governmental strategies which are driven by legitimacy deficits and the recalibration of responsibilities to which they have given rise. Importantly in the context of a political agenda dominated by a neo-liberal ideology, the above strategies and trends resonate with, and draw upon, critiques of representative forms of democracy and established notions of crime control and justice.

This review suggests that O'Malley is correct in his argument that the current shifts in criminal justice policy are not merely the product of technological developments but are allied to the 'uneven and negotiated (and thus partial) implementation of a political programme' (1992: 258). What influences the spread of technologies is most likely to be their appropriateness for particular ends. This, he contends, 'in large measure will be related to political struggles which establish programmes on the social agenda' (O'Malley 1992: 258). However, he is wrong in his over-emphasis on both the ideological coherence of this programme and the nature of its direct linkage to unfolding social patterns. First, as I have hoped to demonstrate, there are important tensions and contradictions within neo-liberal political strategies (Levitas 1986a). On the one hand, there are tensions between the morally-toned desire to punish and managerialist impulses to 'smooth administration'. On the other hand, there lies the 'struggle between risk and sovereignty' (Simon 1988): the dispersed nature of risk prevention strategies and the state's traditional claim to monopolize the use of force in the maintenance of order. Secondly, the process of change is not always or necessarily being driven by political forces. There is a danger that in a quest to engage in critical archaeology we may find politics buried wherever we dig. As I have sought to show, many of the changes are occurring at an arm's length from the state, by private interests (corporate and individual) and in private settings. There are deeper forces at play, which question the capacity of the state, under the pressure of such forces, to steer the emerging governmental processes (a subject to which we return in Chapter 6). They also question the very concepts of 'community' and 'partnerships', the nature of the practices to which they give rise, and the manner in which the coalescence of sometimes countervailing forces impacts upon such practices.

4

Partnerships, Conflicts, and Power Relations

Social institutions such as the police, the probation service, and other criminal justice agencies, mould and constrain the actions and attitudes of the individuals that constitute them. Through processes of socialization and cultural assimilation the appropriateness of certain activities, regulations, and practices is conferred upon, and internalized by members of social institutions. Communal stories, collective interpretations about the world, routine practice, and internal rules reinforce and rearticulate, in changing circumstances, the taken for granted nature of such activities, actions, and 'self-knowledge'. These are legitimating devices, which often cohere around notions of rightness and justice. 'Categories of thought', 'expertise', and 'identities' are produced and confirmed through such institutional processes. Whilst we need to be wary of an overly deterministic or functional interpretation of 'how institutions think' and act, Mary Douglas provides a useful insight into the ways in which institutions help construct, but do not determine, social reality for their members.

Any institution that is going to keep its shape needs to gain legitimacy by distinctive grounding in nature and in reason: then it affords to its members a set of analogies with which to explore the world and with which to justify the naturalness and reasonableness of the instituted rules, and it can keep its identifiable continuing form.

(1986:112)

These insights provide a useful background against which to begin to consider the 'Byzantine complexity' of inter-organizational relations within the criminal justice enterprise.

In this chapter I change tack somewhat in order to consider the ways in which rank and file criminal justice personnel understand, experience, and engage with the growth of the 'partnership' approach to crime prevention and control. With reference to both qualitative and quantitative data collected from related research projects, I will explore the nature of structural, cultural, and conceptual conflicts and tensions which exist between different criminal justice agencies. The impact of task specialization, notions of expertise, and differential organizational functions produce a complex and fragile web of inter-organizational conflicts and incongruities, as well as alliances. It is on top of this that the implementation of incantations to 'partnerships' are being played out. To assess the nature of these conflicts, this chapter will begin with an examination of the different assumptions that police and probation officers, as 'stereotypical' representatives of divergent agencies involved in partnerships, hold about 'appropriate' preventative measures and crime causation. These will be connected to other 'latent oppositions' around which conceptions of justice have been constructed. Perceptions of mutual suspicion and distrust will be considered and the importance of interpersonal and inter-organizational trust relations explored. Ordinary officers' hopes and aspirations for, as well as fears and concerns about, the rhetorical shift to 'partnerships' are examined and evaluated.

The practices of inter-organizational partnerships and the views of agency personnel will be analysed in relation to a number of recurring themes. First is the nature of power relations which give rise to, and which are structured around, these 'latent oppositions' and sites of conflict. Differential power relations—both inter-organizational and interpersonal—mould and influence the resultant processes of policy formation and implementation. Consequently, the manner in which conflicts and tensions are managed in routinized social action and the strategies to which they give rise, will constitute a major focus of this chapter. In this regard the implications of different modes of conflict management are considered with particular regard to their (in)formality and strategies of conflict avoidance. A second recurring theme is the way in which the inter-organizational relations, expressed both through conflicts and allegiances, are in part determined by intra-organizational factors. Hence, the nature of *intra*-organizational tensions and their implications for *inter*-organizational practice will be evaluated. Finally, some of the more general ramifications of 'partnerships' and the practices to which they give rise will be considered with particular regard to the blurring of organizational boundaries, the incorporation of particular interests and agencies into the crime control arena, and the possible dominance of a particular vision of crime control and appropriate interventions.

The two pieces of empirical research reported in this chapter are different yet complementary. The very nature of multi-agency work produces two distinct subjects for research. First, there are those designated front-line officers (at different hierarchical levels) engaged in specific 'formal' multi-agency projects. This group is the subject of qualitative observational fieldwork and in-depth interviews in the research case studies. Secondly, there are the remaining 'ordinary' officers (also of different hierarchical levels), potentially engaged in 'informal' inter-agency relations but not necessarily involved in 'formal' partnerships. The survey sought to tap the views and experiences of this group of main grade probation officers and rank and file police officers. Whilst there are clear signs that the partnership approach has been taken on board by police and probation managers, agreements and policies struck between managers can be difficult to implement at the front-line level of service delivery (Hope and Murphy 1983). In many instances the implementation of inter-agency co-operation requires the, often ongoing, renegotiation of any such agreements at various different organizational levels. The perceptions, attitudes, and actions of 'ordinary' mainstream officers, therefore, are integral to an understanding of the way organizational change is fought over, negotiated, and resolved.

Apart from some notable exceptions (Ortet-Fabregat and Perez 1992; Rutherford 1993), there has been surprisingly little comparative organizational research into differences and similarities between the attitudes and experiences of criminal justice personnel to broader policy changes which transcend specific agencies. In part this may be due to the difficulty in constructing such research given the different standpoints and understandings of personnel to their work within diverse criminal justice agencies. However, comparative research of this kind affords an important insight into the ways in which broad policy initiatives are refracted through organizational, cultural, and managerial lenses.

This dual research strategy arose out of a recognition that the study of inter-organizational relations requires a grounding in the various internal organizational contexts themselves. Pearson *et al.* correctly note that, 'what often appears as *inter*-organisational conflicts are sometimes more appropriately understood as *intra-*organisational conflicts' (1992: 65, emphasis in original). In order to take this insight seriously the research strategy outlined in this chapter seeks to focus the gaze of inquiry simultaneously inside and across institutional boundaries. I begin by examining the survey data and the issues raised therein, before going on to consider the findings of the observational research and the in-depth interviews with designated front-line inter-agency officers.

A Survey of Police and Probation Officers

Whilst inter-agency work often involves a plurality of organizations, the police and probation service were chosen as the subjects of the survey research for a number of specific reasons. Initially, it was not possible—particularly given the resources available but also because of the linguistic and conceptual difficulties of constructing a sufficiently detailed questionnaire which adequately makes sense to officers of differing organizations—to survey more than two key organizations. Consequently, a process of selection of some kind was required. The basis of this selection was premised, first, upon the fact that, as we saw in Chapter 2, both the police and probation service have been pushed by the present government to the forefront of resourcing and implementing local partnerships in a variety of criminal justice fields. This momentum is set to continue in the foreseeable future with significant impact upon the work and practice of both organizations throughout the country. Secondly, the police and probation services are marked by very different training, occupational socialization, cultures, philosophies, and working practices. Significantly, both organizations are structured by distinct gender relations and themselves are gendered in different ways (Sampson *et al.* 1991; Heidensohn 1992). They represent, at least symbolically, important polar interests within the system of crime control and the criminal justice process. They are traditionally associated with competing perspectives, understandings, and conceptual definitions. This creates considerable scope for inter-organizational conflict, both imaginary and real, and highlights the tensions, problems, and possibilities associated with inter-agency work. Finally, in the county in which the survey was conducted both the police and probation service were actively involved in resourcing and implementing a number of high profile, formal inter-agency crime prevention initiatives. These are the subjects of the qualitative data to be considered. These initiatives were well publicized within both organizations and provided a useful reference point around which to focus questions about inter-agency relations.

The survey fieldwork was conducted in early 1993. Questionnaires were distributed to 240 police officers of the ranks of constable, sergeant, and inspector in proportionate numbers to their numerical size throughout the force. In all, 170 police officers returned completed questionnaires (over 10 per cent of the force total), constituting a response rate of 71 per cent. The questionnaire was distributed to all 109 full time probation officers within the county. The only exception was the Chief Probation Officer. Seventy six questionnaires were completed representing a 70 per cent response rate. As a condition of the research the identity of the county is undisclosed. However, in terms of national police and probation comparisons it is in no sense exceptional.

Responsibility for Crime Prevention

The survey findings suggest that both police and probation officers consider crime prevention to be a legitimate part of their work. Only 3 per cent of police and 12 per cent of probation officers answered that 'no one' within their respective organizations should be responsible for crime prevention. Given the traditional police mission, the police response is not particularly surprising. However, the small number of probation officers who consider crime prevention not to be a legitimate part of probation work represents a major recognition of the growing importance of crime prevention and the probation service's role therein. Moreover, as many as one third (33 per cent) of probation respondents said they believe that all probation officers should be responsible for crime prevention, as against just over half (51 per cent) who thought that it should be the responsibility of specialist probation officers. These findings would appear to support the view of other commentators that there is a considerable awareness among probation officers of their possible contribution to crime prevention (Laycock and Pease 1985; Geraghty 1991).

By contrast, as we have already seen, the debate over whether crime prevention constitutes an organizational specialism or an element of general police work-loads, has a longer and more vexed history. The force in which the survey was conducted was no exception in regard to the nature and size of crime prevention as a specialism. At the end of 1992 approximately 0.8 per cent of the total force was designated to crime prevention. Fewer than 4 per cent of the police officers surveyed had worked in designated crime prevention at any time in their careers. The findings suggest that nearly three times as many police officers think that crime prevention should be the responsibility of all officers (71 per cent), as against those who think that it should be the responsibility of specialist officers alone (25 per cent). Police respondents in the survey appear to share a sense of ambiguity about the appropriate place of crime prevention within the police organizational structure and functional tasks.

Crime Prevention as a Contested Concept

Despite, or maybe because of, the growing involvement of a variety of agencies in the field of crime prevention, different images and conceptions of crime prevention abound (Bottoms 1990). The term 'crime prevention' is itself the subject of hotly contested debate. Many protagonists prefer to refer to the term 'community safety' or even the broader notion of 'urban regeneration' (see Osborn and Bright 1989; AMA 1990; Morgan 1991). As a consequence, widely divergent practices are subsumed under the label of 'crime prevention' work (National Audit Office 1992). It is an open-textured concept, the notional boundaries of which are particularly vague. Hence, that which is done in the name of crime prevention can be, and often is, extended to encompass almost any form of 'good work' or intervention which is perceived to have some beneficial impact on the physical or social world for the local residents or targeted populations.

Officers' views of crime prevention revealed in the survey reflect this diversity. Most importantly, the survey findings highlight the importance of different organizational roles for perceptions of crime prevention. When asked to identify, from a preselected list, what they consider to be the five most effective 'proactive' preventative measures, very clear differences in the views of police and probation officers emerge. Unsurprisingly, given their different training, organizational priorities, and traditional cultures, they adhere to very different interpretations of crime prevention.

Table 4.1 shows that police officers' preferred preventative measures are primarily of a *situational* kind: measures which increase the likelihood of detection and reduce the opportunities for crime through the manipulation of environmental and situational factors (Clarke 1995). Police officers were less likely to prioritize broader forms of social intervention, which seek changes in social behaviour through interventions in the social fabric (Bottoms 1990). Consequently, five of the eight most preferred proactive measures mentioned by police officers are principally concerned with situational factors. By contrast, probation officers preferred *social* crime prevention measures. However, a significant number of probation officers also identified measures which increase the risk of detection as being an effective means of crime prevention.

Table 4.1. Crime prevention measures—percentage response as 'one of the five most effective' measures, by organization

	Police (%)	Probation (%)
More police officers on the beat	83	44
Improved domestic security	53	47
Media campaigns	44	27
Neighbourhood watch	37	31
Targeting youths at risk	36	35
Social education programmes	33	52
Surveillance cameras (CCTV)	31	12
Improved architectural design	28	33
More leisure facilities	12	33
Employment/job creation schemes	3	41
Anti-discrimination policies	2	71

Clearly some crime prevention measures do not fit neatly into this dichotomy of situational and social type, but rather combine certain elements of each. However, despite some commentators' criticisms (Forrester *et al.* 1990: 47), what is most valuable and enduring about this conceptual distinction—particularly for our comparative purposes—is that it explicitly recognizes and embodies different assumptions about an aetiology of crime and understandings of 'community' (see Currie 1988). These assumptions would appear to relate to the different perspectives held by police and probation officers. Despite a perceived growing 'common interest' in crime prevention and increased governmental pressure for such agencies to work collaboratively in the field of crime prevention, fieldworkers in the police and probation service start out from what are conflicting premises. They have contested understandings of what constitutes 'appropriate preventative interventions' which are clearly structured by the organizational roles which each performs.

Theories of Crime Causation

Given that crime prevention measures embody certain assumptions about the causality of crime, it is not surprising that the differences between police and probation officers' notions of crime prevention are reflected in competing explanations of the causes of crime. The survey findings suggest that officers' views regarding the causes of crime vary significantly according to professional role.

Table 4.2 outlines those factors which officers perceived to have 'a considerable impact' on the level of crime within the county. Generally, police officers placed greater emphasis on a *deterrent model* which relates crime to a breakdown of coercive prevention,

TABLE 4.2. Explanations for the causes of crime—percentage response as having a 'considerable impact' on offending, by organization

	Police (%)	Probation (%)
Too lenient sentences	84	10
Lack of parental discipline	76	36
Drugs/alcohol abuse	70	71
Greed	35	18
Unemployment	34	72
Carelessness	20	10
Poor street lighting	11	10
Poor schooling	11	26
Individual psychological disorders	10	18
Poverty	10	45
Not enough for people to do	9	20
Poor leisure facilities	9	8
Poor housing	5	28
Lack of religious beliefs	4	5
Lack of equal opportunities	1	27
Experience of discrimination	1	15

i.e. the lack of deterrent punishments and parental discipline. This model finds less favour among probation officers. While 84 per cent of police officers said that 'too lenient sentences' have a 'considerable impact' on the levels of crime (the most frequently cited of the factors identified), only 10 per cent of probation officers held the same view. Similarly, only 36 per cent of probation officers believed that 'lack of parental discipline' considerably impacts upon offending, as against 76 per cent of police officers. This model highlights a belief in the human choice in the criminal act and 'sanction-oriented compliance' on the part of the citizens. From this perspective, it is believed to be the fear of punishments which discourages deviant activities. Therefore, crime is the product of a failure of criminal justice policy to build up effective deterrents to crime. This failure of sufficient deterrent is reflected both in the perceived lack of severity and the lack of certainty of punishment. This approach was also reflected in the more qualitative responses of police offices when given the opportunity in the questionnaire to express what in their opinion causes people to offend. For example a constable of twenty-five years' service articulates this model, suggesting that offender motivation is caused by offenders having 'little fear of being caught and *if* caught little fear of punishment *if* convicted.' This model was alluded to, albeit in different ways, by the majority of police officers.

Probation officers, as Table 4.2 shows, tended to emphasize the *social and environmental causes* of crime. Unemployment was the causal factor most referred to by probation officers. Nearly three quarters (72 per cent) of all probation officers said that they believed 'unemployment' to have a 'considerable impact' on crime. Among police officers this figure drops to a third of those interviewed (34 per cent). Nevertheless, the fact that one in three police officers recognize unemployment as a considerable factor in the cause of crime represents a significant minority view. Other social factors, as Table 4.2 shows, however, carried considerably less weight among police officers.

In the more qualitative responses this concern with social and environmental causes translates among probation officers into an understanding of 'blocked opportunities'. This model sees crime occurring where material circumstances block cultural aspirations and where non-criminal alternatives are absent or less attractive. The lack of legitimate opportunities for attaining widely held goals, it is suggested, leads individuals and groups into illegitimate paths. This perspective was present in some form in the majority of proba-tion responses and is illustrated by the following female court welfare officer's suggestion that there is a 'large gap between life expectations and [the] ability to achieve these by legitimate means . . . [there is a] political agenda that encourages selfish exploitation rather than caring for individuals.' A number of other probation officers suggested that 'blocked opportunities' amount to a 'growing sense of alienation of young people' and a feeling of 'exclusion from mainstream society'. For some probation officers these extrinsic pressures manifest themselves through individual offenders' 'lack of boundaries'. This identification of the need to develop 'boundaries' has a central, traditional place in probation work (Fielding 1984). For some, this 'lack of consistent boundaries' is a product of early socialization, including factors referred to by probation officers, such as 'poor schooling, rejection, truancy, alcohol, and unemployment'.

Explanations which articulate social and economic causes of crime received mixed and somewhat contradictory reactions from police officers. For some, 'poverty' and sociological theories are seen as mere excuses for offending. This is supported by the lack of a deterministic causal relationship between poverty, social disadvantage, and offending. The following comment by a sergeant of twelve years' service, illustrates this point: 'There are plenty of poor, honest people, so I feel that poverty, etc., is an excuse rather than a reason, particularly with a generous welfare state.' In accordance with Fielding and Fielding's findings (1991: 43) a number of police officers in the survey explained and justified their own views on crime causation by reference to their own experiences of learning to distinguish 'right' from 'wrong'. The following comment by a constable of nine years' service, who had worked elsewhere for many years before joining the force, illustrates this point:

I did not offend prior to joining the police force and come from a lower working-class background. However, to use this as an excuse to commit crime I find obscene and a slur upon the millions of good people from similar backgrounds.

Other officers, however, were more sympathetic to the idea that crime is a product of socio-economic disadvantage. In agreement with a number of other officers, a sergeant of fifteen years' service, made the following point:

In my opinion, current crime trends are affected by several factors, most of which are socially caused. Trends such as increases in single parent families . . . and the recession which has caused increased unemployment at a time when government policy suggests [that] the unemployed are responsible for their own situation and altered benefits.

Finally, Table 4.2 also includes a third set of intermediary explanations which fall into an *individual pathology* model of causation, with its emphasis on psychological disorders, substance abuse, and 'greed'. Here there appears to be a greater degree of overlap and consistency between the responses of police and probation officers. Among some probation officers this individual pathology response presents itself as problematizing the very notion of causation. For example, one officer stated that:

I don't accept the word 'causes'. 'Influences' would be a more appropriate term since there is some choice involved. I also don't think it possible to isolate singular influences. I believe individuals are influenced to offend by a combination of personal, social, societal, and circumstantial factors varying between individuals.

To some extent this questioning of causation raises self-doubts as to the role and effectiveness of probation work. At another level, however, it reinforces and legitimizes the individualistic nature of much probation practice and the emphasis on working with individuals on a case by case basis.

These more qualitative responses give a less equivocal understanding of police and probation attitudes to, and explanations of, criminal motivation than a deterministic notion of organizational functions would have it. They point to some of the tensions and contradictions between the views of officers. However, very clear organizational understandings persist and present themselves as predominant factors in explaining how personnel from different agencies come to partnership relations with preconceptions of 'crime' and what constitutes 'appropriate' preventative interventions. These conflicting viewpoints are embedded in organizational imperatives and cultural assumptions.

Inter-agency Relations and the Partnership Approach

Findings from the survey suggest that probation officers place greater importance than their police counterparts on the role of inter-agency work within their respective organizations (see Table 4.3). More than twice as many probation officers (66 per cent) said that 'liaising with other criminal justice agencies in multi-agency cooperation' was 'very important', as did police respondents (31 per cent). This may be explained partly by the greater experience of such work that individual probation officers are exposed to in their routine duties.

When officers were asked for their views about the level of

TABLE 4.3. The importance of multi-agency co-operation, by organization

	Police (%)	Probation (%)
Very important	31	66
Fairly important	47	30
Not very important	15	4
Not at all important	3	0
Don't know	4	0

priority given by senior officers to liaising with other criminal justice agencies, the responses were mixed. Table 4.4 shows that the largest response from both police and probation officers was that the 'right priority' is given to liaising with other criminal justice agencies (42 per cent and 63 per cent respectively). It also shows that police officers were evenly split on those who considered that 'too high' or 'too low' a priority is accorded to liaising with other agencies by senior officers. A significantly larger number of probation officers, on the other hand, considered the level of priority given to be 'too low' or 'far too low'.

TABLE 4.4. The level of priority given by senior officers to liaising with other criminal justice agencies, by organization

	Police (%)	Probation (%)
Too high/far too high	21	4
The right priority	42	63
Too low/far too low	19	20
Don't know	18	13

Beyond the fixed choices offered by questionnaire responses, officers were asked to write down briefly, in their own words, their views on the growing role of inter-agency work within their own organization. These more qualitative responses give greater insights into some of the complex and sometimes contradictory attitudes, sentiments, and concerns expressed by officers. The responses suggest that the levels of resistance and support for inter-agency co-operation vary within, and between, both organizations.

'Nothing Much Has Really Changed'

Some officers were sceptical about the impact that the partnership approach has had upon their organization. This scepticism
expressed itself in two principal ways: first, in the view that nothing
much has changed, except at the level of rhetoric and language, and
secondly, in more cynical views about the 'practical and realistic'
possibilities of genuine inter-agency co-operation. The former
response was more prevalent amongst probation officers and the
latter amongst police officers. Both represent a pragmatic, down-to-
earth approach to multi-agency relations. As noted in Chapter 2, the
greater historical involvement of probation officers with other agencies, principally in the voluntary sector, questions the novelty of a
partnership approach for the probation service. It suggests to some
that this may reflect a change in terminological emphasis, represent
a formalization of pre-existing informal relations, or even be a
metaphor for wider change (Nellis 1995a). Reflecting upon this
uncertainty, a male main grade probation officer of five years'
service asked: 'The expectation is that the role of multi-agency work
is growing. But has it not always been there?' This question was
answered in the affirmative by a main grade woman field probation
officer of twenty three years' service:

I have not noticed much difference in multi-agency work. [I] have always
worked with a bias towards community. [There was] much greater community involvement in the '70s—employees, landlords, etc. . . . Now these
are non-existent: several charities no longer exist, and several resources
[are] no longer available.

The second sceptical response, which views a 'co-ordinated' approach as a fine sounding 'ideal' but largely impractical, is essentially
pragmatic and anti-theoretical. In this vein, a male police inspector
of nine years' service commented:

There is clearly a place for this, certainly in an 'ideal' world. However, I
believe the service needs to focus first upon its 'core business' of responding to calls and requests for assistance from the public . . .

This understanding was more prevalent among police officers. It
appears to be expressive of what Reiner refers to as 'a kind of
conceptual conservatism' (Reiner 1992b: 128). This may reflect the
greater emphasis on empirical reasoning within traditional aspects
of core police culture, which stress 'common sense' and 'experience'

over formal training and academic theories, to which probation officers are more exposed and with which they are more comfortable. Representatives of this perspective among the police largely were sceptical of what one detective constable described as, 'new high-falutin ideas originating from mostly unknown academics and alleged captains of industry'. Nevertheless, this scepticism was also held by some probation officers. For example, a male senior probation officer of twenty four years' service commented that: 'It remains an ideal yet to be achieved. Most aims of the criminal justice system have little if any conception of "team work" and are concerned only to further their vested interests.' This suggests a certain 'impossibilism' and a comprehension of criminal justice as an internally conflictual and competitive enterprise, a subject to which I return later in this chapter.

Hierarchical Relations and Resistance

Respondents expressed a number of views concerning what they considered to be the appropriate hierarchical level within each organization for effective inter-agency relations. The following comment by a police constable reflects the view of a number of other police and probation officers: 'The biggest problem with multi-agency approaches is that it is aimed high . . . too high in the rank structure'. It was also suggested that inter-agency work is often located in over-formalized settings. Often the two are inter-related, requiring junior officers to re-establish and renegotiate relations at a lower level. Numerous officers concluded that this left 'partnerships' remote from the day-to-day work of front-line officers. A sergeant offered the following insight:

Perhaps rather than multi-agency meetings between executive level officers we should have a few more meetings at the 'sharp end' level. Hopefully this might allow front-line troops to get to know their opposite numbers and to appreciate the problems that others face.

Similar views were also expressed by probation officers.

Hierarchical resistance to a partnership approach was seen to be particularly problematic by those police officers who firmly supported the recent policy shift. A male sergeant of fourteen years' service, in contrast to the earlier comments, believed in the need for greater formality in order to overcome resistance:

Multi-agency has hardly taken off. The concept is not taken seriously enough by middle and senior officers, this results from ignorance and lack of understanding. For it to work, there must be enforced responsibility for projects rather than the rather lack-lustre informal approach to new ideas and initiatives. Also, in my view, there remains strong cultural resistance and indifference to the multi-agency approach.

In his comments he is keen to distinguish his own views from those of many colleagues. In doing so, he highlights the different hierarchical levels at which resistance to, as well as support for, partnership work may occur. This was a view supported by only a small number of other police officers, usually those who were committed to working with other agencies and frequently those who had experienced such work at first hand in some designated capacity.

'System Co-ordinatation'

Those officers who hold a supportive or 'benevolent' view of an inter-agency approach, tend to emphasize the managerial benefits of the co-ordination of criminal justice agencies, along the lines of the 'system failures' thesis. This perspective, with its emphasis on the smooth running of the interdependent parts of the whole 'system', is illustrated by the following comments from a woman police constable of four years' service:

[It is] much like giving a service to the public which involves five different companies, or rather, marketing a product which has five different parts all made in different factories. If those factories don't confer and discuss, how do you know that the pieces will fit together? You'll end up with five wrong parts and no end product that is of any use. Collaboration can only make lives easier and decisions better.

This is the 'rational organisation of an industrial enterprise' model (Peters 1986: 32) *par excellence*, applied to the criminal justice context. The main emphasis here is upon ending what one police sergeant called the 'parochial isolation' of individual agencies and, in its place, harnessing the expertise of the various criminal justice 'departments' to work together in a well co-ordinated fashion towards the same corporate goal:

Each agency has a lot to offer in providing solutions for problems and each is likely to approach the problem from a different perspective, which could provide a viewpoint on the problem which would otherwise not have been considered.

(Male police sergeant of 15 years' service)

A similar perspective is to be found among probation officers:

I regard this as a positive aspect of our work. We cannot be 'experts' at all types of intervention and therefore [we] need to include the work of specialists in our plans. Also, it's positive in terms of passing information, seeing other perspectives, and being challenged on our own views.

(Female main grade probation officer, of two years' service)

This concern with the smooth management of criminal justice was referred to by other police and probation officers who also alluded to a 'systems' analogy. For example, one probation officer suggested that an inter-agency approach, 'will help reduce duplication and make better use of specialisms', while another referred to it as the 'maximum use of the most relevant resources'. This largely uncritical acceptance of an inter-agency approach denies, or at least marginalizes, the existence of structural conflicts between criminal justice agencies. Conflict is either considered to be unproblematic or is something which can be removed, circumvented or defined away.

Information Exchange and Confidentiality

The connection between the removal of any duplication of roles and an increased flow of information between agencies, alluded to earlier, was made more explicit by other respondents:

[It] has removed a lot of work from officers who wasted time trying to contact the right people at social services, etc. We now have a direct link. Much better than a faceless person on the telephone. [This] helps with co-ordination and continuation. From a police point of view, if no offences were disclosed the file would invariably rot in a bottom drawer but the offender or person in trouble might still require advice or assistance. Now this can be discussed and passed to the correct department.

(Male constable of sixteen years' service)

Information is a prime commodity among criminal justice agencies. Securing information from other agencies is particularly important among police officers who identify rules which restrict information exchanges as a hindrance to the pursuance of their job. Witness the following comment by a male sergeant of seventeen years' service:

I accept that there should be liaison. However, until full co-operation is achieved no useful purpose will be gained, especially in relation to the probation and social services. Their lenient, 'wet' approach when accompanying juvenile offenders to the station only heightens the frustration officers feel. Also their non-disclosure policies in relation to certain information creates barriers. In my service I have met what can only be described as 'anti-police' probation and social workers, and this is not a rash statement built on ill-informed chit-chat. I can cite a number of occasions when minor information has been refused about a particular individual because it may infringe his/her civil liberties, even when the aim of asking the questions would be beneficial to the person concerned. I am all for a person's legal rights to be preserved, but 'Joe Public' needs and deserves more consideration, and these two departments are not assisting. The flow of information is still very much one way in their favour.

However, information is not exclusively a police concern but is also prized by probation officers. While some police officers see multi-agency collaboration as a means of gaining greater information from other services, for probation officers information exchange throws up complex and important issues of confidentiality. These sensitive contentions are also substantial components within the legal framework upon which contemporary notions of a judicial balance of interests are founded. Claims to confidentiality and information exchange, therefore, also give rise to inter-organizational conflicts and tensions as agencies pursue their own agendas.

Conflict

As in the case of confidentiality, inter-organizational conflict can be viewed as a necessary part of the process of justice, through the expression of divergent interests, or it can be seen as a negative frustration of that process: either an element in a complex balancing act or friction in the smooth running of a machine. The latter can often be another expression of the 'system failures' thesis. These different understandings of conflict were expressed by respondents. A male sergeant of twelve years' service, supportive of a multi-agency approach, identified vested interests as the cause of conflict:

Because each agency has its own priorities and aims, each is generally suspicious of the others' intentions and the final result they are searching for. This is based simply on the fact that the person involved, because they have chosen to work for a particular agency, believes their goals are the right ones for a given situation. If all agencies were to come under one body, each being a stage in dealing with the problem and each agency being given a clear direction within the body, then aims and ultimately achievements may, or should, go a step closer to creating a better society.

A female constable of two years' service, on the other hand, identified different roles within the criminal justice system as the cause of conflict:

Problems are faced quite frequently by police officers who have to deal with, for example, social services, who, in fairness to both parties are all just doing our jobs, but [we] seem to obstruct each other due to a conflict between their priorities and our priorities.

This idea of conflict as a fundamental and potentially necessary aspect of criminal justice was alluded to by a police constable of twelve years' service who had the following to say:

The police service as a whole has to work together with other criminal justice agencies . . . However, a lot of police resources are deployed in the 'gelling' of the separate agencies when generally the work the police do (i.e.) arrest and process criminals, is directly at odds with the views and objectives of the other agencies (i.e.) the probation service, social services, etc.

However, once conflict is recognized as an intrinsic or important element of inter-agency relations, the questions which automatically follow, are how that conflict is, or should be, managed and subsequently, how consent is to be constructed. These questions are posed implicitly by a male constable, of seven years' service.

There has been and will continue to be an expanding role of multi-agency work as problems faced by all agencies increase, with the greater problems faced by the modern society i.e. increased drug abuse . . . unemployment, the lessening of government intervention in the welfare state, etc. This multi-agency work is important but we must find a common ground on which to make it work as many of the differing organisations (i.e. police and social services) have totally different ideas on how problems should be dealt with.

The complexities inherent in the construction of consent against the background of divergent standpoints and competing interests are the quintessence of inter-agency relations. A male main grade probation officer of five years' service alludes to the difficulty in securing such consent:

Undoubtedly, a wider perspective on offenders can produce more effective intervention, not only in terms of multi-agency co-operation but in addressing the complexity of issues that may surround any individual. However, obtaining consensus on policies, approach, and objectives [in] inter-agency [work] can be difficult, and [is] often avoided.

The central importance of strategies for managing conflict will be examined and evaluated in greater detail later in the chapter with reference to the observational and interview research data.

Trust Relations

One way in which inter-organizational conflict expresses itself is in the form of 'distrust' and mutual suspicion between personnel from differing organizations. Mary Douglas correctly notes that 'writing about co-operation and solidarity means writing at the same time about rejection and mistrust' (1986: 1). The survey findings suggest that the majority of police officers disagreed with the statement that, 'probation officers and social workers defeat justice by helping the criminals'. While 55 per cent of police officers said that they simply 'disagreed', a further 8 per cent 'strongly disagreed', as against 11 per cent who 'strongly agreed' and 21 per cent who 'agreed' (the remaining 5 per cent were uncommitted either way). This represents a considerably less dismissive view of probation officers and social workers than that reported by Fielding (1988: 69). By contrast, probation officers appear to hold more cynical views of the work of police officers. The majority of probation officers agreed with the statement that, 'police officers defeat justice by concentrating on getting convictions'. While 16 per cent 'strongly agreed' and 51 per cent 'agreed', only 16 per cent 'disagreed' and 10 per cent 'strongly disagreed' (the remaining 7 per cent were uncommitted either way).

In open-ended responses police officers mentioned a number of factors which for them result in feelings of distrust of probation officers. For some this was said to stem from the perceived unwillingness of probation officers to release information. A number of police officers referred to probation officers' concerns for their clients' interests as amounting to a desire merely to 'keep people out of prison'. Further, a number of police officers referred to the fact that the probation service work to office hours unlike themselves who are 'open 24 hours a day'. The following comment by a police constable illustrates this sense of frustration:

[There] appears to be a lot of take and no give on behalf of other agencies. Because the police are always available, rightly so, to the public, we often deal with other agencies' problems in the first instance, with little response from the other agencies, i.e. 'Sorry, we only work Monday–Friday, 9–5.'

Probation officers, on the other hand, referred to the 'secretiveness' and 'suspicion' of police officers as constituting grounds for mutual distrust. This is not helped by the belief that the police are highly impersonal, as one probation officer said, 'you can never contact the same one twice'.

Consequently, distrust was seen to give rise to conflicts. Some officers put this down to ignorance and a lack of understanding of both the aims of other agencies and the way they work. A male constable of four years' service stated that, 'I am sure a better knowledge and understanding of the problems each agency has to deal with would eventually lead to all round better relationships'. As a remedy for distrust, some officers saw inter-agency relations as a means to an end, as well as an end in itself. Their argument is as follows: through better inter-agency relations, greater understanding develops between the agencies, hence better inter-agency relations, and so on. It is conceived of as a self-reinforcing process. The logic of this view is expressed by a male senior probation officer of twenty-two years' service:

Multi-agency work gives a new breadth to our work, and allows us to gain additional insights from seeing a situation from another person's, or agency's, perspective. We also benefit from the greater trust which develops between agencies, and the breakdown of unrealistic stereotypes.

A police constable of eighteen years' service expressed a similar view from a police perspective:

The police force must move with the times and liaise with other agencies because one factor to low morale is not understanding why other agencies make certain decisions, making officers quick to dismiss the efforts of these agencies perhaps through ignorance of working practices and general bigotry.

'It Diverts Energies'

For a number of respondents a principal concern is that inter-agency crime prevention represents an unnecessary departure from the perceived core functions of their respective organizations. Among probation officers this often means interfering with client-based work. For police officers this translates into what is seen as an interference with 'real policing', the moral mission to which some officers subscribe on joining the force (Fielding 1988). This is illustrated by the following comments by a male constable:

Police officers should concentrate on their specific role, i.e. preserving life, preventing, and detecting crime, keeping the peace. There are vast numbers of officers engaged in other tasks to the detriment of the service (steering groups, review bodies, resource units, etc.) . . . We exist for the children and pensioners, let us get on with it.

A male constable colleague of sixteen years' service goes on to outline the manner in which inter-agency work is seen to infringe this mission:

There are now so many people collaborating with other agencies that there are fewer 'real' policemen doing what they're paid to do. That is increasing the pressure on those of us that are still 'real' policemen.

It is interesting to note that in many such police responses, 'core policing' is directly associated with notions of masculinity, while much inter-agency work is identified as 'women's work'.

From a somewhat different understanding of gender, voices of concern were to be heard among probation officers. A number of them identified inter-agency co-operation as 'undermining' their 'core professional role' and as constituting an unwarranted depart- ure from 'client supervision'.

Blurring Organizational Boundaries and Roles

A related concern is that inter-agency work begins to blur tradi- tional distinctions between criminal justice agencies. This blurring of organizational roles and boundaries, as a cause of concern, unites both police and probation officers. From the survey, 88 per cent of police officers agreed with the statement: 'police officers are increas- ingly required to adopt a "social services" role', of whom 34 per cent 'strongly agreed'. By contrast, 11 per cent disagreed, of whom only 1 per cent 'strongly disagreed' (the remaining 1 per cent were uncommitted). In response to the statement: 'probation officers are increasingly required to adopt a "policing" role', the level of agree- ment among probation officers was not as high but was prominent nevertheless. Some 68 per cent of probation officers agreed to some extent with the proposition, of whom 17 per cent 'strongly agreed'. Just over one quarter (26 per cent) disagreed to some extent, of whom only 4 per cent 'strongly disagreed' (the remaining 6 per cent were uncommitted). This appears to suggest that issues of role confusion and organizational boundary blurring represent import- ant anxieties for both groups of officers.

This concern was also reflected in the more open-ended respon- ses. Some police officers appeared acutely concerned that they may be losing their own distinct identity and autonomy. Their main concern was their belief that they are being asked to take on more 'social work' type functions. As one officer put it, 'the police seem to be expected to think and act as a social worker (especially if it's after 5 p.m.)'. A significant number of police officers were particularly concerned that the growing emphasis upon multi-agency community crime prevention was shifting policing away from its traditional detection and law enforcement role. This is reflected in the following comment by a police inspector of eighteen years' service:

In general terms I feel the [multi-agency] trend is to be encouraged and if correctly approached the concept has much to commend it. I have some concern, however, that the police service is 'losing its way' somewhat, and that there is considerable pressure for us to move away from our traditional 'enforcement' role. That is fine to an extent but I am left with a feeling that since we have embarked on the multi-agency path (particularly in respect of dealing with offenders) we have abdicated our responsibility to the public to prosecute offenders within the community in favour of considering the needs of the offender. This is a generalisation, of course, but it is a view that I know is shared by many—police and public.

Here, a multi-agency approach is seen as tantamount to the 'socialization of criminal justice policy', whereby policing priorities are captured by social issues and sociological concerns. This view is also emphasized by a male constable of twenty-five years' service:

The police force is *the* law enforcement agency and we are losing our way. We are getting involved in tasks that are the province of the social services and other agencies: these tasks are all very worthy but do they require a policeman to perform them? Collaboration is fine but do we want the police to be an 'arm' of the social services?

This fear dovetails with earlier expressions of anxieties regarding the dilution of 'real' policing, loss of organizational autonomy and shifts in professional responsibilities. This is, to a large degree, a plea for a mythical past, as policing has always involved an important social service function (Kinsey *et al.* 1986; Reiner 1992b). These views may tell us more about the attitude of some police officers to the status accredited to certain aspects of police work than they do about the changing nature of policing. Nevertheless, these comments reflect deep anxieties within certain groups of police officers who are antagonistic towards current changes.

From a somewhat different perspective, probation officers share this fear of role transformation and the blurring of organizational

boundaries. A number of officers were concerned with the potential 'diminution' and 'dilution' of the traditional core offender-
orientation of the service. The following comments by a female
main grade probation officer of fifteen years' service illustrate this
concern:

To some extent it is right to have a wider perspective than the offender
only, for example, victim and society as a whole. However, I would not
wish to see concentration on offenders diluted too much—this is where
our primary skills lie.

A main grade male probation officer of twenty years' service re-
emphasized this point in his view that: 'I am in favour of partnership
working, provided it enhances rather than simply replaces our
work.' The fear here is potentially the inverse of that of the police,
the 'criminalization of social policy'.

A number of probation officers referred to the need to maintain
strict boundaries in the face of this process of blurring. However,
the complexities involved in the preservation of distinct organizational roles, within a framework of a 'corporatist' strategy, are
alluded to by a female senior probation officer:

[Inter-agency work is] a very important issue. The service, by the nature of
its history, feels it ought to do it all. We can only achieve this in a multi-
disciplinary way but with a need to preserve the probation services' own
significant contribution to the issue. We do not help ourselves by being
insular or by adopting other disciplines' values. A difficult balancing act!

The balancing act to which she refers lies at the very heart of inter-
agency work, involving the competing tensions of independent
interdependence within and between criminal justice agencies.

Loss of Autonomy, Accountability, and Shifts in Responsibility

Finally, the problems posed by managing these tensions and conflicts
raise additional concerns. Two such concerns which are implicit in
fears about blurring organizational boundaries, are the potential
loss of autonomy of agencies and shifts in responsibility as resulting
from increased inter-agency work. A number of police and probation officers were worried that multi-agency partnerships represent a means by which responsibility and greater work is placed
upon their own organization. A male constable of six years' service
took up this position arguing that:

It would appear that the police service is fast becoming the 'lap-dog' of all other agencies, not really being asked their opinion but being required to do other people's dirty work, which in turn demoralises the 'front-line troops'.

A male sergeant colleague of twenty years' service reinforced this message, commenting that, 'multi-agency collaboration means more work for us, less for them'. Interestingly, however, a female main grade probation officer of five years' service made a similar observation in relation to her own organization. She suggested that inter-agency work 'means each agency trying to persuade the other that it is *their* problem'.

In addition to shifts in responsibility being viewed in a negative or defensive light, one male police constable of five years' service suggested that multi-agency co-operation implies, or requires, a significant shift in responsibility on behalf of the public in relation to crime:

This aspect would be more generally accepted by police officers at the 'sharp end' of things if . . . they weren't expected to be social workers, first-aiders, crossing patrol officers, etc. by the public, i.e. if the public took more responsibility for their own activities, lives, etc. Then we would be able to spend time more creatively rather than acting as nursemaids to society.

Finally, the issue of organizational autonomy is well illustrated by a female main grade probation officer of five years' service. Significantly she relates this to questions of organizational accountability:

At a time when my own professional role is being undermined by 'accountability'—meaning more forms from H.Q.—I find the government's willingness to pour money into the black hole of quasi-independent organisations is to have no accountability.

Clearly the implications of partnerships for both political and organizational accountability (a theme I discuss in detail in Chapter 7) are of fundamental importance.

The survey findings confirm the very real differences that exist between police and probation officers' understandings of crime prevention and the causes of crime. These differences reflect contrasting occupational socialization, roles, and objectives. They structure competing conceptions and definitions of 'appropriate' social interventions. In so doing, they produce sites of inter-agency conflict. These conceptual and definitional conflicts are the stuff of inter-agency work. And yet, as we have seen, in spite of their different training, priorities, and cultural traditions, police and probation officers do share certain similar perceptions, overlapping aspirations, and fears regarding the growth of a 'partnership' approach. They share uncertainties as to its impact upon their work and the future direction of their occupation. These 'shared uncertainties' transcend organizational roles and confuse managerialist and normative debates within and between institutions. They represent expressions of conflicts between morally toned urges to punish and the forces of expediency and management which run throughout criminal justice institutions. These ambivalent and incongruous tensions are clearly identifiable in the survey responses. They represent a fundamental aspect of society's cultural sensibilities towards criminal justice and the question of punishment. As Garland argues:

> To some extent, institutional divisions (between court and prison, police and prosecution, probation and parole, etc.) help contain these conflicts, quarantining the different objectives into different segments of the system. But these boundaries merely structure these conflicts and make them manageable, rather than resolving them in any permanent way.
>
> (1990: 192)

Holdaway suggests that these 'shared uncertainties' may form the basis of greater mutual understanding and trust, and thus establish the 'setting for the shared exploration of developments in inter-agency policy and practice' (Holdaway 1986: 154). What the survey findings show is that in order to understand better the nature of inter-agency relations, we need to identify both the similarities and continuities, as well as the points of departure and conflict, between different agencies.

Partnerships in Practice

In their views, hopes, and anxieties the survey respondents raise a number of salient and important questions concerning the nature of 'partnerships' in practice. I will now explore some of these issues in greater detail through the examination of the observational and interview data from both the crime prevention case studies and the victim/offender mediation research. A brief description of each of the research case studies, the names of which are fictitious, can be found in Appendix A. I will draw upon the research findings to evaluate the ways in which policies in relation to 'partnerships' are translated into routinized social action. I will consider the manner in which conflicts and allegiances are managed in practice, together with how key front-line officers make sense of 'partnerships' and the strategies to which they give rise.

Ideal Types of Partnerships

Until this point, I have used the terms 'partnership', 'multi-agency', and 'inter-agency' interchangeably as in the literature (Liddle and Gelsthorpe 1994a: 4). It is, however, worth drawing attention to the very real differences between conceptions of 'partnership' work. It is useful to make a distinction between two different 'ideal types' of partnerships. Rather like the distinction between 'multi-disciplinary' and 'interdisciplinary' studies, we can distinguish between, on the one hand, *multi*-agency' relations which merely involve the coming together of a variety of agencies in relation to a given problem, and, on the other hand, *inter*-agency' relations, which entail some degree of fusion and melding of relations between agencies (see Crawford and Jones 1996:30–1).

'Multi-agency' relations, therefore, exist simply where more than one agency contributes to an initiative. Formal, as well as informal, contact is likely to be located within existing organizational structures, rules, and practices. Officers within each organization whose professional expertise is considered relevant to crime prevention are identified often as 'link' personnel. Their core tasks remain largely unaltered, as multi-agency work is grafted onto existing practices or those existing practices are redefined. This understanding of 'partnership' work is lucidly outlined by a council officer from the Illsworth estate-based crime prevention initiative:

Partnership means putting everybody's role into perspective and fitting it together so they don't need another job specifically, they need to understand how they fit in and then do their job in an open and public framework, so in effect turning up at the [initiative] and making sure that people take a corporate approach is all that's needed in addition to their existing tasks. Doing the same task a different way is how I perceive it.

This model is representative of a number of crime prevention projects from the research case studies, many of which drew together senior officers from various relevant agencies in a policy making capacity. Thus, for example, the Arlington Racial Harassment Project and the Westbridge Drugs Initiative both sought to 'pool data', as well as to influence and co-ordinate the policies of the incorporated agencies—around issues of racial harassment and drug prevention and safety respectively—by bringing together relatively senior officers. This was achieved without significantly changing the tasks of the individuals concerned. For those involved, this constituted 'just another meeting' (Arlington police inspector) which did not alter existing core tasks, practices or lines of accountability. Similarly, this is the rationale and working practice of Safer Cities, steering committees. It is also the type of collaborative work involved in most mediation partnerships, which usually take the form of advisory or management committees. These committees bring together 'experts' or those who have some form of leverage—be it conceptual or material, for example, in a resource or gatekeeping capacity—on the issues involved. As well as seeking to raise the profile of mediation within the incorporated agencies—much like an approach to racial harassment or a specific drugs policy—these multi-agency committees lend legitimacy and support to the endeavours of, and the aims promoted by, the designated schemes.

In contrast, at the other end of the ideal typical continuum, 'inter-agency' relations are those networks which interpenetrate and thus interrupt 'normal' internal working relations. New structures and forms of working may arise and operate outside the participating organization's core structures, roles, and practices. Individual officers from the key organizations may be relieved of their core professional duties and take on new duties, defined by the new structures. This may involve the formal secondment of officers to the designated project, as a recognition of the extent to which their new tasks lie outside core organizational work and practice. Consequently, inter-agency relations involve a degree of blurring of organizational boundaries and an associated loss of organizational autonomy. For example, on the Greengage Bicycle Theft project the police officer involved found himself working with, and supervising, offenders on community service orders who were using their time repairing and painting bicycles for the project. These were tasks with which he was very unfamiliar, as a police officer, and which involved him in new ways of working and thinking. As an interesting aside, the police officer later resigned from the police, in part due to ill health, and subsequently went on to train as a probation officer, having been interested by his experience on the project.

On the Tenmouth Burglary Reduction Initiative this fusion of roles was taken even further. It was a joint initiative between the police and the probation service to replicate the successful Home Office Kirkholt demonstration project (see Forrester *et al.* 1988; 1990). The scheme involved the police and probation service seconding full time officers to work alongside each other. Over two years, under the supervision of a multi-agency steering committee, they built up a crime profile within the area by interviewing victims of burglaries, their neighbours, and apprehended offenders about local offending and modes of prevention. The aim was to involve the community in identifying and implementing pertinent policies on the basis of the data collected, targeted particularly at repeat victims. This involved the participating officers in very different roles. The probation officers, for example, were required to engage in extensive work with victims and to adopt a 'community perspective'. It also entailed the establishment of new formal line-management and accountability structures, as noted by one of the police constables seconded to the project. 'I think you've got to change the rules slightly when you're running a project like this'. This was the result of the more genuinely *inter*-agency approach adopted by the project.

Inter-agency linkages may be housed at both an organizational and spatial distance from the key participating agencies, with symbolic and practical effects. On the Tenmouth project, for example, officers worked out of a 'neutral location' provided by a local business. This allowed one of the front-line officers on the project to comment that:

An independent office has given the project an independent identity, it says we are here, we're set up, we've got an office and here's what we are doing. Senior officers can actually visit it and see something positive, but also I think the workers are quite comfortable and there is no threat posed by the others there [probation officers to the police and vice versa], they are not a spy in the camp.

Consequently, 'trust' tends to become a more important ingredient in the case of inter-agency relations. The greater interdependence of organizations and personnel places considerable import upon devices for coping with the consequential lack of power, autonomy, knowledge, and information which it brings. It is here that the conditions for the requirements of trust are ripe. Individuals working on such projects often occupy an ambiguous organizational position, at the periphery of their own organization. The development of a clear project identity may develop as a common symbol or representation of these new and emerging interpersonal trust relations. Nevertheless, this can give rise to novel conflicts between 'project loyalties' and 'organizational loyalties'. Tensions may lead project workers to prioritize project goals at the expense of their parent organizational goals. So, for example, there was a continual source of tension on the Tenmouth project where officers frequently identified project goals as taking precedence over conflicting organizational needs. The officers' shared commitment to the project often meant that they would manipulate their own organizations in order to achieve these new goals. The senior police officer commented:

we shared a lot of confidences about what was going on in each others' organisation and we were able to contrive and force issues—playing one organisation off against the other so that both organisations agreed . . . I have to say that we were a bit devious, that we would play one assistant chief constable off against another assistant chief probation officer . . . as a result what was said to one caused the other to do something and we got our way.

Through these and analogous probings and joint commitments, the boundaries of interpersonal and transorganizational trust relations are tentatively constructed. Although inherently this occurs upon fragile foundations, given the 'latent' structural conflicts which frame the nature of inter-organizational work. Here, in addition to the officers' mutual trust and personal commitment, there appears to be an emerging loyalty to the new inter-agency unit although this was neither absolute nor unconditional. These tensions indicate that such inter-agency linkages, as in the Tenmouth case, are likely to be unstable and potentially short lived.

Clearly, not all partnership initiatives conform neatly to one or other of these 'ideal types'. Similarly, they are not mutually exclusive but may co-exist within a given initiative, they may fuse and overlap. Nevertheless, I suggest that they are illustrative of, and epitomize, certain tendencies and differences in the nature of collaborative work between criminal justice agencies. They also identify the different demands placed upon key agency workers in their working relations with other agencies and across organizational boundaries. Consequently, the ability of front-line workers to go beyond their professional roles, in order to develop and maintain interpersonal trust relations with 'outsiders', is more important a characteristic of 'good' *inter*-agency relations, than it is in the case of *multi*-agency work. So, for example, on the Tenmouth project, the ability of the probation officer to 'get on' with ordinary police officers in the canteen was identified as an important aspect in the early success and acceptance of the project. This was certainly not something that the majority of her probation colleagues either would have been able or willing to do, as noted by colleagues. A senior police officer stressed the importance of this characteristic:

I think the way [the project] was accepted at Tenmouth Police Constabulary was due not just to [the police officer] but also the way the probation officer had got on well with the police. When you are working with other agencies you do need the ability to switch into their culture, know what makes them tick and understand it. [The seconded probation officer] would often come in for coffee or lunch and would sit in the [police] canteen and wouldn't sit with me, but would go and sit over on that table with two or three constables, and that had quite a beneficial effect on, not just publicising the project, but here's a probation officer who hasn't got horns coming out on the side of their head or something like that . . . This actually helps.

(Chief Inspector, Tenmouth police)

This 'reflexivity' appears to be an important element in monitoring interpersonal trust relations across organizational boundaries (Giddens 1990: 36–8). In this instance the ability of the probation officer not to appear hostile to police officers as a member of the 'opposite side of the camp' (Tenmouth, police constable), was an important aspect of building trust in inter-agency work, particularly given the background of mutual suspicion noted earlier.

Intra-organizational Relations

Gender Relations

Gender relations constitute a particularly prominent arena, albeit often ignored, in which intra-organizational relations can significantly affect the nature of inter-organizational work. Organizations are both constructed by, and in turn construct, gender relations. This is particularly evident in criminal justice where notions of masculinity and femininity are both prevalent and suffused within legal norms, moral values, and institutional practices (see Gilligan 1982; Heidensohn 1986; Daly 1989; Smart 1989). Gender relations magnify and distort, and in turn are magnified and distorted by, inter-agency relations, as experiences within a given organization are carried over into working within and between organizations. We have already seen in the survey responses—supported by a wealth of research (see Heidensohn 1992; Walklate 1995: chapter 4)—how police culture celebrates values of masculinity. Moreover the dominant cultural ethos exhibits significant elements of sexist prejudice, homophobia and 'old fashioned machismo' (Reiner 1992b: 124–5). In the previous research example from the Tenmouth project, the female probation officer had to negotiate the sexism of the police canteen, drawing upon her own experiences. Within the gendered world of policing, tasks and roles which depart from the 'masculine', action-oriented emphasis on 'chasing criminals' are considered to be less important, as 'social work' and 'not real police work', hence 'women's work'. Consequently, much inter-agency work, which stands at the periphery of both the police organization and 'core' policing, is viewed as such. Therefore, it was not surprising that within the police forces in the research sites there was a high overrepresentation of women police officers working as designated front-line inter-agency workers. This was particularly evident where more genuinely 'inter-agency' projects required the police to operate outside traditional core organizational structures, roles, and practices. Further, other agencies which adopt a more 'caring', less 'punitive' approach to suspects and offenders often are constructed, by police officers, as portraying 'female' characteristics, a view reinforced in the research when individual police officers came into contact with those agencies only to find, within their ranks, a significantly higher proportion of women officers. Within policing, inter-agency work frequently was seen as simultaneously a pejorative form of 'women's work'—in that it did not constitute 'real police work'—and celebrated as a task which women do better. A male chief inspector from the Tenmouth project explained the over-representation of women officers involved in the project, as follows:

In my experience women police officers are not necessarily better at gathering information, but I think that once they've got the information they can process it better than men. In terms of dealing with the whole business of information gathering, male police officers—in my experience —have a shorter attention span. Women, I think, are better at working towards long-term goals.

This example highlights that the relationship between front-line inter-agency workers at the periphery of an organization and core agency officers is not one of neat correspondence and should not be taken for granted. As a result of intra-organizational cultural perceptions (often overlaid with notions of gender) front-line inter-agency workers may be unrepresentative of the wider membership of a given organization.

However, gender relations, as well as producing sites of conflict between agencies, also constitute the locus of shared experiences and forms of allegiances across agency boundaries. My research findings accord with those of Sampson *et al.* (1991), who suggest that women's experiences of marginalization and discrimination within their own organization have a significant impact upon inter-agency co-operation. They conclude that:

These experiences mean not only that some forms of inter-agency work are severely limited by the avoiding action taken by women workers in order to minimise potentially discriminatory encounters, but also that as a means of countering their marginalisation women workers will establish different types of alliances with workers in other organisations.

(Sampson *et al.* 1991: 115)

These networks may cut across structured power relations between agencies. Hence, inter-organizational trust relations, simultaneously, are gendered. This is not to suggest that all women who work across organizational boundaries do so in similar ways. Rather, the experiences of women working in large organizations often contribute to shared understandings of ways of working, frequently resulting in creative strategies of conflict avoidance and informal networking (issues to which I return later).

Cultural Perceptions

Organizational divisions of labour and resources, together with the status perceptions to which they give rise, can generate important intra-organizational conflicts which seriously affect inter-agency relations. For example, the Tenmouth project was caught up in conflicts which had their origins in the internal status perceptions of crime prevention within the police. These seriously affected, and in turn were affected by, the nature of resultant inter-agency relations. In order to invert the prevailing caricature of crime prevention work within the police—so aptly described by Harvey *et al.* a 'sort of pre-retirement course for experienced but tired detectives' (1989: 88)—the senior police officer involved in the project recruited, as the second officer, someone widely recognized throughout the local force as destined for higher office. He had hoped that the association of such a 'high flyer', would raise the profile of crime prevention within the force. However, the organizational preference for officers to have worked in CID before promotion and the cultural celebration of detective work, resulted in the seconded officer's removal from the project. The senior police officer explained the reasons for the move and (in his own typically understated manner) its impact:

For personal career development reasons [she] was taken off [the project] and she is now in CID. We see her as a bright star in the future, and the police service wanted to develop her career in personal terms. And this had, again, an unfortunate effect on the project. A slight impetus was lost . . . but unfortunately the old culture of the police service meant that she needed to get wider experience of CID.

The subsequent withdrawal of a central and prominent figure on the project precipitated an immediate crisis at the next management committee meeting. The probation service threatened to withdraw their seconded officer and terminate the project. This was exacerbated by the, almost simultaneous, replacement of the senior police officer (quoted above), although this had been known and expected for some time. Future relations became strained as the change of personnel was felt to be down-grading of the general police commitment to the project. The removal of two individuals with whom important interpersonal trust relations had been forged further frustrated relations. The nature of the tensions and the importance of sustaining trust were illustrated in a discussion with the senior probation officer on the project. When asked about the panic that the changes had caused the probation service, the senior probation officer involved said:

I don't think that would have happened if [the original senior police officer] had been at that meeting. [He] and I would have got up at the end of that meeting and said, 'what the hell's going on?', because I didn't know either. I don't think [the original senior police officer] would have made a move until I had come back to him with an answer.

Question: Do you mean that you would have operated informally?
Yes, that's right, because we have been working together for much longer and are much closer as far as our trust goes. [The new senior police officer] has just been moved to a post he is not comfortable with, with many distractions. And I'm just one of the many new things that he has got to take on board. I don't think he'd had enough time to suss me out.
Question: Are informality and trust quite important then?
Oh, yes. We'll soon be starting project number two and we're building on the same model, and I'm doing that with [the original senior police officer] again and that's based on trust, because he and I don't have a difficulty.

This example is illustrative of the way in which inter-organizational conflicts may have their origins in intra-organizational tensions. It also highlights the importance of trust relations as the premise for working collaboratively across agency boundaries.

Power Relations

Pearson and colleagues (1992: Blagg *et al.* 1988; Sampson *et al.* 1988; 1991) correctly identify power as the central aspect in the study of inter-organizational networks. Relations of power between institutions, they suggest, exist at 'a deep structural level'. Importantly, power relations are neither evenly nor randomly distributed but are differential. They go on to add:

It is power differentials running between different state agencies which influence other symptomatic forms of inter-agency conflict, such as struggles over confidentiality and privileged access information.

(Sampson *et al.* 1991: 132)

My own research findings endorse this emphasis. Institutional and structural power differences exist between agencies and other organized interests incorporated into multi-agency work. Human and material resources, access to information, and claims to 'expertise', all affect the capacity of agencies and interest groups to achieve desired outcomes. Some individuals and groups are in more favourable structural positions and better able to appropriate specialist knowledge than others. The police, for example, given its size, hierarchical structure, and working patterns is able to deploy, with considerable ease, human (and to a lesser extent material) resources very rapidly, in large numbers, and in flexible patterns. This often gives the police a lead position in crime prevention projects and accords them the symbolic stick of withdrawal, one which can be waved when deemed necessary. It also leaves the police often frustrated at the relatively slow pace at which decision making and human resource deployment occur in other agencies. This in turn may provide the seeds of new inter-organizational conflict. Further, as a result of their function and organizational location within the criminal justice system, the police have a huge informational advantage over other agencies and groups in relation to matters of crime and its prevention.

In the field of mediation partnerships, given mediation's awkward relation with the formal criminal justice process, a prominent source of 'powers of leverage' lie in, and through, referral relations. Consequently, mediation schemes are reliant upon maintaining good systems of referral (which often differ from one scheme to the next). Agencies that refer cases for mediation, whether or not attached to the prosecution or sentencing process, therefore exert considerable power over mediation schemes and their success (at least defined in quantitative terms). The police as key 'gatekeepers' to the criminal justice process hold important defining powers. They act as an initial filter of cases, consequently imposing their own definitions of appropriateness. This is particularly evident in victim/offender mediation initiatives, many of which are reliant on diversion related referrals. Here it is predominantly the police who screen referrals. However, it would be wrong to suggest that this power is always deployed in the pursuit of organizational interests. A Juvenile Liaison Officer, related to the Leighdale Mediation Scheme explains:

I select them [cases] if I think that it is likely to get some response, particularly from the parents. If I think they may be interested in making some reparation or that it may be useful for the young person to get to understand what they did to their victim, how they affected them. But I don't see them [the offenders] they're just files that come across my desk. I just make a judgement on the basis of the information given to me in their papers. I don't keep any records on who I select or why. There are no guidelines. If it looks suitable I refer. But it all depends on whether I've got the time to select files . . . I haven't sent any for 2 months because I've been too busy. I haven't got the time to sift them out.

A managerial rather than ideological logic is at play here. With the collapse of the case referral panels in the area and the considerable reduction in related staffing, the Juvenile Liaison Officer was likened, by a local Juvenile Justice worker, to a central 'processor of decisions', driven only by a managerial desire for 'consistency'.

This view was further illustrated during the course of the research. One of the co-ordinators of the Leighdale Mediation Scheme became particularly concerned that, as a consequence of my asking 'too many awkward and difficult questions' (in her words) of referral personnel in relevant agencies (notably the police), inadvertently I might have been threatening the existence of established referral channels, and ultimately the future of the scheme. She explained:

You've got to tread carefully, because, you know, many of the people don't think about why they are referring. They don't ask themselves 'what is this all about? Is it in the interests of the police? of victims? or offenders?' or those sorts of things. They do it because their boss told them to. If they start to think too much about why they are doing it, they may not wish to continue.

Some schemes, such as the two research case studies, tried to avoid this over-reliance upon the police by diversifying referral points through different agencies. One of the co-ordinators of the Oldcastle Victim/Offender Mediation Service, likened this to 'not putting all our eggs in one basket'. Consequently, considerable effort was invested in the process of multiple referral points, even when on occasions it appeared to run counter to the initial aims and ideology of the project. Often this is done in the hope that firm and enduring interpersonal trust relations, absent in the relationship with the police officer cited above, can be established. One of the co-ordinators of the Leighdale scheme explains:

It's difficult establishing referral systems . . . sometimes the people we're using are not the right people in the right places . . . and you've got to tread carefully, because they can always withdraw their goodwill and then you've got to start all over again.

The problem of referrals is also an issue for many community mediation schemes, particularly those willing to accept police referrals. For example, a co-ordinator of the Northolt Community Mediation Service had to invest considerable effort in trying to 'persuade and educate' the police (her words), at various different subdivisions, not to refer what she believed to be the 'wrong types of cases'. The concern, as she saw it, was that the police might use community mediation as a potential means of redefining criminal cases as civil disputes, to be dealt with by means of negotiation in the shadow of the courts. Experience had shown her that 'non-serious' cases involving established, particularly familial, relations between victim and offender were being redefined as disputes, in order to be disposed of.

In addition to the police, other agencies hold considerable sway over mediation schemes. For example, the Northolt Community Mediation Scheme became highly reliant upon the Environmental Health department of the local council. By contrast, the Leighdale Victim/Offender Mediation Service went through a torrid relationship with the local Youth Justice department which, for a significant period of time, refused to make any referrals to the scheme. Later, it decided to make only post-sentence referrals. This rupture arose out of a single case referred by Youth Justice workers to the mediation service, in which a number of youths had pleaded guilty to an assault, but who, in the view of the mediators and scheme co-ordinator, were not taking the mediation process seriously. In addition, they were believed to be fabricating stories that the victim had written to them to forgive them. Consequently, this understanding of their participation was included in the report submitted to the court. Subsequently, the boys received reasonably severe sentences, which Youth Justice workers blamed upon the mediation service reports. The co-ordinator gave her interpretation of events:

In this case I spoke to the PO [probation officer] concerned after we had written the report and I said 'should I send it in?' and the PO said 'just put it in'. So I did. They [Youth Justice] just want positive reports . . . He's [the head of the Youth Justice team] sent round a memo to tell all his staff not to refer pre-sentence . . . because in the report we didn't say what they wanted to hear, it had negative elements.

The head of the Youth Justice Team, however, explained it thus:

We've run aground on two or three occasions where it's been pre-sentence. And I think, to some extent, that's fine if the young person co-operates, the scheme feeds into court the fact that he appears to be genuinely feeling remorse because the offender has done this or that . . . If it goes the other way and if the young person, for any reason, doesn't co-operate and then a report goes in . . . I feel very uneasy about that. And so, I think simplistically I would prefer to draw it out of our system. So as not to allow those situations to arise, by making it post-sentence only.

This example highlights the structural power of gatekeeping agencies. However, power differentials express themselves in a variety of forms.

Organizations bring to 'crime problems' competing claims to

specialist knowledge and 'expertise'. In the field of crime prevention, the police, planning departments, and architects are often in dominant positions given the predominance of situational and architectural notions of prevention, particularly those deploying forms of technology. They are able to claim, and often are accorded, an 'expert' status in the field of prevention, despite the emphasis on 'common-sense' knowledge, both within policing *per se* and much crime prevention theory. The police, specifically, have an ability to define and defend a range of problems and tasks, and to acquire new ones in terms of security and prevention (Ericson 1994: 158–9). Specialization in crime prevention, together with the wealth of (statistical) information about crimes available to the police, have allowed designated police officers to become 'experts' in prevention and control. They are the new 'security professionals'. In the face of this 'expertise', other partners in inter-agency work are often left muted.

For example, the situation in which the probation officer on the Tenmouth project found herself, highlights this self-fulfilling process. From her own perspective:

My probation officer training really leads me to think that unless you are going to make wholesale changes in the way society views crime—things like masculinity, maturity, adult responsibility—then you will never really be able to make anything but superficial changes to patterns of crime. In a way this project struggles with that part of my way of thinking . . . I think that [the project] and some of the people involved in the project are anxious that something practical should be done and I would say that there is a limit to that, but I think that I am *learning* about crime prevention . . . I came into the project with very little knowledge of crime prevention per se, whereas *the police have that knowledge* . . . I think that people [on the project] perceive crime prevention very much in the police view of locks and bolts and burglar alarms. (emphasis added)

What is interesting here is that her years of experience of working with offenders and confronting offending behaviour were not seen as particularly relevant to, or in any way informing, 'crime prevention'. Crime prevention for her had become synonymous with police thinking and knowledge, which was primarily 'practical', technological, and concerned solely with target hardening. Consequently, she was 'sent on an "in house" police training course' in order to 'learn about crime prevention' (her own words).

However, while the police were often able to use their resources to define policy and set broad agendas, they found themselves to be in less powerful positions in relation to specific dealings with housing and planning departments, whose 'expert' knowledge, particularly on council estate-based projects, was rarely challenged. A similar police silence often descended in debates over health issues concerning drugs and the prescription of 'clean alternatives' (on the Westbridge Project). Further, the police were often reliant upon local council 'know how' when it came to seeking sources of funding, although as Reiner (1991) notes, this is an area of growing police 'expertise', particularly at senior levels.

Conceptualizing Inter-organizational Power Relations

There is a predisposition in some of the research literature to conceptualize power as largely conflictual, constraining, and repressive. For example, Pearson et al. (1992) tend to emphasize power embedded in structures which appear as external restraints upon action. Following Foucault (1979), we need to understand power not just as prohibitive but also as productive: power is creative and enabling as well as constraining. In their over-emphasis upon the conflictual and constraining nature of power relations, Pearson et al. (1992) underestimate the creative and productive nature of action within structural constraints. Such an approach leaves us only a partial understanding of the operation of power in inter-organizational contexts. As Lukes points out, social life involves 'a dialectic of power and structure, a web of possibilities for agents, whose nature is both active and structured, to make choices and pursue strategies within given limits, which in consequence expand and contract over time' (1977: 29). Power, therefore, is a relational concept which is not static but, to a certain degree, fluid. It shifts in balance over time and space.

Differential power relations encompass the relative capacity of orgnizations and actors, drawing upon material and human resources, to achieve desired outcomes. In a multi-agency crime prevention context, this frequently involves the ability of different organizations and actors to impose their definition of a situation upon others and to realize their strategic interests. Giddens correctly notes that, 'power is the means of getting things done and, as such, directly implied in human action' (1984: 283). 'Getting things done' through partnerships (as we will see in the next sections) takes on various different forms and strategies. In multi-agency crime prevention, and to a slightly lesser extent mediation, power often is exercised through *the power to define*: to set broad agendas, determine the contours of policy and direct resources. But it also expresses itself in more specific and temporal strategies of action, in definitions of 'crimes', their 'appropriate solutions', and legitimate 'community'. Hence, power in inter-agency contexts is neither a permanently possessed fixture, exercised for unidirectional ends, nor is it wholly pluralistic. Power and control refer to a set of diverse social practices which are not resolved in any unilinear direction, albeit bounded by important structural constraints. Hence, the study of power within inter-agency relations must concern itself with the particular alignment of social relations in given contexts.

The 'Creative' Management of Conflict

As a consequence of their conceptualization of power and conflict, Pearson *et al.* (1992) focus, almost exclusively, upon instances in which latent structural conflicts are realized and played out in, and through, human interactions: where structural oppositions appear at the 'surface level' in the form of overt conflict. However, whilst they are correct to note that these oppositions are 'always latent' (Sampson *et al.* 1988: 482), the important question, for our purposes, is how these oppositions relate to, and are embedded in, *routinized social action*. The issue of how deeper level oppositions are negotiated in non-overtly conflictual interactions, is one that commentators largely seem to ignore. Consequently, they fail to address sufficiently practices of conflict avoidance and the creative management of conflicts 'off stage' in discreet settings which control their impact upon broader inter-organizational relations. This is not to say that the expression of latent structural conflict is a nonessential aspect of inter-organizational relations, for, as I hope to have shown, it clearly is. Rather, this represents only a partial understanding of the dialectics of power relations. Latent structural conflicts can be, and often are, managed through creative strategies which do not result in the expression of overt conflict. In the quest to understand power relations in inter-organizational settings, we need to look behind the substance of conflict and the occasions upon which it is realized, at the complex processes through which conflict is often hidden in routinized action.

This creativity is an important aspect of working within the tensions and oppositions that exist within and between agencies. By creativity, I refer to the ability of senior managers and front-line inter-agency workers to manage the tensions and challenges posed by working across agency boundaries whilst securing, albeit limited, goals and strategies. As Rutherford suggests in his recent study of criminal justice practitioners, one perennial challenge faced by such criminal justice personnel is, 'how to work *creatively with the inherent tensions*, affording legitimacy to both independence and interdependence' (Rutherford 1993: 126, emphasis added). Such tensions do not only constrain the deployment of human and material resources but also provide opportunities for new modes of working. My research findings suggest that there is, first, an awareness of sites of conflict, and secondly, considerable creativity among inter-agency workers in negotiating the deep structural oppositions that exist.

At this point it is important to stress that the notion of creativity, as I use it, carries no normative judgement of its moral value. It is not to be treated as a necessarily positive endorsement of innovative working practices. On the contrary, many forms of creativity evidenced in the research, resulted in working practices which were frequently unaccountable, often took place behind the backs of agency and community representatives and posed complex questions for procedures aimed to ensure confidentiality. It is the nature and consequence of these creative practices, and in particular their implications for organizations' own strategies and interests, which are of paramount importance.

For example, the initial aim of the Tenmouth Anti-Burglary Project had been to agree a corporate plan of crime prevention measures for implementation during the lifetime of the project. As the data piled up the project reached a series of impasses over the extent of the recommendations to be jointly agreed and the nature of their implementation. Issues such as how to address the lack of support for victims, the perceived need for improved security measures in private rented and local authority housing, and the form that 'community building' in the area should take, remained unresolved, as did questions concerning who was to fund improvements and resource any new services. The senior police and probation officers involved in the management of the project, when confronted by these problems as well as the pending withdrawal of commitment by their organizations, jointly renegotiated the initiatives' objectives.

Over a drink it was transformed from a practical crime prevention initiative involving the implementation of locally researched recommendations into a research project alone, with no formal implementation stage.

The redefinition of the scope and nature of the Tenmouth project enabled the police and probation service not only to 'save face' but to pursue with renewed vigour the notion that what was being done was genuinely about 'the community' and in their interest. Thus the redefinition of the project was later 'sold' to other members of the inter-agency committee in terms of the recommendations being 'handed over to the community' (both phrases were used frequently by officers on the project). Thus the implementation stage was to be the community's responsibility and no longer that of the key agencies involved in the project, for whom the project was to be 'put to bed' (Chief Inspector, Tenmouth police). Later, at a public launch and to significant media acclaim, the findings of the two year project were duly 'handed over to the community'.

The creativity of practice, more often than not, takes a pragmatic and managerial form. It tends to be about 'getting through the day's business' and meeting managerial objectives, rather than pursuing any moral or political mission. For example, at the Arlington Racial Harassment Monitoring Project, one of the officers from the local authority was prevented by her own organization from revealing any information about the number of incidents of racial harassment between council officers within her department. The way in which she managed the tensions between the demands of confidentiality from her own organization and the wishes of the multi-agency forum, allowed her to maintain her active involvement in the forum, whilst appearing to follow her organization's guidelines. She achieved this by providing 'general information' rather than 'specific detail' about the number of racial incidents reported and by asking for this information not to be officially recorded in the minutes. This example illustrates the way such tensions are managed through a negotiated process of pragmatic compromise. Compromise often takes place informally and, in this instance, unobserved by the host organization. This presents problems for accountability (an issue I consider in Chapter 7) as well as for formal safeguards of due process concerning confidentiality.

A further consequence of the notion of creativity, as I use it, is that it implies a certain degree of reflexivity on the part of the actors involved. It implies that management and front-line workers are (to an extent) aware of, and monitor, the latent sites of inter-agency tension and conflict. This awareness of potential conflict was well illustrated on the Westbridge Drugs Project. Here, a council officer devised a complex series of strategies to recruit the local health authority to support his own objective of the limited availability on prescription of certain street drugs for local addicts. Far from assuming that their support would be immediately forthcoming he explicitly worked from the premise of conflicting priorities. He devised a high risk strategy in which he spent some time building up what he referred to as an 'arsenal' to use against them in order to ensure their supportive involvement. This 'arsenal' largely comprised activities which took place unbeknown to, and outside, the formal multi-agency committee and included a local press campaign criticizing aspects of the health authority's policies. While this strategy yielded a degree of success the council officer was well aware of the fact that it could have resulted in more entrenched conflict. While the research revealed only a limited number of examples in which conflict was managed in such a deliberate and utilitarian manner, nevertheless agency workers frequently adopted similar but more everyday routines.

Multiple Aims

One general strategy for managing the conflicting interests of the parties and the differential power relations that exist between them, is the 'smörgasbord tactic'. This involves initiatives in claiming a multiplicity of aims and objectives in the hope that given organizations or interests can identify themselves with at least one of the stated aims: that there is something on the menu for everyone. This 'multiple aims' approach is prevalent among most crime prevention projects as well as mediation schemes. The research case studies were no exception. A cursory glance through publications which list the aims of such schemes should immediately alert the cautious reader to the fact that the aims are rarely prioritized and are often contradictory and ambiguous. At a practical level this approach may have much to commend it, as a way of 'getting things done', or even getting people around a table to start the process of communication and to begin the exploration of any common interests. However, rather than resolving conflict, this strategy seeks to mask it in a conceptual fog. As a consequence, 'different interest groups pass each other like ships in the night' (Sampson *et al.* 1988: 488); that is, at least, until the fog lifts, or the ships inadvertently collide.

However, whilst multiple aims enable mediation schemes and crime prevention initiatives to draw upon a wide and diverse audience for support, they also constitute their Achilles heel. In seeking to meet the divergent aims that they proclaim, these schemes are pulled in different and often competing directions as they attempt to satisfy the divergent demands of their different constituencies. First, multiple aims increase confusion and ambiguity, which for some may be their explicit purpose. However, muddying the waters in the long-term is likely to damage trust, rather than enhance it. It does not constitute the foundations for constructive conflict management. As in the earlier cited Leighdale mediation scheme and the Tenmouth project, it may merely postpone the day of reckoning and exacerbate its consequences. Secondly, multiple aims pose particular problems for evaluation and monitoring (Merry 1992; Crawford and Jones 1996), which as a consequence may give rise to new sources of conflict, particularly in an age of management by objectives and outcomes. One of the most telling findings of the recent research on mediation and reparation schemes (also belatedly becoming apparent in relation to crime prevention) is the lack of correspondence between mediation *rhetoric* and *practice* (Davis *et al.* 1988; Marshall and Merry 1990; Davis 1992: 209). An empirical mismatch between what is said and what is done may serve only to undermine longer term normative arguments. This may be exposed by practical experience as well as methodologically rigorous research. Often, such research as there has been, has revealed the frailty of the thin strands which hold together the awkward alliance of supporters of mediation. The danger is that in attempting, or rather claiming, to do too much, mediation and reparation initiatives, like their crime prevention siblings, will all too often end up falling between numerous stools, simultaneously disappointing advocates on many fronts.

Conflict Avoidance and the 'Goal of Unity'

A more specific and persistent strategy, evident in partnership work, is that of conflict avoidance. Rooted in the very notion and practice of a 'partnership' approach lies a distinct philosophy. This is an 'ideology of unity' (see Crawford 1994a: 504) which claims the capacity to reduce conflict through the co-operation of diverse professional and interest groups in an homogeneous body with 'corporate' aims. It is one to which inter-agency personnel and participants in multi-agency crime prevention work often subscribe, or to which they are obliged to subscribe by the exigencies of 'incorporation'. This ideology of partnership practice is grounded in pragmatic and managerialist assumptions. It tends to silence very real inter-organizational conflicts. This it does, first, by excluding 'non-consensual' or antagonistic voices—who are either never included in the process, or who subsequently withdraw from it—and, secondly, through the working assumption that an homogeneity of interests actually exists: that 'we *are all* partners against crime'. And yet this assumption is made without ever really scratching the surface of what it is *we* take crime, criminality, and justice to mean, what interests *we* may serve and where conflicts, as well as commonalities, may exist.

In this light, conflict and competition are perceived to be the enemies of effective partnerships, despite the fact that they structure the material and ideological relations which exist between organizations involved in partnership work. In their place appeals to 'consensus' and the 'goal of unity' have become the established credo. Consequently, around the tables of multi-agency forums the supposedly adversarial nature of relations between criminal justice agencies is being reconstructed, without the form and substance of what is emerging in its place ever really being considered. In the sphere of crime prevention and control this quest for 'unity' poses serious questions, not only about the effective and constructive negotiation of conflict, but also the finely balanced tensions between the independence and interdependence of criminal justice agencies. It raises questions about the 'discipline of incorporation' (Crawford 1994a) and loss of autonomy, both recurring themes of ensuing chapters. In the stampede for 'unity' vital safeguards of due process, accountability, transparency, and individual rights may become trampled underfoot. Further, as we shall see in Chapter 5, the 'goal of unity' has considerable implications for the social processes of exclusion and inclusion through which 'community' is constructed.

One pre-eminent expression of the 'goal of unity' is the practice of conflict avoidance. Given the deep structural oppositions that exist, what is often most striking is the absence of overt conflict at observed inter-agency forum meetings. More often than not, conflict is defined away or circumvented. This is illustrated by one example, of many, drawn from the fieldwork. At a meeting of the

Arlington Racial Harassment Monitoring Project, the various agency representatives were unable to devise an agreed set of categories for the variety of ethnic minority groups resident in the borough. The agencies present at the meeting had different practices for recording the ethnicity of the victim and offender and used different terms to describe social groups. The police, for instance, had six categories of ethnicity as against the local authority's nine. It was suggested by a representative of a particular ethnic minority group that victims should be allowed to self-identify the ethnic group to which they felt they belong. This was dismissed as 'impossible' by the police as for them to do so would contravene the police's own policy, may 'offend the victims', and could 'create a perception of police racism'. These organizational differences were size-stepped by the 'agreement' that it should be left to individual agencies to code the ethnic origin of victims and offenders in accordance with their own criteria. During the period of the fieldwork, the issue was never again raised given its likelihood to give rise to 'unnecessary conflict'. The consequence of this 'non-decision' was that the dominant power of police recording practices remained unchallenged and unchanged. As Lukes notes, the power of *non*-decision making is an important element in the exercise of power itself (Lukes 1974). Thus 'doing nothing', while appearing to be non-conflictual, is also an important aspect of ongoing power relations between agencies.

In other instances conflict was avoided by the creative construction of the agenda or even the omission of certain items from agendas. On some occasions, contentious issues were not recorded in the official minutes. More often than not, however, conflict merely was deemed not to be 'appropriate'. As a member of the Northley Multi-Agency project commented: 'We did not all give up our valuable time to come here and argue'.

(In)Formal Relations

A further strategy of partnership practice, evident in relation to particularly problematic issues, is that they are managed 'off stage' in private settings. This strategy seeks to avoid overt conflict by controlling the impact of resultant decisions upon the 'corporate' body. Decisions are taken 'elsewhere' in more informal and exclusive settings, and subsequently presented as uncontentious, requiring no further consideration. This 'informal' management of conflict was prevalent in the research case studies.[1] Frequently, 'shadow' meetings took place which were rarely mentioned or reported at official committee meetings. This kind of unaccountable informal decision making process usually involved the most powerful parties in the partnerships. On occasions they occurred at crucial and strategic moments in the life of a project. For example, in the Tenmouth Anti-Burglary Initiative, in connection with the redirection of the project referred to earlier, senior representatives from the police and probation service circumvented the agreed formal procedure of regular meetings. Their informal meeting in the police bar, in which they put their 'cards on the table' was a discussion to which the other agencies, most notably Victim Support and the local authority, were not privy. Their own particular concerns about the project were given no voice as the change of policy was presented as a *fait accompli*. The contents of their 'frank discussion' were never subsequently placed on the forum's agenda nor referred to in an open forum meeting. Importantly, this meant that the community representatives were denied any say in this major shift in the direction of the project. Thus the two officers involved were able to control the impact of their joint decision and limit any resultant conflict, particularly from the community representatives who were subsequently asked to resource much of the future crime prevention work.

On other projects, policy decisions were taken in informal settings or through 'unofficial' conversations, often over the telephone. Many of these significant moments of conflict management and policy formation were never made public or reported to wider partnership members. In all these examples, informal inter-agency relationships tended to increase power differentials between agencies. Access to, or inclusion within, the relevant 'shadow' informal arenas, are themselves powerful resources in inter-organizational relations. As a result, those excluded from such informal discussions, either by default or by design, are marginalized and disempowered. For those included in the discussions, social power is left largely unregulated and unlimited. Consequently, not only do informal arrangements tend to fail to address or mitigate differential power relations, they are more likely to exacerbate them.

---

[1] This has also been the experience of inter-organizational relations outside the specifically criminal justice field. See, for example, Mabbott's research findings in relation to the practice of City Challenge (1993: 29–30).

This is particularly problematic when combined with the earlier noted strategy of multiple aims. Where the aims of the project are open-textured and vague, as in many community crime prevention partnerships, this may allow significant changes in direction or objectives, without all members realizing what has happened, as in the Tenmouth situation cited earlier. A further example of this took place at the Illsworth Crime Reduction Project. Due to cut-backs in local authority funding, the council officers slowly began to close down the project, removing the assigned worker to another crime prevention project which had maintained its funding. However, the council officers did not wish to close down the project officially because this, they felt, would not be politically expedient. One council officer commented:

Politically, we can't wind it up, because [the Chair, a senior local council-lor] won't let us. He doesn't want to be seen to be not providing something in his area. It's a waste of time if there is no money—and there is no money ... It is just not important any more. We'll let it die ... slowly stop arranging meetings and the like.

(Council Officer, informal conversation)

The process of inclusion here, as elsewhere, would appear to have a number of tiers and is tied up with knowing the 'rules of the game', all intrinsically bound up with relations of power.

Informal relations, especially in the field of criminal justice, may circumvent formal procedural safeguards. This raises particular issues regarding the exchange of sensitive information which, as respondents from the survey noted earlier, often is the prized and sought after possession of criminal justice agencies. In addition, it poses problematic questions concerning possible implications for confidentiality and individual liberties. For example, on a number of occasions at the Illsworth Project, officers from the local authority and the police were witnessed discussing 'problem families', by identifying youths and homeless people on estates. When this was raised at meetings, officers described the people in neutral terms and did not identify them by name. However, both council and police officers were observed taking time before and after official meetings to share information more casually. In one instance, a housing officer discussed with the local Home Beat Officer a 'need assessment' interview with a homeless couple who were squatting on a nearby estate. In breach of the housing officer's own guidelines on confidentiality, hearsay information was exchanged which may have mitigated against the couple receiving any housing priority.

Conceptualizing (In)Formality

Consequently Pearson *et al.* arrive at what they acknowledge to be a contradictory conclusion regarding 'the question of hierarchy: formality and informality' in inter-agency relations (1992: 63). They declare that:

On the one hand, informal systems of inter-agency working and information exchange are risky encounters which can endanger important confidentialities and might even sometimes constitute a threat to civil liberties. On the other hand, more informal and fluid systems of inter-agency relations seem to offer a more workable basis for communication and negotiation.

(Pearson *et al.* 1992: 64–5)

Whilst identifying an important dilemma within inter-organizational relations, they appear to conflate and confuse a number of issues. First, they fail succinctly to explicate the conceptual distinction between 'informality' and 'formality', rather they are left as taken for granted categories. And yet, secondly, they implicitly conflate formality with organizational hierarchy. Thirdly, in suggesting that informal relations offer a 'more workable basis for communication and negotiation', they appear to celebrate 'informality' and confuse it with an ends-orientation, which I would argue is not justifiable. What is needed is greater conceptual clarity. Here, Atkinson (1982) provides a number of useful insights. Using conversation analysis, he suggests that there may be 'methodic and identifiable procedures' in both professional and lay interactions available to actors for the categorization of certain action as 'formal'. Most particularly, he notes that formality is associated with the extent to which relations depart from 'a taken for granted model of everyday conversational interaction' (Atkinson 1982: 114). These conversational interactions will be different in divergent organizational and social contexts. In multi-party settings, Atkinson suggests, many 'formal' interactional practices may be related to resolving the general problem of 'shared attentiveness' or specific dimensions of it (1982: 97). Similarly, it could be argued that the formalization of the mediation process (itself too often incorrectly categorized as 'informal'), through rules of engagement in face to face encounters between the parties (see

Quill and Wynne 1993), has much to do with 'turn taking', allowing the parties to have their say and mitigating power differences. All of these elements of 'formality' may play important roles in the effective achievement of certain tasks, most notably the socially constructive negotiation of conflict.

Armed with these conceptual insights, a number of related issues become clearer. First, we can see that 'formality' and 'informality' are not 'all or nothing' concepts and are more fluid than Pearson and colleagues suggest. Secondly, 'formality' is not directly linked to organizational hierarchy. Whilst it is clear that many multi-agency forums involve senior officers in a policy making capacity and lower ranking officers at the level of implementation (all of which may require the renegotiation and/or distortion of policy), this is as true of policy implementation within organizations as it is between them. Any overlap between organizational hierarchy and formality is more the product of policy implementation processes, than the characteristics of (in)formality. Thirdly, 'formality' may serve an important role within multi-party interactions, particularly where professionals of different agencies (with different organizational languages) are concerned, and even more so where the public are involved (Atkinson 1982:114). A significant level of 'formality' (defined as departures from conversational interactions) may be a prerequisite for communications and negotiations across organizational boundaries, as well as between criminal justice agencies and the public. A degree of 'formality', therefore, may be fundamental in mitigating power relations—particularly those which coalesce around notions of expertise and control of knowledge—within partnerships.

There is a persistent danger, among critical commentators, of celebrating the 'informal', whilst simultaneously identifying 'formality' with pejorative terms. This trap Pearson and colleagues implicitly fall into, particularly in their desire to commend bonds of 'mutually supportive inter-agency relations among women workers' (Sampson *et al*. 1991: 132). This is a trend which critical writers need, and are beginning, to address (Abel 1982; Matthews 1988; Merry and Milner 1993). While it is clear that a greater degree of informality in settings may be more conducive to 'getting things done' at the level of practice, they may be less suitable in the context of policy formation. Here, elements of formality may constitute fundamental aspects of constructive and democratic negotiation. Genuinely 'informal' interactions, therefore, may need to be bounded by more formal procedures and practices, in the name of transparency in the management of conflict. 'Informality' too often leaves differential power relations unchecked, hides decision making processes from any review, and removes them from any democratic input or control. I am not seeking to replace a celebration of the 'informal' with that of the 'formal'. Rather, we need to look at, and be critical of, the quality of negotiation and the conditions under which constructive and meaningful negotiation can prosper. Negotiation needs to be, in part, normatively driven, bounded by notions of 'ethical practice', openness, accountability, and reviewability. It should not be merely ends-oriented, as is the case of much inter-agency practice, particularly under the pressing weight of the 'goal of unity'.

However, a dilemma remains which may lie at the heart of the contradiction that Pearson and colleagues note. We need to consider to what extent 'formality' interrupts or interferes with trust. To put it the other way round: is 'informality', through sustained conversational interactions, an important element in building and sustaining trust? If so, then we may need to consider 'formality' and 'informality', not as alternatives but as complementary processes. What is clear, however, is that given the secrecy, lack of visibility, accountability, and reviewability of much informal decision making, it is questionable whether it can ever conform to such standards. 'Getting things done' is synonymous neither with adhering to long standing commitments nor with 'doing the right thing' by conforming to equitable, open, and inclusive processes.

Conclusions

The survey findings reported in this chapter confirm the very real differences that exist between police and probation officers' understandings of the causes of crime and 'appropriate' preventative interventions. Similar conceptual divergences exist between other organizations involved in partnerships in the field of criminal justice. These differences constitute important sites of ideological and organizational conflict around which inter-agency relations are structured. They reflect differing organizational roles, priorities, and perspectives. However, in the views expressed by survey respondents, they identify an awareness of conflict and inter-organizational tension, and its grounding in both imaginary and real aspects of the complex organizational matrix of criminal justice. Respondents identified important concerns regarding the potential implications of partnerships for their own organization and practice, most notably the blurring of organizational boundaries and functions, and the loss of organizational autonomy.

These issues were considered in the light of the practice of partnerships. The relevance of trust relations, raised as an issue by a number of survey respondents, has been seen to be a significant element in the practice of working across organizational boundaries, particularly between agencies where high levels of distrust and lack of knowledge exist. We have seen the ways in which intra-organizational tensions can themselves significantly find effect as, and influence, inter-organizational conflicts. Managerial priorities, cultural perceptions, and gender relations may all impact upon the nature and ability of individuals and groups to work within and beyond organizational boundaries. Inter-agency conflicts, therefore, are both constituted by, and constitutive of, intra-organizational tensions. This suggests, first, a need to clarify from the outset the objectives, working practices, and lines of accountability of any inter-agency work, as well as the definitions of key concepts relevant to the initiatives, including locality, types of crime, and forms of intervention selected. Secondly, it suggests a need for the appropriate selection of front-line officers from the different agencies who are sufficiently reflexive to transcend their organizational roles and cultural identities, and to monitor the impact of their own work upon personnel of other agencies.

Perversely, however, the current climate of 'new public management' fostered by the present government, has done much to exacerbate inter-organizational conflict and undermine open and constructive inter-agency relations. This managerialism encourages the adoption of a rigid *intra*-organizational focus, with its emphasis on internal performance, value for money, hierarchical control, and the clear distribution of authority and responsibility (Rhodes 1995: 14). Managerialism thus produces the seeds and extends the impact, of new conflicts. Its fixation upon a results-orientation undermines and marginalizes the need to address the nature and quality of conflict negotiation and the maintenance of trust relations over time. 'New public management' (NPM), as Rhodes notes, 'is inappropriate for managing inter-organisational networks but, more important such networks undermine NPM with its intra-organisational focus

on objectives and results' (1995: 15). Whilst the partnership approach envisages corporality and holism, this can be undermined by
the managerialism which underscores the NPM reforms, with
its emphasis upon the management and measurement of intra-
organizational performance. Further, there is an ambiguous current
which flows out of the government's attempts to inject a more
competitive, commercial ethos into public services, and at the same
time to encourage co-operation between potentially rival agencies
and sectors. This is dramatically accented in the process of competitive tendering for central government funds and exacerbated by
the non co-terminus geographical boundaries of criminal justice and
other relevant agencies. As a consequence, agencies involved in
partnerships may find themselves involved in intra-organizational
competition, or may abandon partnerships because of the conflicts
of interests that competitive tendering may bring. These and other
tensions are played out in the multi-agency forums of criminal justice
around the country.

Given the level of 'latent conflict' between organizations which
sit down together at the tables of partnerships, the central issues are,
first, the need to recognize the existence, and identify the sites, of
conflict, and secondly, to consider the manner in which conflict is
then managed and regulated and in which these 'latent oppositions'
relate to, and are embedded, in routinized social action. With reference to the fieldwork, I have illustrated a number of strategies
through which conflict is managed. The three most prominent
strategies are the use of 'multiple (ambiguous) aims'; conflict avoidance; and the 'informal' management of disputes. I have focused
upon their problematic nature and implications. I will return to this
theme and its implications for accountability in Chapter 7.

For the moment, however, we can draw out some initial lessons
from the research data and preceding discussion. First, there is a
need for less ambiguity of purpose and greater conceptual clarity.
Room needs to be made in inter-agency relations for constructive
debate concerning the competing contributions, priorities, and aims
of the agencies involved. Secondly, I have tried to show that rather
than addressing the fundamental causes of conflict, inter-agency
'partnership' practice often revolves around obfuscation and conflict avoidance. What is most striking given the structural tensions
which exist between agencies, is the absence of overt conflict. Under
the burden of incorporation and the 'ideology of unity', inter-agency

workers develop what are sometimes highly 'creative' strategies for defining away and circumventing conflict. Often these are driven by managerialist ends. This does not mean that conflict is negotiated or resolved, rather, it is left unaddressed. This leaves structural conflicts and power relations unmitigated. Hence, within inter-agency relations there is too often a working assumption that conflict hinders effective multi-agency relations, that is a 'bad thing'. The search for consensus which does not address structural (or even interpersonal) conflicts, as is the general practice, is less likely to be effective in the long run. Similarly, there is an assumption that 'formality' gets in the way of efficient inter-agency relations. And yet, as I hope to have shown, there are significant elements of 'formality' which may play important roles in the effective achievement of certain tasks and may be a prerequisite for communications and negotiation across organizational boundaries, as well as between criminal justice agencies and the public.

Where structural oppositions, divergent values, and professional missions exist, conflict may in fact be a desirable product of inter-agency work. Conflict may be the healthy expression of different interests. It is, therefore, important that these differences should not be ignored or defined away in the search for inter-agency consensus. Rather, they need to be recognized and addressed. Mutual recognition of difference represents a more preferable premise for inter-agency relations than either an assumed consensus or an ends-oriented 'goal of unity'. The latter often hides conflict below the surface and seeks to manage real structural opposition in ways which are often unaccountable, informal, and invisible to external scrutiny: consequently, differential power relations are left unregulated and unchallenged. In contrast it is important that conflict is negotiated in an open, accountable and socially constructive manner which seeks to include the parties and which recognizes and appropriately compensates for power differentials.

5
The Contestable Nature of 'Community'

Never was the word 'community' used more indiscriminately and emptily than in the decades when communities in the sociological sense became hard to find in real life.

(Hobsbawm 1994: 428)

'Community', as we saw in Chapter 2, has become the policy buzz-word of the 1990s, the antidote to the *fin de siècle* crisis of modernity. In criminal justice rhetoric and practice, 'community' is both a signifier and referent around which complex contradictory effects, meanings, and definitional struggles coalesce (Stenson 1993: 171). In this chapter, I will consider the nature of 'community' to which appeals are made in criminal justice discourse and policies, and the institutionalization of 'community' in actual practices. Or to re-phrase this as a series of questions: why community? what is meant by community? and whose community? This will involve a consideration of the possible and actual contribution of 'community' to the practices of social order and crime prevention. In other words, what is it that 'community' has to offer crime control?

I will address these inter-related questions at a number of different levels. I will examine some of the understandings and conceptualizations of 'community' within dominant political and intellectual discourse along with the assumptions which underlie them. The aim will be to expose some of the hidden theoretical and practical presuppositions and the ideological strategies which they serve. Tensions between the normative and empirical aspects of appeals to 'community' will be considered: both what 'community' ought to be, and what it is. In doing so, I will explore the contribution of communities to crime control and prevention, drawing upon insights from both the crime prevention and the mediation research case studies. This will require a consideration of the nature of

community representation and participation, and the correspondence between community representatives and the communities that
they represent. In the discussion of the role and place of community
in mediation, this will be supported and enhanced by a consideration
of the findings of a survey of mediation schemes' Annual Reports,
from around Britain. This will focus on the various uses and conceptualization of 'community' in the reports most notably the role
of the mediator as a symbolic representative of the 'moral community'. This will be extended by an evaluation of the specific place
and meaning of 'community' within the growing communitarian
movement and its influence on criminal justice policies.

The Nature of Community in Policy Discourse

A close examination of Conservative government and opposition
parties' publications and policy statements in the field of crime
control and prevention, identifies a number of recurring assumptions upon which appeals to community are premised. These
assumptions, it will be argued, derive from certain ideological
understandings of the nature of crime, community, and their interconnections. Consequently, King is correct to note that in the past
seventeen years, Britain has witnessed a central government for
whom 'law and order'—given the anxieties, fears, and outrage that
it can evoke—has constituted a powerful vehicle for the dissemination of its own political ideology (King 1989). However, neither the
coherence nor the effectivity of that vision, as shown in Chapter 3,
should be assumed or taken for granted. Rather, I will hope to show
that at the levels of policy and local practice, whilst a dominant set
of understandings and images prevail, they are escorted by a host of
complex contradictions, inconsistencies, and sites of resistance.

The following quotations from leading figures in the two major
British political parties over recent years set the tone of dominant
political appeals to 'community' and their connection with crime
and its prevention (see also Home Office 1994; Labour Part 1995a;
1995b; Mandleson and Liddle 1996; Blair 1996; Liberal Party
1996).

We need to look to individuals . . . to help us re-build those values and a
sense of individual responsibility which prevents crime from taking a hold.

It is only when these values fail that we come to rely upon the police and the courts. Rebuilding values will in many cases, also involve rebuilding communities. Crime flourishes in neighbourhoods with shallow roots, where there is little sense of pride or loyalty and where the disapproval of neighbours does not matter . . . In these places litter, for example, is not just a sign of local authority inefficiency but a potent symbol of the 'couldn't care less, let someone else clear it up' attitude to life. In many of these places the sense of community has been lost . . . The restoration of the values and standards of behaviour that should form the foundation for any 'community' is a moral imperative which we must pursue in the coming years . . . At the very centre of our ideas on how to control crime should be the energy and initiative of the active citizen. His or her contribution must be mobilised and should be the core of the radical rethinking we need on prevention and control of crime.

(Patten 1988: v–vi)

Aggressive begging, along with graffiti and, in some cities, 'squeegee merchants' all heighten people's fear of crime on the streets . . . The result is a vicious circle in which people use the streets less, society becomes atomised, and community life breaks down.

(Straw 1995a)

We need to do what we can to recreate the sense of obligation through the generations. We also need to be aware of our duties as good neighbours . . . The strongest communities exist where voluntary collective action is most apparent. In rolling back the State we have rolled forward the scope for voluntary local collective action. We have given individuals far more scope for getting involved.

(Howard 1994)

Britain must move back towards mutual responsibility if it is to re-establish vibrant community life . . . We need to break out of the language of dutiless rights and begin to insist upon mutual responsibility. Rights and duties go hand in hand . . . the community should expect responsible behaviour from all.

(Straw 1995b)

The similarities and continuities in the above message both express the established mainstream political consensus on the appropriateness of a 'community' approach to crime, and the fact that 'community' signifies and references divergent attractions, meanings, and strategies. What the 'community' constitutes, its boundaries or the values and interests it prioritizes are rarely explicated. Nevertheless, a number of interconnected political and ideological assumptions can be identified.

A Lack of Community Leads to a 'Spiral of Decline'

Underlying policy initiatives around crime in the community, as in the above extracts, is the prevailing idea that crime results from a failure or breakdown of community life. This degeneration is traditionally associated with a failure of processes of communal socialization and informal social control. Distant echoes from Chicago School sociologists can be heard in the notion that crime is associated with 'disorganised communities' (Skogan 1988; 1990). Community reorganization, from this viewpoint, acts to counter the degeneration associated with crime, on the presupposition that it is an inherent capacity of communities to mobilize their own resources of social control. Through informal community controls, it is anticipated that the primary of the normative, law-abiding consensus of the community will be asserted. These ideas connect with, and reflect the influence of, Wilson and Kelling's (1982) 'broken windows' thesis. According to this, communities are seen as occupying a pivotal role in halting moral decline, the regeneration of neighbourhood life, and the prevention of crime, by exerting their moral authority. Communities are identified, therefore, as a powerful site of social order and control.

Within the 'broken window' thesis, and British policy rhetoric which draws upon it, community degeneration is viewed as both the social cause and the effect of crime and the fear of crime. Crime is the product of disorganized communities and, at the same time, it is disorganized communities which create the conditions for crime to flourish. The regeneration of community is the proposed solution to halt and reverse the cycle. This process embodies a dual understanding of community. It assumes a definition of community as both a shared locality—in purely territorial terms—and a shared concern or 'sense of community' (both points to which I return). It starts from the premise that mere proximity generates—or at least should generate—shared concern. It goes on to propose that the combination of individual actions and behaviour, together with informal social processes of control to which those acts give rise, will help reconstitute and reassemble a 'sense of community'. Consequently, 'community' constitutes a means to an end, and an end in itself. It is both the vehicle to a better life and the better life. Means and ends have become badly confused. With such circularity, it is hard to recognize and separate off implementation problems associated with community programmes, as they constitute as much a failure of theory as of practice (Hope 1995a: 23). It is not apparent, therefore, whether community regeneration or the reduction of crime is the primary aim, as they are seen to march hand in hand. In practice, however, they are not the same thing and, by contrast, they are often in tension, or at least ambiguously inter-related. This is especially problematic for practitioners—given the open-textured nature of both community and crime prevention—in that it exaggerates the multiple aims which often obscure strategies. The tension between means and ends, as a result, creates additional problems for monitoring and evaluation, as 'success' becomes so multi-layered as to be virtually meaningless (Crawford and Jones 1996).

Further, approaches that identify 'community' as a force of organization, tend to focus upon the *internal* attributes of 'community', its collective sense, social institutions, structure, demographic composition, and so on. Efforts at community organizing rarely, if at all, acknowledge, or seek to address, *external* forces and dynamics which often undermine—especially in high crime areas—those efforts. However, the power of private capital and property interests, resident mobility—particularly changing patterns of tenant allocation in public sector housing (Bottoms and Wiles 1986)—unemployment, social exclusion, and poverty, will all impact upon internal community relations, potentially increasing social and cultural disorganization (Hope 1995a: 34).

More Community Equals Less Crime

The 'broken window' thesis assumes a direct causal relationship between a lack of informal social control—in other words a lack of 'community'—and the existence of high levels of crime. It is empirically questionable, however, whether there is any direct link between incivilities, crime, fear of crime, and informal social control. 'Broken windows' do not necessarily have the same effects in different neighbourhoods. The way communities perceive crime and other social problems may be refracted through the political and social resources available to that community (Lewis and Salem 1986). Contrary to Wilson and Kelling's model, crime does not have a uniform impact upon community life. Foster's (1995; Hope and Foster 1992) ethnographic research on two crime-prone, public sector housing estates in England, exposes this fallacy of the 'broken windows' thesis. Foster found that informal control mechanisms were not absent in all high crime areas, challenging the assumption that they are lacking in poor communities torn by crime. Moreover, on one of the estates, the impact of crime was to a large degree contained, principally by local, mutual support networks. Crime, she concludes, is not always damaging *per se* so long as other mediating factors cushion its impact (Foster 1995: 580).

In addition, the logic behind this association between the lack of 'organized' community and crime is that, conversely, more community equals less crime. Community, in this context, is cleansed of any negative or crimogenic connotations and endowed with a simplistic and naïve purity and virtue. This benevolent understanding of community is highly misleading. In some instances 'community', i.e. its communal normative values, itself may be the source of crimogenic tendencies. Recent British research into criminal subcultures has reiterated the long established criminological truism that the collective values of a community may serve to stimulate and sustain criminality (Hobbs 1988; 1995; Foster 1990; Robins 1992). This paradox has been particularly clearly noted in research on football hooliganism (Williams and Taylor 1994). For, in that context, it is the celebration of a particular (male) community and of cultural traditions, which is perceived as 'problematic'. Williams *et al.*, for example, note that:

much of the behaviour involved in football hooliganism seems to reflect less the simple *lack* of local community attachments than it does the strength of *particular kinds* of local identifications and experiences.

(1988: 170, emphasis in original)

Rebuilding communities as a set of shared beliefs is not, therefore, synonymous with the creation of social order. This has been acknowledged by some criminologists recently, in their recognition of 'community crime careers' as a valuable category of analysis (Reiss 1986; Bottoms and Wiles 1986). This concept shifts attention away from a focus on *more*, or *less*, 'community' as the key to criminality, towards an understanding of a neighbourhood's crime patterns as a complex whole. A 'community crime career', therefore, is the summation of the consequences, whether intended or not, of the way a multitude of actors interact in an historical process (Bottoms and Wiles 1992: 25). This identifies the importance of an understanding of social relations within an area and, more import-antly, also how these relations are shaped by the wider socio-economic environment, most notably the urban market.

Community as a Set of Attitudes

As suggested earlier, the dominant discourse assumes 'community' to be a set of shared attitudes. Consequently, reference frequently is made to the importance of a 'sense of community'. 'Community', thus understood, is more than geographic location, it exists where members of a social grouping *feel* bound together by shared interests or identity. Therefore, communities take much of their character from the way in which their members think about and 'imagine' themselves (Anderson 1983). Community boundaries form around what its members share in common, or are 'imagined' to share, and how this differentiates them from others who are not members. Crime control policy (as identified in the extracts cited earlier) seeks to create and foster 'spatial communities', whereby a common sense of belonging to a geographical neighbourhood constitutes a defining criteria in the construction of communal identity and boundary formation. Consequently, a 'sense of pride or loyalty', 'mutual responsibility', and individuals showing that they 'care' about the place in which they live, are all prerequisites for a 'sense of com-munity' and the local moral regeneration which it sustains. Here we see the 'activation of individual commitments, energies, and choices, through personal morality within a community setting' (Rose 1996). The 'community' constitutes an acceptable collective imagery for energizing and catalysing individuals.

I will return to the issue of 'spatial communities' later. For the moment, however, I want to focus upon this generalized assumption that communities can, or should, be 'imagined', and therefore, that their construction and sustenance merely involve an attitude shift. Communities are, by and large, associations and groups of people which gather around certain interests, characteristics or identities, which may be based on lifestyle, culture, religion, ethnicity, occupa-tion, place of residence, and so on (Bell and Newby 1971). These social identities are accorded significance, both internally and externally. The process of ascribing significance involves the con-struction of 'boundaries' of inclusion and exclusion, but which need not be spatially constrained. An important element in this process is the establishment of a sense of 'belonging'. The way in which communities think about and imagine themselves and others is an evident part of community life (Crowe and Allan 1994). However, social identity, as a state of mind, whilst an important empirical aspect of 'community', fails sufficiently to explain the nature of a community's capacity for informal social control or its ability to address and organize around issues of crime and its prevention.

Currie (1988) has forcefully revealed the inadequacies of such a conception of 'community' in the field of crime prevention. He identifies two distinct 'visions' of community crime prevention in order to illustrate the very different understandings of 'community' upon which they are premised. The differences between the two visions impact upon, and contain, the capacity of communities to address issues of crime. In the Phase 1 vision, 'community' is under-stood, as in dominant policy discourse, in symbolic terms—a 'social-psychological view'—as a set of collective attitudes. Here, Currie suggests that

Community, in brief, is in people's heads. Consequently, if you wish to improve community conditions you are in essence in the business of changing attitudes, or altering the symbols of community, in the hope that improved interpersonal relations will follow. In the ideal scenario you may thus start a benign cycle: improved attitudes lead to better behaviour, which in turn enhances people's conception of community, which in turn . . .

(1988: 280–1)

Phase 1 is most clearly typified by Wilson and Kelling's 'broken windows' model and by much situational crime prevention, particularly of the 'defensible space' type on large public sector housing estates. In my research, this notion—of community as attitudes which need to be implanted in a locality—was prevalent in all the case studies. For example, a council officer on the Illsworth Project articulated this approach:

the function of community representation is to try, and by involving those opinion-formers in the local community, somehow spread the awareness that something is happening, to get the feeling out there that something is happening, that something is being done, that people do care about the area and to get the area *up* rather than *down*, and in order to encourage that feeling in the wider community you have to start with the rep[resentative]s.

This 'trickle down' understanding of community representation suggests that an attitude shift is a, if not *the*, fundamental element in reversing the cycle of urban decline. Currie admits that this 'sense of identity' is a component of what a community is (1988: 281). However, he suggests that this represents only a partial account. Further, it is arguably one that, by itself, does not constitute the most significant element for the purpose of crime control. This type of understanding of community, with its emphasis on the symbolic, lacks what Currie calls 'structural awareness'. This he illustrates by contrasting it with a Phase 2 vision. Here, 'community' is seen in:

> much more structural, or institutional terms not just as a set of attitudes we can 'implant' or mobilise, but as an interlocking set of long-standing institutions which in turn are deeply affected by larger social and economic forces ... real communities thrive or fail to thrive, become healthy or pathological, mainly as a result of the strength or weakness of these basic institutions—work, family and kin, religious and communal associations, a vibrant local economy capable of generating stable livelihoods.
>
> (Currie 1988: 282–3)

An understanding of 'community', particularly in the field of crime prevention, which fails to move beyond Phase 1 thinking and which lacks a structural or institutional awareness will only ever be partial. Unfortunately, much of the dominant policy analysis is locked into Phase 1 thinking alone. However, a Phase 2 understanding of 'community' recognizes the potential to build upon the limitations of current conceptions of 'community', in order to embrace strategies which are more concerned with the empowerment of groups and the construction of vital social institutions. 'Community', even in the Phase 1 vision, does not constitute a discursive closure. Rather, it is open-textured, allowing important alternative perspectives to coalesce around it. Phase 1 and Phase 2 are not necessarily mutually exclusive, but collide and produce important sites of conflict amongst and between publics and professionals, where the politics of community can be, and sometimes are, contested. As a site of resistance to dominant prevention policy, Phase 2 thinking offers a space, albeit limited, for more constructive visions and strategies.

Community as Place

The shift in criminological concern from *criminals* to *crimes*, people to places, has been dramatic over the last two decades (as noted in Chapter 2). Space, rightly, has come to be recognized as a critical variable in understanding and mapping the incidence of crime, together with its prevention. Urban geographers have been instrumental in asserting the importance of 'place' in criminological theory, both in terms of the spatial distribution of offences and offenders as well as their explanations (Evans *et al*. 1992; Bottoms 1994). As a result, the contemporary criminological talk is of the 'patterning of offence locations' (Bottoms 1994: 602), the 'crime area distribution' (Wikström 1991: 191), 'hot spots' of crime (Sherman *et al*. 1989) and other spatial characteristics. However, theories of situational crime prevention in general, and 'defensible spaces' in particular, have come to revere the importance of the spatial. Often the result has been to focus exclusively upon spatial characteristics at the expense of social factors. In its excesses, crime and prevention have become overly 'spatialized'. Consequently, 'community' in crime prevention is defined, almost exclusively, in geographical terms and so spatial attributes are both the principal defining characteristics of scheme boundaries and the point of entry for most interventions.

At the level of practice this produces a number of tensions. These boundaries are often arbitrary—imposed by the constraints of funding or political niceties—and often mean little in human terms. They frequently create sources of local jealousy and conflict in relation to bordering areas. These largely revolve around whether vocal neighbouring residents wish to be included in, or excluded from, community crime prevention projects. For example, on the South Ornley Burglary Project a neighbourhood watch co-ordinator campaigned vigorously and successfully, for over a year, for the inclusion of his neighbouring area into the project. By contrast, other residents of his area were concerned about the association with crime that their locality might be given by the extension of the project. Consequently, there was little take up of the subject in his area.

Similarly, the Tenmouth project did not emerge around any 'natural' boundaries. The boundaries that were established arose as a consequence of local conflict and political expediency. Initially, the seconded probation officer had identified a small area of the city of Tenmouth as having a high rate of domestic burglary, based on an examination of police statistics. However, this created a local controversy when the chosen area became publicly known. Local residents expressed considerable concern at their area being the focus of a crime prevention initiative. Many of them thought that it would suggest that the locality was a 'high crime' neighbourhood and give

it an adverse reputation. It was feared that the locality might subsequently become stigmatized and that house prices might be
threatened. In response, the project leaders decided to broaden the
scope of the initiative to include two additional police subdivisions
of south and central Tenmouth, which included a further eight local
authority wards, in an attempt to address the residents' concerns by
watering down the focus of the project.

When placed in the context of competitive tendering for small
amounts of government money, the emphasis on the spatial leaves
local residents and workers in contradictory positions. In order to
attract the funds, they are forced into cataloguing and highlighting
the problems in the area. This often requires agency workers to
over-emphasize the negative aspects of a given community. To use
the language of the Illsworth council worker cited earlier, they need
to put an area 'down' in order to get the resources to try and pull it
'up' again. The politics of attracting funds may involve media
scrutiny and unwanted publicity. On the Churchway Project, for
example, the publicity generated by the process of attracting funds
was seen as involving an ambiguous logic, by the local residents. A
tenants' association representative on the project explained:

The media has been particularly useful at the beginning of the project
when the residents had wanted to draw attention to the plight of [the
area]. However, the media is a double-edged sword in that they also only
ever want to hear bad news and always paint [the neighbourhood] as a
terrible place.

As the target of agency initiatives and public attention, the area
developed what for many residents was an unwanted notoriety. The
outcome of this process, other community representatives explained, was a desire on the part of some people to leave the area,
particularly when insurance companies began refusing to renew
contents insurance policies, a further product of the 'spatialization'
of crime and risk assessment.

Other initiatives were plagued by similar problems and concerns
about the fear of labelling a neighbourhood as a 'high crime' area,
particularly through high profile interventions. Consequently, the
connection between crime and 'spatial' communities is both
inherently problematic and a 'double-edged sword'. It carries the
imminent capacity to stigmatize whole areas. The very recognition
that crime is a problem in a given area can be enough to set in

motion a series of processes which may be eventually self-fulfilling, as an area gains a reputation for crime.

What is clear is that government policies and the actions of agencies can have an important influence upon the make-up and nature of communities. The provision of resources is particularly fundamental in this regard. Resources from governmental and other agencies may contribute to the construction of community boundaries and the promotion of either competition or collaboration between different groups (Jeffers *et al.* 1996: 123–4). On the one hand, the existence of scarce public resources can provide the basis for the establishment of an identifiable community and can encourage collaboration. This was the case in Churchway, which actually transcended two local authority boundaries but which was seen to be an ideal site to attract City Challenge funds. The two local authorities, as well as different subdivisions of the police and social services departments, consequently 'came together' and 'buried their differences' for the sake of mutual advantage. However, on the other hand, competition for resources, particularly of the type currently popular in government circles, can increase conflicts within and between groups and organizations. As we have seen, it can create intergroup jealousies and rivalries as well as further intensify social polarization (an issue to which I return in Chapter 8).

Community as a Defence Against 'Outsiders'

The dominant thinking and practice of community crime prevention perceives strong communities to be a means of defending internal members against an exterior threat. 'Community' in this sense is defined negatively, through reference to 'others'. Community members recognize themselves as a collective, as 'us' in contradistinction to 'them'. Consequently, 'insiders' only exist because there are 'outsiders' and so 'community' may be based less on what people share in common than upon their difference in relation to 'others'. And yet, this external threat, whether imagined or real, constitutes a shared value which can serve to reinforce a 'sense of community'. In the context of crime, this notion of community as a defence against 'outsiders' arises from, and reinforces, a fundamental misunderstanding of the relationship between offenders and communities. The offender is viewed primarily as an 'outsider' against whom the 'community' needs to defend itself. This model of the connection between 'community' and crime is explicit in the idea of neighbourhood watch, in which members of the communities are expected to look out for 'strangers' (Currie 1988: 281). Similarly, notions of 'defensible space' assume 'insiders' to be law-abiding, whilst 'outsiders' are to be viewed with suspicion as the embodiment of potential danger against which private space needs to defend itself and over whom it needs surveillance. There is no sense of offenders being internal to, and members of, communities. This is highlighted by the story circulating on one of the research sites which, whether true or not, is nevertheless illustrative. The newest technology had been installed in a small block of council flats, which had undergone the full rigours of redesign in accordance with Coleman's version of 'defensible space'. A CCTV monitor installed in each flat granted the occupants surveillance over the entry point to the block. Regardless, a spate of burglaries occurred within the block. The culprits, who subsequently were discovered to be two brothers living in one of the flats, had used the technology to monitor the movements of other residents before breaking into their flats whilst they were out. This illustrates the perplexity which confronts notions of 'defensible space' in relation to 'insiders'.

This conception of 'community' as something that needs to be defended from an external threat, is more persuasive in suburban neighbourhoods where the outside threat is represented by a dangerous external 'other'. Here, 'community' connects with prejudices about 'respectability'. It presupposes a clear demarcation between criminals and law-abiding citizens, and yet is blind to the fact that many of those who may regard themselves as 'respectable' may be guilty of committing white-collar, road traffic, regulatory or other criminal offences which go undetected. However, as an ideology, this conception of 'community' is pervasive also in inner-city neighbourhoods. For example, on the Churchway Anti-Crime Project, it became a commonly accepted piece of 'public wisdom', amongst both agency workers and community representatives, that the drug dealers and prostitutes (the focus of the project) came from 'outside' the area. People spoke of 'outsiders invading' and 'taking over the area'. Thus, one member of the group commented angrily at a forum meeting that: 'We want our area back. Our area has been taken over by drug dealers and by prostitutes, none of whom live in this area.' Some agency workers privately admitted that, on the contrary, many of the prostitutes and drug dealers were local residents. However, few agency workers were willing to challenge this 'accepted wisdom' in public. Consequently, the prostitutes themselves were excluded from representation at the crime prevention forum, despite a number of approaches from the English Collective of Prostitutes, and the fact that many of them not only worked in the area but also lived there. On other research sites similar perceptions existed. For some, the pre-eminent task of community crime prevention was, as one tenants' association representative from the Illsworth project put it, 'to keep *them* out of *our* community'.

Community as Homogenous

Connected with this is the notion, prevalent within dominant policy understandings, of 'community' as an homogenous entity. Communities are perceived to be synonymous with like-minded people, or neighbourhoods with universal interests. This connects with, and serves to reinforce, the 'ideology of unity' discussed in the previous chapter. As with organizational communities involved in partnership networks, at the level of local lay communities this assumption tends to silence very real intra-community conflicts. It does so by excluding 'non-consensual' voices and working from the premise that an homogeneity of interests actually exists. This increases the tendency towards conflict avoidance. It presents particular problems for policing and crime prevention as they are inherently grounded in social conflict, which involves the policing *of*, and interventions *against*, certain individuals and groups of people. Where intracommunal conflicts are not addressed, more powerful interests are able to dominate over other less powerful groups, often resulting in the policing of the latter by, or in the name of, the former. This reinforces the construction of 'insider' and 'outsider' distinctions, which in turn strengthens assumptions of homogeneity.

In this context of defended communities, 'strangers' are more easily identified in culturally homogenous areas. In ethnic and culturally heterogeneous areas, such as the neighbourhood which was the focus of Merry's ethnographic work, it is harder for residents to know 'whether an outsider they observe is a dinner guest or a thief' (1981: 232). It is not surprising, therefore, that community crime prevention programmes—neighbourhood watch most notably—are easiest to establish within those localities which conform most closely to a rural idyll of homogeneity (Skogan 1990). Where diverging interests exist and cultural identities clash, establishing community organizations is much more complex. This is particularly so with regard to conceptually vexed issues such as crime and incivilities. Low-level nuisances, which dominate the public agendas of community-based crime prevention initiatives (as in the research sites), only serve to expose the problematic definition of crime. The lack of agreement over the priorities which should be given to crimes and incivilities in some communities only serves to reinforce the notion that incivilities, like crimes, have no 'onto-logical reality' (Hulsman 1986: 66). This is especially evident in culturally diverse neighbourhoods where, more often than not, little consensus about incivilities is apparent (Matthews 1992: 35). For example, what was seen for some residents in the Parkland Manors neighbourhood to be a serious and criminal nuisance, fly posting, was for others a 'respectable and honest way of earning a living' (in the words of one resident).

In addition, crime simultaneously impacts upon groups within neighbourhoods in divergent ways and gives rise to different responses within communities. In some neighbourhoods this can further exacerbate any attempt to construct an uniform or cohesive community response. The type of street crime that disrupts a neigh-bourhood's sense of order is perpetrated, largely, by a particular constituency within the community, young men. Moreover it dis-proportionately affects the lives of other identifiable groups within the neighbourhood, most notably women and the elderly (Crawford *et al.* 1990). Hence, the demographic make-up of a community can play an important role in the nature of the crime problem and of informal responses to it (Foster 1995: 580). Beatrix Campbell (1993) has vividly documented the way in which gender constitutes an essential dynamic through which the differential impact of, and response to, crime and poverty within peripheral communities are constructed. In her account of the disturbances in many British cities in 1991, she highlights the way in which community space can be, and often is, the site in which one segment of the community, the 'lads', seeks to re-establish its control by 'creating chaos' (Campbell 1993). In the face of this, she argues, other constituencies within the community are forced to deploy subtlety and ambiguity in their responses. In the gendering of reaction to adversity, she argues, it is frequently the mothers, through their experiences of moving within and between the boundaries of the public and private spheres, who comprise the 'spinal column' of community action. The problem for public agencies, themselves highly gendered, is how to connect with and support these informal networks.

Consequently, understanding how 'masculinity' constructs often different and dominant responses to pauperization and relative deprivation, as well as being reconstituted by them, comprises an important foundation for making sense of intra-community conflict and internal polarization within marginal neighbourhoods (Campbell 1993; Newburn and Stanko 1994). So too does a comprehension of the gendering of community responses, and how they connect and can be facilitated by statutory, voluntary, and private organizations. In considering the internal composition of existing communities, therefore, it becomes clear that they are not homogenous but heterogeneous. Neither are communities always the utopias of egalitarianism which some might wish but are hierarchical social formations, structured upon lines of differential power relations, most notably as feminists have argued, upon lines of gender, but also upon lines of ethnicity, age, class (if these social categories are not in themselves grounds for exclusion), and other personal attributes and identities.

Community as Public Space and the Silence of Private Danger

'Danger' in this conception of community is defined not only as emanating from 'outsiders', but also as existing 'outside'. It is assumed that danger inhabits public spaces, not 'private' domains. Contrary to empirical evidence which suggests that much violent offending takes place within familiar and familial relationships (Russell 1982; Hanmer and Maynard 1987; Yllö and Bograd 1988), offenders are conceptualized as strangers who inhabit public spaces. The home, by contrast, is viewed as a place of safety, a refuge from the violence and unpredictability of strangers in strange, and by definition, 'dangerous' places (Stanko 1990a). There is a missed connection between public crime and private danger (Stanko 1990b: 150). Consequently, private arenas and the (abuse of) 'private' power relations that reside therein, all too often are ignored within community safety agendas. As a result, much domestic violence and sexual harassment is left unaddressed by community crime prevention. Perversely, therefore, 'community' can be, and has been used as, a shorthand term for 'individuals in public' in which the victimization of women and children by 'known' offenders is marginalized.

In addition to the silences with regard to crimes which occur in 'private' settings, there are also absences from crime prevention agendas in relation to less visible forms of criminality (Walklate 1991: 219). Hence corporate crimes, like other types of crime which occur 'behind our backs', are marginalized by the shift to community crime prevention. Ironically, this has occurred just at a time when greater public and legal concern appeared to have been developing in this regard. Given the dispersed impact of much corporate criminality, it is less easy to see how it can gain a strong foothold on local community crime prevention agendas. The growth of local ecological and environmental pressure groups, however, points to the possibility for progressive developments in this field.

Community as a Prioritization of 'Moral Order'

In the context of criminal justice, 'community' is often a motif which seeks the prioritization of order maintenance over the goal of law enforcement. This is explicit in the arguments underlying Wilson and Kelling's (1982) 'broken windows' thesis together with the 'zero tolerance' strategies to which it has given rise, and implicit in the philosophies and practices of community policing (Fielding 1995). The latter assumes that order must be achieved to gain the consent and co-operation of the 'community', on the back of which efficient enforcement may proceed. Disorderly behaviour—from youths hanging around streets and drunks to 'squeegee merchants' (Straw 1995a; 1966)—it is argued, violates community expectations of what constitutes appropriate civil behaviour (Kelling 1987: 90). This higher order value trumps individual civil rights. Wilson and Kelling (1982; Kelling 1985), therefore, advocate aggressive order maintenance activities by the police against those perceived to be engaging in disorderly conduct. Kelling recognizes that this form of order maintenance is controversial, because there are no clear and consistent definitions of what constitutes disorder and because the legal justification for police intervention is unclear (Kelling 1987: 94–5). Many behaviours which may create disorder are not illegal. However, the moral arguments—e.g. that community expectations of order are more fundamental than individual rights to behave in a disorderly fashion—together with the pragmatic crime control arguments—that the reinvigoration of order will reduce the fear of crime which will, in turn, reduce the level of crime (the 'broken windows' thesis)—appear to outweigh these vexed issues. However, there is an additional problem which Kelling fails to acknowledge, i.e. the absence of consensus about what it is that constitutes disorder. This in turn raises the further crucial question: whose definition of 'order' should be accorded priority? Is 'order' that which the youths are engaged in when 'doing nothing' hanging around street corners, as they may perceive it to be, or do they represent an infringement upon the order of others? For example, one of the research sites, the Parkland Manors, had a high student population as a consequence of which there were tensions with local youths, who saw 'their area' increasingly transformed for the student market. In that context, the question 'whose order?' tended to become defined in terms of the conditions under which students could live free from anxieties about the safety of themselves and their property. Little concern was accorded by agency personnel to the disorderly conduct of students themselves, or the disorder created by the annual clearing out of debris onto the streets from student residences at the end of the academic year.

Here there is an unwarranted slippage between topography and moral order. Community as a prioritization of order implies that dominant 'communal' values are to be accorded preference over and above individual lifestyles or minority identities. This has problematic implications for civil liberties, as order maintenance may require the police or other authority to use extra-legal measures. This echoes the communitarian calls for a greater emphasis on responsibilities rather than rights (to which I return later in the chapter). Often this assumes that the two are in some sort of hydraulic relationship, whereby more of the one inherently leads to less of the other. Thus, for some, communities are best served by reducing the rights of suspects or defendants and increasing the responsibilities of 'at risk' or 'dangerous' populations. In this logic, civil rights come to be seen as inimical to public or communal safety. 'Community' in this context can act as a kind of consequentialism which prioritizes an ends-orientation over and above any concern with due process. Order is the prevailing priority. How it is achieved is relegated to the 'back seat'. The danger is that in this kind of utilitarianism the 'community' becomes a justification for greater punitiveness and arbitrary policing.

Community as a Resource

Explicit in a number of the quotations with which I began this chapter is the notion that the community has untapped resources which can be mined and utilized. 'Voluntary collective action' is seen as the under-exploited 'rough diamond' of civil society, which can be polished and turned to the provision of essential local goods and services. For neo-liberals 'voluntary collective action' is seen to have been buried deep under the rubble wrought by a culture of dependency on the welfare state. From the perspective of 'New Labour' and the centre left of politics, it is viewed as having become hidden beneath the excesses of the 'free market' society in which individualistic forces have been allowed to run rife, destroying the fabric of 'collective civil action'. For both, however, it constitutes a source of resources to which the state must turn, given the nature of the current fiscal crisis.

Hence, in the 'double-speak' of criminal justice rhetoric, the notion of 'community ownership' frequently translates into 'the community must mobilize its own resources'. The 'responsibilities' and 'obligations' to which politicians refer as the hallmarks of 'community' membership, are the human and material costs of crime prevention. However, the conception of 'community involve-ment' implicit within most crime prevention project is a passive one, which casts the community in the role of recipient of a set of mechanisms. This is what Rosenbaum (1987) refers to as the 'im-plant hypothesis' of crime prevention, whereby prepackaged pro-grammes are implanted into local social environments. This was evident in the research case studies. For example, the principal aim of Tenmouth Anti-Burglary Initiative was, according to its own publicity, 'community ownership'. Repeatedly, reference was made to the project being 'handed over to the community' when the initial work of the seconded officers was completed. However, there was a marked lack of any significant implementation of the mechanisms identified and proposed by the project. Reflecting upon this, the senior police officer on the project described—with an uncanny awareness of an 'implant hypothesis'—the tensions which arose out of transferring a set of mechanisms into an area together with the simultaneous expectation that the community will take over respon-sibility and 'ownership' of those preordained structures:

But when you talk about community, people smile and it's a nice sort of friendly thing, but if you just leave it [the project] out there in the community it just withers away and dies. You need someone to pour some water on it and fertilise it. But not *own* it! That is the great difficulty with neighbourhood watch, that the police, to promote it, have tried to own it too much, and now we are having to withdraw our ownership of it because we don't have the resources and it's withering . . . We need to water and fertilise it [the project] in a way in which it doesn't deplete our resources but allows it to blossom out there in the community.

As with many 'implant' projects, there was little community involvement during the life of the project, largely because the technical parameters of the project had already been set, in that it was conceived as a replication of the earlier Home Office funded Kirkholt project (Forrester *et al.* 1988, 1990). Consequently, when the time for 'community ownership' arrived and the project workers, as well as agency support, were withdrawn, the aims and ideals of the project, like the proverbial plant, largely withered and died.

This approach to 'community' as something to which responsibility can be transferred after a short initial period of funded assistance, is an aspect of a much wider short-termism which pervades crime prevention thinking in Britain. This outlook is evident in both funding and evaluation processes. The short-termism of evaluation tends to prioritize easily quantifiable, hence, physical or situational type interventions, at the expense of longer-term strategic and structural approaches, which potentially offer the least tangible short-term results (Crawford and Jones 1996). As the Morgan Report noted, there is a risk that the perceived need for short-term, quantitative evaluation will encourage community crime prevention activities, 'which are easily monitored rather than those which are relevant to the longer term social needs of the neighbourhood, which may not be susceptible to simple evaluation' (Morgan 1991: 22). This 'project driven' approach, in a simplified and caricatured form, involves: targeting an area; intervening in that area; getting a result; and moving on. In the process the community is rendered responsible for the future maintenance of the 'good work' undertaken during the project. If community crime prevention is to be about the broader process of developing institutions and structures of 'community' (Currie 1988) and local empowerment, then it will need to go beyond short-term evaluation and funding, and involve residents in monitoring effects on an on-going basis.

This notion of 'community' as a resource reaffirms a self-financing philosophy. Communities are being asked to help themselves in the prevention of crime, although the nature of the resources communities have at their disposal is rarely articulated. This approach gives a pivotal role to private business, voluntary bodies, and 'active citizens'. It presumes that all the necessary resources for successful crime prevention pre-exist within the community and only need to be harnessed. It presupposes that these resources will be given willingly and freely, but ignores, as was repeatedly illustrated in the research sites, 'the fact that the cost of tapping resources can considerably exceed the value of the benefits received' (AMA 1990: 19).

Rosenbaum concludes his review of the North American literature on community crime prevention asserting that, 'politicians must be disabused of the notion that community "self-help" and "volunteerism" are free' (1988b: 379). Implicit in this is a failure to recognize that some communities are more capable of tapping resources and informal community control than others. More importantly, those communities with the most severe crime problems are most likely not only to have fewer resources at their disposal, but also to lack even the most elementary social structures upon which community crime prevention can build. Time and again, research has exposed the dilemma that community responses to crime are easier to gene-rate in exactly those areas where they are least needed and hardest to establish in those where they are most needed (Rosenbaum 1988a; Skogan 1990). One American commentator has put it more simply,

the literature suggests that the sine qua non of community organising is an already organised community; that of crime prevention, an area not subjected to crime. So, too, appears to be the case with community polic-ing, which like its predecessors does best in the areas that need it least.

(Buerger 1994: 411)

Appeals to 'community' have come to be seen in economic terms as potentially cheaper alternatives to existing state institutions. They presuppose that communities have an inherent capacity to mobilize their own material and human resources of social control in order to keep initial 'implant' projects going. Neighbourhood self-sufficiency appears to be the ultimate goal, and the cost imperative seems to be the driving force in the process.

The Nature of Representation and Participation in Community Crime Prevention

Community Representation

The social processes of inclusion into community partnerships also entail the exclusion of certain interests. Importantly, they involve a process of 'social closure', albeit partial and contested, as opposed to open, pluralistic competition. They exclude as well as include. Organization, for instance, is a prerequisite for any interest being represented. The ability of certain interest groups to organize around, and define, issues of crime is of paramount importance in attaining a voice. However, as a consequence, the exclusion of disorganized interests differentially impacts upon those already politically marginalized and social disadvantaged: the unemployed, the homeless, black people, youths, and women trapped in abusive familial relationships. This has particular implications given the dominant association between crime and disorganization noted earlier. By implication this process of inclusion involves a redefinition of the participatory trappings of 'citizenship', in which the least powerful and most disorganized sections of society are increasingly excluded from partnership structures. The significance of organization was alluded to by a member of the local authority on the Illsworth estate-based crime reduction project, while explaining the nature of community representation on the inter-agency steering committee:

So you are looking at a range of the organised groups in that particular geographical area that represent some part of the community that has a right to a voice. What you find is that they don't really *represent*, but apart from that you have the whole private sector people who are privately renting, of which there are quite a few in that area, they don't get represented because they don't have an organisation to represent them.

Interestingly, the issue of organization potentially leaves public sector tenants in a more powerful position than those in the 'disorganized' private rented sector. This raises implications for these, and other, interest groups which cannot easily or effectively be organized around issues of crime and, consequently, are rarely incorporated into crime prevention initiatives. Exclusion is not so much an unfortunate by-product of the practice of community-based crime prevention initiatives but an essential element of its operation. The important lesson for community partnerships should be how to limit exclusion through integrating strategies which seek to ensure representativeness.

However, as with other 'consultative' groups, multi-agency forums generally fail to confront the problems relating to the unrepresentativeness of community representatives (Jefferson *et al.* 1988;

Morgan 1989). Those representatives within such forums tend to be drawn from very specific and limited interests within a locality. They work within highly undemocratic networks of special interests, in which agency workers often act as gatekeepers (Fyfe 1992). The senior police officer on the Tenmouth project explained the *ad hoc* manner in which community representatives were sought and invited onto the multi-agency forum:

Obviously we wanted it to be a community-based project. We realised that we would have to walk away from the project and so we would need rep[resentative]s from the community. Now, obviously that's terribly, terribly difficult. We had a very committed Neighbourhood Watch co-ordinator. She was very happy to take part [Tenmouth] has an ethnic minority population of about 10 to 11 per cent. The area of the study was showing a particular burglary problem in the densest area of population of ethnic minorities. There was a lot of time and pavement walking trying to get rep[resentative]s. Our first approach was to the local Commission for Racial Equality and unfortunately, the CRE worker had too many other commitments to devote proper time to the project. Although, initially they were keen to come on they couldn't commit themselves to it. They had too much other work. Our next option was to approach one or two other members of the ethnic community. We didn't have a lot of success, but we finally approached some one I knew and his wife. He's a solicitor and she's very prominent in the Afro-Caribbean community. And then, after the committee was established, some 6 to 9 months later, a black youth and community worker joined.

Inclusion may have more to do with personal relations with key agency personnel, noted activism or previous 'good' service in other fields of 'voluntary' community work, rather than any notion of representativeness. Such networks are largely self-perpetuating, self-justifying, and rarely challenged. Taylor aptly summarizes the nature of relations of representation in this context:

These relations are characterised (very much like the local television news programme and its relationship with its audience) by a nervous and hyperactive *belief* in the existence of a close and responsive relationship rather than by *demonstrable* relations of real solidarity.

(Taylor 1995a: 416, emphasis in original)

In a number of research sites the same representatives—often drawn from an informal list circulated between agencies—appeared on various different local consultative committees. This was noted by a police officer on the Arlington Racial Harassment Monitoring Project:

The thing that worries me about the make up of a lot of these groups is that it is the same people, whatever meeting I go to, and I sometimes wonder and worry about what their ulterior motive is.

This state of affairs was frequently explained by the need for people who 'understand' the administrative procedures, language, and practice of local agencies. A level of 'understanding', therefore, can become a filter for inclusion. Even if this is not an active decision taken by agency personnel, it is often self-imposed and self-fulfilling. In the research sites community representatives 'dropped out' complaining that they were 'bored and couldn't understand what was going on' (Tenmouth community representative).

Inclusion, as Sampson *et al.* note, is also bound up with powerful agency definitions of the 'respected' and 'respectable' (1988: 489). 'Troublesome' groups are marginalized, ignored or overlooked. This was frequently justified on the grounds that multi-agency partnerships are about consensus building (the goal of 'unity' discussed in Chapter 4) and that such 'troublesome' groups would merely disrupt an established consensus. Most glaringly, this affects youth groups in all their guises, which are often perceived to be potentially 'troublesome' and thus are conspicuous by their absence from community crime prevention schemes.

Yet agency personnel were well aware of the lack of genuine community representation. Whilst this was the source of a certain degree of embarrassment, agency personnel tended to explain and justify the problem in one of two ways. First, they occasionally blamed the community itself for not having in place proper democratic structures through which representatives could be rendered accountable. As a council officer on the Churchway project explained: 'It is up to the local forum. If they don't like the way in which they are being represented they could change it.' This was not seen to be something that the agencies collectively through the multi-agency forum should, or could, encourage and facilitate within the local community, but was something the community had to work out for itself. Here again the problem of disorganization compounds matters. Further, this approach ignored the fact that traditional, local democratic structures through local councillors often were deliberately not included in the decision making process, nor were there formal lines of accountability to them.

Secondly, some agency personnel pointed to the 'impossibilism of representation' to explain the unrepresentative nature of incorporated community members. According to this viewpoint, 'true representation' is impossible, so why waste the effort trying? Numerous professionals, when questioned about the lack of community representation on the initiatives, reflected the view of one of the agency workers on the Churchway project, who stated: 'I mean it's always going to be a problem that you can't get a true representation of the people in the area.' Others merely retorted that 'you can never really be representative'. This was a justification for 'doing nothing' to ensure greater representativeness. And yet, perversely, it was also given as the reason for excluding certain troublesome groups, such as the exclusion of the English Collective of Prostitutes from the Churchway project. A key figure from the local authority in the area explained:

I happen to think that the English Collective of Prostitutes are an irrelevance because I don't believe they are actually working with the mass of women. I mean they're a political group, they don't really impact on people's lives round here. So they wouldn't give a genuine representation of prostitutes in the area anyway.

Whilst 'genuine representation' is inherently problematic, the above statement signals a catch-22. If representation is an 'all or nothing' concept, which can rarely if ever be attained, then the question remains, why establish structures of representation which clearly cannot adhere to this ideal and at the same time seek to claim to represent actual community interests? Legitimate local representation presents important challenges to local agencies in terms of how they construct and incorporate democratic processes into community representation (to which I return in Chapter 7). It also highlights the necessity for a more rigorous understanding of both the limits and possibilities of genuine representation and one which overcomes the ostrich stance of 'impossibilism', but engages with the inherent associated difficulties which give rise to it.

Crime Prevention and Community Participation

Community participation, like that of other organizations in partnerships (as we saw in Chapter 4), is structured by differential power relations. The resources available to the different agencies, their appeals to 'expertise', and their grasp of the technical language in which much debate is couched, leave community representatives in relatively powerless positions. This relationship was succinctly summarized by one member of the Tenmouth project, in which she described, 'professionals as people with the capacity to do things and the community [as] there to have things done for them.' Nevertheless, the distinction between formal agency and community representatives is by no means clear cut. Representatives of voluntary organizations, local charities, and institutions like the churches sit uncomfortably in relation to state/civil society and lay/ professional distinctions. The boundaries between these are significantly more blurred than might appear at first sight. The differential power relations between agencies contributing to a given project mean that complex relations of dominance exist in regard to both the policy formation and implementation processes. Despite claims about the importance of 'non-expert' lay input, an association with 'community' can reduce the influence of an organization over more powerful bodies. For example, a community worker, employed by the local authority on the Churchway Anti-Crime Project, expressed frustration at her relative impotence in influencing decision making:

And because I think our organisation is community based, we're managed by local residents, I think they [the police and other local authority departments] probably feel there is a lack of professionalism and so we're not given an equal role.

In this instance, as she suggests, too close an association with the community led to a marginalization from the central decision making processes. She continued:

Where are the decisions being made? because they're certainly not being made at the working party from what I can gather. And I'm not sure how much they [senior council officials] meet with police outside those meetings, but something must be happening to make it work, I don't know whether they just go away and do their thing and then come back and say, 'well this is what we've done'.

Research observations of the working party meetings and interviews with other key personnel tended to support her implied suggestion that those outside the key agencies were not privy to decision making processes. This experience was mirrored in other research sites. For example, on the Tenmouth project this was openly acknowledged by the agency personnel, as in the following comment by the seconded police officer:

There isn't anything for them [the community representatives] to do. We are collecting the data, and we are now analysing the data. I think when the results are published and it is decided what sort of course of action to take as far as putting measures into effect, then they will come into their own. I suppose that it's a bit unfair on them to say: 'Well, just sit back for nine months or whatever it is, and we'll call on you again'. But I think that that is just the way it is.

This impacted upon the attendance of the community representatives at the steering group which gradually declined until there was only one person from the community regularly attending steering group meetings. This experience was replicated on the Arlington Racial Harassment initiative, where the administrator of the project explained:

It's an oil and water mix. Officers fit these things into their busy schedules and they have to put up with the rep[resentative]s moaning. The rep[resentative]s fade away, because with these big unwieldy committees there is no role for them. And then you have attendance problems.

Many representatives found the language, style of working, and resourcing to be both alien and very frustrating. As one representative on the Illsworth Crime Prevention Project explained, with ironic use of obtuse language: 'I'm an action person . . . the problem is it [crime prevention] gets "fundified". I hate funding.' This often left community representatives feeling as if they had very different priorities from those of public agencies involved in the partnership. This may serve to heighten the politics of crime and problematize existing legitimacy deficits. As one community representative (on the Illsworth Project) commented on her experience: 'We want miracles and they want an easy life.'

  Community participation itself impacts in different ways upon the other parties within partnerships. This is due to, first, the different dominant conceptions of 'community' held by the organizations and their personnel and, secondly, the competing understandings of the nature and role of community representation and participation within the process. 'Community' fits into specific crime prevention, and more general organizational, strategies in separate but overlapping ways. For example, police and probation officers bring very different notions of 'community' to their work.

For probation officers, their individual and client-centred approach to work renders 'community' immediately problematic. A 'community perspective' is not something to which most probation officers traditionally ascribe. 'Community' is something from which their clients often feel estranged and disconnected (Sampson and Smith 1992: 107). For probation officers, 'community' may be something that their 'clients lack'. However, for them to say exactly what that constitutes is a more complex question, one from which they often shy away. Consequently, probation officers are generally less comfortable, not only with the notion of 'community' but also in interactions with community representatives themselves.

For police officers, by contrast, 'community' represents a common referent for their work. Police officers frequently seek justification for what they do 'in the name of the community'. The 'community' is often referred to as symbolic legitimation, particularly for contentious aspects of police work (Morgan 1989; Fielding and Fielding 1991). The moral order of the 'community' is a benchmark against which police seek to be judged as opposed to the interests of specific individuals, or even minority groups within the community. The 'community' is even called upon as the higher moral ground on which claims to cleanse abuses of police power are sometimes made. This is captured, for example, in the contradictory phrase used by the Metropolitan Commissioner of Police, 'noble cause corruption' (Condon 1993)—the idea that police infractions of the law may be morally justifiable in the name of the wider community interest—which has passed into common police parlance. What the 'community' consists of, in this context, is usually taken for granted and rarely elucidated. In reality, however, it constitutes a highly specific reference group, one which is bound up with notions of 'the respected and the respectable' (Reiner 1992b).

Despite competing conceptions of 'community' amongst agencies involved in 'partnerships', such as the police and probation service, they share, and are bound together by, a much wider policy agenda in which 'community' participation connects with questions about their own legitimacy. Whilst agency representatives talk about the need for 'local input' and 'knowledge of local conditions' within the decision making process, more often than not such an input merely serves to justify decisions taken elsewhere. In reality, the attraction of community involvement, for the agencies, is for them to be seen to be 'doing something'. Community representatives act as 'messengers' in this regard, disseminating an image of activity. Community involvement also feeds into 'public relations' exercises which are becoming increasingly important facets of modern organizations, including those in the criminal justice field. As a consequence, there is an attempt to catalyse the 'community' into a shift in attitudes and values, both in terms of how agencies are viewed and how the public ought to view their own responsibility. This is closely tied to issues of legitimacy and power, both connected properties of social organizations (Sparks and Bottoms 1995: 48). At one level, it is concerned with meeting public expectations of action. At another level, it is concerned with the rearticulation and dissemination of what public (and to a lesser extent, private) agencies perceive to be the legitimate expectations that the public should hold for them. As one agency worker sardonically explained: 'the difficulty with the community is they've got such bloody silly expectations'. Community involvement, therefore, is a means of managing and controlling expectations. This point was recognized by an agency worker on the Churchway Anti-Crime Project, who candidly commented that:

as well as being a good way of consulting and trying to arrive at some joint decisions, it's a very good way of controlling people . . . if bureaucracy does not want to discuss but at the same time wants to be free from accusations of being insensitive, it's an ideal model.

What is important is that the inclusion of local interest organizations and community representatives in partnership schemes carries with it attachment to those structures and participating agencies. As such, it constitutes a form of 'local corporatism' (Crawford 1994a). Through 'partnerships' organized community interest groups are incorporated into the processes of policy formation and implementation. Within corporatist theory (which I consider in greater detail in Chapter 6) incorporation carries with it the assumption that those interest organizations accept responsibility for, and have the capacity to implement, agreed policies (Cawson 1985; 1986; Schmitter 1974; 1985). Consequently, 'incorporated' organizations are given a privileged 'public' status which grants them certain powers—including access to policy formation—while at the same time conferring on them responsibilities and obligations, in terms of ensuring the implementation of, and compliance with, 'public' policy. This is done to some degree on behalf of the state's interests rather than the direct interests of the organization's members. Thus, 'corporatism' entails a degree of external intervention in processes of 'private' and intra-organizational decision making.

The practical implications of incorporation are dependent, in large part, upon the ability of those incorporated individuals to control and regulate their members and, therefore, it is conditional upon the nature of the relations between the 'representatives' and those that they represent. For incorporation to have a 'regulatory' effect, this need not necessarily be a relation of correspondence, but rather one which holds a capacity for suasion over those who are represented. Incorporation is neither a necessary nor an inevitable product of membership. Clearly, those representatives who represent no greater interests than their own incorporate no wider constituency. Thus, a senior police officer on the Arlington Racial Harassment Monitoring Project berated the lack of genuine incorporation of community groups beyond the individuals on the committee in suggesting that:

Now, what they [the multi-agency forum] don't look at is to actually say to an organisation which has nominated 'A' to represent them, does 'A' go back to that organisation asking for input from them? I doubt it because, from my perception of the majority of community organisations, they have rep[resentative]s on committees and they never take it back to those communities.

However, other representatives, most notably those of tenants' and residents' or ethnic minority groups—due to the nature of their relations with their members—can incorporate large constituencies. As a result, these may become tied to, and enmeshed within, the dissemination and implementation of local policy initiatives.

Hence, in a number of the research projects, community representatives were called upon to contain and regulate their members' demands, as well as to convey what they could legitimately expect from the multi-agency forum. One tenant representative on the Illsworth estate project was forced to defend and justify the actions of the forum to a group of angry residents. She insisted later that she did not agree with the policy nor thought it to be appropriate, but felt compelled to defend the actions as they were being undertaken in the name of the forum of which she was a member. For some community representatives this disciplinary strain was too much and resulted in their attendance at meetings trailing off.

Some commentators have highlighted the manner in which even oppositional community groups can become co-opted onto formal agendas (Santos 1982; Cain 1988). In turn, they can be transformed from sites of alternative ideologies into supplements and extensions to the dominant formal system (Cohen 1985; Nelken 1985). While this is an ever-present danger it is not an inevitable consequence of incorporation.

Mediation and Appeals to 'Community'

Appeals to 'community' find expression in mediation at a number of different levels. These are connected to, but somewhat different from, the understandings prevalent in dominant community crime prevention discourse. In examining the understandings of 'community' and their connections with mediation, I will draw upon the research case studies and a survey of Annual Reports and related statements of 'aims and objectives' of neighbourhood and victim/offender mediation schemes in England. The survey was conducted in 1994, using the Mediation UK list of affiliated members. All schemes were contacted and asked to provide a copy of their latest Annual Report or most recent description of the schemes' aims and objectives, together with any associated publicity material. Responses were received from thirty of the forty-eight schemes to which requests were sent. This represents a 63 per cent response rate. A list of the schemes which replied and provided the documentation upon which the survey is based is set out in Appendix B.

Community as Empowerment Through Communication

The involvement of the parties in the process of disputing through mediation is seen by proponents to be an essential element of community membership (Wright 1990: 76–7; Christie 1977). Disputes and crimes arise where 'normal' community controls have broken down (Abel 1973). Consequently, the response to crime is an activity which is conducted on behalf of the community and reflects a community's moral sensibilities. Conflict processing is, therefore, a highly *communal* act. It strengthens and reaffirms communal bonds. It represents, not only, a 'potential for activity, for participation' but also it allows the parties 'opportunities for norm-clarification' (Christie 1977: 7–8). Hence, it is argued, that the process of mediation—through party participation in conflict negotiation—is itself socially constructive. Resolving a conflict between parties is a means to an end. It is understood as instrumental to the construction of shared values and commitment among the local community of residents. Consequently, mediation is believed to empower the parties and the wider community through a heightened form of communication. Hence, a mediator from the Southwark Mediation Centre is quoted in their documentation as saying: 'Mediation is important because it is a powerful tool for relieving some of the stresses suffered in the neighbourhood and can contribute to the building of a harmonious community.' In this light, mediation is viewed as empowering the parties. It is an aspect in a wider ideology of 'social transformation' (Harrington and Merry 1988). On the one hand, mediation is seen to be 'an age-old practice, natural to any functioning community' (Sandwell Mediation Scheme Report 1993). And yet, on the other hand, it is something that, as a society, we appear to have forgotten about—either because community has broken down or because the courts and other professionals have appropriated the role from communities—hence the need for schemes to restore people's capacity for mediation. The Sandwell Mediation Scheme goes on to declare:

Modern communities rely too much upon the intervention of formal agencies and professional workers to solve their problems and conflicts. Community mediation advocates a return to community control over local disputes.

Moreover, the large majority of neighbourhood schemes in the survey identified, in some way, 'strengthening the bonds of community' as an aim to which their service is committed. This is believed to occur either by solving interpersonal conflicts and thus alleviating tension or, more often, through 'mediation as education'. Here, mediation is seen as a medium through which people can learn to communicate their feelings. It enables them to have the ability to solve their own problems in the future. To this end, a significant minority of neighbourhood schemes actively 'teach' or 'facilitate' mediation skills in schools and other local institutions. Victim/offender mediation schemes, by contrast, were more likely to emphasize their impact upon the community by stressing the influence of mediation upon offending behaviour. Some victim/offender schemes, however, also referred to their potential impact upon 'community safety' more generally, by addressing victims'

fears and anxieties. Consequently, if they do not reduce the incidence of local crime they may reduce the fear of it, thus impacting
upon community cohesion.

However, social transformation and community empowerment
through mediation are difficult to assess. Clearly, the parties may be
given a greater sense of control, but the extent to which this has an
enduring impact is less evident. The somewhat pessimistic conclusion reached by Yngvesson, in relation to the San Francisco
Community Boards, was that community empowerment may be
possible only for a privileged 'internal community' of volunteers
rather than the external 'community of neighbours' (1993: 381).
Certainly, considerable effort is made by mediation schemes, particularly those that rely upon volunteer mediators, to making them
feel part of a 'community of mediators'. To this end, particular
attention is accorded to mediators' own 'personal growth'. Considerable space, within most scheme Annual Reports and analogous
documentation, is given over to the mediators themselves, their
experiences, views, commitment, training, and so on. Thus, as a
mediator quoted in the Southwark Mediation Centre documentation declared: 'I find mediating in disputes to be very rewarding. I
have gained immensely from being a mediator because it has helped
broaden my understanding about dealing with people on a personal
level.' Similarly, the Northolt Community Mediation Service, from
the research case studies, organized various social events, group
workshops and training sessions aimed at bringing the volunteer
mediators and management committee together 'to give them a
sense of belonging' (in the words of the scheme co-ordinator).
However, Yngvesson (1993: 381) suggests this internal community to be largely an exclusive one. Consequently, the aim of community empowerment through communication for the internal
community of volunteers and scheme workers may be a more easily
obtainable goal and one which is given greater priority than the
empowerment of the wider community of residents.

Community as Obligations to Others

The restorative priorities of mediation identify the importance of
ongoing and future relations, the mainstay of 'community'. Mediation seeks to give prominence to mutual responsibility, shared
values, and interconnectedness. This finds expression through different, normatively informed notions of justice, which emphasize

the reparation and restoration of communal bonds in response to crime and harm, rather than retribution through punishment (Zehr 1990; Wright 1991). Thus, an importance is accorded to inter-personal accountability through interparty dialogue. This carries with it a role, and concern, for the wider community. Therefore, 'encouraging the parties to acknowledge their own responsibility' (mediator, Leighdale victim/offender scheme), is an important pre-requisite for individual empowerment through mediation and a recognition of a connection to a wider community. This sense of obligation or responsibility resonates with appeals to community in mediation, which are consequentialist by way of their future-orientation.

However, it embodies a tension between voluntarism—the indi-vidual autonomy of the parties in the process of resolving their dispute—and the type of communication which they must accept as a premise for mediation—mutual responsibility, a concern for the future, and the importance of how their actions impact upon others. The ambiguity lies in the fact that this requires a shift from one dialogic frame to another, and yet it is one which in the spirit of voluntarism must be freely embraced. However, in reality, this transformation of the self may not be forthcoming and may require encouragement by mediators.

Consequently, victims and offenders may feel a suasive com-munity pressure to enter into the mediation process, as their actions have potential consequences for others. Further, this consequen-tialism implicitly, and sometimes explicitly, is referenced and rein-forced within mediation practice. More often, this suasive potential is likely to affect the victims of crime who may, and often do, feel that through their meeting with the offender(s) they may be able 'to help' them confront their offending behaviour thus resulting in fewer 'victims in the future'. One of the co-ordinators of the Leigh-dale victim/offender scheme explained:

The reason why a lot of victims agree to face to face [mediation] is that they put on their 'community badge', you know, do their bit for the community . . . It never ceases to amaze me the amount of forgiveness in victims. As an experienced mediator, the most common reason why victims want to meet offenders is to try and persuade them to stop offending, not to get 60 quid out of them, or not to shout and scream at them, but to try and persuade them to stop. I think that in comparison with probation officers, police officers, teachers, social workers, that victims are better placed to say: 'Please stop', because what the offender did was to them.

Similarly, offenders may need to be encouraged, or may feel the need, to 'help the victim get over what has happened to them' (mediator, Leighdale victim/offender scheme), by explaining their actions and answering the questions which the victim may have about the offence.

In neighbourhood mediation the context of this future-oriented 'mutual responsibility' is somewhat different. It is not necessarily bound up with the establishment of 'wrongdoing' and 'blameworthiness' which criminal activities carry, at least for the offender. Nevertheless, in victim/offender mediation, while this places the parties in uneven positions, it can act as a powerful leverage upon which the acceptance of responsibility, by the offender at least, can be constructed. The parties in neighbourhood disputes may feel less willing to accept mutual responsibility and look to the future if blameworthiness has yet to be established in any authoritative way.

Mediators and the Moral Community

Proponents of mediation argue for the need to involve 'community' representatives as third party mediators in the disputing process (Danzig 1973; Shonholtz 1987; Grönfors 1989). As such, mediation is often seen as a critique of established forms of dispute processing which are overly professionalized (see Crawford 1996b). The courts and the criminal justice processes are both spatially and, more importantly, socially disconnected from the disputants and the 'community' out of which disputes arise. In this regard, mediators are deemed to constitute important 'community' bonds, to embody, both figuratively and literally, the 'community'.

In the survey responses, nearly all neighbourhood mediation schemes emphasized the importance of local 'lay' people or 'volunteers' as mediators. Here, the mediator often aspires to represent the community—even if only symbolically—to be *from* and *of* the community. This approach permeates local victim/offender as well as neighbourhood, mediation practice. This notion of the mediator as intrinsically connected to the community through their attachment to the local neighbourhood was referenced, in some form or other, in the majority of survey responses. For example, Southwark Mediation Centre's documentation stated: 'All of the Centre's mediators live in the local area and they therefore have the kind of experience that enables them to sympathise easily with the difficulties that they mediate.' However, this attachment causes mediators to occupy, simultaneously, two related but tensed positions. On the one hand they are seen as symbolic representatives of the 'moral community'; on the other hand they are cast in the role of the disputant's social peers, as somehow *like* the disputants. Mediators are deemed to share certain characteristics with, and to be representative of, the same community. In many situations these two positions may dovetail neatly. However, there are important differences and tensions between them. The first position is a normative judgement of the appropriateness of certain behaviours and how to respond to them. The second, by contrast, is an empirical relationship between the mediator and the parties, albeit one which takes a variety of forms, whereby 'likeness' may be understood in terms of shared geographic proximity, socio-demography, cultural identity or ethnicity.

The resultant ambiguities in the connections between mediators and 'community' give rise to theoretical and practical questions about mediators' roles, their social legitimacy, and relations to the parties. First, to what extent do mediators have the authority to force settlements, to encourage the parties towards certain 'desirable' outcomes? Secondly, should mediators be, at least ideally, representative of all 'ordinary' community members (a 'unity' perspective) or of a specific segment within that community (a 'diversity' perspective)? Thirdly, is voluntarism an essential element of representativeness in the mediator role? Or, to put it another way, does representativeness erode with professionalization? Let us consider these inter-related issues with reference to the research findings.

All these questions reference and come together around the processes of mediator selection strategies, as mediators replicate the various meanings of 'community'. The co-ordinator of Oldcastle Victim Support (a member of the advisory committee of the victim/ offender mediation scheme) identified the important place of the connection between volunteers and the 'moral community', undifferentiated by culture and ethnicity. He saw this as transcending the work of both Victim Support volunteers and mediators, in responding to victims of crime:

They [victims] need to have their faith in the community as a whole restored. I think that's what volunteers are doing, they are almost representing the community at large and helping them to restore the faith of that individual in that community. Because it is only one isolated maverick within the community that has hurt that victim, and the rest of the community is basically OK. That's what we're saying.

Here, it is implied that voluntarism—in the sense of volunteers, rather than individual autonomy—is an important element in constituting the representativeness of the 'moral community'. Consequently, many schemes deliberately seek to recruit 'ordinary lay volunteers'. However, two understandings of community representativeness are present in the use of volunteers. First, 'the community' is viewed as a geographic location which is structured, essentially, by homogenous interests. Thus, a representative mediator (like a community representative in crime prevention) may be any 'right-minded' person who is from, i.e. lives in, that community and who shares broadly its values. Symbolically, they are 'representative' by means of their 'ordinariness', rather than any specific relation of 'likeness' they share with the parties (outside of shared residence within a potentially large and socially diverse geographic area). A senior probation officer, with management responsibilities for the Leighdale project, outlined what he saw as the value of such 'ordinary' community volunteers as mediators:

I'm not convinced that paper qualifications actually deliver the competencies ... for this sort of work. I believe that there is something very special about ordinary people being involved in these processes. Always, the Borstal boy could say to me that I'm getting paid to do this job. Which in some ways was a statement about, 'you don't really care, you don't want to make a difference because you're doing it to pay your mortgage'. It wasn't true, but I believe that's important. That cannot be said for somebody who comes to a job not paid and actually wants to do the work. They're also *of* the local community, they live in it, they experience the crime. Now, you can say that probation officers do as well, but to a degree they [volunteers] are coming out of the community, they're an important link with it and there are some tremendous talents there, and some very natural bits that actually work. They don't carry a lot of the problems, the wrong sort of professionalism with them, which are anti-human anyway.

A second understanding of 'community' is to be found where schemes recognize a diversity of social identities within the locality and seek to accommodate them, through 'representation', within the body of mediators. This approach was adopted, at least as an ideal, in most schemes in the survey and the research case studies. In practice, however, it may co-exist alongside 'unitary' interpretations. From the survey, Plymouth Mediation Service was unexceptional in its declaration that:

> We wish to recruit a volunteer force which, so far as is possible, represents a cross section of the communities which we serve. This inevitably means that our volunteers will include: the retired; the unemployed; single parents; those with families; those with their own transport and those without; those in part time work and those employed full time.

Other schemes, like the Newham Conflict and Change Project and the research case studies, identified the importance of specific criteria of 'likeness' in terms of differences in ethnicity and culture. As a result, they are committed to the development of a diverse pool of volunteers and to selecting mediators who 'match' parties as far as possible. The central dilemma here is how far diversity can, or should, be recognized and accommodated without fracturing a sense of a unified 'moral community' to which mediation accords. Further, which forms of social identity constitute a significant group within a locality, such that it should be represented among mediators? What criteria denote significance?

The answer to the first question may well be 'the more the merrier'. In the context of representation within community crime prevention projects, this may make sense and have some value. However, as with other dispute processing mechanisms, mediation is based upon a central 'triadic relationship' (Shapiro 1981: 1). This is an inherently unstable relationship, with an ever-present threat that the triad will break down and turn into a relationship of two against one. Therefore, the mediator is not merely in a unidimensional relationship of correspondence but one which at its most simple involves two sets of relationships which often are in tension with each other. The victim and the offender may not only be in conflict as a result of the acts which brought them to the mediation, but also may have very different social identities or come from divergent social, cultural or ethnic backgrounds. Many schemes' use of two (or in some cases three) mediators for face to face mediation sessions does allow multiple identities to be represented and hence a certain degree of 'balance'. Nevertheless, the problematic relationship between representativeness, likeness, and legitimacy remains. The possibility of 'triadic breakdown' raises questions about the legitimacy of mediation for the different parties in dispute.

It also problematizes the nature of the social relationships between the third party mediator(s) and the diverse interest constellations which find themselves represented in the disputes brought before them. In addition, the essential 'logic of identity' tends to generate dichotomy rather than unity within the 'community of mediators'.

This notion of 'representation as difference' should alert us, not only to the co-existence of diverse communities within a geographic area, but also to the different cultural meanings that may be attached to 'community' within and between cultural groupings. For example, the Oldcastle Victim/Offender Mediation Scheme covered an area with a large Asian population, amongst whom the scheme was having difficulty finding recognition. One of the co-ordinators, himself of Asian descent, reflected upon the difficulty and the great efforts that he was having to put into working with the Asian community, given a perceived cultural resistance of the notion of mediation as a legitimate alternative either to the formal system or to informal community controls:

The fear I have there is that people think: 'Well, who are these people? We can sort it out in our own community.' In two cases that I've attended that was the reaction. 'We'll sort it out in our own community' . . . But community is crumbling [amongst Asians in Oldcastle], to be quite honest, it's crumbling. There might be a few there who say: 'We'll deal with it in our own community', but quite honestly, I don't think so. I would have believed it 5 or probably 10 years ago. But now, the youth are growing up and a lot of crimes are committed by Asians in [Oldcastle]. Because they have their freedom and obviously if you tie somebody up, as soon as they get their freedom they are going to run wild. That's what is happening in [Oldcastle]. They are not going to be listening to elders.

This suggests not only a cultural understanding of community, but also one which may be overlaid by generational differences. This cultural resistance to mediation—due to its perceived encroachment upon more genuinely informal modes of dispute processing—also presented problems for recruiting volunteers. The same Oldcastle co-ordinator explains:

I have two Asian volunteers, who speak most of the Asian languages. I'm looking for more. I'm looking for Asian, females as well, to come forward. It's hard to recruit them. Very difficult. I remember when I used to do voluntary work they [people in the Asian community] used to ask me, 'Oh, you are doing voluntary work, how much do you get paid?' You know, it's hard to tell them you are doing it for nowt. It's hard getting people from the Asian community. There is still a lot of development work to be done.

This insight raises problematic questions about the nature of correspondence between 'voluntarism' and 'representativeness', both of which implicitly underlie most appeals to 'community' in mediation. The importance of human agency, consent, and voluntariness of the parties as prerequisites for community or individual empowerment is inextricably connected with the idea of the mediator as volunteer. And yet, the very unrepresentativeness of most 'ordinary volunteers' poses dilemmas for mediation. This reality has required some mediation schemes to look to other ways of attracting mediators from the diverse groups which are traditionally under-represented among volunteers. A co-ordinator of the Leighdale Victim/Offender Mediation Service explained the dilemma:

If all you can do is offer people voluntary work then you are only going to get the kind of people that really you don't want. You're only going to get the white, middle-class volunteer, who can afford to be a volunteer, we don't want that, obviously we want a cross-section of the community, we want people with experience, we want people of all ages and so, if you look at our mediator group I think we're as near as probably we've ever been to achieving a reasonable cross-section of the representative community of [the area]. What we do lack, and I think everybody is saying and certainly other mediation schemes say the same thing, is that we cannot attract the ethnic groups—for some reason we cannot do that—we attract the ethnic groups but for some reason the Probation service generally is bad at keeping black volunteers, and I personally think that's probably to do with there not being an opportunity for people to move into paid employment.

To address this gap, the scheme paid its core mediators an hourly fee (primarily restricted to those mediators with significant experience, although limited by budgetary constraints). The same co-ordinator went on to explain the rationale:

Most people who come to us, they know that they're coming as a volunteer to start with, but if they know that at some stage they're going to be paid, we've got a better chance of keeping the ones who turn out to be effective mediators, if, at the end of the day, they're going to be able to develop and move on to paid work . . . So you know, it's a bit of a myth that everybody wants to be a volunteer and that you can start schemes like this and other schemes, and I think it's a bit of a management myth that people like that exist, I don't think that they actually exist. The people who do exist to be volunteers are the ones, to be quite truthful, you don't want so many of because they're not representative of the community.

As a realistic means of achieving the desirable 'representative-ness' among the body of mediators, this strategy has much to commend it. However, in turn it produces an hierarchical élite among the community of mediators, potentially reinforcing differences between them. In addition, it acts as an important control mechanism over mediators. It allows scheme co-ordinators to make judgements about competence and effectiveness of specific mediators. Those mediators who, on the basis of staff assessment, are not believed to fulfil the required characteristics, can be left to drift among the marginal category of volunteers, while those who do, are moved into a paid position and thus accorded 'core' status. In the name of improving the standards of mediation practice this may be a useful inducement, and yet it may serve to undermine the very 'likeness' between mediator and the parties. The problem is that by paying mediators, schemes may begin to erode the very attraction of mediators as disputants' social peers, their symbolic lay connectedness. Consequently, mediators may begin to look and behave more like 'quasi-professionals' than ordinary lay people. The proliferation of guidelines on training and standards of 'good practice' has led some commentators to the perception that we are witnessing a reformalization and reprofessionalization of mediation, which runs counter to the informalizing and deprofessionalizing declarations of many schemes and aspirations of early proponents (Sarat 1988; Harrington and Merry 1988).

The recognition of multi-cultural heterogeneity and the notion of 'representation' as difference raises a number of normative, as well as practical, dilemmas. Is the logic of representation an acceptance of the normative values of the given group or association? Should mediation be culturally relativistic in its approach to outcomes? In other words, is an agreed settlement acceptable, purely because the parties have exercised their own agency and judgement in the process? Or should the process and outcome accord to some standard notion of acceptability? Here, mediators face a central dilemma, 'to settle a case without imposing a decision' (Silbey and Merry 1986: 7). As a result of this, Silbey and Merry suggest, coercion of some form is an essential prerequisite of mediator settlement strategies (1986: 13).

The British experience suggests a certain diversity of approach at the local level. An examination of mediation schemes' own literature suggests that some are keen to emphasize the cultural flexiblity of mediation as a model of conflict resolution. The following extract from the Bristol Mediation documentation serves as an example:

We will build on our contacts with minority and ethnic groups to work on appropriate conflict resolution processes to ensure a culturally representative mediation group ... We will develop appropriate models of mediation conflict resolution for different communities.

In this context, being 'quick to judge' and 'jumping to conclusions' are viewed as undesirable traits of mediators and ones which training and assessment both seek to limit and reduce. In its place, 'listening', 'understanding', 'empathising', and 'human sympathy' are accorded significant weight. The rhetoric of mediation suggests it to be a culturally transferable and relativistic tool. However, the observational research experience suggests a more complex picture. Whilst mediation seeks to be an open process unconfined by cultural or normative assumptions, in reality, it is forced to do so. First, as we have seen 'community' itself has different cultural meanings and thus its appeal within mediation carries different emphases. Secondly, it is set in a wider context of a relationship with the formal court processes, from which it derives many of its mythologies and imageries of appropriateness (Fitzpatrick 1992). Mediation stands, not in opposition to, but rather in the shadows of, the court. At a practical level, administrative limitations and constraints often require the development of subtle mediator settlement strategies. For example, in Leighdale, where they pay their core mediators per hour, they have restricted individual mediators to a maximum of ten hours work per case (including assessment, groundwork, and face to face contact). If mediators clock up longer hours they do so in their own time. In this context it is unsurprising that mediators deploy the use of 'inducements', 'incentives', and occasionally 'coercive sticks', particularly in initial preparatory assessment meetings with the victim or offender. The emphasis given to preparing the parties for face to face mediation, particularly in victim/offender work, has been seen to be, and sometimes is, a means of 'educating' the parties about what is 'acceptable' (see Davis 1992). This usually involves encouragement of the offender to challenge his/her own criminal behaviour and take responsibility for its impact. For the victim, more often, it is about tempering their anger and looking to the future.

Nevertheless, by contrast, there are elements of mediation practice which embody clear values of appropriate behaviour in the parties, particularly the offender, including their willingness to 'accept responsibility', 'challenge their own offending behaviour', 'see the consequences of their actions', 'accept their problems', and 'show remorse' (all phrases used by respondents). This awkward balance between, on the one hand, a relativistic empathy and acceptance of the agency and outcome of the parties and, on the other hand, a moral judgement of appropriateness both in the process and outcome, is a tension which lies at the heart of the mediator role.

Further, there is a troublesome contradiction. The more attached to the 'community' mediators are, the less likely they are to hold the required 'detached stance' which constitutes a central value in establishing mediator neutrality and legitimacy. The more mediators represent interests or value systems, the greater the danger that the triadic relationship will break down, or will be perceived to have broken down. As Harrington and Merry have commented in relation to the American experience: 'Precisely because of their participation and membership in the community, it is difficult for them to assume the required detachment' (Harrington and Merry, 1988: 730). However, as they go on to suggest, ironically, it is the interest in providing neutral and detached mediators that increases the pressures to develop a core of professional mediators. Their claims to expertise as specialists in mediation set them apart from that 'community'. Over time, many schemes come to rely upon a group of 'core' mediators who are semi-professionals by virtue of their work turnover, their training, and experience.

A second contradiction exists between the analysis of the problem —that there is a loss of sociability upon which conflict is constructively negotiated in some neighbourhoods—and the solution, i.e. settlement by mediators well integrated into the local community so that their actions are rendered legitimate. This is particularly clear in the earlier discussion of the cultural resistance to mediation among members of the Asian community in Oldcastle. If there are already existing figures within the local community who are sufficiently legitimate in their own authority, then it would seem that local sociability has not altogether broken down and mediation could take place outside formal schemes attached to systems of criminal justice. Or, if there are no sufficiently legitimate agents within the community, it is questionable whether any scheme will be sufficient to manufacture such legitimacy. The concern is that the legitimacy of mediation schemes derives not from their moral attachment to community but from the (coercive) authority that stems from their attachment to the formal criminal justice system.

The Involvement of Extended Community Members

There is a final sense in which certain forms of mediation appeal to 'community'. That is through the involvement of wider community members in the disputing process, not as mediators, but as 'secondary' parties to the dispute, incorporated by way of their 'communal' connection to the primary disputants. This wider involvement of community members in the disputing process, while recognized by legal anthropologists as a fundamental element in many pre-industrial societies (Llewellyn and Hoebel 1941; Danzig 1973; Snyder 1981), has only recently been revived in advanced capitalist societies. To some extent, neighbourhood mediation is capable of incorporating wider community members at a local level. For instance, one case dealt with by the Northolt Community Mediation Service involved disputes between a number of local residents on a particular street concerning noise and nuisances. Rather than deal with the specific case as a discrete incident between two parties, the co-ordinator and mediators sought to open it up as part of a wider, ongoing series of disputes. Consequently, whole families were invited to the mediation session, for which the mediators had to find a large enough room and lay on a crèche! The wider community as parties to the dispute were thus involved in the resolution process, were able to 'have their say' and be a part of the agreed settlement.

However, more dramatic developments have occurred in New Zealand and Australia where Family Group Conferences (FGCs)— or community conferences as the Australians prefer to call it—have taken off in recent years (see Alder and Wundersitz 1994; Braithwaite and Mugford 1994; Strang 1995; Hudson *et al.* 1996). 'Community' in this context has a different place and meaning from that in traditional victim/offender mediation. Based upon Maori traditional practices FGCs have become a part of the established juvenile justice system since 1989 in New Zealand, where either they take direct referrals from relevant agencies or act as a form of diversion from the court process. The New Zealand model of FGCs entails a meeting at a time and place chosen by the family of the offender. It is attended by the young person, his/her wider family, persons who may be key supports in the offender's life, the police, the victims and his/her family and supporters, and the youth advocate (young person's lawyer) where one has been appointed. It is arranged by the Youth Justice co-ordinator who acts as facilitator and mediator, although he/she can invite others to act as facilitator, especially if this is culturally important (see Morris *et al.* 1993). Somewhat different models exist in different states in Australia (see Hudson *et al.* 1996) and separate yet related developments have occurred in Canada under the label of 'sentencing circles' (LaPrairie 1995). A common aim is to draw extended family and community members into the process of finding resolutions and redress to crimes. The idea is to assemble actors with the closest relations and social interdependencies to the principal disputants, most notably with a view to bringing together those people with the best chance of persuading the offender of the irresponsibility of a criminal act (Braithwaite and Mugford 1994: 142). FGCs and community conferences have received a favourable reception in Britain amongst some senior criminal justice practitioners (see Burnside and Baker 1994; Pollard 1996) and recently a number of initial experiments have been established, for example, through Bristol Mediation (see Mediation UK 1995: 8–9) and through the establishment of a NACRO working party.

This is not the place to consider the implications of FGCs and community conferences for crime prevention, nor the strategies of reintegrative shaming with which they are associated (see Crawford forthcoming); here I want only to examine the particular concept of 'community' that they embody. This conceptualization of 'community' goes beyond locality and embraces a multiplicity of groups and networks to which, it is believed, we all belong (Strang 1995: 16). It does not rely upon a fixed assumption of where a 'community' will be found. Rather, it develops upon the notion of 'communities of care'—the networks of obligation and respect between the individual and everyone who cares about him or her the most—which are not bounded by geography (Braithwaite and Daly 1995: 195). In this, it marks a significant development in the understanding of contemporary communities. These 'communities of care', it is argued, are more relevant to contemporary modern living in urban societies. They encompass an expanded notion of 'community' which, in part, is a subjective one, in that the ascription to community membership or social identity is personal and not necessarily one which carries any fixed or eternal attributes of membership. In other words, 'communities of care' do not carry connotations of coerced or constrained membership. This is one of their appeals.

Community conferences and FGCs, it is argued, go beyond some of the limitations of traditional victim/offender mediation through their involvement of wider community participants with whom the parties have a 'relationship of genuine care'. First, they open up what can otherwise be a private process (Braithwaite and Daly 1994: 206–7). Secondly, in doing so, they can limit the power which mediation accords to professional mediators. Thus, both the power of mediators is curbed, and the process is open to greater public scrutiny. Thirdly, they confirm accountability upon those citizens who have concern for victims and offenders. 'In contrast to mediation, conferences are designed to encourage community dialogue' (Braithwaite and Daly 1994: 207). Finally, they address the potential unequal bargaining power of the parties, by incorporating extended members.

Communities and Communitarianism

The understanding of 'community' in FGCs and community conferences explicitly draws upon communitarian literature and the conception of 'community' therein. At this stage it is worth considering briefly the tenets of communitarianism, particularly as expounded by its leading advocate Amitai Etzioni (1993; 1995; 1996, see Crawford 1996a). In doing so, I am not suggesting that all proponents of FGCs and community conferences accept all the elements of such a vision of communitarianism, which is itself the subject of debate (Waltzer 1990; Bell 1993; 1995), but rather that as a dominant representation of communitarianism, that vision exposes and highlights some of the salient issues and problems implicit in the conceptualization of 'community' to which it appeals. It also allows a consideration of a version of communitarianism which has found a favourable reception in many influential quarters of policy making, particularly within the British Labour Party.[1]

[1] In Britain the Demos political think tank has done much to promote communitarian philosophy and the work of Amitai Etzioni in particular. More recently

Crime, as a compelling symbol of lost community, has a particularly salient place in communitarianism. The doubling of recorded crimes in the UK in the years between 1979 and 1990, and the dramatic rise in crime in the USA in the 1980s has been seen as symbolic of the erosion of traditional communities and the social cohesion that they are said to sustain. The perceived decline of a 'sense of community' and the fracturing of actual communal institutions in the late twentieth century, are associated in the minds of communitarians with a crisis of social regulation. Other expressions of this crisis of modernity are to be found in separation, divorce, privacy, political apathy, untamed consumerism, and narcissism (Lasch 1980). 'Community' aspires to be the exact opposite of fragmentation, 'the home of coherence, connection, and narrative capacity' (Waltzer 1990: 9). Hence, the rallying cry of the communitarian movement is 'the community is itself a good—conceivably the most important good' (Waltzer 1983: 29).

The place and understanding of 'community' within communitarianism is premised upon the existence of a permanently tensed relation between individuals and the society of which they are members. This tensed relation between 'centripetal forces' of 'community' and the 'centrifugal forces' of autonomy, expresses itself in three elements which lie at the heart of what Etzioni (1995; 1996) prefers to call 'responsive communitarianism'. The first element is the understanding of the self as 'socially situated'. Individuals, it is argued, are members of one another, they are ontologically embedded in a social existence (Walzer 1990). Even an individual's own liberty is socially situated. Braithwaite, for example, prefers to refer to liberty as 'dominion' in order to differentiate it from liberal notions of autonomy. Whereas the liberal conception of liberty is the freedom of an isolated, atomistic individual, the communitarian notion of liberty is 'the freedom of a social world' (Braithwaite 1995: 279). Thus we gain our initial moral commitments from the communities into which we are born and which, over time, are reinforced by other forms of community membership: 'Communities speak to us in moral voices. They lay claims on their members. Indeed, they are the most important sustaining source of moral voices other than the inner self' (Etzioni 1993: 31). The second

Demos has entered the crime policy debate in Britain elaborating its own brand of communitarianism with the publication of a pamphlet entitled 'The Self Policing Society' (Leadbeater 1996).

element, therefore, is that as individuals owe their values to, and are dependent upon, their social situation. Consequently, a degree of commitment to the communal good has a moral standing. The final tenet of Etzioni's communitarianism is that it is neither possible, desirable nor morally justifiable to absorb fully members' identities, energies, and commitments into the social realm. This assertion acts as a corrective to the excesses of 'community'.

Hence, the communitarian agenda asserts the need to restore communities and their moral voices (Selznick 1995). This requires a greater emphasis upon individual's responsibilities towards, rather than rights over, their communities (Etzioni 1993). The reinvigoration of 'community' facilitates social control mechanisms such as FGCs which are more conducive to, and more effective when drawing upon, communitarian cultures (Braithwaite 1989b: 100). Strong communities can speak to us in moral voices. They allow the policing *by* communities rather than the policing *of* communities (Strang 1995: 217). There is a virtuous circularity in this argument, whereby we gain our moral sense from the communities to which we belong, subsequently, investing in those communities is a moral act which, in turn, strengthens the bonds through which communities speak to us. Thus, 'community' is an end in itself, as it is the product of our moral voices, and a means to an end, in that our moral values are attainable because of the social pressures which 'community' brings to bear on its members.

The relationship between 'centripetal' and 'centrifugal' forces— order and autonomy; responsibilities and rights—lies at the heart of communitarianism. Crucially, it is not a zero sum relationship, whereby more of one results in less of the other, nor is it a mutually enhancing one. Rather it is seen as a relationship of 'inverting symbiosis', whereby 'the two forces are mutually enhancing up to a point, and then they can turn antagonistic' (Etzioni 1996: 7). Importantly, this recognizes the issue, too often missed by those politicians who have taken up the communitarian baton, that the erosion of individual rights is *neither* the premise nor prerequisite for the establishment of greater social order or mutual interdependency. However, the point at which both the common good and the individual members' autonomy turn from being mutually enhancing to antagonistic is left largely unexplained (Etzioni 1996: 9). We are given little by way of criteria upon which to assess or recognize such movements, beyond extreme cases of societal anarchy or totalitarianism. However, one factor which is deemed to limit the potentially oppressive power of communities is our ability to belong to multiple communities in different fields of social life, as residents and family members, employees, members of religious, political or cultural groups, and so on. One form of community membership acts to limit the potentially negative impact of others.

However, within communitarianism, and Etzioni's version in particular, there is a slippage between a sociological and ideological understanding of 'community': between what 'community' *is* and what it *ought* to be: the empirical authenticity of 'community' as distinct from its normative appeal (Frazer and Lacey 1993: 154). This is evident in the argument that 'community' is inherently volitional, comprising a collection of similar people who have voluntarily chosen to be together on the basis of some shared commonality. If this is so, then what exactly is that community's normative suasion and moral value? How much compliance and discipline can a 'community' command if individuals are free to move, like butterflies, from one to the next? Communities, in order to hold some normative sway over their members, must, to some degree, be able to exact a measure of compliance, by means of regulation, sanction, and/or coercion. Further, this returns us to the problematic assumption, noted earlier, that 'community' can merely exist inside peoples' heads. The notion of identity inscribed within Braithwaite's 'communities of care', is a subjective one, in that the ascription to community membership is personal and not necessarily one which carries any fixed or external attributes of membership. In other words, 'communities of care' do not carry connotations of coerced or constrained membership because membership is freely chosen by the subject. Far from constituting 'communities of fate', it is argued, these are chosen with pride. This, naturally, is one of the appeals of the notion of identity and yet it is also its weakness. For as 'community' is subjectively ascribed, there is little by way of external criteria through which the nature of community can be assessed. Community here begins to look more like bilateral relations of trust than 'semi-autonomous social fields' which have rule making capacities, and the means to induce compliance, but which are simultaneously set in a larger social matrix which can, and often does, affect and invade it (Moore 1973: 720). Moreover, if 'community' is a free-floating social identity, internally ascribed and easily escaped, as Braithwaite and communitarians more generally imply, then, like dominant rhetoric, it fails to accord to 'community' any significant structural or institutional characteristics around which the suasive capacity of communities is constructed and maintained. In addition, the ideal of unrestricted entry to, and exit from communities needs to confront the empirical reality of exclusion, differential power relations and coercion with communities (I return to consider the implications of these insights for an understanding of community in Chapter 9).

This leads us into a circular argument whereby the fact that people are able to choose voluntarily to belong to one community or the next, gives rise to the absence of coercion, and the absence of coercion means that people are free to choose whether to engage in certain activities, hold certain views or even whether to continue to be a community member. Empirically, such a claim is dubious as we have seen. For example, certain people in geographic communities do not have the freedom of mobility. Voluntariness suggests alternative choices. If one inhabits a 'community' to which exit is not easily available, there may be no alternative to the dominant moral voices and their suasive capacity. Communitarians, like Etzioni, seem to want it both ways. The present weakness of 'community' is simultaneously seen as 'the problem', the cause of most contemporary social ills, and its saving grace, in that people are assumed to be able to switch and move freely between communities if they disagree with their practices or values, and/or remain within a 'community', and dissent from the dominant moral voices therein. After all, the ability of a 'community' to bring social pressures to bear upon its members, its suasive capacity, is its enduring appeal. However, it simultaneously constitutes its fear.

Communitariansim raises important questions about the nature of inter (as well as intra) community relations. These, however, it fails sufficiently to address. The salient issues can be analysed at two levels. The first is at an horizontal level which involves the nature of the relations between one 'community' and the next. Here, communities have potentially divergent values and conflicting interests. They may be antagonistic or in competition for scarce economic resources and political power. Consequently, the absence of a theory of power and political economy, as in much communitarianism, is particularly problematic in its failure to make sense of, and hence mitigate, differential power relations. Consequently, Etzioni's brand of communitarianism disconnects a concern for community (dis)approval from a concern with political and economic inequality both of which, Braithwaite rightly argues, should be at the core of a progressive criminology (1995: 279).

The second level of analysis is a vertical one, concerning the nature of the inter-relationships between different hierarchical formations, between communities and the wider 'community of communities', the nation state. Here, the concern is with how specific communities, with their own moral codes, fit within an overarching set of institutions. From an economic perspective this questions the extent of state interventionism on behalf of communities. From a political perspective it problematizes the nature of the state's regulation (and 'policing') of given communities in the name of the collective national (or even international) cultural identity. It interrogates the extent to which the state adheres to either a 'multiculturalist' or 'universalist' approach to communities' cultural and moral differences.

In all these regards, communitarian conceptions of 'community' pose more questions than they answer. These questions and the implications to which they give rise, however, will constitute the central recurring themes in the ensuing chapters.

Conclusions

Within the diverse appeals to 'community' in criminal justice discourse and practice, as we have seen, there is considerable conceptual obfuscation, not least in what 'community' is taken to mean. A quarter of a century ago Bell and Newby (1971) declared there to be no satisfactory definition of what 'community' is. This would appear to be as valid today. They identified over ninety definitions of 'community', in which 'the one common element in them all was man (sic)!' (1971: 15). In this chapter, I have not sought to define comprehensively the term 'community', rather, I have outlined a number of competing contemporary conceptualizations of 'community' in criminal justice discourse and practice. From this review, what becomes clear is that 'community' acts as a genial host which is accompanied by layered ideological assumptions and presuppositions all seeking to serve ulterior political aims, strategies, and interests. This is not to suggest that actual communities always conform to these assumptions, nor is it to suggest that community participation in institutions of crime control does not contribute to effective crime prevention or a sense of justice. It is, rather, to suggest that certain implications flow from the prevailing ideological terrains out of which appeals to 'community' continue to bloom and flourish, as well as the governmental strategies through which they are given voice. The consideration of these implications is the primary focus of the next three chapters.

As we have seen, 'community' in policy discourse is conceptualized as both something in need of regeneration and also that which constitutes the existing moral fibre of society. 'Community' is viewed as a social and moral good in itself, as well as a means of achieving certain policy goals: the reinvigoration of 'moral authority'; citizen empowerment; the relegitimation of public institutions; the transfer of responsibilities from the state to individuals and groups for their own security; and as a source of resources to be tapped and exploited. In the ensuing confusion between means and ends, 'community' is largely cleansed of any pernicious or crimogenic connotations. The need to restore a 'sense of community' around issues of crime and its control, therefore, implies an assumption that high crime areas lack sufficient 'community'. The dilemma that policy discourse has struck is that, on the one hand, the answer to the question: how to prevent crime? is, through the regeneration of 'community', whilst on the other hand, the answer to the question: how to regenerate community? is, the prevention of crime. The problem in practice, therefore, is how to break *into* this virtuous circle of 'community', when at the same time its absence is perceived to be the source of the problem. If 'community' is in need of regeneration, it is questionable whether the arrival of intermediaries—be they crime prevention partnerships, mediation schemes or FGCs—in the current ideological climate, will have the sufficient legitimacy or resources to empower community self-responsibility. Here, the empirical weakness of 'community' collides with its normative appeal.

This goes to the crux of issues of community representation and participation, which this chapter has sought to consider. The research evidence raises serious questions about the representativeness of community representation as incorporated into new intermediary, partnership structures. The failure of crime prevention schemes to address, meaningfully, issues of community representation (both symbolic and real), therefore, is especially problematic. The 'ideology of unity' which underlies appeals to 'community' and yet which confronts a background reality of social conflict and diversity, presents dilemmas with regard to the exclusion of certain interests and the nature of subsequent participation. Intra-community relations need to acknowledge dissent and negotiate the conditions under which mutual co-operation and respect can begin to be constructed. In order to establish and maintain nuanced forms of legitimacy, 'community' initiatives need to spell out clearly how they come to know what that 'community' wants by way of order, its needs, and its sense of justice. Without this, legitimacy remains precarious.

In addition, the research has exposed tensions between 'community' and 'voluntariness'—in the sense of volunteers as people and in the sense of an individual's own capacity for self-volition and agency—which are problematic and also a constraint upon the actualization of strategies of community crime control. The weakness of community action is that it lacks authoritative means to mobilize resources above and beyond that which can be procured on a voluntary basis. More often than not, this has led to an understanding of 'community' as a 'sense', inside people's heads. This 'sense', it is believed needs to be implanted in the appropriate populations resulting in a desired shift from a 'concern with self' to a 'concern with others', or to use Etzioni's language, from 'I' to 'We', 'rights to responsibilities' (1993: 26–7). And yet, exactly how this crucial step is to be taken without infringing upon, or interfering with, the sacred cow of 'voluntarism' remains a vexed issue. Moreover, such an approach tends to see 'community' as a set of attitudes rather than institutions and structures which need to be constructed and maintained in order to enhance members' capacity for self-empowerment. In other words, the nature of 'voluntarism' and the conditions under which it can be realized are rarely confronted. 'Collective voluntarism', therefore, often translates into a means of governing individuals through 'imagined' communities.

Finally, against the background of increasing social fragmentation and popular disenchantment with public institutions, 'community' appears to offer an attractive means of (re)creating cohesion across a fragmented society. However, the tendency of 'crime' as a category to bifurcate the 'normal' (law-abiding individual) from the 'pathological' (criminal) has serious implications for the formation of community boundaries, around distinctions between 'insiders' and 'outsiders', as well as the nature and practice of actual community involvement. A prevailing concern, therefore, is that, through the incorporation of vocal and powerful interests, minority and dissenting voices may become trampled under the hooves of a community's sense of 'moral order'.

6

Fragmentation of the State?

Since the eighteenth century, the state has come to be seen as the central institution of politics. It became the effective—although not exclusive—field of political action with regard to most sectors of social life. The capitalist nation state was a pre-eminent 'power-container' which 'ensured much greater social integration across time-space than had previously been possible' (Giddens 1994: 92). Most notably, this came to be epitomized through the nation state's monopoly of public power and law. Policing and crime control represent pre-eminent and central symbols of state sovereignty. However, as we saw in Chapter 3, the expansion of private security, the emergence of strategies of 'government at a distance', and the new governance of risk and protection have presented considerable new challenges to the state's authority and capacity for governing. They have also fractured any notion of a real state monopoly of effective power. Many of the trends, outlined in Chapter 3 and illustrated in the subsequent Chapters, draw upon an explicit, or at least an implicit, critique of the established bureaucratic state apparatuses. They are, therefore, in many senses 'anti-statist'. Simultaneously, considerable new challenges have presented themselves from above and beyond, as well as below and within, the territories of the nation state. The development of supra-national—political, legal, and economic—institutions has questioned state sovereignty within its own borders. Even in the fields of criminal justice and crime control, often seen as the last bastions and central symbols of state sovereignty, supra-national institutions have problematized the state's capacity for monopolistic control (Walker 1993; Sheptycki 1995; Anderson *et al.* 1995).

As sociological commentators have noted, these processes of 'globalization' and 'localization' are not necessarily antagonistic but often are interconnected through pressures towards social and system integration. This, Gidden (1984) refers to as, 'time-space distanciation', whereby social systems are stretched across time and space. The 'disembedding' nature of the global economy, through 'new circuits of global capital' (Lash and Urry 1994: 1), connects with a sense of local contextuality for members of society in their routinized day-to-day activities. The importance of 'locale'[1]—or what Taylor *et al.* have more recently described as the local 'structure of feeling' (1996: 5–12)—remains an essential part of how ordinary people make sense of the world.

And yet, paradoxically, as many commentators have argued, these dual developments of 'localization' and 'globalization' have made the state neither redundant nor ineffective. The state remains a fundamental 'power-container'. Giddens has insisted that 'the ever increasing abundance of global connections ... should not be regarded as intrinsically diminishing the sovereignty' of states, but rather seen as 'in substantial part the chief condition of the world-wide extension of the nation-state system in current times' (1985: 5; see also Hirst and Thompson 1995). Consequently, the central question that this chapter will seek to address is to what extent the current shifts and developments are fragmenting or undermining the power of the state. Whilst acknowledging the importance of 'globalization'—a subject worthy of in-depth consideration in its own right—I wish to reflect on the nature of social relations and challenges to the nation state from within its own boundaries, as represented through appeals to 'prevention', 'community', and 'partnerships' as well as the institutions to which they give rise.

In Chapters 4 and 5 we saw, illustrated through the empirical research findings, the nature of interactions in and around 'community partnerships', and analogous administrative arrangements. We noted the importance of differential power relations, especially as embodied in the social processes of exclusion from, and incorporation within, these emerging intermediary structures. We began to sketch out and identify some of the specific strategies to which dominant power relations have given rise and their potential implications. This chapter will attempt to take this analysis further and engage with key theoretical debates concerning the location of social power—with particular regard to the formation and implementation of local crime control policy—and the manner in which it has been transformed by recent developments. The chapter, therefore, will seek to answer the following related questions: who is setting and

---

[1] Giddens defines 'locale' as a 'physical region involved as part of the setting of interaction, having definite boundaries which help to concentrate interaction in one way or another' (1984: 375).

determining policy agendas? and who is actually steering the policy process? I will address these questions at two distinct analytical levels. First, at an hierarchical level, I will examine relations between the central state and local intermediary bodies. Secondly, I will go on to consider the implications of the research findings for the nature of relations at the local level, within and between the local state, interest groups, and associations within the new policy partnerships. In particular, I will examine the extent to which the private business sector has become involved in shaping the policy process. Finally, I will examine broadly some of the possible implications of the earlier insights for the form and substance of the policies themselves. In other words, are changes in the hands controlling policy significantly affecting the content of crime control and 'public' policy outcomes and practice?

'Governing at a Distance': The Role and Capacity of the Central State

The current crisis of crime control would seem to expose the modern nation state's real incapacity to maintain one of its principal functions, the maintenance of public law and order. Despite the prolific and sustained reference to some form of 'crisis' within criminological literature (see Sparks 1994: 18–20, for a critique of the contemporary use of the term 'crisis' within criminology), there appears to be little interest within criminology for any sustained questioning of one of its most taken for granted assumptions: the direct connection between the state, law, and order. It is, therefore, to social and political theory to which we need to turn for assistance in making sense of the considerable expansion in the nature and range of organized groups and institutional forms at the interface between state, market, and civil society. Consequently, I will consider three important recent contributions to concerns about modern governance and understandings of the changing role of the state and the policy process: the 'policy networks', 'governmentality', and 'neo-corporatist' literature. These will be evaluated before the primary focus is shifted to the question whether modes of 'government at a distance' in crime control and prevention represent a weakening or strengthening of the capacity of the nation state.

Policy Networks

A fruitful source of theoretical analysis is to be found in the 'policy networks' literature. Rhodes (1981; 1991), a leading exponent of 'policy networks', has argued that recently the nature of central-local relations has been transformed. Given the complexity and specialized nature of policy making, it has become fragmented and disaggregated into discrete sectors. Here, 'policy networks' have emerged which bring together a 'cluster or complex of organisations connected to each other by resource dependencies and distinguished from other clusters or complexes by breaks in the structure of resource dependencies' (Benson 1982: 148). Marsh and Rhodes (1992b) distinguish between subsets of policy networks: 'policy communities' and 'issue networks'. These typologies constitute end points along a continuum. They are employed as descriptions of key characteristics of groups and organizations which coalesce around the policy making process at the sub-central government level (Rhodes 1991). 'Policy communities' are networks in an economic or professional sector which are characterized by stability of relationships, continuity of highly restricted membership, vertical interdependence, and a considerable degree of integration and insulation from other networks (Marsh and Rhodes 1992b: 251). Further, members are seen to share basic values, they all have access to resources and there is generally a balance of power amongst members. 'Issue networks', by contrast, are primarily involved only in policy consultation, they are characterized by a large number of participants with a limited degree of interdependence, access fluctuates significantly and contacts shift in frequency and intensity. Here, a measure of agreement exists, but conflict is ever-present and power relations are unequal, reflecting unequal resources and access (Marsh and Rhodes 1992b: 251).

These concepts, or more properly 'metaphors' (Dowding 1995), are useful in analysing 'partnerships' in criminal justice fields. They are 'both encompassing and discriminating in describing the policy process' (Atkinson and Coleman 1992: 156). They are 'encompassing' in that they refer to a variety of actors and relationships in the policy process beyond the bureaucratic state apparatuses, and 'discriminating' in that they suggest different types of networks in different fields and with divergent, interactive relations. They see the relationship between the state and civil society as 'richly varied and deny that there is any advantage in working towards a single model' (Atkinson and Coleman 1992: 156). In so doing, the 'policy network' literature identifies a central problem of government as being how to steer disaggregated structures of interdependent organizations (Marsh and Rhodes 1992b: 266). It highlights the kinds of issues which we have seen in Chapters 4 and 5 to be pertinent in the analysis of relations within community partnerships in the field of crime prevention. Most notably questions of: how inclusive/exclusive? how internally integrated? and who wields power? are at the forefront of distinctions between 'policy communities' and 'issue networks'. In this regard, the partnerships outlined in Chapters 4 and 5 approximate more closely to the 'issue networks' end of the continuum than the 'policy communities' end point, although, as the insights from the research suggest, these typologies may not be mutually exclusive as two tiers of networks (one more formal than the other) may emerge. This idea of typologies as 'non-exhaustive' is something that Marsh and Rhodes recognize (1992b: 255). A core and periphery or a formal (open) and informal (shadow) set of processes may form around the distinction between members with greater or less resources and influence.

Underlying a 'policy networks' approach is a concern with the ways in which interdependencies and processes of exchange can be maintained in stable relations. In this regard, policy making is viewed as negotiation within the 'rules of the game' (Rhodes 1981). The 'game-like quality of network management' (Rhodes 1995: 17) has led commentators to draw upon 'game theory' in order to identify and understand the choices of individuals and organizations (see Axelrod 1984; Hargreaves Heap et al. 1992). Commentators have used games like the 'Prisoners' Dilemma' to show a broader conception of self-interest, by which co-operation emerges out of mutual interests and behaviour on standards that no one individual or organization can determine alone.[2] Crucially, this has exposed the importance of *reciprocity* and *trust* to exchange relations in

[2] The Prisoners' Dilemma is a non co-operative game involving the interaction of two players in which the 'rules of the game' are such that the players are not able to make binding agreements with each other, but must act independently. The result is always mutual dissatisfaction. The game is designed to show that co-operation would be more beneficial to the parties. The provision of public goods and the conditions for participation in collective action, it is argued, are inescapably bound up with attempts to solve the Prisoners' Dilemma (Hargreaves Heap et al. 1992: 99 and 144–8).

networks. Trust operates in environments of contingency and complexity within modernity. Trust, it is argued, reduces complex realities far more quickly and economically than prediction, authority or bargaining (Powell 1991: 273). The importance of both trust and reciprocity were evident in the empirical research examples cited in Chapters 4 and 5. However, we also saw how inaccurate it is to characterize networks in terms of collaboration and co-operation alone. Conflict is as important an element of network relations as is concord.

The typologies advanced by Rhodes and Marsh also confront a number of difficulties when viewed in the light of the empirical research evidence cited so far. For example, they fail to separate off the cohesiveness of policy networks—their stability, integration, and exclusivity—from the question of dominant power relations. Consequently, 'policy communities', while being cohesive, simultaneously are characterized by an *equal* distribution of power and access to resources. There does not appear to be the possibility of 'policy communities' which are also structured by differential power relations.

Further, whilst the 'policy network' literature is useful in analysing internal relations of interactions within partnerships, it is less useful in terms of the analysis of external relations—such as how certain groups get to be included or how they relate to central state authority—which by definition will serve to construct, delimit, and license those internal relations. Given the fragmented and disaggregated nature of networks and policy communities, the policy network literature tends to reinforce an image of pluralism in relations with the state. There is a tendency to see a variety of organizations and interests as in open competition with each other for scarce resources. Rhodes and Marsh (1992), for example, suggest that the best way to describe the overall structure of policy domains is as 'élite interest group pluralism'. There is an associated tendency to disconnect policy networks from broader political institutions and discourses, which leaves 'a rather anaemic view of the state' (Atkinson and Coleman 1992: 164). It ignores the fact that fundamental assumptions about the nature of relations and their structure are derived from macro-political discourses and arrangements. The focus upon interaction across the state-civil society divide can serve to obscure the structural conditions and normative context under which those interactions occur. Hence, Rhodes's (1991) claim that network theory is a meso-level concept, neutral in relation to theories of the state runs the risk of falling into a 'floating eclecticism' (Jessop 1995: 318).

Further, there is insufficient interest within the policy network literature in dynamics of social and political change, a point which Rhodes and Marsh themselves recognize (1992: 15). This is not surprising given that 'policy communities' are seen, in part, as a barrier to change. The literature tends to be content with describing interaction rather than shifts and transformations within them, as well as those outside which may impact upon them. Most notably, for our purposes, the manner in which processes of inclusion and exclusion change over time and the nature of power relations, as well as their implications for policy, are crucial issues which need to be addressed. There is also the largely neglected question of how political ideas change and shape networks, an omission which is symptomatic of the lack of connection to broader macro-political discourses (Atkinson and Coleman 1992: 173). Nevertheless, the 'policy networks' literature has forced a reconsideration of the policy process and the role of formal state institutions therein.

Governmentality Thesis

The expansion of an 'intermediary' or 'hybrid' sphere which links and invades the public and the private spheres has led other commentators to begin to question the value of concepts like the state and civil society. Rose and Miller, for example, have argued:

> The language of political philosophy: state and civil society, freedom and constraint, sovereignty and democracy, public and private plays a key role in the organisation of modern political power. However, it cannot provide the intellectual tools for analysing the problematics of government at present. Unless we adopt different ways of thinking about the exercise of political power, we will find contemporary forms of rule hard to understand.
>
> (Rose and Miller 1992: 201)

The governmentality literature has added considerably to the study of the problematics of political power and government (Burchell *et al.* 1991; Stenson 1993; Rose 1994; 1996; Barry *et al.* 1996). In so doing, it also shares certain commonalities and concerns with the governance literature generally. It draws its frame of reference from

Foucault's (1991) understanding of 'governmentality' as the management of populations through technologies of power around a conceptual triangle of 'sovereignty', 'discipline', and 'government' (1991: 102). According to Foucault, since the eighteenth century we have seen the 'governmentalisation of the state'. And yet, paradoxically, it is the 'tactics of governmentality' which have allowed the state to survive, rather than the state itself having produced 'techniques of government'. Consequently, in order to understand 'government' in the era in which we live, there is perceived to be a need to refocus the frame of analysis away from the state towards 'governmentality' which is 'at once internal and external to the state' (Foucault 1991: 103).

Rose and Miller (1992), as leading exponents of this approach, have sought to begin to outline an agenda which breaks out of the philosophical opposition of state and civil society. Their concern is with the exercise of power beyond the state. They suggest that:

Political power is exercised today through a profusion of shifting alliances between diverse authorities in projects to govern a multitude of facets of economic activity, social life and individual conduct. Power is not so much a matter of imposing constraints upon citizens as of 'making up' citizens capable of bearing a kind of regulated freedom. Personal autonomy is not the antithesis of political power, but a key term in its exercise, the more so because most individuals are not merely the subjects of power but play a part in its operations.

(Rose and Miller 1992: 174)

Hence, power is constitutive of individuals and collectivities. Consequently, those working within this frame of reference have sought to explore the manner in which technologies of power and 'technologies of the self' produce forms of disciplinary 'normalization' (Donzelot 1979; 1991; Rose 1992; Miller and O'Leary 1994; Hunt and Wickman 1994). Rose and Miller (1992; Miller and Rose 1995) suggest some ways of analysing these moving elements of political power, at the heart of which lies a concern for the 'problematics of government'. They argue that government is connected to the 'activities of expertise', the role of which is not to construct an 'all-pervasive web of "social control"', but to enact 'assorted attempts at the calculated administration of diverse aspects of conduct through countless, often competing, local tactics of education, persuasion, inducement, management, incitement, motivation and encouragement' (Rose and Miller 1992: 175). They go on to show how problematics of government can be analysed through 'political rationalities'—the changing discursive fields within which the exercise of power is conceptualized—and in terms of their 'governmental technologies'—the strategies through which authorities seek to give effect to governmental ambitions—as well as their interdependencies, the articulation of which is said 'to enable us to begin to understand the multiple and delicate networks that connect the lives of individuals, groups and organisations to the aspirations of authorities' (Rose and Miller 1992: 175–6). The focus on technologies and rationalities of government is believed to be better suited to capture the dispersed nature of political power.

By their analysis, Rose and Miller have contributed significantly to contemporary conceptualizations of political developments occurring 'at arm's length from the state'. In so doing, they rightly problematize the overly neat distinctions between state and civil society which have structured political analysis for so long. In its place, they identify an important field of investigation which offers the opportunity of enabling us to analyse alliances and unities within regulation and authority in institutions both within and outside the state. Further, they draw to our attention the active part played by expertise and the dynamics of administration, as processes capable of generating their own logics of development. Finally, they also connect the exercise of power with specific political values, purposes, and ends. All of these, as we have seen, are central elements within the study of 'community partnerships' in the field of crime control and prevention.

However, there are a number of crucial difficulties in their approach. First, explicit in their rejection of 'sociological realism' (see Curtis 1995: 577–8), is a tendency in their analysis to ignore the lived experiences of material realities, the interactions, interpersonal behaviour and the meanings accorded to them by actors (O'Malley 1996: 312), so pertinent in the 'policy networks' literature. Their focus upon 'rationalities' and 'technologies' leads, at least implicitly, to an assumption as to the effectivity of regimes of authority. For example, they declare that since the eighteenth century 'those seeking to exercise power have sought to rationalise their authority, and these rationalities have a systematicity, a history and an effectivity: enabling the exercise of government and its critique' (Miller and Rose 1995: 591). And yet, one might ask the question, effectivity for whom? Are the governmental strategies effective in regulating those that authorities seek to govern? If so, the space for resistance, in reality, appears limited, whilst the governed are cast in the mould of 'cultural dupes'. Moreover, their approach appears to sideline fundamental questions of legitimacy. Rather, we need to ask: does the exercise of power command popular support? and what is the basis of power's authority? If, by contrast, the 'rationalizations' to which Rose and Miller refer are deemed to be effective only in themselves (in terms of their own frames of reference), then we might want to question any presumption of the smooth institutionalization of such strategies. Years of criminological research have shown that it is unwarranted to assume that implementation will necessarily proceed in a logical sequence (see Hope and Murphy 1983).

This brings us to a second obstacle in Rose and Miller's analysis. The political rationalities that they identify ('liberalism', 'welfarism', and 'neo-liberalism') are too all-encompassing. Their 'systematicity' is overarching and accorded undue prominence. They yield an homology and coherence which, on closer examination, they do not deserve. Where in this framework of analysis is the space for contradiction and unintended consequences? Further, like Foucault before them, there is a tendency to over-rationalize power and its exercise. There is little place for the presence of non-rational and irrational forces and values, particularly problematic in any analysis of criminal justice. Further, through the notion of political power circulating in 'projects to govern', they imply elements of intention and calculation which are not, by necessity, always evident in the exercise of power. By contrast, any analysis of governmental strategies must be sensitive to the complexities and nuances of the policy formation and implementation processes. It must allow for political and ideological contradictions, the gulf between rhetorics and practices, potentially countervailing institutional strategies, unintended consequences, as well as the knowledgeability of 'lay publics' and their capacity to resist. Conflicts and collisions between governmental strategies and reality are conceived primarily in terms of the 'failure' of programmes. However, as O'Malley notes:

To think in terms of failure puts the emphasis on the status of the collision from the programmer's view point, and consequently reduces resistance to a negative externality. No space is created for a productive and incorporative relationship with resistance—such as would exist where rule and resistance form each other reflexively.

(1996: 311)

Thirdly, their focus upon 'language', to the exclusion of a 'realist' account of social behaviour and action, is problematic. 'Language', they declare, 'is not merely contemplative or justificatory, it is performative' (Rose and Miller 1992: 177). It is within the discursive field of language, 'that "the State" itself emerges as an historically variable linguistic device for conceptualising and articulating ways of ruling' (Rose and Miller 1992: 177). In over-privileging 'language', particularly in its textual form of official documentation and discourse (O'Malley 1996: 311), they fail sufficiently to acknowledge the significance of the dissonance between what people say they do, or will do, and what they actually do. Again, this is particularly troubling within the criminal justice context. There is a sense in which, within some of the governmentality literature, 'the rhetorical' and 'the real' are conflated and confused. Consequently, the space for human agency appears limited in the face of all-embracing discourses, technologies, and political rationalities (Curtis 1995: 581–5).

Finally, in an attempt to identify the importance of modes of 'government at a distance' we should not lose sight of the 'state' altogether. To argue that the state has no 'essential necessity or functionality' (Rose and Miller 1992: 176) is to overstate the problem. Whilst the state may have been over-prioritized and taken for granted within political theory, it remains a meaningful concept, even if of diminishing significance and in constant need of problematization. In fact, it is debatable whether Rose and Miller actually escape from the state/civil society dichotomy which they deride. Their continued reference to 'beyond the state' accords to the state an enduring conceptual utility, even in its absence.

Neo-Corporatism

The conceptual development of neo-corporatist theory shares much with the 'policy network' literature. It is important to stress, first, that neo-corporatism as a descriptive tool is distinct from the macro-level forms of tripartism of the 1970s, which brought together government, business, and trade union representatives. Secondly, the development of neo-corporatism is not necessarily incompatible with the rise of neo-liberal ideology (Cawson 1985; Harden 1988: 38–9). Neo-corporatism, at a meso-level, involves a blurring of the public and private spheres (Schmitter 1974; 1985). It highlights the dual processes whereby *private* access to *public* policy formation is facilitated, as is *public* access to *private* policy making and implementation. In so far as private interests are incorporated into the policy formation processes, they are granted a certain 'publicness'. Schmitter's early definition usefully sets out the conceptual contours of the term:

Corporatism can be defined as a system of interest representation in which the constituent units are organised into a limited number of singular, compulsory, noncompetitive, hierarchically ordered and functionally differentiated categories, recognised or licensed (if not created) by the state and granted a deliberate representational monopoly within their respective categories in exchange for observing certain controls on their selection of leaders and articulation of demands and supports.

(1974: 93–4)

The notion of 'local' neo-corporatism highlights the uneven, contested, and plural nature of power relations within local policy institutions. It describes the twofold process involving the representation of organized interests and the *control and regulation* of members via intermediary interest associations. Consequently, 'intermediation' embodies the fusion of policy formation and implementation in the relationship between groups and the state, as I have argued elsewhere:

Corporatism highlights an organisation's capacity both to represent its members' interests and to discipline and control them as part of a negotiated interaction with other groups. This interaction focuses attention on the nature of the relationship between organised interests and the state. This is understood, however, not as a relationship in which the state merely directs the interest associations, nor is it one in which state agencies are 'captured' by private interests. Rather, corporatism implies certain weaknesses as well as strengths within the state.

(Crawford 1994a: 502)

Consequently, it involves a 'centrifugal dynamic' (Cawson 1982: 41). Hence, as Cawson suggests, a central component of the corporatist research agenda comprises the uncovering of the 'rules, or logic, of collective action where exchanges take place across the threshold of public power' (1985: 7). In focusing on these 'osmotic processes' within and between organizations, the state, and the community, neo-corporatism—as a model of analysis—forces an interrogation of: the blurring of organizational boundaries; the manner in which inter-organizational relations are constitutive of, and constituted by, intra-organizational relations; the role of the state in the regulation of 'private interests'; power relations in and around corporatist structures; the process of interest group incorporation; the form of control over members' behaviour; the responsibility for the implementation processes and its legitimacy.

Importantly, neo-corporatist theory has identified tendencies towards 'social closure' (Cawson 1986) and 'monopolistic control' (Schmitter 1989) as dynamic processes. These give prominence to the importance of boundary changes and pressures exerted by those 'outside' pressing in—what Atkinson and Coleman refer to as 'excluded but attentive' publics (1992: 176)—as well as those 'inside' keeping others out. Hence, neo-corporatist theory injuncts an interrogation of the characteristics of the excluded and the structures of power which shape modes of exclusion as well as inclusion. In doing so, it adopts a more 'institutionalist' approach, in that it suggests that behaviour cannot be understood exclusively either in terms of the (rational) choices and preferences of individuals or by reference to the impositions and identities of organizations (Schmitter 1989: 61). As institutions, 'partnerships' occupy an intermediate position between two sets of autonomously constituted and resourceful actors from which they draw resources: individuals/communities and state authorities (Schmitter 1989: 62). They depend upon the former for membership and the latter for recognition. And yet, the analysis of intermediary institutions is reducible to neither. It cannot ignore the calculations, preferences, and routine actions of individuals any more than it can the discourses, strategies, and structures of powerful state and private organizations.

Streeck and Schmitter (1985) suggest that a fourth ideal type of 'associative order' needs to be added to the familiar trilogy of 'state', 'market', and 'community'. This allows a theoretical space for the emerging patterns of interaction between private interests and public authority. It permits an understanding of the 'amorphous complex of agencies with ill-defined boundaries performing a great variety of not very distinctive functions' (Schmitter 1985: 33), without rejecting wholly the established conceptual trilogy. Rather, it seeks to problematize and question—under pressures of social change—the inter-relations, fusions, and tensions between 'state', 'market', and 'community'. Neo-corporatist theory identifies 'private interest governments' as agencies of 'regulated self-regulation' (Streeck and Schmitter 1985) with devolved public responsibilities.

The state, hence, continues to occupy a pivotal place as a 'licensing' and 'steering' institution as well as a resource. Streeck and Schmitter see the state's role as an active one, both in facilitating and authorizing the institutional and administrative characteristics as well as systems of (self-)regulation of interest group associations (1985: 25–6).

Importantly, as with the governmentality literature, neo-corporatist theory both connects dynamics of development and change to external political ideologies, as well as to internal logics of corporatist institutions. In relation to the former, it sees policy outcomes in the light of the uneven and partial implementation of political programmes without reducing outcomes to them. In relation to the latter, it suggests the need to analyse the logics of 'membership' (processes of inclusion and exclusion—'representation'), 'influence' (power, participation, and control), and 'secrecy' (its association with democracy and accountability, which I examine in greater detail in Chapter 7). These logics may at times be antagonistic.

Corporatism has been criticized for being too rigid a metaphor for government-interest group relations (Rhodes 1985; Jessop 1990). In response, types of corporatism have been developed which emphasize tendencies within corporatist arrangements. For example, Crouch (1983) distinguishes between 'authoritarian corporatism' and 'liberal corporatism' as points on a continuum. The variables of which are: first, the nature of membership discipline and, secondly, the degree to which incorporated groups actually represent the interests of their members. This highlights tensions within corporatist administrative structures between the power of 'public' and 'private' interests whilst emphasizing their partial and unresolved nature. Consequently, at one end of the continuum stands 'authoritarian corporatism' which is all discipline and no representation, whilst at the other end is 'liberal corporatism' embodying greater representation and less discipline.

In terms of the variances of interaction within intermediatory bodies, neo-corporatist theory has much to learn from 'network theory', without losing sight of the distinctions and interconnections between the causes, defining conditions, and consequences of corporatist arrangements (Schmitter 1989). The more central role of the state within neo-corporatist theory, which simultaneously problematizes the notion of the state as an homogenous entity, poses difficulties as well as opportunities with regard to a macro theory of the state. As with the policy network literature, it is in continual danger of slipping into either liberal pluralism or an instrumentalist Marxism (Jessop 1990). Finally, there is a concern, which in part stems from its conceptual genesis, that neo-corporatist theory tends to over-prioritize formal policy arrangements at the expense of more informal and fluid processes. As we have seen, the process of incorporation itself may be multi-layered.

Synthesis

All three of the above bodies of theoretical literature, whilst partial in their own ways, can significantly help us make sense of the changing nature of social governance in the field of crime control as elsewhere. Their strengths and weaknesses lie in their emphases upon different aspects of the phenomena under enquiry. The 'policy networks' literature identifies the importance of specificity and the given nature of interactions within a particular policy sector. Therefore it warns us against reification and over-generalization. The 'governmentality' approach points to the importance of political and ideological programmes and the intersection of professional, 'expert' knowledge and 'technologies of power'. It cautions us to look deeper for 'hidden' relations, to the way in which knowledge informs power and constitutes subjectivities within regimes of control. It alerts us to the impact of new technologies and knowledge as constituting a field of power relations through which subjects are constructed as responsibilized, risk avoiding, and security conscious. In so doing, it seeks to connect modes of control with ideological programmes. Finally, neo-corporatist theory reaggregates the state as a central political institution and 'power-container'. In so doing, it addresses a concern that the previous two approaches may have thrown out the conceptual baby with the bath water of governance. It identifies the important space that new structures occupy, whilst focusing attention upon the ways in which they are constructed and constrained by external forces—the dynamics of social change— most notably, the way in which structures of power are shaped by forms of exclusion from political processes.

Collectively, these insights draw our attention, not to a return to pre-eighteenth century relations between state, market, and civil society, but rather, to a reordering of those relations as a result of which we are witnessing the emergence of new forms of 'government at a distance'. These extend and problematize existing institutions. They identify and highlight not only 'a new set of things to look at', but also the need for 'a new way of looking at things'. One central question, which all three approaches call into consideration, is the extent to which—under the shifts to which they accord significance—the state's capacity to govern is becoming stronger or weaker.

Weakening or Strengthening of the State?

Rhodes (1994) suggests that 'policy networks', new public management, and privatization programmes, together with pressures of 'globalization' and 'localization', reduce and erode the central state's capability, and identify its limitations to marshal and manage sectoral hierarchies. He argues that we are witnessing the 'hollowing out of the state' whereby:

fragmentation constrains the centre's administrative ability to co-ordinate and plan. Diminished accountability constrains the centre's ability to exercise political control. In sum, current trends erode the centre's capacity to steer the system—its capacity for governance.

(Rhodes 1994: 149)

Jessop (1993) connects this change in the form of the state—its 'hollowing out'—with a change in its scope of intervention. This emerging state form—which he refers to as a 'Schumpeterian workfare state' in order to distinguish it from a 'social welfare state'—he suggests, is in 'terminal decline' (1993: 17, 34). He goes on to outline the fundamentals of this transformation:

the hollow state metaphor is intended to indicate two trends: first, that the national state retains many of its headquarter functions—including the trappings of executive authority and national sovereignty as well as the discourses that sustain them; and, second, that its capacities to translate this authority and sovereignty into effective control are becoming limited by a complex displacement of powers. The resulting changes in the formal articulation and operational autonomy of national states have major repercussions on forms of representation, intervention, internal hierarchies, social bases, and state projects across all levels of state organisation.

(Jessop 1993: 22)

In the field of crime control many of these 'hollowing out' processes are less developed than in other spheres of social life. Consequently, they have received little criminological attention (although see Bottoms and Wiles 1995). However, in one recent review Cope *et al.* (1995) have argued against the conception of a 'hollow state', preferring the notion of a 'lean state'. They correctly point to the fact that the 'hollowing out' thesis fails to identify sufficiently counter-trends towards increasing central control that seek to enhance the policy making capacity of the state (Cope *et al.* 1995; Leishman *et al.* 1996).

In the criminal justice field, trends towards increased central control are undoubtedly evident. In Chapter 2 we saw the increasingly interventionist role of the Home Office over the past twenty years or so, most notably in the areas of policing and probation work. Similarly, in Chapter 3, we noted the expansion of government appointed 'quangos' and Next Step agencies which appear to have further strengthened central control. In addition, a multiplicity of new national structures and institutions have been established to co-ordinate criminal justice, such as the National Criminal Intelligence Service, the National Reporting Centre, the National Co-ordinator for the Regional Crime Squads, the Crime Prevention Agency, the National Crime Prevention Centre, and so on. Control by the Home Office over senior appointments has tightened significantly, the appointment of chief constables is a notable example (Reiner 1991; Wall 1994) and has been extended further by short-term contracts for senior personnel under the Police and Magistrates' Courts Act 1994. Moreover there has been an increasing use of national objective setting and standardization procedures, supported by inspecting and auditing mechanisms. National objective setting, for example, is a central element of the Police and Magistrates' Courts Act 1994, which requires local police authorities to establish a local plan for the police (in consultation with the chief constable) including key objectives laid down by the Home Secretary (Loveday 1995: 143). More generally, criminal justice institutions, in accordance with the logics of 'new public management', have been encouraged (some might say cajoled) by the Home Office to produce statements of organizational objectives and priorities. This has been augmented by standardization processes which often take the form of government charters and circulars, national codes and standards, performance indicators, and 'good practice' guidelines, all of which have proliferated. The effect and implementation of standardization and objective setting procedures have been enhanced by various monitoring, auditing, and inspecting procedures, such as the use of the Audit Commission, National Audit Office and Her Majesty's various Inspectorates (of Prisons, Probation,

Constabulary, and so on). These controls over national policy agendas are justified, frequently, in the name of 'universal consumer satisfaction'. They appeal over the heads of individual organizations directly to the 'customer' (Keat 1991a). And yet, through these processes the centre exerts considerable agenda setting and mobilizing powers, which influence the implementation process through the 'policing' and regulation of standardization and objectives.

Similarly, the devolution of budgets, at a time of financial stress and accompanied by the proliferation of accounting technologies, has not merely 'liberated' budget holders but has tied them into 'centres of calculation'. Budgetary devolution embodies a double-edged logic. It simultaneously constrains the use of professional discretion and heralds a loss of trust in welfare professionalism. As a consequence, as Miller and Rose note: 'Professional discretion is shackled not by attempts to claim jurisdiction over the content of expert judgement, but by encircling expert judgement within the discourse of budgetary calculation' (1991: 133).

Some criminological commentators have interpreted these and other centralizing processes as evidence not of a weaker state, but of a state which is expanding its capacity under a 'mask' of destructuring and decentralization (Gordon 1987; Jones 1993; Christie 1993). Jones, for instance, has argued that, despite a

powerful rhetoric of community participation and 'consumer responsiveness' the old hierarchy still operates within the same power structure 'behind a false front' . . . Central government has devolved some powers in order to maintain its dominance.

(1993: 188).

Certainly, the rhetoric in which the Police and Magistrates' Courts Act 1994 was swathed emphasized devolving powers and managerial freedom, despite the significant centralization that they entailed. Garland (1996) in a recent article appears to go some way towards endorsing Jones's 'false front' proposition, but correctly draws back in suggesting that whilst the state is experimenting with ways of 'governing at a distance', the success of such strategies should not be taken for granted:

The state does not diminish or merely become a nightwatchman. On the contrary it retains all its traditional functions—the state agencies have actually increased their size and output during the same period—and, in addition, takes on a new set of co-ordinating and activating roles, which in time develop into new structures of support, funding, information exchange or co-operation. Where it works—and one should not underestimate the difficulties involved in making it work—the responsibilization strategy leaves the centralized state machine more powerful than before, with an extended capacity for action and influence. At the same time, however, this strategy serves to erode the notion of the state as the public's representative and primary protector.

(1996: 454)

The 'more-powerful-extended-state' argument—rather like an inversion of the 'hollowed-out-weaker-state' perspective—appears to imply an overly unidirectional understanding of unfolding power relations. These are implicitly conceptualized as 'all or nothing' strategies, in which power is a zero sum game: put simply, increases in central state power are understood as resulting directly in decreases in local sites of power (and vice versa in the 'hollowed-out-weaker-state' perspective). However, there is a more complex displacement and restructuring of powers in process. Further, the 'expanding state' thesis embodies a number of other problems. First, it implies too rational an intention and too united a purpose on the part of the state. Secondly, it assumes a level of effectivity of government intention which is empirically dubious. Thirdly, it accords undue significance to the reading of legislation which is the traditional tool of central state authority but which, in many fields, is increasingly becoming supplanted by the role of 'policy' in all its guises. Legislation, in turn, is increasingly authorizing, licensing, and inspecting rather than directive. Fourthly, it ignores the blurring of the state/civil society dualism and the emergence of an additional associative or corporatist order. Fifthly, it disregards the fact that many recent developments have their origins at a considerable distance from the central state. For example, private policing and private zones of governance have not directly filled a vacuum left by the state, but rather have created their own spaces of governance (Shearing 1992). The dynamic for change lies not wholly within the state but, as the governmentality literature recognizes, on occasions originates far from it. Finally, the 'expanding state' thesis overlooks real processes of devolved powers (O'Malley and Palmer 1996), local institutional frameworks, and individual 'consumer' sovereignty, albeit given the differentiated ability of individuals to assert claims against the state which is premised upon their capacity to reproduce the attributes of the abstracted 'consumer' (Keat 1991b; Abercrombie 1991).

Osborne and Gaebler (1992) offer a somewhat different insight in response to the question, does a smaller, less interventionist state mean a weaker state? The answer they give is an emphatic 'no'. Using the analogy of a rowing boat, they suggest a need to separate the 'steering' activities of government from the 'rowing'. 'Steering', on the one hand, involves policy formation—leading and setting norms or agendas—as well as catalysing and facilitating change. 'Rowing', on the other hand, concerns policy implementation and service delivery, the 'doing' of things (1992: 34). Governments that 'steer' more, but 'do' less, are not weaker but stronger. 'After all those who steer the boat have far more power over its destination than those who row it' (1992: 32). This analogy acts as a useful way of making sense of the current 'responsibilization strategies' which accompany appeals to 'community', 'prevention', and 'partnerships'. As a metaphor for the intended direction of government policy it appears highly apt.

Cope *et al.* (1995) adapt this line of argument to the British criminal justice context, notably recent changes to policing, in which they identify both centralizing and decentralizing tendencies. As a consequence, they argue, we are seeing the emergence of a 'leaner state'. As important an insight as this is, it tends towards an over-intentional and functional understanding of change. Like Jessop's speculative account, which assumes that the resultant 'rearticulation of political capacities' somehow constitutes a more 'appropriate general state from' for the new order of things in a post-Fordist era (1993: 11–12), it is ultimately circular and unduly functional. Cope *et al.* seem to get carried away with the managerial rhetoric of 'hiving off' and 'down sizing' which it is said results in a 'rejuvenated', 'fitter and stronger', 'leaner and meaner' state, as if it had returned from a health farm or been force-fed with British Steel advertisements! They conflate intentionality with effectivity. Whilst Jessop's functionalism is economically reductionist, Cope *et al.*'s is politically reductionist. In their quest for functional utility, neither appears to allow sufficient space for *contradiction* or *unintended consequences*, both of which the more sophisticated sociological (and criminological) theorists continue to caution against ignoring (Hunt 1981; Cohen 1985; Garland 1990). As Giddens rightly warns, 'knowledge of social life transcends the intentions of those who apply it to transformative ends' (1990: 54).

Shearing (1996), aware of such dangers, differentiates two distinct processes of change. These he identifies as first, 'state rule at a distance' and, secondly, 'private government'. The former, he suggests, gives birth to 'a system of rule that uncouples the "steering" from the "rowing" of policing and locates the responsibility for "steering" with the state and "rowing" with citizens' (Shearing 1996: 85). These are state-initiated developments of 'rule at a distance'. What is privatized here is the business of policing. 'Private governments', by contrast, 'deploy rule at a distance strategies that allocate the "rowing" of governance, including policing, to others' (Shearing 1996: 86). Here, that which is privatized is both the business and direction of policing. What is important in Shearing's conceptual separation is its acknowledgement of the limitations as well as the strengths of state power in relation to this growing complex 'associative order' of governance. It is useful in identifying the locus of motivation and dynamic for change, either 'within' or 'outside' of the state. However, it fails sufficiently to grasp the fused and contradictory nature of developments across the state (public) and civil society (private) divide. It unduly accepts the separation of 'rowing' and 'steering' as both possible and/or desirable. Consequently, such a bifurcation lacks an adequate acknowledgement of, on the one hand, the state's role as an active one in facilitating, authorizing, and regulating systems of 'private government', and on the other hand, the impact of the process of incorporation of 'private' interests into partnerships in crime prevention and control. Through incorporation, simple lines of motivation are confused, along with the policy formation and implementation processes.

Osborne and Gaebler's (1992) metaphor is itself too rigid a description of the policy process. It oversimplifies complex and controversial relations between the actors. It fails to grasp, adequately, the fact that policy does not reach its desired targets in a simple 'cause and effect' manner. As Deakin and Walsh have reported in relation to the Health Service reforms, delivery systems once set up have begun to exhibit a tendency to develop their own dynamic (1996: 35–6). Moreover, in practice, it is becoming harder to distinguish those who are 'rowing' from those who are 'steering'. It is here that the concept of neo-corporatism is so useful in its identification of, first, the conflation and fusion of policy formation and implementation processes at the meso-level, and secondly, the nature of 'regulated self-regulation' which much 'private interest government' heralds in relations with macro-political institutions.

As we have seen, recent developments in crime control and policing involve both a decentering and recentering dialectic, and yet centralization and devolution are not mutually exclusive, but in many fields of criminal justice may be complementary processes (McLaughlin and Muncie 1994: 137). More importantly, as I have sought to show throughout, the trends are not merely *upward* (to the nation state or even supra-national state) or *downward* (to localities, communities, and consumers), but also *outward* into the new policy networks of 'partnerships' which are increasingly re-figuring relations between centre and periphery in the criminal justice complex. Fragmentation, therefore, has complex effects. There is no unidirectional tendency, but a plurality of tendencies. The central state's capacity in some spheres of operation is being diminished, in others it is being intensified, and in others it is being refashioned. Strategies and institutions of 'regulated self-regulation' and 'private interest government' do not fit neatly into traditional hierarchical relations but rather reconstitute them.

Consequently, as Garland argues, state sovereignty over crime is simultaneously denied—as being 'beyond the state'—and symbolic-ally reasserted—through periodic episodes of hysterical and populist denials of the state's limitations (1996: 462). Limitations of tradi-tional criminal justice, i.e. police and punishment, are recognized in certain instances only to be discounted or ignored in others:

[A]lthough this contradiction is sometimes rationalized as a 'policy of bifurcation' [as in the 1991 Criminal Justice Act], its real routes lie in the political *ambivalence* which results from a state confronted by its own limitations.

(Garland 1996: 462; emphasis in original)

This dualistic denial and recognition produce volatile shifts in the state's presentation of its own capacity for effective action in crime control.

Who's Steering at the Local Level?

Within the local 'policy communities', the above issues beg the crucial question: which interests are dominant at the local level? The answer is neither straightforward nor uncontested. As we saw in Chapters 4 and 5, the research findings highlight a number of general issues concerning relations *within* the 'policy communities' of inter-agency crime prevention. There are clear structural power differentials between organizations and groups, which impact upon and influence policy outcomes. This occurs, first, through the processes of inclusion into, and by definition exclusion from, decision making processes. Partnerships create 'privileged oligarchies' (Marsh and Rhodes 1992: 265). They involve an element of 'social closure', although this is neither rigid nor complete. These new forms of administration, therefore, favour established interests which are already significantly powerful enough to be included and to participate within the processes of policy formation and implementation. They preserve and extend the power of 'local élites', with privileged access to decision making processes. Secondly, the differential power relations construct and constrain the nature of interactions and participation within partnerships. They structure the relative ability of organizations and groups to define policy and to determine what constitutes 'appropriate' crime prevention. The existence of layers of (in)formal relations within partnerships and the tendency to avoid conflict, which we noted earlier, only serve to reinforce power differentials and associated processes of exclusion. Despite the apparent critique of 'expertise' implicit in appeals to 'community' and 'partnerships', it remains a fundamental element in the exercise of power at the local level. Whilst the knowledge relationship would appear to have been transformed in the rhetorics of 'partnership'—which privileges the importance of shared, holistic, and lay knowledge—the reality remains heavily reliant upon expert knowledge which marginalizes any significant community input or control. Rather than the end of professional expertise, 'partnerships' reconstitute a new model of professionalism.

Private Sector Involvement

One topic which has not been considered thus far is the potential impact of private sector involvement upon the steering of policy at the local level. The private sector, as well as being seen as a part of the problem given the perceived unwillingness of many within business to acknowledge their responsibility for the prevention of crime, is also envisaged as part of the solution, as a key component of 'community partnerships'. In the government's handbook, entitled 'Practical Ways to Crack Crime', it declared:

Crime prevention is as crucial in the workplace as it is in the home or neighbourhood. Reducing crime is as much a part of good management as prompt delivery, good staff relations and other accepted management functions . . . Crime outside the workplace, in the community, can affect business too . . . Companies can play a big part in local crime prevention projects. By doing so they will improve the quality of life for their employees and clients alike. They will also nurture goodwill and enhance their prestige in the local community.

(Home Office 1991: 37–8)

The 'responsibilization' of the business community has been a constituent part of government strategy. To this end, the government has encouraged the establishment of various 'Business Watch' schemes, as well as crime prevention panels and Crime Concern, which have sought to provoke and facilitate private involvement.

An important element of the ideology of 'new public management' has been not only to introduce private sector ideas and methods of working into the organization and delivery of public services, but also to introduce private sector finances into the funding of crime prevention and business people into policy making roles. Hence, a central component of the Police and Magistrates' Courts Act 1994 sought to incorporate people with private sector backgrounds into local police authorities (Loveday 1995). The underlying idea is that people with private sector experience will bring with them a more businesslike approach to the problem of crime. I will consider the impact of the wider ideological 'marketization' and 'commodification' of crime prevention which this heralds in Chapter 8, but for the moment I want to consider the specific and direct involvement of private sector funding and the incorporation of business people within crime prevention initiatives with reference to the research findings.

As we saw in Chapter 5, the notion of 'community as a resource', which underlies much dominant crime prevention thinking, reaffirms a self-financing philosophy which relies heavily upon the inherent capacities of communities and/or their ability to tap the private sector for support. The consequent involvement of the private sector has had substantial implications for the types of interventions prioritized by schemes. Corporate sponsors tend to prefer one-off short-term contributions which are easily quantifiable and which have tangible outcomes. They are less willing to contribute to core funding, the impact of which may be less easily measurable. Further, expenditure on capital projects is more often forthcoming from businesses than usual operating costs, with the practical result that resources from the private sector are more likely to take the form of investment in technological hardware rather than investment in people.[3]

In addition, the process of harnessing private sector contributions can be very time consuming, whilst over-reliance upon businesses as a major source of resources can be counterproductive. For example, the Tenmouth Anti-Burglary Initiative was continually delayed and eventually redefined largely as a result of operating on a 'shoe-string' budget which expected major material resources from the private sector. These were either not forthcoming or, when they were, actually added to the time delays. The project also experienced the withdrawal of commitments from the private sector which undermined much of the work that had been done. The catalogue of difficulties confronted by the project illustrates the crucial role of funds for the implementation of community crime prevention strategies and highlights some of the problems associated with a self-financing philosophy. Further, it illustrates that the level and continuation of commitment by the private sector in crime prevention funding is subject to fluctuations in the local economy and may not be conducive to long-term strategic approaches. Durability, as the Morgan working group noted, requires established resources (1991: 23). It concluded that, 'excess reliance should not be placed on sponsorship' (Morgan 1991: 19).

The Northley project co-ordinator, for example, confessed:

by far and away the hardest part of the job is trying to get money out of the business community. It's very time consuming and often for very little or no reward. For example, I gave a lunch time presentation and display to a group of business people and they all ate the lunch and commented on what good work we are doing, but none of them were willing to stick their hands in their pockets or contribute anything.

For the purpose of encouraging private business involvement, the Northley police seconded an officer to work one day a week for the scheme. He was given the specific task of attracting financial assistance, funding, and equipment from the business sector to assist a wide variety of community safety schemes across the city. After eight months work, he produced an interim report which was submitted to the partnership forum. It acknowledged, frankly, the

---

[3] This is not true of all commercial involvement. Some notable companies with traditions for philanthropic work specialize in secondments and investments in labour, for example Cadbury's and Marks & Spencer.

difficulties associated with levering in financial or other commitments from private businesses:

Businesses, in general, are unable or unwilling to donate to projects. A large amount of energy is required to produce small rewards ... The business sector in [Northley] has not yet recognised its responsibility for tackling crime issues, which is beyond that of alarm systems and private security ... We have found that there can be a lot of work in tailoring schemes to their interest. Some companies expect [the Northley Project] to guarantee crime reductions and have difficulty in understanding quality of life issues.

The experiences of Crime Concern and many Safer Cities Projects reflect similar difficulties in raising and maintaining private sector funds. Writing about the experience of Crime Concern, Jon Bright, the then Director of Field Operations, concluded:

Apart from relatively small charitable donations, most serious company giving is usually determined by an assessment of the community relations, or less frequently, marketing benefits, that might result from a proposal. This normally excludes long-term funding of 'problem-oriented' initiatives in high crime areas.

(Bright 1991: 72)

The process of 'tailoring' can have a very real impact upon policy outcomes. For example, the installation of CCTV cameras around Northley city centre received greater interest from the private sector than did work in peripheral high crime estates. Not only was this 'closer to home', but also it constituted a high profile initiative with public relations and publicity potential.

This points to a number of broad implications. First, the involvement of the private sector is likely to constrain and distort the types of crime prevention interventions adopted by schemes, notably those heavily reliant upon business contributions. It is likely to prioritize interventions into the physical environment which are short-term, visible, tangible, and may be subject to some kind of quantitative assessment of effectiveness. Put simply, private sector input inclines towards situational rather than social prevention. Moreover, secondly, it is likely to act as a restraint upon long-term projects, given fluctuations in business performance and market benefits.

However, thirdly, its impact should not be over-exaggerated. It would be wrong to suggest that in all fields of crime prevention and control the private sector is rushing into partnerships and heavily investing their resources. Many in the private sector are unwilling to fund activities which they consider to be the legitimate responsibility of government (Bright 1991: 72). This is particularly true of crime prevention and control outside the regulation of businesses' own physical space, property, and employees. In the current climate in which a plethora of voluntary, charitable, and intermediary institutions are all chasing the 'same slice of the corporate sponsorship cake', issues of 'crime' are not high on the agenda of many in the private sector, except in so far as they seek to reduce their own direct loss from it. Crime is a 'dirty' and 'unglamorous' subject. It is also one traditionally and symbolically associated with state sovereignty. As one member of the Northley project (with experience of working with the voluntary sector) commented, 'In the current highly competitive basis it's [i.e. crime prevention is] not very marketable. It's not small and cuddly!'. Some business commentators are even hostile to the very idea of private sector involvement in community safety issues. They see appeals to the responsibility of the private sector as 'an attempt to achieve public policy on the cheap and on the side' (Brittan 1993). Nevertheless, this does not mean that private sector involvement will leave crime prevention virtually untouched. On the contrary it is clear that in the future governments (of any of the major political parties) will increasingly look to the private sector to fund a significant proportion of crime prevention and community safety.

The Criminalization of Social Policy?

One question that the preceding discussions beg, is whether broad policy outcomes are being transformed by the fact that 'partnerships' draw together organizations and groups working in diverse areas of social and public policy, specifically around issues of crime. The blurring of organizational boundaries and roles, identified in Chapter 4, has ramifications for the general direction of policy outcomes. Is the effect of blurring a diffused one or one which pulls policy in particular directions?

There is a concern that under the aegis of 'community partnerships' in the field of crime prevention we may be witnessing the 'criminalization of social policy' (Pearson 1983: 239; Blagg and Smith 1989). This concern can be analysed at two conceptually distinct, yet inter-related, levels: first, with reference to the targets of central government and charitable funding, and secondly, at the level of negotiations between the parties involved in 'partnership' arrangements. There is a real anxiety that the high degree of influence given to 'crime prevention' may result in social policy, its direction and funding, being redefined in terms of its implications for crime. This is rendered all the more worrying given the place of inequality within both neo-liberal ideology and the dominant Durkheimian discourse of 'social (dis)integration', which underlies much of the liberal left thinking (see Levitas 1996). Inequality, in this context, increasingly is viewed as something which is a 'problem' only because, if extreme enough, it is disruptive of social order, or at least perceived to be potentially disruptive (as in the fear of crime). It is not seen as either, first, an integral feature of a capitalist, free market, economy, nor, secondly, as a 'cause for concern' in its own right.

Crime is not only an indicator of social ills but, more importantly, has become a defining factor in the allocation of resources. This is illustrated by the prominence accorded to the issue of crime within City Challenge and the Single Regeneration Budget Challenge Fund.[4] The fact that the money is not channelled through traditional 'law and order' mechanisms—in other words the police working alone—only serves to make this more palatable. An example is the Churchway Anti-Crime Project the *raison d'être* of which was to identify an area and its crime problems for the purpose of subsequent proposed Single Regeneration Budget funding. Further, there has been a profusion of ideas about crime control into routine decisions about urban planning, architecture (see Department of the Environment 1994), and the design of 'public' facilities and amenities, many of them imported from the USA (Davis 1990: 223–36). The built environment, as a consequence, is becoming saturated with crime and disorder prevention features.

A potential consequence of according to crime a central place in the construction of social order is that fundamental public issues may become marginalized, except in so far as they are defined in terms of their crimogenic qualities. The danger is that, as a consequence, we may come to view poor housing, unemployment,

---

[4] The fact that there are to be no new Safer Cities Projects and that the funding is to be subsumed within the general Single Regeneration Budget, only serves to reiterate this point. In essence, the loss of the Safer Cities projects, as a distinct crime prevention initiative, means that 'crime' will have fully penetrated social policy as it becomes a defining part of the wider process of urban regeneration.

racism, failed educational facilities, the lack of youth leisure opportunities, and so on, as no longer important public issues in themselves. Rather, their importance may be seen to derive from the belief that they lead to crime and disorder. The fact that they may do exactly that is no reason not to assert their importance in their own right. The fear is that social deficiencies are being redefined as 'crime problems' which need to be controlled and managed, rather than addressed in themselves. This would represent the ultimate 'criminalization of social policy'.

Nevertheless, there are countercurrents. The malleable nature of crime prevention work also creates a limited space for resistance and the flexible reinterpretation of local policy among alternative lines. This point was noted by a community worker on the Churchway project:

I do think that most of the things that you can apply for, you can word in such a way that it can sound as if it's to do with crime prevention. You can blur the edges a bit, but not completely.

This space for resistance is constrained not only by the organizational priorities of powerful agencies, but also by the prevailing technicism, short-termism, and project-orientation within crime prevention practice. Within that limited space, however, more progressive practitioners in the research sought to divert crime prevention funding to what they saw as 'social ends'. A council officer from the Illsworth Crime Prevention Project explains:

Crime prevention is actually about social interaction . . . and we're getting it through actually, no, we're not just talking about going down and keeping a few tenants happy; no, we're not just talking about having a few bobbies on the beat; no, we're not talking about busting a few people who are a pain in the arse to everybody; and no, we're not just talking about better lighting and locks . . . we're actually taking about social processes here and that crime, as somebody . . . once said, is a metaphor for a lot of other social problems.

As constrained as this alternative vision is, its existence plays an important role in the conflicts and sites of resistance within and between agencies. What these alternative visions often amount to in practice, as in the Illsworth example, is no more than using crime prevention funding as a means of resourcing social provisions against the background of a general lack of such social funding. This is recognized by the response given by the same council officer, when asked how the local communities viewed their scheme:

[T]hey realise of course that if there is a multi-agency initiative in their area then they've got a fighting chance to get some resources put into their area. And . . . you know they've a fighting chance of something happening for the better in their area.

Thus 'crime' becomes a lever for acquiring scarce funding for socially deprived areas. However, in a post-welfare economy which has experienced the recent decimation of welfare policies, this strategy is itself bound up with contradictions. This competitive quest for diminishing resources, rather than being an indictment of the lack of social provisions, has become the means of managing the fall out of a market economy from which large sections of the population are marginalized. As such, multi-agency crime prevention initiatives are in danger of becoming part of the broader management and administration of the social crises induced by post-welfarism and the market economy.

At the micro level, interactions and negotiations between organizations incorporated into (as well as, by definition, those excluded from) partnership arrangements impact upon the general drift of policy outcomes. This is particularly so given the nature of structural power differentials between the parties as discussed in Chapter 4. Most particularly, the power of the police to define issues of crime in addition to their informational advantage raises fears that their dominance in partnerships may encourage further the 'criminalization of social policy'. Most notably, this often leaves the police in a considerable position of power, particularly given their ability to draw very quickly upon human resources, their gatekeeping role within the criminal justice system, and their claims to expertise in crime prevention and detection (Ericson 1994). Shearing notes that by and large the 'partnerships' of community policing are not ones in which the control of policing is shared equally between the partners. 'They are instead, partnerships in which the police are steering partners while the citizens are rowing partners' (1995: 5). A senior police officer on the Northley project was very clear that what he was looking for in relation to drugs policy was 'concessions to confidentiality'. He saw a 'corporate approach' as one which, by necessity, sacrifices certain individualistic procedural barriers for the sake of 'the wider community'. To this end he prepared a discussion paper on drug policy, the aim of which was: 'To push the other agencies as far as they will go in conceding confidentiality. To see what level of intrusion they will accept.' The aim here was very explicitly to co-opt other agencies into a 'law and order' approach to issues of crime. Given the 'leadership' role of the police on many partnerships, this frequently can be the practical outcome. However, blurring can have more complex effects. It can work to prioritize aspects of social issues and influence police practices in the reaction to crime. Thus, for example, on the Westbridge Drug Project the police were successfully encouraged to suspend law enforcement to allow health aspects of drug abuse to be given priority. Similarly, the experience of multi-agency domestic violence projects around the country has been to raise the profile within criminal justice organizations of domestic violence and responses to it, although even in this context the issue of criminalization or decriminalization remains a vexed one.

Nevertheless, the impact of partnerships upon policy outcomes is real and can serve to extend a particular vision of crime control within local agendas. As we have seen, these visions tend, largely, to be pragmatic and managerial. The forms of intervention tend to be short-term and situational. Those interventions which are more amenable to simple evaluation so beloved by funding bodies, the commercial sector, and the media are consequently accorded priority. As such, they tend to focus on target hardening, 'designing out' crime, and other 'technological fixes' at the expense of interventions which question the social causes of crime.

Conclusions

As a note of caution, there is a danger in over-interpreting the proliferation of 'partnerships' and community involvement, both as something 'new' (a point made by respondents to the survey recorded in Chapter 4) and as always according to idealized schema or arrangements. There is an ever-present hazardous lure in getting carried away with rhetoric. The philosophy of 'partnerships' is more widely extolled than practised (James and Bottomley 1994: 165). As the co-ordinator of the Northley project wryly noted to me, 'there are plenty of "paper partnerships" around'. This experience is not limited to the field of crime prevention and control (see Hirst 1995). Organizations are only too aware of the fact that if they want to access external funds in the current policy era it is imperative that they appear—at least on paper—to be in 'partnership' with other relevant organizations and to be engaged in some form of 'community consultation' (whatever that may represent). Scratch the surface of some formal 'partnerships' and you will often discover a fiction created for a particular audience. Further, as we saw in Chapter 4, agreements struck in 'partnerships' frequently have to be renegotiated at rank and file levels within organizations where resistances abound. Nevertheless, even the rhetoric has practical effects. The dramatic rise in the ideology of 'partnership' and appeals to 'community', as well as the actual institutionalization of practices, are set to increase rather than diminish in significance and effect.

Against this background, arguments about the demise and decline in state power may be premature and over-exaggerated. The public sphere has never had an absolute and unconditional monopoly over policy in the past, even (and particularly) in the sphere of crime control (South 1988; Johnston 1992). There is a danger in over-emphasizing the extent to which the trends outlined so far represent a fundamental breach in relations between state and society. We need to be careful lest such an assumption wrongly implies a total rupture with the past and posits 'neo-corporatism' as a total system of governance. The novelty of these arrangements and processes can be over-emphasized. They may be better understood as representing new, partial elements within the existing economic and political formation which co-exist alongside other (older) modes of administration and regulation.

7
Questions of Accountability

A significant insight of neo-corporatist theory, which augments an understanding of contemporary partnerships in crime prevention and control, concerns the questionable compatibility of neo-corporatism with democracy and, therefore, queries as to its longer term legitimacy (Schmitter 1989: 58; Habermas 1989b: 61). In this chapter, I will consider the implications of the developments and trends in the local governance of crime outlined in the preceding chapters for forms of accountability and notions of democracy. This I will do at two levels, first, in relation to organizational accountability, and secondly, with regard to political accountability. I will critically examine the implications of neo-corporatist trends in order to expose a number of problematic issues surrounding accountability and democracy. I will then go on to consider how partnerships might be rendered more accountable. Consequently, I will explore the need for positive political thinking about the democratic principles that ought to underpin 'partnerships', before outlining some of the recent contributions to how one might begin to build such institutions, their limitations, and possibilities.

None of the following discussions, however, should be taken as suggesting, either deliberately or otherwise, that we have left behind a 'golden age' of accountability in crime control and policing, nor that we are heading down an inevitable path. There is a dangerous assumption, evident in many recent criminological debates about policing and democratic accountability, that somehow, if we could only turn back the clock to pre-Thatcherite days, then we would have restored democracy to policing. The appeal to (often local) democracy in this mythical 'golden age' thesis, is both hollow and problematic. The flawed nature of the historic tripartite system of police accountability has been well documented (Jefferson and Grimshaw 1984; Lustgarten 1986) and, as I intimated in Chapter 2, accountability in crime control generally has long been a vexed issue. Furthermore, as I have hoped to show throughout, the trends outlined in this book point to a number of tensions, ambiguities, and path-dependent possibilities.

Organizational Accountability

In the ensuing discussion of organizational accountability I intend to differentiate between two inter-related facets of organizational accountability: first, in terms of responsibility for, and openness in, the process of inter-organizational decision making and its impact on organizational accountability, and secondly, in terms of 'financial' and 'managerial' accountability within organizations. All too often, the former is ignored or subsumed under the rubric of the latter. My purpose, therefore, in disaggregating the two types of organizational accountability, is to highlight the importance of the former and suggest that in order to understand forms of accountability we need to recognize these two component parts, how they are inter-related, either by serving to undermine or reinforce each other.

Inter-organizational Accountability

Organizational changes heralded by 'new public management' were supposed to increase organizational accountability, by specifying criteria for success, providing greater information, freeing managers to manage, and through financial accounting procedures (see below). However, their focus is wholly intra-organizational and, as such, they fail to grapple with the complexities which inter-organizational networks cause for (both internal and external) accountability. Partnerships mean that policies are increasingly made in conjunction with other organizations and, as such, impact upon intra-organizational relations. Partnerships and policy networks blur organizational boundaries and increase the interdependence of the included parties. This, after all, is part of their appeal. In doing so, however, they muddy the waters of organizational accountability. In contemporary 'partnerships' there is no single identifiable agency or actor which is accountable for the outcomes of policy implementation. This gives rise to what Rhodes has identified as,

'the problem of many hands' where so many people contribute that no one contribution can be identified; and if no one person can be held accountable after the event, then no one needs to behave responsibly beforehand.
(Rhodes 1995: 15)

Joint and negotiated decisions tie the parties into corporate policy and outcomes, but fail to identify lines of responsibility. Institutional complexity further obscures who is accountable to whom, and for what. Consequently, as was argued in Chapter 6, the attempt to distinguish between operational and policy issues in the face of blurring and shifting relations is doomed to lead to greater, rather than less, uncertainty. Ambiguity is the resultant order of the day. As Peters comments:

> under the present conditions authority can hardly be located any more: it has become shared, parcelled, delegated, conditioned, subjected to approval and correction, steered by publicised or secret departmental guidelines and circulars. In a word: authority has become elusive.
>
> (1986: 34)

This leads to a second issue, 'the problem of invisibility'. In Chapter 4 the research findings highlighted a number of practices in inter-organizational relations which all undermine 'transparency' that is fundamental to organizational accountability. First, is the failure within policy networks to specify clear collective aims and strategies. Often there may be no agreement as to the desired outcome or how to measure it. This is particularly the case in the field of crime prevention where monitoring and evaluation are usually weak and rendered problematic by the multiple (often conflicting) aims and strategies, and the open-endedness of what 'counts'. This malleable essence allows a flexibility in the criteria of evaluation and consequently in that which is described as 'successful'. Secondly, the practice of conflict avoidance tends to result in pragmatic compromise, rather than negotiation involving the open exchange of conflicting interests and competing objectives. This further clouds accountability in the decision making process by undermining any notion of normative regulation. The proliferation of 'policy' only serves to increase the dissonance between rhetoric and reality: presentation and behaviour. Thirdly, as we have seen, there is a tendency for *real* decision making processes to occur in private, informal settings. Informal power relations are encouraged and nourished by the practice of conflict avoidance in inter-agency relations. They give rise to the establishment of second-tier informal relations which are both private and exclusive. As such, they supplement and yet undercut formal decision making processes. Access to these second-tier or 'shadow' processes becomes an important additional filter for inclusion/exclusion. These kinds of informal contexts hide decision making processes from any review, shield them from the democratic gaze, and compound problems of confidentiality where they exist. Ends-oriented, performance-related accountability tends to ride roughshod over the procedural norms of good public accountability. If, as Rock (1990) suggests, 'independent interdependence' is the 'weak force' which binds the criminal justice system together, then these forms of organizational accountability must constitute key safeguards which prevent the 'weak force' from snapping.

Financial and Managerial Accountability

'Value for money' disciplines introduced initially into criminal justice by the Financial Management Initiative of the early 1980s have been extended by 'new public management'. As we have already noted, criminal justice agencies, along with other government departments, have been required to develop objectives, and means of assessing and measuring performances in relation to those objectives. The Audit Commission and Her Majesty's Inspectorates have been used as crucial external inspecting mechanisms with the aim of encouraging the spread of objective-driven performance and generating a performance conscious culture, most notably within senior management, but ultimately throughout public sector organizations. This 'value for money' approach is rooted in a notion of financial accountability. It also has the associated attraction of management accountability by rendering the measurement of outputs and outcomes, throughout an organization, accessible to management, and thus allowing them to manage more effectively. It enables 'auditing' and 'stewarding' by management. Accounting technologies hold out the possibility of securing the 'responsibilization' of individual action, by constructing 'calculable selves' and 'calculable spaces', loosely linked to each other by 'networks of calculation' (Humphrey *et al.* 1993; Miller and O'Leary 1994).

This form of organizational accountability, it has been argued, has implications for external as well as internal audiences (Audit Commission 1988; Davies 1990). It generates data and information upon which customers can assess performance, lobby for change, and so on. Hence, it is argued that financial and managerial accountability, through forms of informational accountability, connect with wider political accountability (to which I return later) (Audit Commission 1990; 1991).

This line of thinking can be seen, for example, in relation to policing, where 'policing by objectives' has been embraced by senior police officers (ACPO 1990) and adopted by forces. One study suggests that between 20 and 30 local objectives are produced annually by police sub-divisions, which amounts to approximately one a fortnight (cited in Weatheritt 1993b: 27). Further, the content of police objectives has been sufficiently extensive to include forms of responsiveness to different categories of users and consultation with local communities, thus incorporating a degree of external measurement in the process. In addition, the proliferation of reports by the Audit Commission, National Audit Office, and Her Majesty's Inspectorate of Constabulary (HMIC), since the late 1980s, has dramatically increased the quantity of numerical data available. Since 1990, Inspectorate reports on forces have been published. This is a practice which dated from the establishment of HMIC in the mid nineteenth century but which had long since lapsed.

Internal research by the police has expanded significantly, with the 'Operational Policing Review' (Joint Consultative Committee 1990) and various local 'customer' surveys. This informational explosion has been extended by the statutory requirement under section 95 of the Criminal Justice Act 1991 to record and monitor information on criminal justice practices by relevant agencies. The aim of the section is to enable awareness of financial implications and to facilitate the avoidance of discriminatory practices. Consequently, Weatheritt notes that 'the push towards police performance measurement, while grounded in the wish to secure management accountability for the use of an expensive resource, has begun to move on to a different plane' (1993b: 43).

Informational accountability is in large part dependent upon access to information, its form, and quality. However, not all information is publicly available (for example, auditor's detailed reports are not published although their main conclusions are, as they are the property of the local authority concerned). Even where inspection reports are in the public arena they are neither written for a lay audience nor to inform public debate. Their audience is very clearly an internal one. In addition, the production of information outside an 'explanatory' or 'co-operative' framework can only ever constitute a weak form of accountability (Reiner 1993). Further, performance objectives in practice are highly flexible, sometimes contradictory and subject to different interpretations, so that 'success' and 'achievement' often become meaningless (National Audit

Office 1990: 21). In addition, information is often incomplete or poorly formulated. In some instances, the greater use of contractual arrangements may actually limit the information available. For example, access to information and open government do not apply in the same way to contractors as they do to local government (Stewart and Walsh 1992: 515). Further, there is little evidence that objective-driven activity in the field of criminal justice and the mass of 'partial' information which it has spawned, have provided the basis for transforming practice or consolidating and learning from 'successful' performance (Weatheritt 1993b: 27; Humphrey *et al.* 1993). Moreover, any change in formal systems of 'objective setting' will have little impact in practice if it does not involve procedures which confront and negotiate with informal, cultural norms, assumptions, and artefacts within organization (see Goldsmith 1990). Finally, without mechanisms for directly linking the setting of objectives with external constituencies in an open manner, the control over definitions of 'success' and 'failure' will remain firmly located within organizational hierarchies. Consequently, these internally derived goals may be more concerned with the projection of an 'image of success' (by lowering expectations and changing goal posts, for example) than with the attainment of 'social' goals.

The language of 'consumer sovereignty' is the principal means through which financial and managerial accountability appeals to a wider constituency. It summons up an image of direct accountability to the consumer by way of organizational responsiveness. Whilst this is a powerful symbolic critique of remote, élitist, and unresponsive bureaucracies (and/or politicians) it is an inadequate grounding for the action of public bodies. Crime control and policing, first and foremost, are tied up with the exercise of coercive powers of the state. In this context, it is not helpful to treat people as customers, as crime control and prevention involve the surveillance, policing, and regulation *of* certain individuals. Those who are consumers of, 'consumed' by, use, or otherwise benefit from crime control services are not an homogenous group with shared values or interests. It is inaccurate to conceptualize certain tasks of crime control, particularly those in which coercive powers are used, as a 'service' in respect of which individuals are merely the recipients. The language of 'customer', which implies individual entitlements, fails to confront the empirical reality that for most people living in urban areas, crime control remains a monopolistic service from which there are no rights of exit. Whilst affluent neighbourhoods may be able to buy in private security guards and thus exit state provision, this option is not available to all. The 'policy networks' of community partnerships may serve merely to reinforce this monopoly control by drawing together public and private provision within a geographical area.

A narrow understanding of performance may only serve to distort organizational activities (Butler 1996) and give a partial picture of what is relevant. We can learn as much from that which is omitted from performance indicators as from that which is included. Judgement, by necessity, will be constructed and contained by powerful interests. Hence, Weatheritt concludes:

> Performance information, whether produced by or for auditors, inspectors, professionals, administrators or politicians is primarily a way of formulating and asking further questions and promoting a dialogue with service providers about the prospects for service improvement. That dialogue may well turn out to be no more than a sterile tussle over disputed meanings. It may fail to take place at all. In policing, the structures for encouraging and supporting such a dialogue at local level are not yet firmly in place; there has not been much evidence of serious local political interest in establishing them; and the nature of policing as a service to some extent militates against the establishment of such a dialogue.
>
> (1993b: 41)

In theory, this is a dialogue that 'partnerships' could help to foster. However, as we saw in Chapter 4, in practice this dialogue is largely absent and in its absence informational accountability remains severely limited.

Political Accountability

As I have implied so far, 'policy networks' and 'partnerships' erode not only organizational, but also political, accountability. At the level of national parliament, the proliferation of agencies and 'quangos' has problematized relations between policy and institutions of political accountability (Plummer 1994), a development further exacerbated by 'the Europeanisation of everything' (Rhodes 1995: 142). Along with changes in the management of public services, this proliferation has challenged the assumption of accountability *upwards*: that accountability of public servants to those who receive a service is through the political process (Stewart and Walsh 1992: 509). The new totems are 'customers', supported by regulators, auditors, and inspectors. In the process, clear hierarchical lines of accountability have been broken. This leads to the problem of 'who is accountable to parliament for what?', as Jordan notes:

> We are told ministerial accountability remains. But in reality it is now accountability *to* the Minister by the Chief Executive rather than accountability *of* the Minister to the House of Commons that is now on offer; these are different.
>
> (quoted in Rhodes 1995: 148, emphasis in original)

The growth of 'private interest government' has left much policy making invisible to parliamentary scrutiny and the surveillance of the public.

At the local level, community 'partnerships' appear to represent part of a broader trend, namely the diminishing importance of electoral channels of representation. The role and powers of local authorities have been dramatically changed and limited in the last two decades. Since 1979 there have been almost fifty statutes affecting local authorities, many of which have restricted their autonomy. Numerous centrally controlled agencies and quangos have been established whose work parallels that of elected local authorities.[1] Several of the new institutions which have been created recently in the field of crime prevention and control have been introduced specifically to limit and circumvent the influence of locally elected representatives and to bypass local government. The most notable example has been the Safer Cities Projects (Tilley 1993). Furthermore, the response of the government to any proposals to increase the responsibility of local authorities in the field of crime prevention has been unequivocally dismissive (Home Office 1992c: 1–2). More recently, the government was partly unsuccessful in its attempt to remove the majority representation of local councillors on police authorities by means of the Police and Magistrates' Court Act 1994, although it did manage to reduce the dominance of elected representatives (Loveday 1995). The absence of involvement of elected councillors is similarly apparent within locally established crime

[1] Outside the specific fields of (although with implications for) crime control and prevention these new agencies include: urban development corporations, programmes for urban development such as English Partnership, Training and Enterprise Councils (TECs), management boards of opted out schools, hospital trusts, and so on.

prevention initiatives, even those set up by local authorities. The research sites revealed a distinct lack of involvement of locally elected representatives, a finding supported by other research (see Liddle and Gelsthorpe 1994a: 15–16). Furthermore, none of the schemes had formal lines of accountability to existing electoral channels of representation.

What is clear is that the legitimacy of these inter-agency networks resides not at a *political*, but at an *administrative* level: in claims to superior cumulative expertise and/or increased effectiveness of service provision. This essential prioritization of non-normative authority, as we have seen, has implications for practice. It means that 'partnerships' embody dynamics which are antithetical to 'transparency', both through the complex and secretive deliberations that inter-agency concertation involves and the selective participation of representatives. The managerial criteria upon which partnerships are founded and sustained detach them from what Habermas refers to as the processes of 'public will-formation' (Habermas 1989a). As a consequence, we are witnessing the emergence of 'privileged oligarchies' inhabited by a 'new magistracy'. Hence, a study by Democratic Audit in 1993 estimated that there were over 70,000 unelected 'quangocrats', more than three times the number of elected councillors (cited in Mandleson and Liddle 1996: 197). This is not to suggest, however, that a previous system of democratic control over criminal justice functioned satisfactorily, but rather that there is evidence of a widening democratic deficit.

Democracy and Crime Control

There is a fundamental but complex relationship between democracy and the 'rule of law' (Thompson 1975; Fine 1984). An aspect of this is that the awesome power of crime control and policing should neither be arbitrary nor captured by partisan interests. Paradoxically, the *political* control of, or influence over, such power exposes the potential for such scenarios. However, this danger is not averted by protecting the autonomy of the professions themselves from outside 'political' authority. On the contrary, as Reiner and Spencer note, this may merely serve as a shield behind which professionals may represent and pursue their own or some other partisan viewpoint (1993a: 179). Furthermore, a similar fallacy underlies the ideology of, and dominant thinking about, 'partnerships': that they should bring together neutral 'experts' or 'right-minded people' with some contribution to make to the crime problem. For, as McLaughlin rightly points out in relation to policing: 'In a demo-cratic polity the fundamental constitutional principle underpinning police accountability should not be that "reasonable people can make anything work" ' (1994: 171). Crime control needs to be connected to processes of 'public will-formation'. Questions about the direction and methods of crime control are not merely technical or administrative ones, they are also intrinsically political. How a society regulates crime tells us much about its political priorities, as well as the nature of social order that it sustains.

As we saw in Chapter 2, crime control is fundamentally tied to politics, institutions of democracy, and their legitimacy. As crime control is inherently grounded in conflict and its regulation, the processes through which consent of the public is constructed and the activities of crime control are accepted as legitimate are central to the nature of the enterprise. The long tradition of a public discourse of 'policing by consent' (Reiner 1992b) raises important issues about the mechanisms through which legitimacy is sought and maintained. This is rendered all the more salient in the changing context of the local governance of crime. Further, legitimacy and consent are bound up with the efficacy of crime control which, as we have seen, relies upon the active support and co-operation of individuals, groups, and organizations. For this reason alone, the Audit Commission (1990) has recognized the need for, and pro-moted, greater public involvement through political institutions, notably police authorities (Davies 1990).

Ideals of Democracy

A common element in discussion about democracy is a distinc-tion between 'utopian' and 'realist' accounts: the former represent 'ideals' or 'ideas' of democracy, while the latter refer more directly to mechanism and institutions of contemporary capitalist societies (Hindness 1991: 174). Both are significant aspects in an analysis of political accountability and crime control. Ideals and values of democracy, as McLaughlin (1994) notes, are all too often ignored within the criminological literature where the notion of democracy is ill-defined. Therefore, before examining some potential 'realist' mechanisms for addressing political accountability, I will begin with a consideration of the 'ideal' values which should underlie the democratic regulation of crime control.

Given that the governance of crime control and policing are inherently about conflict—the policing and control *of* certain groups, individuals, acts, and behaviours—democracy must involve more than responsiveness to locally elected bodies. The dangers of 'participatory pluralism' turning into 'populism' are ever-present, particularly in times of social fragmentation and mistrust (Jordan and Arnold 1995: 171–2). Politicians can exploit, all too easily, the widespread fears and anxieties that crime can engender. In so doing, they can mobilize coalitions against minorities, in which the 'politics of enforcement' become the rhetoric for channelling intergroup antagonisms (Jordan and Arnold 1995). The 'immediacy of the question of power' (Panitch 1986: 46) can become blinding when mixed with the powerful rhetoric that crime evokes. Hence, there is the need for a robust democracy which protects against majoritarian domination. It requires an understanding of what Jones and colleagues have referred to, in the policing context, as 'a set of criteria for the purpose of testing how far the arrangements for making policing policy follow democratic principles' (1994: 44). The criteria that they set out are: equity, delivery of service, responsiveness, distribution of power, information, redress, and participation (Jones *et al.* 1994: 42–8). The authors fittingly emphasize that these are relatively open and contested categories, and that their list is neither exhaustive nor an end point in debate, but rather an attempt to clarify what is meant by 'democracy' within the context of contemporary policing and crime control.

Importantly, the notion of *equity* which runs throughout 'idealist' democratic theory, is placed first in the order of priority. However, in the context of crime control and policing, as Jones *et al.* note, equity is itself problematic (1996: 190–1) because: first, certain aspects of crime control are adversarial and conflictual, whilst others involve the provision of a service—different members of the public have different needs which themselves may change over time and space. In other words, some people are the targets of 'control' or surveillance on behalf of others. Secondly, there are important distinctions to be made between equity of provision and equity of outcome. This second point raises distinctions between conceptions of justice, whether what is being sought is, on the one hand, formal and individualistic justice or, on the other hand, substantive and distributive justice. In the context of crime control, this begs the question whether, as a society, we wish to recognize the unequal social distribution and impact of crime and victimization (which for many people compounds their existing social disadvantage and political marginalization) and seek to control it so that its negative impact is more evenly distributed. This, in turn, may involve the politically awkward activities of redistributing or 'deflecting' victimization (Barr and Pease 1990). These issues lie at the heart of the discussions in Chapter 8 about social justice. For the moment, I want only to acknowledge the problem that in order to recognize the different crime control needs of groups and to go some way towards addressing existing inequalities, this must override equity in a formal sense. Rather, democracy must embody a notion of 'complex equality', whereby 'different goods are distributed for different reasons by different agents to different people', so that no single group of people is dominant across the spheres of social life (Waltzer 1983).

And yet, as Jones *et al.* note (1996: 189), this can produce tensions when the 'needs' of victims are juxtaposed against those of offenders. These will at times, although not always, be in conflict. This tension can be mitigated, however, by a focus upon *prevention* rather than enforcement, and *reintegration* rather than exclusion. One of the most important recent lessons of criminological research has been to show that victims and offenders frequently occupy the same social and geographical spaces and often share the same economic and political disadvantages (Jones *et al.* 1986; Young 1986; Crawford *et al.* 1990). Consequently, collective provisions which target areas with high levels of victimization may serve, simultaneously, to address the needs of both offenders and victims.

In their seven other democratic criteria, Jones *et al.* (1994; 1996) identify key components necessary in the democratization of partnerships in crime control and prevention, the absence or presence of which has been noted in earlier discussions. I am not going to attempt to make detailed evaluation of the priorities which Jones and colleagues accord to different criteria, but I will pick out of their discussion a number of points of particular relevance for partnerships, which have not been considered thus far. First, the 'distribution of powers', as the research evidence presented in Chapters 4 and 5 highlights, must be a fundamental and defining principle in the democratization of partnerships. Conflict is inevitable and therefore what is needed are mechanisms and processes for moderating power so that it is not concentrated in too few hands, as at present. This will involve both the greater incorporation of otherwise excluded voices and formal procedures for equalizing involvement and participation. One might want to argue that the distribution of power should be second only to equity in priority in the list of criteria to which Jones *et al.* refer, as all the other criteria will be dependent upon, and in large part determined by, the constellation of power relations.

Secondly, as already implied, the notions of 'service delivery' and 'responsiveness' both beg the question, delivery for, and responsiveness to, whom? Here, the danger in the field of crime control lies in prioritizing individual (particularly victim's) or market solutions, with little regard for a 'social purpose'. The importance of overlapping tiers of government between the national, or even supra-national, and the local (to which I return below), is paramount in reinforcing, at each turn, a 'social purpose'. It needs to embody a notion of *citizenship* which is multiple—political, economic, and social—and multi-layered (Bader 1995: 212), which values complexity and equality on behalf of all its members. Hence, 'citizenship' rather than 'consumerism' is the preferred basis for inclusion and constitutes the ideological terrain upon which tolerance for 'diversity within unity' is constructed. As Waltzer notes:

what marks a democratic political community is the recognition that all those social transactions that drive citizens towards the margins, that produce a class of excluded men and women ... are everywhere and always in the life of the community unjust.

(1993: 64)

As a political ideal the state—at different levels and in different spheres of activity—is, or rather should be, entrusted with the moral task of promoting and defending, values of diversity and equality. This role requires the state's prominent involvement as an authorizing, licensing, and subsidizing institution, which regulates, at an arm's length, developments in the various 'associative orders' in accordance with such values (Hirst 1994).

Thirdly, 'service delivery', 'responsiveness', and 'information' are all inter-related. In the long-term they rely and impact upon each other. Good information is crucial for balancing and negotiating between the competing demands of 'service' and 'response'. It is also fundamental to the assessment of good performance in meeting the priorities so negotiated. What is more important, as I have already suggested, is that this should take place within an open dialogue between the different constituencies—as 'citizens' not mere 'consumers'—and the service providers. This process of giving an account and listening to what is said about it, in a continuing relationship, lies behind what Simey refers to as the 'principle of stewardship' (1988: 237).

Finally, the concept of 'redress'—in which the ultimate sanction is removal and replacement—is important and yet complex in the field of crime control. Given the near monopoly that the public sector retains in the provision of essential services, ideas of 'democracy as competition' are limited. Whilst an individual, organization or community may be able to terminate a contract with one private security company (due to poor service delivery or whatever) and enter into another, this right of entry and exit is not available for some people nor is it applicable to certain criminal justice practices. Further, whilst it may be possible to remove certain incompetent individuals—for example a manager of the police or probation service—it is harder to deal with more structural institutional incompetence which runs deeper than a few individuals. This is different from the situation with regard to political élites, where whole administrations can be removed and replaced by new ones.

Jones and colleagues have helped steer debate towards the need to connect notions of democracy in crime control with conceptions of social or distributive justice. What their complex criteria embody are both elements of procedural and substantive justice. My own research suggests the need to maximize the opportunities for participation while constructing minimal, yet critical, limitations on the nature and form of participation. In order to protect against majoritarian rule and safeguard vulnerable minorities from the coercive and oppressive power of communal morality, there is simultaneously a need for a socially inclusive process—particularly with regard to traditionally neglected and suppressed groups—with procedural mechanisms governing conflict negotiation and communication, which seek to mitigate power differentials and structure the normative boundaries of the process. Furthermore there is a need to ensure a minimum respect for diversity in both process and policy outcomes. The problem, as Loader notes, is that an overriding concern with principles of substantive justice which curtail the outcomes of the policy making process in terms of their content, has anti-democratic implications: 'The greater the level of anterior constraints placed upon practices of democratic deliberation, the more the impetus towards them, and the possibilities manifested by them, are lost' (Loader 1994: 533). This tension is not easily resolved but, nevertheless, is fundamental to the present day need for an appreciation of an interconnectedness between conceptions of democracy and social justice.

There is, also, a fundamental tension between, on the one hand, the democratic logic of equality and, on the other hand, the liberal logic of liberty. This tension as Chantal Mouffe argues is one that we should value and protect, rather than try to resolve, because 'it is constitutive of pluralist democracy' (1993: 150). There is a need to secure pluralism and diversity by locating individual rights outside the reach of majoritarianism. But, by the same token, there are dangers of according such significance to a set of 'rights' that they may entrench inequalities and foster individualism. Thus, the universalism of citizenship must be sufficiently fixed to protect against populist advances but also must remain indeterminate 'since it is this indeterminacy that is the condition of existence of democratic politics' (Mouffe 1993: 147). Further, we need to recognize disagreement and contestation in politics, and the potential existence of violent and dominating forces with which rational political debate can make little advance. Thus acceptance of the 'rules of the game' must constitute a basis for inclusion within the process. This is not, therefore, an argument against all forms of exclusion, but rather one for a clear recognition for the conditions and justification upon which exclusion is founded.

Finally, the spatial dimension of democratic processes and the interrelationship between different layers need to be recognized, particularly given simultaneous pressures towards 'globalization' and 'localization'. Crime remains fundamentally local in nature, and therefore a considerable emphasis within a democratic input must remain at the local level. The central state retains an important guiding and regulating function. Within the constraints imposed by the democratic gaze it sets standards and universally acceptable rights and redress. Above the nation state pressures towards Europeanization and globalization in crime control also need to be matched by mechanisms of accountability (Walker 1993). However, there is also an important intermediary tier between local and central government, that of regional government. This has tended to be ignored in the discussion of crime control and policing and yet is important for a number of inter-related reasons. First, it is at this level, rather than at the national level, that genuine mediation between localities can occur. Local interests and priorities will differ significantly, particularly given the spatial polarization of inequality (the impact of which I consider in detail in Chapter 8). Similarly, the crime control activities in one locality may have a spillover effect into the next. It is at a regional level that a vision of crime control which extends beyond the parochial and embraces a 'public purpose' can properly emerge. In part, the significance of the regional level is dependent upon the unit at which the description 'local' is set, something which proponents of 'community initiatives' rarely specify. And yet, if localization is genuinely bound up with aspirations of participation, by necessity it will have a reasonably specific geographical focus. Secondly, some criminological commentators have suggested that particular characteristics of regions themselves might have an impact on victimization, in addition to the characteristics of smaller areas contained within them (Smith 1986; Trickett et al. 1995). Thirdly, the existing institutions of criminal justice have important regional structures, which need to be co-ordinated and rendered co-terminous if local partnerships are to function effectively. The French process of decentralization in the 1980s offers a partial model in this regard (Norton 1994; Lazerges 1995). What is required, therefore, are a series of interconnected tiers of democratic processes at the local, regional, national, and international levels: at each level concerns for 'social' justice will confront distinct considerations and implications whilst impacting upon those above and below.

Local Democratic Mechanisms Reinvigorated?

Given the geographically focused nature of much crime, there is a clear need to reinvigorate local democratic institutions. The preoccupation within criminological literature has been concentrated solely around issues of police accountability. Whilst this is of fundamental importance, given the dominant police role in crime control and their *de facto* leadership of many community-based initiatives, it is insufficient in itself. First, it fails to confront the reality of contemporary networks and partnerships where, at least formally, authority is 'parcelled' and 'shared'. Secondly, it accords to the police lines of accountability, which can only serve to legitimize, strengthen, and entrench their existing dominance of crime control and prevention in multi-agency networks. This might merely hasten the 'criminalization of social policy'. For these combined reasons the democratic net needs to be cast wider to incorporate all the parties within networks of local governance in crime control. In this, I am not arguing that the democratization of networks should replace, or act instead of, mechanisms for the democratization of the police—or for that matter other bureaucratic (public sector) organizations—but that it should supplement and support such processes.

Furthermore, in the changing socio-political landscape, new mechanisms of local political accountability must involve more than turning back the clock. The challenges are more complex, and require more constructive and imaginative thinking than that. Calls to reconnect local public policy making to established channels of local representation—through local authorities—whilst important, are also only partial. We need to acknowledge that local authorities have not always proved themselves capable of running services competently, nor have they provided effective long-term strategic oversight. One-party rule at both the local and national level often leaves little incentive for elected leaders to perform well. It may also lead to crime control within a given area merely reflecting the values of the dominant party in control. The power and disciplinary control of established political parties have tended to silence certain debates, pacify participation, marginalize minority interests, and reinforce the social exclusion of dissenting voices. A comparison with other countries shows that Britain has one of the lowest average turnout percentages for local elections, which stands at 40 per cent (Rallings *et al.* 1994: 18). The 'immediacy of the question of power' can serve to obscure both long-term strategic needs and the incorporation of diverse social interest. All to easily in this context, crime can become a political football in which politicians seek to outbid each other in presenting a 'tough on crime' image and pandering to punitive populism. Hence, traditional calls for greater 'political accountability' have tended to be formalistic (Brogden *et al.* 1988: 190). They have prioritized the form of 'representative democracy' with little regard to the substance and content of the democratic input or the kind of crime control and policing outcomes to which it gives rise.

In sum, there appears to be a twofold 'crisis of representative democracy'. At one level, as Jefferson *et al.* argue, this crisis involves 'the inability of existing democratic mechanisms to adequately represent the interests and aspirations of the most disadvantaged and least powerful segments of British society' (1988: 91). At another level, as I have sought to show, the contemporary policy formation processes and 'conversations that matter' are shifting and increasingly occurring in new networks outside the 'political sphere' and shielded from any 'democratic gaze'. Some commentators have begun to grapple with these issues in an attempt to think through how to render neo-corporatist 'partnerships' more democratically accountable and at the same time incorporate the interests of the politically marginalized.

Local Surveys

Recently, the use of local crime surveys has been heralded as an important new 'democratic instrument' (Young 1991; Crawford *et al.* 1990). Jock Young has argued that they can provide 'a reasonably accurate appraisal of people's fears and of their experience of victimisation' (1992: 50). This allows us to go beyond the abstraction of aggregate national statistics, which are misleading given the highly geographically focused nature of crime (see Young 1988; 1991). Surveys can play an important role in grounding policy in the specific social context of an area. They can provide important local information to supplement forms of organizational accountability and against which performance indicators can be constructed and measured. As such, they can be used as a partial corrective to the inadequacies of national data and local organizational assumptions. They can also serve to limit the informational advantage of the police and other agencies by providing an additional source of information about the level of victimization and people's experience of it. Surveys can supplement existing forms of community consultation, for example, in examining the correspondence between the representatives and the represented. On the basis of these insights people can also begin to examine other ways to involve marginal groups within processes of consultation.

However, their value should not be overstated, they cannot provide a blueprint for local policy. They involve complex methodological problems (see Sparks 1981a). The ability of surveys to tap the social complexities of crime, how it is experienced, its subjective and cultural meanings, and social reactions to it, is limited (Hough 1986; Genn 1988). Crime surveys are less able to map certain forms of criminality, particularly those without a direct or identifiable victim, and so can serve to reinforce the absence of certain crimes from local crime prevention agendas (such as corporate criminality). In addition, crime surveys—because they rely on victims for data about offending—have a tendency to prioritize the situational circumstances of an incident while marginalizing the motivation of the perpetrator and associated social issues. There is a danger that an over-reliance upon victimization survey data by crime prevention policy makers will over-emphasize the attributes and standpoint of the victim. This danger is evident in the tendency in much crime prevention work to highlight the 'life style', 'situational', and 'opportunity' factors in the commission of crimes. As a partial corrective to this tendency, some initiatives have supplemented victim surveys with surveys of known offenders (Forrester *et al.* 1988).

There is also the reality that people's subjective experiences of crime are themselves partial and do not translate unproblematically into socially just policies (Brogden *et al.* 1988: 189). As already noted, the crime control needs of people living within a given area will differ markedly. Surveys only represent an aggregation of individual responses, not a 'community' response. While they may tap unconsulted individual voices, it should not be presumed that those individuals collectively represent the 'community' or even particular 'communities'. Surveys map individual responses and attitudes, not notions of mutuality and solidarity which are collectively determined.

Furthermore, surveys vest considerable power in those who frame them, as well as those who subsequently interpret their findings. Surveys are not neutral instruments but are, in part, ideological constructs. So far as they do constitute part of a 'consultation process', they embody political choices about what data is sought, how that should be elicited, and what questions should be asked. The questionnaire is not an open conversation, but imposes a 'fixed rigidity on social life that it in fact does not have' (Giddens 1984: 330) and invests the researchers with power to structure and determine the range of answers available to the respondent. The proliferation of 'customer satisfaction' surveys, the primary purpose of which appears to be purely justificatory of existing practice, should warn us to think critically about their value.

Surveys leave unresolved the more difficult and yet fundamental issue of their interpretation, how to negotiate between the conflicting interests and demands to which they give rise. The prioritization of policies merely on the basis of numerical support or majority consensus may lead to a form of majoritarianism in which minorities' interests are abandoned. This is particularly pertinent given the thin line that exists between 'popular' and 'populist' policies. Further, in the policing of communities the temptation exists to distinguish clearly between 'respectable' fears and anxieties, and those 'unrespectable' concerns of the 'criminal classes'. As a consequence, surveys could serve to marginalize further those most socially excluded. Hence, as argued earlier, clear principles of social justice are required as the basis upon which to negotiate conflicting interests at the local level.

However, surveys do inform us of whether interventions would, or would not, carry public support which can itself be crucial to the success or failure of policy interventions. They offer a means through which otherwise unconsulted voices can at least begin to be heard. It is often the most marginalized and powerless who are exactly those local people who have the greatest experience of crime, its control, and related problems in their area. Surveys can constitute a moment, albeit a small one, in a process of 'negotiation' in the balancing of interests. As such, they need to be situated within, and part of, a wider political project concerned with an open and reciprocal dialogue. Surveys leave many considerations about their context, framing, purpose, and use unanswered. Consequently, we should be as cautious about their potential contribution to local democratic crime control as we should be to acclaim their promises.

Independent Monitoring

Some commentators have seen independent monitoring groups as constituting 'the *only effective* means by which police operational policies and practices can be opened to public scrutiny' (Scraton 1985: 176, emphasis in original). Given the lack of public visibility of much that occurs within criminal justice—from policing to prisons—and the informational advantage of public bodies, there remains a crucial role for the external monitoring of what is done in the name of the 'public' under the aegis of crime control. This is even more so given the sheer quantity of information available, and the democratic value of good quality information. Dedicated monitoring organizations, by focusing their resources on a limited range of specific issues, can play an important part in sifting, checking, evaluating, and responding to the information produced by and for inter-organizational networks. They can also commission and produce 'alternative' forms and sources of information. Hence, single issue pressure groups, civil liberties organizations, reform bodies, and local police monitoring groups all have a fundamental role within the democratic process. As representatives of individuals and groups which otherwise lack the power of representation—because they are marginalized, disadvantaged or disorganized—they can act as an element of a wider 'conscience' and inject a deliberately critical insight into the nature of a 'public purpose' within the context of crime control. As such they are an important constituent part of a public civic polity.

The central problems with monitoring groups are: how do they gain and maintain sufficient levels of funding and, simultaneously, pursue an independent role? who monitors the monitors? what is the nature of the correspondence between the monitors and the people they claim to represent? and, how do, or should, they influence future policy making? The same questions can, and should, be asked of official audit and inspection bodies such as the Audit Commission, the National Audit Office, and HMSIs. However, monitoring by definition is reactive to policies set elsewhere and may only be concerned with very narrow or sectional interests. As such they do not constitute a civic polity but fragments within one. Rather than being an answer in themselves, they raise important issues about how to place the interests of the politically excluded and marginalized voices onto local agendas. The incorporation of such groups into partnerships, providing they are accorded significant involvement, may add to the ability of partnerships to identify and, therefore, address the full range of competing interests and demands against which difficult priorities need to be negotiated.

Citizens' Juries

'Citizens' juries' have been advocated as a possible means of involving local people in policy making. They have been used in Germany and the United States in diverse fields of policy (Stewart *et al.* 1994), and have been introduced recently as an experiment in local democracy in crime control in Britain, most notably in a high profile initiative to tackle drug-related crime in Lewisham (Camp-bell 1996). The process is designed to test local views on a variety of policies by exposing 'jurors' to evidence presented by various 'experts' and interested organizations (Stewart *et al.* 1994: 1). Juries do not replace representative democracy but inform it of the con-sidered views of citizens formed after deliberation. Ideally, jurors are selected either at random from the electoral register (as in Germany), or as a representative sample of the local population, controlling for criteria such as ethnicity, age, gender, and education (as in America, where sampling occurs by the use of telephone surveys). The number of jurors is variable, in America they have been between twelve and twenty-four, while in Germany they usual-ly have twenty-five members (Stewart 1996: 33). They can 'cross-examine' witnesses and moderators assist them in drawing up recommendations. The fact that 'jurors' are compensated by pay-ment for their efforts resolves some of the problems associated with 'voluntarism' and the unrepresentativeness of 'volunteers' that undermine traditional consultative arrangements (as discussed in Chapter 5).

At a time in which the 'legal' jury is the subject of severe criticism (see Roskill 1986; Findlay and Duff 1988), the rise of its 'political' equivalent may appear somewhat strange. Nevertheless, the model allows for an informed dialogue to begin to take place, albeit with a limited number of people, which goes beyond people's 'common sense' and seeks to establish 'good sense' (Brogden *et al.* 1988: 189). By necessity this should involve the consideration of wider social implications beyond the merely parochial. It is also argued that juries can restore a vital element of deliberation to the demo-cratic process and encourage a habit of citizenship at the local level (Stewart 1996: 32). However, representativeness remains prob-lematic, as does the inclusiveness of those 'experts' consulted. Simi-larly, the problem of differential power relations between 'expert' witnesses and lay 'jurors' raises issues as to whether jurors are able, or willing, to arrive at independent decisions or whether they will merely act as a rubber stamp for policy predetermined 'elsewhere'. Citizens' juries so far do not have a good record of effecting change, either in Germany or the US (Milne 1996: 8). They could be regarded as expensive talking shops used to legitimate unpopular policies. Indeed, the very name 'jury' is misleading since a legal jury has the power to make decisions that must be implemented, whereas a citizens' jury's recommendations are not binding.

Furthermore, the terms of reference of the jury will be set by others and may be restrictively or narrowly defined. The role and influence of moderators remains ambiguous. In addition, there remains the danger of majoritarianism which fails to accord significant protection to minority interests, even though members of a jury may express different views in the final report. This is an issue which the 'legal' equivalent, in part, addresses by requiring unanimity or at least a substantial majority consensus (ten out of twelve) before a decision is reached, albeit potentially at the expense of integrity within the process. Related to this, again of significance in legal debates, is the question of openness of the decision making process and its reviewability. For example, the hearings conducted at the Lewisham drugs-related crime reduction experiment were held in private (Campbell 1996). It is unclear whether the decision making processes are themselves bounded by any democratic values. Although, according to supporters great stress is laid on maintaining the integrity of the process in both America and Germany, in part due to the fact that juries are conducted by independent centres with no particular view to support (Stewart 1996: 34). Nevertheless, there is the problem that if citizens' juries do find themselves in a position to influence important policy issues, they may come under direct lobbying pressure from organized pressure groups. Vested interests may seek to influence jurors' decision making in ways which may be difficult to regulate. Finally, a jury, as a short-term, one-off event, fails to construct the basis for an ongoing, long-term dialogue between local people and the relevant institutions. Like surveys, if used sensitively and constructively, juries may introduce an interesting level of experimentation in local democracy, in which ordinary people can potentially have a considerable influence upon local policy agendas. However, their inherently short-term essence and practical ambiguities limit the significance of their scope and contribution.

Processes of Contestability

Geoff Mulgan (1993) writing in a working paper for the Demos centre-left political think tank, has suggested that one way out of the contemporary deficit of accountability and legitimacy may be through the construction of processes of 'contestability' and competition. Mulgan's particular concern lies in relation to the proliferation of quangos, but similar arguments can be extended to other forms of 'partnerships' and policy networks. He argues that democracy is predicated on competitive processes and the public's power to remove unpopular governments. He believes that ultimately it is only the threat of ejection which makes politicians act efficiently and in the public interest (Mulgan 1993: 6). His model of 'contestability' involves two essential elements. The first is an appointments process which he calls a 'democratic version of competitive tendering' (Mulgan 1993: 7). An Appointments Commission would need to be established, drawn from national and local government, and other agreed representatives. The Commission would scrutinize and select a contractor from amongst bids put before them. Bidders would be required to set out their plans, including the targets that they aim to achieve, and the criteria and indicators by which they would wish to be judged. It is argued that such a process encourages creative 'coalition building' between interested groups, makes the criteria of evaluation transparent, and renders the selection procedure 'democratic in spirit' (Mulgan 1993: 8).

The second element in the process allows voters dissatisfied with the performance of a local quango or 'partnership' the power to call a local referendum on whether it should be allowed to maintain its contract or funding from government. This can be triggered if 2.5 per cent of the relevant population covered by a particular body sign a formal petition calling for the change in the make up of the board. It is argued that the very existence of this 'negative authorization' and process of 'management by exception' would be a powerful incentive for quangos and 'partnerships' to ensure responsive local governance. Hence, 'the power of the boot' is held up as a threat of 'last resort' (Mulgan 1993: 9).

Mulgan's proposals, whilst attractive in their attempt to combine democratic accountability with basic efficiencies of 'good governance', are limited by a number of problems with particular regard to crime control. First, as Mulgan recognizes, if the threshold of dismissal (i.e. his suggestion of 2.5 per cent) is set too low there may be a danger of excessive instability, and conversely, if set too high there may be a danger of inertia within the process. Secondly, the power proposed is neither creative nor proactive, but rather is wholly negative and reactive. It is concerned primarily with the criteria that Jones *et al.* (1994: 1996) refer to as 'redress' and subject to the same limitations identified earlier. It is not a power to set agendas but to respond to agendas set elsewhere. Democratic power needs to be structured as an enabling, as well as a limiting, force. There is only a tangential democratic input into the appointment process outlined by Mulgan, even if greater transparency may encourage grass-roots pressures for certain contract criteria to become recognized, or to be a prequisite for selection. Thirdly, there is the possibility that the bidding process will not generate options of sufficient quality, or that no suitable alternative to the established contract holder can be found. This is particularly problematic in the field of crime control where the existence of alternative providers may not be forthcoming. For example, it would be hard to imagine that a multi-agency group of police, probation officers, social workers, and housing officers set up to tackle crime on a public sector housing estate could be replaced by an alternative group with access to the same organizational resources and facilities. Such a scenario would be an organizational nightmare of internal competition. And yet, one might imagine a security firm succeeding in bidding for a contract to police a certain area in competition with the public police. The experience of 'Community Force' in Sedgefield suggests that this may not be such a far-off possibility. Mulgan's response to this problem is to assert the need for a credible default option which could involve local authority management (1993: 10). In the field of crime control it is difficult to see how this could constitute a credible option.

As I have sought to show through my emphasis upon mechanisms of govern*ance* rather than govern*ment*, we should not presume that the processes requiring democratization are anchored primarily, or in any simplistic way, in the sovereign state. The contract with government may not be the sole or even primary source of funding. Many contemporary 'partnerships' have highly complex relations with central or local government and unlike some quangos these are neither directly nor simply contractual. Consequently, the power of government to enforce 'the boot' may be limited or even unrealistic. Finally, the boundaries, constituencies, and therefore the possible electorate, of given 'partnerships' are often (deliberately) ambiguous. Mulgan's proposals are really only applicable to clearly defined geographical areas.

Democratic Partnerships

None of the above are solutions in themselves to the democratic deficit in crime control. The changing nature of socio-political relations may require multiple strategies to reinvigorate local democracy. Nevertheless, it is vitally important that commentators are beginning to recognize the problematic nature of the relationship between 'partnerships' and democratic accountability, and acknowledging the need to think politically about the democratic principles that underpin those 'partnerships'. The democratization of 'regulated self-regulation' and 'private interest government' is a fundamental prerequisite for the transformation of existing institutions into the 'ideal' forms of social and economic governance that Hirst (1994) envisages in 'voluntary self-governing associations' or as promoted by communitarians as 'self-governing communities' (Etzioni 1993). Where I part company with these visions is in a particular sensitivity to the problematics of democracy in the field of crime control. This arises from an empirical concern as to the actual relations within and between associations and communities, and the power of crime to divide (which I began to explore in Chapters 4 and 5, and will consider in greater detail in Chapter 8). As a consequence, I have outlined a vision of democracy as communication, defined not in terms of popular majorities but in terms of the quality of decision making that arises out of the interaction between the governing agency and the intermediary representative bodies organizing the activity being governed. In this, the adequate flow of information as a process of effective two-way dialogue between the agencies and the public is crucial. Hence, I have outlined both a much more prescriptive notion of democracy, in its form and content, than either Hirst or the communitarians, and one in which the state—at local, regional, and national levels—continues to occupy a significant interventionist regulatory, mediatory, and facilitatory role.[2]

[2] Hirst's associationalism extols the virtues of 'participation' as a democratic ideal, one which is particularly problematic in a crime control context. In his vision the state, over time, cedes functions to voluntary associations which are self-governing and pursue benefits for their members in co-operative ways which are more effective than individual action. Nevertheless, even Hirst recognizes the need for a 'common public power' (1994: 33). The essential bounding mechanisms of associations are limited to two requirements. First, that they are *voluntary*, i.e. they must be freely chosen by individuals for the purpose of their own interests. Secondly, there must be an unconditional *right of exit*, the legal defence of which

Further, it needs to be recognized that it is easier to render 'communities of place' democratically accountable than communities of interest, identity or concern. First, their boundaries are more fixed and hence more easily identifiable, even if often they are politically arbitrary. Secondly, they relate to, and can complement, existing channels of representation through local authorities, which are themselves based on 'a sense of place' (Stewart 1996: 38). However, there is an associated danger that in recognizing communities of place, other communities, which may be increasingly relevant in contemporary social life and which transcend geography, will be neglected or shielded from the 'democratic gaze'.

Conclusions

As we have seen, current trends towards neo-corporatist partnerships and policy networks signal a significant detachment of governance from institutional structures of 'public will-formation'. In its place is a technocratic and managerialist image of crime control which extols the disciplines of financial accounting and 'corporative expertise'. Hence, we have seen a move away from 'political' forms of accountability towards 'financial' and 'managerial' models. Simultaneously, there is a transfer of normatively regulated powers to systems that function with little regard for the quality of decision making processes and communication. In sum, current trends suffer from a severe democratic deficit to the extent that one might predict, in the long-term, that if not addressed these will translate into legitimacy deficits. Questions about the direction and methods of crime control and prevention are inherently political and not purely technical or administrative. Consequently, there is a pressing need for the democratization of partnerships and policy networks.

However, this is not to hark back to a mythical golden age of democracy in crime control. Rather, I have sought to identify the need to grapple both with the current changing sites of governance and the deficiencies with existing and traditional democratic institutions. In relation to the former, we need to acknowledge that the

by the public power, 'is more important than any positive interventions by the public power to ensure that the association is democratic' (1994: 51). He goes on to argue that the rules applied to the governance of association must be 'as few as are consistent with preventing them oppressing their members and denying them choice' (1994: 51–2).

sites of power are shifting and that the contemporary processes of policy making of import are occurring in novel and non-traditional settings. In relation to the latter, we need to recognize the failure of traditional structures of local representation to encourage participation, include marginalized voices, and foster kinds of socially just policy outcomes, particularly in the field of crime control.

And yet, we cannot dismiss all recent trends as inherently anti-democratic. Forms of informational and organizational accountability can supplement political processes. Financial accountability and 'consumer sovereignty' have done much to expose the shortcomings of a patronizing traditional welfarist relationship between the state and the individual. They have highlighted the need for a reciprocal relationship between service providers and citizens, one which embodies responsiveness and redress, both of which we have seen to be key elements in progressive notions of democracy. And yet, in the context of a neo-liberal hegemony the 'mesmeric grip of accounting' (Humphrey *et al.* 1993), performance indicators, and individualized choice have undermined other forms of political accountability. Similarly, the role of 'trust' and the space for a 'public purpose' have been dealt a severe blow. There is a need to work with and against the ambiguities of financial accountability and the contradictions of the recent managerialist reforms. Hence, the criteria of performance and service delivery, as elements of reciprocity, both have a democratic place so far as they are constituted around an informed and ongoing dialogue between service providers and public. As Kaser has suggested there is an overwhelming need to reclaim the 'politics of value' from within notions of 'value for money' (1988: 53).

The debate about the possible mechanisms through which new modes of governance can be rendered more democratically accountable, particularly at the local level, is only just beginning. In this chapter, I have considered and critically evaluated only a few of the possible alternatives. This review highlights that the reinvigoration of democracy requires imaginative thinking and experimentation as many of the old certainties have been shaken by the rearticulation of relation across the threshold of the state, market, and civil society. This is not to suggest that traditional models of representative democracy are redundant, far from it, rather they need to be complemented by additional layers and dimensions of political accountability. Different models may prove to be more relevant to different policy sectors and different localities. What is clear is that, in relation to crime control and prevention, democracy needs to be robust to secure pluralism and diversity by locating individual rights outside the reach of moral majorities. Hence, there is a pressing need to move beyond majoritarianism and the individualistic language of 'consumer', to incorporate a 'public purpose' which constantly seeks to pull 'citizens' away from the margins of society.

8
Local or Social Justice?

In this chapter I will take an avowedly jaundiced view of some of the path-dependent possible implications of recent developments in the governance of crime and appeals to 'community'. Particular concern will be given to issues of *social* justice and responsibility. In part, what follows will be a deliberately speculative account which does not constitute a 'history of the present', but rather the identification of a sometimes loose constellation of tendencies, trends, and forces, not all of which are necessarily pulling in the same direction at the same time. The aim, here, is to accentuate the darker and sombre forces at play as a sobering device, in order to begin to debate, engage with, and fashion ways of avoiding such scenarios. In doing so, it is my contention that dystopian futures are intrinsically avoidable given sufficient political insight, will, and commitment. At the heart of this lies a need to think more normatively and politically than hitherto about the principles of a public civic polity and simultaneously to engage with the transformations to local governance and the current trends in social and economic life.

The chapter commences with a discussion of shifts in responsibility heralded by recent developments and their possible implications both for the commodification of security and the evaluation of 'success' and 'failure' in crime control policy. In an individualized and market-driven context, in which potential victims are charged with the responsibility for their own safety, what is the role of a public polity and what are meant by notions of social justice? In this light, the implications of marketization on the construction of 'community' will be considered. Given some of the logics and dynamics of recent developments, as outlined thus far, we need to consider a further series of questions: what might the future landscape of the city look like? How might the various communities within and around cities interact and inter-relate? Is crime an appropriate subject matter around which to restore bonds of community? And if so, to what kinds of communities might this give rise?

It will be argued that, against the background of social polarization and the spatial concentration of poverty and wealth, the politics of 'community' invites and expresses the power to exclude. Security, or at least a sense of it, may become a predominant characteristic in the map of future social relations, particularly in urban areas, with insulation from undesirable 'others' as its defining logic. In this light, 'appeals to community', given the exclusivity and localism they breed, may be antithetical to social justice.

However, it is not my intention to suggest that community participation is neither a legitimate nor appropriate response to crime. A cursory glance at the history of social control must provoke an acknowledgement that 'community' always has been, and will continue to be, a crucial, if not the fundamental, site of social control. Hence, community disapproval against crime must be an essential element in prevention strategies. Rather, it is my intention to identify some of the possible implications of the present appeals to community in crime control and the shifts in responsibility that they herald. In the rush to appropriate the 'community' and 'partnerships' as artillery pieces in the new 'war on crime', too many issues have been ignored without due consideration. So far I have sought to expose some of the ideological underpinnings which lurk in the inky waters of conceptual obfuscation. The contention of this chapter is that we need to be as aware of the social hazards of appeals to 'community' and 'partnerships' as we should be ready to celebrate their virtues.

Shifts in Responsibility for Security

As we have already seen, 'responsibilization strategies' are a key element in the current governance of crime. Private individuals, groups, and associations are being entreated and summoned to play an active role and accept their own greater responsibility for crime prevention. Where government ministers and chief police officers once claimed that the task of policing should be left to the 'professionals', now they claim that 'policing cannot be left to the police alone' (Home Office 1993b). The 'community' and public, previously defined as recipients of a service—a conception supported and extended by the establishment of the welfare state—more recently have been called upon, in various different ways, to join the 'fight against crime'. Now crime prevention is to become a part of the 'routine day to day practice and culture' of individuals and agencies (Home Office 1993c: 16). This is tantamount to a redrawing of the boundaries of legitimate public intervention. In this context, 'community' is the principal site around which legitimacy is being sought for a new relationship between state, market, and the public. 'Community', as we saw in Chapter 5, is the contested terrain upon which a recalibration of public expectations in service delivery is being played out.

Indeed, the 'attitude shift' which, constitutes an integral aspect of dominant accounts of 'community' (discussed in Chapter 5), is in reality little more than the acceptance of a redefinition of the limited responsibilities for the state by groups and individuals. A prominent police chief constable recently commented that an essential element in the future role of a chief constable will be 'managing public expectations and perceptions' (Butler 1996: 227) rather than passively responding to them. Community initiatives allow relevant criminal justice agencies simultaneously to be seen to be 'doing something' (in an effort to meet public expectations of, and demands for, action) and to attempt to rearticulate and redefine the boundaries of the public's legitimate expectations of state agencies. Community involvement is, therefore, a means of managing and steering expectations. In this new relationship the financial burden of private and group security is no longer the state's alone. 'Community' incorporation has become a means of shifting the cost away from formal state agencies and onto individuals and communities.

And yet, responsibility not only carries the burden of cost but also is accompanied by the weight of blame for failure. The Safer Cities co-ordinator on the Churchway project alluded to the significance of this shift:

that's part of the whole interesting thing, for the last half decade of, you know, 'law and order is not just a matter for the police', a limited truth, but it's now really getting to the point where you're beginning to wonder if it's a matter for them at all, or [if it's] everybody else's problem.

Now (as was suggested in Chapter 3), crime prevention has become the responsibility of potential victims. This is the message of the Home Office's handbook 'Practical Ways to Crack Crime' (first published in 1989) which through various editions has sought to shake the general public out of its perceived apathy towards the protection of self and property. The primary responsibility for preventing opportunistic crime now lies with potential victims who have been thus armed with practical advice. The victim, rather like the offender assumed to inhabit the world of situation crime prevention, is cast in the role of the 'rational choice actor'. He or she is notionally free to make choices as to what level of security is desired, by weighing up the costs and benefits. Victimization, thus envisaged, becomes the outcome of rational choices—whether or not to purchase security devices, visit particular places or engage in certain 'lifestyles'—for which the victim bears ultimate responsibility. In this logic 'carelessness' becomes the catch-phrase of victim blaming. This has been evident in successive government advertising campaigns, under the now long-standing banner of 'together we can crack crime'. The latest 1996 version suggests quite bluntly that those individuals who fail to join neighbourhood watch schemes— or by implication those communities in which such schemes never get off the ground—are actually colluding with the criminals, literally giving them 'a helping hand' in the commission of their offences.

Through analogous 'responsibilization strategies' and the devolution of certain powers and duties for the management of crime prevention to local neo-corporatist structures, both government and state agencies have increasingly sought to distance themselves from association with failure and blame. This decentralization results in:

a pluralization of the centre, enabling the problems of the state to rebound back on society, so that society is implicated in the task of resolving them, where previously the state was expected to hand down an answer for society's needs

(Donzelot 1991: 178)

The conceptual confusion surrounding 'community'—both as a means and an end, and the virtuous cycle within which community and prevention are symbolically connected—provides an ideological terrain upon which it becomes easy for certain socially deprived areas, which do not accord with the idealized notion of the community-crime prevention equation, to be written off as beyond redemption. This creates ripe conditions in which 'social problems' can be seen not as the product of government policies but of poor moral standards within communities. Hence, certain communities line up alongside offenders as blameworthy for *their* 'crime problem'. Here community blaming marches hand in hand with victim blaming (Walklate 1991: 209).

These 'irredeemable' communities are 'Britain's dangerous places' (Campbell 1993), where marginalized youths (neither full consumers nor citizens), vagrants, drug abusers, prostitutes, and so forth are identified as the architects of neighbourhood change and economic decline, rather than as its victims. Alongside them are those forced to share or inhabit the same spaces and those unable or unwilling to flee, and yet powerless to make a significant difference. This pathological understanding of 'community' has the potential not only for undermining the tolerance of diversity in heterogeneous communities through 'norm enforcement', but also for creating modern 'no go' areas in and around our major cities (a theme to which I return later in this chapter).

Both 'failed' individuals and communities in the present neo-liberal political climate, which celebrates autonomy, choice, and responsibility, come to be seen as culpable, liable, and thus justifiably blamed, for their own marginalization and exclusion. They are constructed as the architects of their own social position, disadvantage, and victimization. As Rose suggests:

Those who were previously the object of a social politics are also reconceptualised within this regime of choice. They are accorded a new personal responsibility for their 'marginalisation' from this new regime of the choosing, consuming, autonomous subject . . . They no longer, as they did previously, serve as a potent reminder of the need for a politics of social solidarity and care: their plight remains, in some sense or other, an outcome of their personal capacities to choose; intervention must on the one hand, limit the social threat that they pose, and, on the other, compel them to accept their responsibility to organise their freely chosen life in a social form.

(1994: 385)

Whilst there are clear dangers, implicit in Rose's statement, in romanticizing the past, what is evident is that an increasing emphasis upon 'autonomy, responsibility, and choice', has marched hand in hand with growing social polarization.

This is neither an argument against greater collective responsibility *per se*, nor a rejection of the language of responsibility in order to turn the clock back to a mythical age in which the central state was responsible for all crime control. Appropriately, the ideals of civic republicanism have at their heart the active and participatory citizen (Braithwaite and Pettit 1990; Braithwaite 1995). Rather, the discussion here should awaken us to the context in which responsibilization is occurring. This is one of power imbalances, differential experiences of crime, and structural inequality. In this context, we need to problematize the conditions under which responsibility, be it collective, communal, familial or individual, can be exercised or maximized (O'Malley 1994b: 23). The central problem for communities which have sought to build social institutions and develop empowerment strategies for their internal members, is that the conditions under which responsibility can be activated, nurtured, and allowed to prosper is continually being undermined. The paradox of community crime prevention, as Hope notes in a recent review of the research, stems from:

the problem of trying to build community institutions that control crime in the face of their powerlessness to withstand the pressures towards crime in the community, whose source, or the forces that sustain them, derive from the wider social structure.

(1995a: 24)

Security as Commodity

The marketization of crime control and prevention has resulted in the commodification of security (Spitzer 1987). Crime prevention has become a growth industry whilst the security market has mushroomed in both size and scope (Jones and Newburn 1995).[1] As a commodity crime prevention holds out the promise that 'security' can be attained through purchase: buying 'expert' preventative technology and security hardware; employing 'trustworthy' intermediary services; moving to 'safe' areas, and so on. And yet, security is more complex a phenomenon than commodification would suggest. By its nature 'security' is defined in relation to an *absence* in time and in space (Spitzer 1987: 47). It is the negative corollary of

[1] Commentators like Christie (1993) and Lilly and Knepper (1992) suggest that what we are witnessing is the displacement of techniques and personnel from the military apparatus, with the decline of the 'Communist threat', to domestic law enforcement in the form of a 'corrections-commercial complex'. In an analogous vein, Cohen suggests that in the USA the cult of national security represented by the Soviet threat may have given way to a cult of personal insecurity which links the dangers of predatory crime with other nameless risks (1996: 10).

fear, risk, and danger.[2] Conceptually, security embodies no positive attributes but rather lacks contrary ones. Security is the quest for a situation or moment in which something undesirable does not exist or does not occur. As such, it embodies elements of subjectivity but is also subject to manipulation on the back of public anxiety. This is not to suggest that anxieties about crime are unfounded (see Crawford *et al.* 1990; Young 1992)—on the contrary for many it is a negotiated aspect of everyday life—nor that levels of crime, notably street crime, do not have direct and corrosive effects upon the social psyche. Neither is it intended to imply a morally abstentionist position regarding the responsibility and blame of offenders for the harm that crime inflicts. Rather, it is to suggest that the impact and experience of this (social as well as individual) harm is (increasingly) unevenly distributed throughout society. It is socially situated. Consequently, it has different cultural inflexions and referents.

Despite the rationalistic tones of much security discourse, security as a commodity is intrinsically related to complex individual and collective sentiments of insecurity, anxiety, and fear, all of which are connected to wider, subjective and non-rationalistic elements of social identity and well-being (Sparks 1992b: 124). Danger has many meanings for people, including, but extending far beyond, crime. It connects not only with experience (both personal and vicarious), local knowledge, tradition, and folklore (Smith 1986), but also with unconscious fantasies, desires, and traumas. Buying 'security' may be a way in which actors can attempt to situate and interpret themselves and the world around them as stable, coherent, and manageable despite, or maybe because of, the realities of uncertainty, fragmentation, powerlessness, and a loss of collective identity. As such it may represent a quest for an unattainable and imaginary idyll in which we seek comfort, reassurance, and order. And yet, security speaks to those seeking it through assurances and guarantees as to its objective effects (Shearing 1992: 401).

Moreover, as Taylor (1996) has argued, these private 'desires' nurtured in respect of everyday life by powerful, suburban middle classes, may have wider horizons, particularly in terms of the future political and economic prospects of a given city. Crime can undermine 'quality of life' concerns and attempts to promote and reposition a given city within national, European, and/or global

[2] Although see Giddens's discussion of the differences between 'risk' and 'danger' (1990: 34–5).

economies. The symbolic and material significance of crime and the fear of crime in different localities, therefore, may be interwoven with other issues to do with 'urban fortunes' (Taylor 1996: 334). It is here that suburban fears, anxieties, and aspirations connect with 'growth coalitions', particularly city-wide partnerships such as the Northley project, which seek to project a certain status image for the city.

And yet, Taylor overplays this connection through an over-emphasis on, first, the relation between commercial businesses and the success of local 'urban boosterism'; and secondly, the sense of loyalty and commitment, within suburban populations, to the city as a place. Large commercial enterprises uniformly do not have such a committed 'sense of place'. They can and do move their operations and headquarters out of cities into safer and more secure environs. Further, he ignores the fact that many in the suburbs do not define themselves as part of the city, but rather tend to define themselves in contradistinction to it. In part this is due to the connections between 'the city' (particularly the 'inner-city') and crime. As important as it is to understand the role of city-wide partnerships in relation to 'growth coalition' and 'urban fortunes', there are powerful economic and 'security' determinants which may render such coalitions precarious, most notably when local factors collide with city-wide interests. The relation between a 'local sense of well-being' and 'the good standing of the broader conurbation' in which suburbs are located (Taylor 1996: 318), is more complex than Taylor suggests: the former can also serve to undermine the latter, particularly when the perceived threat to the local sense of well-being derives from its relationship with the broader conurbation (as in Northley).

The symbolic embodiment of danger is often represented through the unknown and the contingent alien 'other'. Despite the empirical research which suggests that danger is most likely to be posed by the familiar and the familial, the figure of the 'stranger' has an abiding hold over our cultural referents of 'danger' as well as policy discourse (Stanko 1990b). Difference, therefore, can be an important signifier through which anxieties are triggered. Merry concluded her ethnographic research in an heterogeneous neighbourhood in an American city, with the summation that: 'Danger encompasses the fear of the stranger, the morally reprehensible, disorderly, or culturally alien person, and the anonymous member of a hostile and threatening social category' (1981: 223). A sense of danger may arise from antagonisms, both real and symbolic, between groups which emerge from class, gender, and cultural differences. In this context, anxiety sells. This is not to suggest that people's fears about crime and victimization are unfounded (Crawford *et al.* 1990; Young 1992). The salience of given risks and fears for individuals is related to the place they occupy within different cultures (Sparks 1992b: 127). They are differently interpreted and mean different things for different groups of people who experience different everyday social realities. On top of this, fears, and anxieties are fed by the seductive lure of 'security'.

Moreover, even 'rational risk assessment' and 'future probability calculations', as Ericson notes (1996), are always inexact. They are best guesses at predicting control over an unknowable, unpredictable, and risky social world (Spitzer 1987; Beck 1992). This requires a leap of faith, one which is always subject to being undermined by new developments or shifts in feelings of (in)security. Consequently, the commodified notion of '*private* security' may itself be an oxymoron (Loader 1997). First, in the sense that it is an unachievable goal: 'a new form of "magic" within a system that eschews the invisible and the unknowable' (Spitzer 1987: 47). Perversely, the acquisition of more and more 'security as commodity', may serve to undermine feelings of genuine 'security' by institutionalizing anxiety (Loader 1997). The 'anxiety market' may have an inexorable ratcheting effect due to the insatiability of security. In this context, 'security generates its own paranoid demand' (Davis 1990: 224). Secondly, on the one hand, 'security as commodity' appears to offer 'consumers' real choices, as to what to purchase, through which they can confront and try to manage the social environment which envelops them. However, on the other hand, these choices carry with them anxieties and uncertainties, and demand further responsibilities and trust. Security as an ideal remains an illusion and one perpetually subject to potential fracturing. Once 'security' (technologies or people) has been invested in, its *failure to secure* may deal a severe blow to any trust relations which that person had sought through expert systems or personnel, ones which subsequently may be hard to repair. In addition, as we have seen, the outcome of these choices—despite the manner in which they may meet a real need in the short-term—serve to undermine 'community' and the possibility for equality (Spitzer 1987: 58). These are individual choices which may impact upon others' security and sense of safety. Hence, in a regime of choice in which security is an exalted—albeit potentially insatiable—commodity there may be an inherent antagonism between *feeling secure* and *being social*. The individualistic quest for personal security may undermine the public sphere and people's experience of it.

In reality, therefore, 'community' often means little more than the sum total of individuals living within a given locality, whilst 'the public' is defined as the outcome of competing individual private interests. In the context of policing and crime control, as in other fields of state performance, the marketization of social life has increasingly created the perception of society as a series of private spheres in which individuals, corporations, and organizations must take responsibility for their own problems. In this context concepts like the 'public good' and 'social value' are seen as merely the outcomes of market processes.

As we saw in Chapter 3, the emergence of 'mass private property' in which much human activity occurs, has further fragmented the notion of a genuinely 'public sphere'. In doing so, it has increased the 'private' power to exclude. A defining feature of such privately controlled public spaces is the lure of 'security' that they appear to offer. The modern shopping mall is the clearest example, incorporating into its very architectural design and fabric the latest social control mechanisms, symbols of security, and 24-hour surveillance. Increasingly, however, other types of 'secure zones' such as private parks, playgrounds, and entertainment venues, are springing up in and around the city. Here, entry is restricted and behaviour monitored. These zones or 'new enclosures' are a far cry from the Habbermasian notion of public space, where 'access is guaranteed to all citizens' (1989a); rather they rely upon and foster exclusion.

The Quest for Security and the Construction of Community

This leaves us with the question which Nelken (1985: 239) poses: is *crime* the appropriate vehicle around which to regenerate communities? And if so, what sort of communities will we be generating through such a focus? As we saw in Chapter 5, one of the dominant meanings of the concept of community is that those who are members of it, those who belong to it, have something in common. This commonality marks off community members from outsiders who do not belong and/or are not permitted to belong. A crucial aspect in the study of communities must be, therefore, not only a consideration of their cohesion but also of their defensiveness. There are dangers that, with *crime* as the focus for the construction of community and social relations which it fosters, 'community'—like 'security'—will come to mean little more than an absence: to mean less what people positively share in common, but inversely, what they are against, the perceived threatening 'outsider'. Their commonality thus becomes their defensiveness. Given the anxieties, fear, and outrage that crime can evoke, 'security'—i.e. the absence of perceived danger—may come to define communities in terms of outsides, about whom community members know little, but whose only defining characteristic is their ability (through fear) to unify and solidify community membership. Here lies the potential space for the emergence of 'imagined communities' (Anderson 1983), no less real for being 'imagined', with little in common but an abiding fear of an increasingly mythical 'other'. The more they retreat internally the more the 'other' takes on a frightening form.

The rhetorical force of the language of 'community', as Lacey has argued, lies in the fact that it speaks to our fears at the same moment as it whispers to our fantasies (1996: 110). It has a 'profound emotional legitimacy' (Anderson 1983: 14), in that it holds out the ideal of genuine human identity, connectedness, and reciprocity precisely at a time in which they appear most absent. Lacey draws upon psychoanalytic theory to suggest that in this relationship between 'self-identity' and 'otherness', signifiers such as 'community' leave an important space for, and speak to, fantasies of the subjects to whom they are addressed. Most fundamentally, ' "community" speaks to aspects of the Real which concern the role of the Other in underpinning (yet constantly threatening) the subject's identity' (Lacey 1996: 112). In this light, 'defended communities' can become self-perpetuating. The external threat, whether actual or imagined, becomes both the reason for, and the means of sustaining, 'community'. Its collective past and future are both defined by the perceived external threat. In such a context, the collective identity which emerges can become idealized, all-pervasive and rigid, the perfect conditions for intolerance of others to breed.

Crime, as the focus of community construction, presents itself as a pre-eminent producer of 'defended communities'. In essence these may be the 'communities of choice' which communitarians and associationalists extol, but in reality their characteristics are closer in resemblance to 'communities of fate' (Hirst 1994). The marketization of social life, and in particular the commercialization of

crime, can affect, and have influenced, the ways in which communities, groups, and organizations constitute their boundaries,
select their members, exclude others, and construct a sense of identity. Marketization has provoked incentives—both costs and benefits
—into the calculation of community formation. As even public
sector institutions are discovering, it is easier and often in their
interests to exclude 'problem' populations. Thus, for schools with
one eye on league tables in a regime of choice, it may not be in their
interests to (re)integrate and (re)incorporate the 'disruptive' and
'difficult' pupils (Blyth and Milner 1993). Exclusion becomes a
defining characteristic of community formation. Jeffers *et al.* conclude their recent empirical investigation into community formation
around race and ethnicity with the following poignant observation:

The logic underpinning the process of group formation and the deployment of more or less inclusive or exclusive boundaries seemed to us to be
a complex by-product of the degree of defensiveness felt by such groups,
combined with the purpose of that mobilisation.

(1996: 120)

Given both the anxieties that crime evokes and its tendency to
bifurcate the criminal from the law abiding, and the 'rough' from
the 'respectable', crime may well be the worst social issue around
which to construct open, tolerant, and inclusive communities. The
preoccupation with security may have less to do with personal safety
than with the degree of personal insulation from certain 'others'.

It is in this dislocation between the social and the communal that
forms of racism breed (Wieviorka 1995). Some commentators have
highlighted the fear that within this context 'community' can become, and may be becoming, a 'new byword for bigotry' (Malik
1995). The danger behind appeals to 'community' is, as Edward
Said suggests, 'that you cannot both "belong" and concern yourself
with . . . [others] who do not belong' (1988: 178). To belong to a
'community', by the process of inclusion may mean to lessen concern for those who are excluded, or at worst to be hostile towards
them. The assumptions implicit in notions of the 'community', of
organic wholeness and of a given fixed collectivity, can be inimical
to a politics of difference (Yual-Davis 1992). For those excluded,
left out, left behind, and left at the margins, those 'foci of identity
may appear as classes used to, as communities of fate and resistance'
(Hirst 1994: 66).

Further, as we saw in Chapter 5, crime as an issue around which to organize communities, can be a double-edged sword in its ability to stigmatize areas. The very recognition that crime is a problem in a given area can be enough to start up a series of social and economic processes which may result in that area becoming associated with crime. Such an association can be a self-fulfilling prophecy as people and capital flee an area through the fear of victimization or in order to avoid any 'secondary' stigmatization.

Social Exclusion and Ghettoization

The most dangerous aspect of 'appeals to community' lies where ideals confront empirical reality. In Britain, like the USA, the idea of 'community' collides with a social and geographical map which is becoming ever more fragmented, economically divided, and socially stretched. In this context, 'community' can be a disabling abstraction whose effect is to obscure the differences and conflicts within and between groups of people which infuse everyday life. Appeals to community, overlaid upon today's social and economic realities, may serve to entrench, extend, and legitimize inequalities. They can all too easily conceal questions about the relative distribution of social and economic disadvantage, including safety from crime. In their most extreme forms they can be an advance guard for a type of spatial apartheid, in which 'security differentials' widen, and the boundaries of community are constructed around 'defensive exclusivity'.

Whilst republican criminology's ideal of a minimalist state response in the field of crime control and criminal justice policy alongside strong state interventionism in economic policy (Braithwaite (1995: 280) is an important long-term aim not to lose sight of, the empirical reality of appeals to community in crime control is a maximization of communal response in relation to crime coupled with an absence of significant external (state) economic interventionism. It is in this context that we need to be cautious of the potential dangers of 'community', particularly its anti-state interventionism.

The Spatial Concentration of Social Disadvantage

The geographic polarization of rich and poor has been a marked feature of socio-economic change in Britain over the last fifteen years (Harker and Oppenheim 1996). The 'Joseph Rowntree Foundation Inquiry into Income and Wealth' (Barclay 1995; Hills 1995) documents an increase in the local concentration and spatial polarization of poverty between the years 1981 and 1991. The Report notes that 'the most striking features since 1979 are the rapid rise in the share of the top 10 per cent and the fall (particularly after 1985) in the share of the poorest fifth' (Hills 1995: 36). Changes in local economy and housing are defining characteristics of this polarization (Power and Tunstall 1995). The decimation of traditional manufacturing industries, particularly mining and shipbuilding, in many parts of Britain has left geographical communities without the economic base around which they were constructed, and with little alternative economy (Hutton 1995). The public sector housing stock has undergone considerable residualization as a result of the 'right to buy' legislation of the early 1980s which led to the sale of a quarter of the national stock. Within this residual stock further residualization is significantly influenced by the 'social market' structured by the housing allocation policies of local authorities and housing associations (Bottoms and Wiles 1986; 1995).

Research conducted for the Joseph Rowntree Foundation into twenty of the most difficult to let estates in England, found evidence of considerable polarization (Power and Tunstall 1995). Unemployment levels on the estates were three times the national average and economic inactivity rose between 1981 and 1991, whereas it fell nationally. On these estates only a very small proportion of the housing stock had been sold to tenants (Power and Tunstall 1995: 4). The authors of the report found that the concentration of lone parents was four times greater, and the proportion of children obtaining no GCSE passes was over four times the average. In some places this concentration effect is overlaid by racial identity, in London, for example, up to 70 per cent of all residents in these areas were from ethnic minorities. The authors concluded: 'The fear of social breakdown resulting from the increasing concentration of the needy and vulnerable households was so acute that special localised measures to reinforce community stability were constantly needed.' (Power and Tunstall 1995: 4). National data also reflects this process of social stretching and the associated concentration effect of poverty and chronic joblessness for the low skilled. In 1989, 10 per cent of 16–19-year-old youths in the labour market were unemployed, by the summer of 1993 this figure had grown to 23 per cent.

Over the same period of time the number of 20–24-year-old people who were unemployed rose from 9.5 per cent to 17 per cent (cited in NACRO 1995: 30).[3] The spatial concentration of poverty has been exacerbated by the growing wealth of some within the population and the flight of people and capital out of certain localities. This 'market residualization' is resulting in a growing social dislocation which is fundamentally spatial in nature (Lash and Urry 1994: chapter 6; Wiles 1992: 63).

Consequently, as a number of reports have indicated, a large and growing number of people are being excluded, not only from schooling, employment and housing, but also from the benefits associated with them (European Commission 1994; Commission on Social Justice 1994; Barclay 1995; Hills 1995). What is especially problematic is the growing disparity between the rich and those who are being left behind. Commentators have suggested that these bifurcating processes are leading to a 'two thirds, one third society' (Therborn 1985), or what the provocative right-wing American commentator, Charles Murray, has recently referred to as the 'New Victorians' and the 'New Rabble' (1995: 16). Significant groups in the population are being socially excluded, geographically isolated, and politically cast aside. Waltzer aptly notes that:

We don't quite know what to call these people—the dispossessed, the underclass, the truly disadvantageous, the socially isolated, the estranged poor—and this confusion about their classification reflects a deeper embarrassment about their existence. For the whole tendency of modern (welfarist or social) democracy, so we once thought, is to make the reproduction of marginality and exclusion increasingly difficult.

(1993: 56)

These 'exclusions' are increasingly being recognized, particularly within Europe, as presenting a significant challenge to modern societies (European Commission 1994; Commission on Social Justice 1994). And yet, even this language, in which a fixed group—the underclass, the 'rabble', the 'one third', or whatever—is identified as excluded, is itself problematic. In its dominant form, first, it obscures the inequalities among the majority, the two thirds or

---

[3] Interestingly, the Rowntree report concludes that: 'Internationally, there has *not* been a universal trend towards greater inequality in recent years, although this has been the case in the majority of countries . . . The *speed* with which inequality increased over the 1980s was faster in the UK than in any other country for which data are available except New Zealand' (Hills 1995: 72, emphasis in original).

'overclass', who are cast as sharing the same experience and values. Secondly, members of the 'excluded' group themselves appear as homogeneous, driven by the same culture and experience (be it a culture of dependency or of deprivation). The experience of community, as we noted in Chapter 5, is not a uniformly shared one. Further, it tends to polarize difference between the underclass and everyone else, who are perceived to be 'doing just fine'. As such, this discourse, as Levitas acknowledges:

allows the recognition of the continuing existence of poverty—which can hardly be disguised—to coexist with arguments or assumptions about the attrition of class and class divisions in the main body of society.

(1996: 6)

Exclusions continue to operate on class lines, albeit overlaid by other multiple forms of exclusion which are expressed in more nuanced ways. More fundamentally, exclusions constitute a defining product of a capitalist economy. However, the dominant discourse tends to assume that inclusion is always beneficial, without regard to the questions, inclusion into what? and, under what conditions? As I have tried to show with my analysis of community partnerships, inclusion and exclusion, whilst fundamental aspects of power relations, should not be the end point of a critical gaze. We need, also, to look to the conditions under which the experience of inclusion operates. This, the dichotomous model of exclusion and integration, as Levitas notes, tends to obscure, and 'therein lies its appeal' (1996: 18).

The Spatial Concentration of Crime

Crime, like poverty and other forms of social harm, is not evenly spread throughout society but concentrated within certain social and geographical areas (Hope 1995b). Crime compounds other forms of social disadvantage. This 'compounding effect' occurs in two principal ways. First, those people who are most likely to be victims of crime are most prone to suffer other social problems, which may increase both the effects of victimization and victims' sense of long-term vulnerability. Secondly, people who are victims of one crime tend to be victims of other crimes or 'repeat victimization'.

Local victimization surveys have for some time highlighted the unequal distribution of victimization (Kinsey 1985; Jones *et al.*

1986; Crawford *et al.* 1990). However, it has taken secondary analysis of the findings from the British Crime Survey to show, despite methodological limitations (see Young 1988), considerable differences in both crime incidence—the average number of victimizations per head of population at risk of victimization, or 'crimes per head'—and *victim concentration*—the average number of victimizations per victim, or 'crimes per victim'—across different areas (Tricket *et al.* 1992). Comparing the 10 per cent of areas suffering the greatest crime incidence with the 10 per cent of areas suffering the least crime incidence, Tricket *et al.* found that there was an elevenfold difference in the prevalence of crimes against the person, and a fourfold difference in property crime (1992: 85). These figures, the authors note, are liable to be underrepresentations. They conclude their analysis declaring:

> The most prominent distinguishing characteristic of the high crime area when compared with the low crime area, therefore, is the relatively widespread extent of personal victimisation. While property crime gets worse in the high crime area, what gets very much worse is the probability of any citizen falling victim to a personal crime.
>
> (Trickett *et al.* 1992: 85)

More recently in a comparison of British Crime Survey findings over time—between 1982 and 1988—Tricket *et al.* (1995) found that the unequal distribution of victimization had increased. By 1988 people living in certain high crime areas were subject to a greater share of the national level of victimization—due to an increasing inequality in prevalence—and within those areas the burden of this increase was being suffered by a small number of households, through an increased inequality in concentration (Tricket *et al.* 1995: 350). This redistribution was shown to have occurred irrespective of the level of the national trend in crime.

The extent of 'multiple' or 'repeat' victimization is something that criminologists have only recently begun to recognize (Sparks 1981b; Genn 1988; Barr and Pease 1990; Farrell 1992), the impact and significance of which is still not fully realized (Farrell 1995). And yet, as a lens of inquiry it offers new insights into, and ways of documenting, victimization (especially through the focus upon victim concentration) and its differential social distribution. There are, however, dangers that the new-found interest in repeat victimization, particularly in its individualistic and positivistic forms, may have the unintended consequence of further stigmatising and blaming victims, by focusing upon individual attributes and 'life-style' of the victim as constituting 'causes' of victimization. More-over, there are dangers that criminological understandings of repeat victimization may enter the very different world of the insurance industry. There they can be used as a means of predicting risk and hence serve to raise the cost of, or conditions attached to, insurance premiums against those already the most vulnerable. Thus, insur-ance can act as a further, perverse, 'compounding effect'. The thin edge of this wedge is already clearly visible. According to a research report published by the Association of London Authorities (1994) residents of whole streets and estates in high crime areas are being refused cover by some insurance companies. The report describes the policy in one large company which allocates certain postcode areas to 'category R' , which means that all requests for insurance there must be referred to head office. The head office has lists of whole streets or estates where insurance is not granted. One insur-ance company employee is quoted as saying: 'There are certain postcode areas in which we consider it undesirable to do business' (ALA 1994).

Furthermore, by concentrating upon attributes of individuals or dwellings, commentators may miss a potentially crucial connection between an individual target of 'repeats' and the area or context in which they are situated. It may be that some 'repeats' tell us more about the locality than they do about the specific individual or household. In other words, 'repeats' may be symptomatic of wider social forces which transcend individuals (their 'lifestyle') or house-holds (their physical characteristics). Nevertheless, at individual, household and community levels, the identification of repeat victim-ization does offer an important, and potentially more egalitarian, basis for the allocation of scarce preventative resources (Farrell and Pease 1993: 15).

Spirals of Ghettoization?

Social and spatial polarization fundamentally undermine appeals to 'community' as a force of *social* cohesion. A particularly problematic aspect of these (old, although increasingly stretched) social divisions of wealth and power is the way in which they fuse with concerns about 'security' and the new-found sense of people's own responsi-bility to prevent or avoid risk. This adds a pernicious dimension to the process of social polarization, in which 'security differentials' become defining characteristics of wealth, power, and status. The formation of ghettos and 'islands of neglect', around which the high waters of 'security' (barbed wire, locks, surveillance cameras, and walled perimeters) separate rich and poor areas, is transforming the experience of poverty and criminal victimization.

Hence, while poverty, for many people who are not trapped by it, is something hidden, something 'out of sight and out of mind', so crime, for those same people, is 'elsewhere', something to be avoided, often by avoiding 'unsafe' places and 'menacing' or 'dangerous' people. Consequently, this polarization is in danger of transmuting the political agenda—at the level of both personal and governmental politics—as many people do not see themselves as occupying the same worlds as the poor and socially excluded. This can have a number of effects. First, ghettoization is likely to accentuate the lack of knowledge that people have about danger, upon which they develop adaptive strategies and negotiate safety (Stanko 1990b). Consequently, the spaces vacated by any intimate knowledge of areas in and around cities are likely to be filled by distorted media representations and generalizations from occasional panic stories. This is particularly probable amongst those people who intentionally flee inner-city areas in the search of suburban tranquillity. Areas that are unknown can more easily acquire a reputation for danger which may be unwarranted (Smith 1986). Greater, rather than less, knowledge of our cities is more likely to breed tolerance. Ghettoization may impact upon people's sensibilities, their cultural beliefs about safety and danger, and the appropriateness of place. Anxieties and fear of crime in the urban 'ghetto' and of the cultural connection between crime and place, will only serve to reinforce the processes of segregation and insulation.

Secondly, ghettoization can lead, and increasingly has led, commentators and politicians to ask what it is about certain communities that results in such concentrations of crime and poverty. Rather than highlighting the fact that the social and spatial distribution of victimization appear to reflect the distribution of access to economic, social, and political resources (Hope 1995b: 10), an increasingly vocal lobby currently asserts that this is evidence of a growing 'underclass'. In this context, the term is used to evoke the idea of a class of people set apart economically, geographically, culturally, and *morally*—particularly lone-parent families—born of a culture of dependency due to over-generous social benefits and welfare

(Murray 1990; 1995; Dennis 1993; Dennis and Erdos 1992). This is not the place to review these debates (see Campbell 1994; Kempson *et al.* 1994; Hobbs 1994), however, what they have managed to do is to reinforce, and give credibility to, the notion of the 'pathological community'. In so doing, they have contributed significantly to a predominant shift in discourse 'from poverty as "our" problem to poverty as "their" problem' (Williams and Pillinger 1996).

At a political level, we appear to be experiencing a reconfiguration of the public agenda away from concerns with socio-economic inequality to the distribution and management of risk. The unequal society is increasingly being replaced by the unsafe, 'risk' society (Beck 1992). The institutions of the welfare state had as their ideal the inclusion of all citizens in the name of social justice. Welfarism sought to spread risks and to protect the most vulnerable. This ideal appears to be in the process of being abandoned in various fields of social life. This is a notable feature of what O'Malley and Palmer refer to as 'post-Keynesian policing' (1996). The welfare ideal is being replaced by a regime which paradoxically extols 'choice' and 'community', but which accords little concern to the conditions under which 'choice' can legitimately be exercised, alongside the construction of open and tolerant communities. People are increasingly united, or separated, included or excluded on the basis of shared risk or a common interest in the distribution of risk. Communities organized around risk and fear produce new (often defensive) solidarities and forms of social cohesion, which can cut across, but also serve to reinforce, traditional social categories and identities.

As the role of the state is increasingly replaced by private insurance in the provision of welfare services, the identification and classification of those most 'at risk' become driven by powerful market forces which will increase the power to exclude. The logic of 'private' insurance is to reinforce demographic inequalities. This kind of 'market residualization' raises the concern that ghettoization, or rather insulation from the ghetto, is increasingly becoming a dominant theme of social existence in urban life (Wiles 1992: 67).

Herein lies the potential space for a vicious spiral of ghettoization to develop (see Figure 8.1). Against the background of existing social polarization, and in a regime of choice where the marketization of public and private safety, and the logics of private insurance prevail, responsibilization strategies and appeals to community form

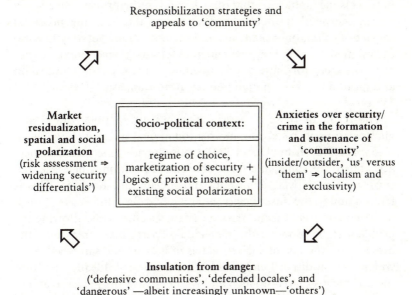

Responsibilization strategies and
appeals to 'community'

Market residualization, spatial and social polarization (risk asssessment ⇒ widening 'security differentials')

Socio-political context:

regime of choice, marketization of security + logics of private insurance + existing social polarization

Anxieties over security/ crime in the formation and sustenance of 'community' (insider/outsider, 'us' versus 'them' ⇒ localism and exclusivity)

Insulation from danger
('defensive communities', 'defended locales', and 'dangerous' —albeit increasingly unknown—'others')

FIGURE 8.1. Spirals of ghettoization

a heady mix. With crime as a focus for the formation and sustenance of 'community', the concern is that anxieties over security will lead to introspective localism and result in defensive and parochial communities. In this scenario, communities which form around insider/outsider—'Us' versus 'Them'—distinctions, which crime encourages, will focus upon insulation from dangerous 'others'. The insatiable quest for 'security' is a powerful dynamic in this process. This, in turn, will encourage market residualization and further social polarizaton. Given the differential ability of communities to prevent crime and purchase security, and the lack of the appropriate conditions under which communal responsibility can be fully exercised, the dynamic of this process can be self-fulfilling. Those who can afford to search for increasingly inventive ways of 'guaranteeing' effective security will do so, and will be encouraged to do so, in the name of their own 'responsibility'. The 'public' police in this scenario will increasingly become a residual force (Reiner 1992a) which patrols the boundaries between the 'security enclaves' and the surrounding 'dangerous places'.

Figure 8.1 should not be read, however, as suggesting that this process is inevitable nor that one element in the process necessarily causes the next. Rather, it is designed to illustrate the potential impact of, often unspoken, social dynamics upon everyday life and the momentum that they can generate within given contexts. However, the seeds for these developments are already visible in Britain and more noticeably in many North American cities (Davies 1990; 1992).

The result of these processes may be further polarization and ghettoization of crime, and the creation of new and more 'ungovernable spaces' (Lash and Urry 1994). Consequently, ghettoization may act, at least for some, as a form of crime prevention, albeit one that is precarious, as well as morally and socially questionable. This is tantamount to the 'fuse society' envisaged by Barr and Pease (1990), in which crime is concentrated in certain specific areas, allowing the problem to be more easily 'managed'. These 'fuse' areas take the pressure off the rest of society, act as indicators and safety valves of wider societal discord and enable greater control. Ideally, the 'fuse society' means that 'both men and women know the places to avoid' (Barr and Pease 1990: 304–5). That is, however, unless by force of circumstances you inhabit, or are required to use, those places. This comes close to Mike Davis's (1992) dystopian American scenario, 'Beyond Blade Runner', in which social polarization and spatial apartheid scar the 'cityscape' along lines of fear. Those who can afford it simply 'pad the bunker' or retreat behind 'mini-citadels', 'gated communities', and 'walled zones' connected by, and traversed through, 'safe corridors'. 'Security differentials' become a defining attribute of this nightmare scenario.

Such scenarios, however far-fetched they may appear now, nevertheless represent the deliberate exaggeration of real life trends. The crucial point, however, is that such developments are avoidable. The key question is whether the political will exists to address these problems and to alter the course we appear to be blindly following.

Furthermore, these trends carry with them their own tensions and contradictions. Shifts in responsibility have also exposed weaknesses within the state. Invocations to individuals and community groups to take greater responsibility for local crime problems, have called into question the ability and legitimacy of the state to 'do the job' of crime control effectively. As a result, as we saw in Chapter 6, there is an erosion of one of the foundational myths of modern society, that the sovereign state is capable of providing security and order through its monopoly of legitimate coercion.

Consequently, volatile new spaces have begun to emerge which have problematized distinctions between official and unofficial local community-based crime prevention initiatives. These spaces have been increasingly filled by forms of extra-state policing and growing vigilantism (Marx 1989; Harrington 1993; Johnston 1994b). Despite the lack of empirical research on the subject in Britain, media reports suggest that vigilantism is on the increase (see Weale 1993; McCrystal 1993; Jury 1993). The nature of the relationship between these developments and state crime control is unclear, as is the extent of their recognition, authorization or legitimization by public bodies. Nevertheless, what this trend suggests is that legitimacy deficits of the state have not been resolved, as such, but rather displaced into new arenas. Vigilantism, as Johnston suggests, represents:

a public unconvinced by the security guarantees given to it by the formal system of justice. In those circumstances, private and popular solutions come to the fore. The private sector offers commercial guarantees of security and, by so doing, regenerates ever renewed demand for the security commodity. Autonomous citizens, by contrast, merely seek to 'do something'.

(1996: 232)

Given the fragmentation and delegitimization of state power which vigilantism evokes, these spaces are inherently unstable as they mix violence (or the threat of it), coercion, and control with popular and populist local politics in a potentially combustible cocktail. The relationship between crime and politics has long been a key criminological concern (Cohen 1996), however, the advent of vigilantism suggests a social order in which there is a collapse of any distinction between the two. It may pave the way for the Hobbesian nightmare, of which Dahrendorf warned in the mid 1980s, of the exercise of private power in the 'war of all against all' (1985: 74).

Whither Social Justice?

This raises the crucial question as to the nature of the relationship between local and social justice. One of the implications of the dominant conception of 'community', as we have seen, is that it reinforces a parochial or localized understanding of crime problems, an important dynamic in spirals of ghettoization. Consequently, solutions tend to be 'particularistic', with little concern for wider social ramifications (Rose 1996). However, security and prevention in one area may have significant implications for, and impacts upon, others.

Crime Displacement

The phenomenon of crime displacement—or 'crime deflection' as Barr and Pease (1990) prefer, whereby a crime which has been prevented is merely shifted elsewhere—has only recently been 'discovered' by criminologists and has begun to be taken seriously in debates about crime prevention (see Pease 1994). Displacement can take a number of different forms including spatial, temporal, tactical, target, and type of crime (Hakim and Rengert 1981). As a consequence, it can be hard to evaluate the extent of the displacement effect of any given preventative measure. What is important is that it highlights the fact that the current unequal distribution of the burden of crime is not inevitable nor immutable but rather, is the consequence of conscious and unconscious policy decisions. This raises fundamental issues about the choices we make as a society in allowing crime to remain distributed in its present uneven pattern. And yet, members of the public often have an astute and very clear understanding of the effects of displacement. It is a subject about which ordinary people are very much aware. Vocal community residents from the research sites were often only too keen merely to move crime out of their area, well aware of the fact that they may not solve the problem but rather shift it on to others.

For example, on the Churchway Anti-Crime Project, the subject of displacement constituted an important source of conflict between community representatives and agency workers. Community representatives wanted the drug dealers, users, and prostitutes to be 'moved out of the area' by co-ordinated police interventions. However, it was felt that the police and other agencies were unwilling or unable to satisfy these demands and that, therefore, a conscious decision had been taken to keep the problems in their area, because it was believed to be easier for the authorities to manage them in that way. One community member of the project commented angrily:

the police know the problems . . . they can deal with it, you know, the minute they clamp down on it, it moves somewhere else. And they're not [clamping down because] it means a big problem for them. So that's another underlying thing the residents always feel that their problems are being kept there because it is manageable within [the area].

Residents were unhappy with suggestions that prostitutes could be displaced off public streets and into private premises within the area because they understood that this would not deal with the associated nuisances: pimps and clients coming and going, discarded condoms, and needles.

In Britain these debates have come to national prominence in relation to prostitution particularly in Balsall Heath, a locality in Birmingham (O'Kane 1994; Milne 1995: 23), and the Manningham district of Bradford (Weale 1995). In both areas local community residents have organized 'peaceful pickets' or 'vigilante patrols', depending upon with whom you speak, in order to 'get rid of the prostitutes and associated problems', and have met with various degrees of success.

Displacement, however, is not necessarily an undesirable consequence of social intervention. Displacement may be a legitimate policy choice. Benign displacement may seek to deflect crime away from vulnerable social groups and into social spheres which limit or serve to redistribute the level or impact of victimization. For example, a needle exchange was proposed as part of the Churchway Project. This caused considerable consternation amongst the community representatives who saw it as something that would attract drug users to the area (a form of negative displacement or 'magnet'). The only way to appease the local uproar created by the proposal was to have a mobile needle exchange which moved around a large area. While this compromise resulted in what some agency workers saw as a potentially less effective service, it could be argued that it was an instance of benign displacement as it distributed more evenly the nuisance believed to be associated with living or working next door to a needle exchange. Yet the meaning of 'benign' and 'malign' displacement may be very differently interpreted by different people and at different spatial or sectoral levels of analysis. For example, the ethics of displacement may be differently understood at a localized level for community residents, as against a broader social level which takes into consideration the equitable social distribution of victimization as a legitimate social good.

In relation to prostitution, for example, there is considerable

debate about the appropriateness or otherwise of 'zones of tolerance', in which prostitution is not prosecuted simply because its
location is perceived to result in a lesser negative impact upon the
wider society and local community (see Lowman 1992; Matthews
1992b). In other words, prostitution is allowed and potentially
encouraged to remain in non-residential areas, such as industrial
estates, where fewer people are adversely affected. This raises a
further debate regarding the level of formality and organizational
hierarchy at which such 'tolerance' should, and/or does, occur. For,
if we accept that the placement of crime is the product of conscious
human decisions, all crime is to some degree or other 'tolerated' in
its location. Balsall Heath or the Manningham area were no more
the 'natural' sites of prostitution than are the places to which prostitutes have moved. Everyday policing, as Skolnick (1966) suggested,
may require a certain degree of such informal, if not formal 'tolerance'. The central issue remains the 'social' criteria upon which
decisions as to where, when, and why, 'tolerance' or discretion are
exercised.

The choices that crime (dis)placement provides are essentially
political. However, as Barr and Pease note: 'Alternative choices
exist, but the will to exercise them probably does not' (1990: 313).
Rather than the more equitable patterning of crime, what appears to
be occurring, whether or not intended, is the inverse. The fact is that
community-based 'partnerships' against crime are hardest to establish in exactly those areas which are most in need of crime prevention: disadvantaged, public sector housing estates, with low income,
high unemployment, heterogeneous populations, and with high
levels of crime, fear, and distrust (Rosenbaum 1988). If communities
are able to displace crime successfully through community initiatives
and 'partnerships', without waiting for political (state) intervention,
it will be the already organized, well resourced, and culturally
homogenous communities with little existing crime which are most
likely to succeed. This in turn, will exacerbate the plight of the
already socially marginalized localities plagued by high levels of
crime and victimization.

Against Localism

This localism is given intellectual and political succour by the excesses of both postmodernism—in the name of *différence*—and
communitarianism—in appeals to revive moral communities. It is a

localism achieved, largely, through the power to exclude. It is a parochialism which is anti-democratic in its rejection of any notion of universality, even as a democratic ideal, thus reducing the space for the development of wider solidarities.

Nevertheless, it is important to recognize that different local areas have different social problems which require different strategies and solutions. Local experiences remain crucial in identifying needs and generating tailored programmes which correspond to the distinctive characteristics of a given locality. However, a sensitivity to local socio-economic contexts and a recognition of a need for greater local autonomy should not hand a *carte blanche* to 'localism'. Decentralized local autonomy which encourages bottom-up approaches to policy making needs to be bounded by principled and normative constraints of social, rather than local, justice.

Instead of localism what is needed are forms of social cohesion which both foster social solidarities yet preserve a cosmopolitan acceptance of cultural difference. This requires a radically different conception of social order in which consideration is given to the conditions under which individuals or groups are prepared to co-operate with one another to reach common goals. It also requires social dynamics of change which seek to increase public interaction between different groups and encourage group and self reflexivity. A social order which structures 'enforced exposure to alternative perspectives' into its fabric (Phillips 1994: 249), in its cities, its parks, and its public spaces as places of celebration rather than exclusion and residualization (as is currently the case), will foster greater social tolerance. This tolerance needs to be simultaneously more extensive and more directive: extensive in the sense that 'toleration is a necessary component in the development of larger loyalties' (Phillips 1994:247); and directive in the sense that it rejects permissive toleration that simply lets people get on with their own private business. Following Mendus (1989), Phillips argues for a toleration which is not a 'frozen' acceptance of difference but which is concerned with change and seeks to challenge forces which undermine a wider sense of belonging (1994: 247). A civic polity which validates difference and yet fosters social solidarity requires the deployment of forms of 'strategic essentialism', which recognizes the silences that essentialist categories, such as 'citizen' and the 'public sphere' embody, but sees them as *essential* to wider political action. It is one thing to recognize the 'other', it is another to claim that the lack of essentialist categories that unite us should necessarily blind us to any notion of collective value or commitment. This is not the sentimental anticipation of some future homogeneity or the wilful wishing away of conflict and difference, but a commitment to a politics which draws upon solidarities and seeks to create the conditions for tolerance, openness, and change. The privatization and marketization of everyday life fly in the face of such a politics.

Differences should neither be denied nor simply celebrated but continually challenged. This challenge of change should seek to disrupt not only the assumptions of dominant groups, but also the parochialism and introspection of less powerful groups. Instead of encouraging those who can afford it to retreat into their 'gated communities' and 'bubbles of security', we need to encourage public interaction between different groups:

> In such contexts, differences can and should generate change: encouraging a reassessment of what may prove unfounded complacencies; and forcing people to reconsider what may be false generalisations from a very limited base.
>
> (Phillips 1994: 249)

These public places will require 'ground rules'—which respect diversity and yet address real concerns as to personal and group security—for which there must be a minimum of solidarity. These rules of interaction will need to be founded upon a minimum agreement about what constitutes a 'public' place, its proper use, and the limits to what is collectively acceptable for it to flourish. The rights of minorities and individuals to live without fear or harm need to be inscribed in 'tougher notions of public space', whereby 'community and security' can be matched with 'the kind of openness that can stimulate a positive sense of challenge and contestation' (Squires 1994: 98).

And yet, such toleration can only co-exist alongside strategies and initiatives which address and seek to tackle differential power relations and social exclusion. The appropriate conditions for forging co-operation across boundaries of difference require interventions to address political and economic inequality and asymmetries of power. In order to counter the inequalities of crime, the lack of material resources, and weak social infrastructure in many of the poorer parts of our society need to be addressed. This will necessitate 'the successful reintegration of the inner-city islands of neglect into the larger community' (Buerger 1994: 430), and the rearticulation of the modern city with a public purpose and a civic tradition.

Following postmodernists in the celebration of difference and diversity or some communitarians in the worship of communal identity, are dangerous paths without an understanding of differential power relations and a detailed map of spatial and social inequality as a guide. As Squires notes:

It is no use simply celebrating unassimilated otherness as though all differences are chosen with pride, are democratic in impulse and glorious in manifestation. What might conceivably make a pluralism radical is an awareness of the existence of structural oppressions and the need to act positively to overcome them.

(1994: 98)

Whilst we need to be alert to the criticisms of grand narratives and essentialism we should not get lost in them. Realist commitments are fundamental to maintaining and supporting normative arguments and sustaining debates about social values and social justice in the construction and implementation of criminal justice policies.

Furthermore mutual recognition of difference is a preferable premise for community involvement than an assumed consensus. The latter often hides conflict below the surface and seeks to manage real structural opposition by often unaccountable, undemocratic, informal, and exclusive means which leave differential power relations unchallenged and unregulated, and exclude many local groups and individuals. There is too often a working assumption that conflict hinders effective crime prevention. Conflict is viewed as pathological, as a 'bad thing'. To ignore conflicts and difference or to define them out of existence in the search for consensus—as too often occurs in practice—leads to an impoverished analysis and forms the basis of ill-conceived negotiation. The important question for consideration, is how to build the institutions and frameworks in which to negotiate conflict in a socially constructive manner, and to seek the connections which link, rather than separate, people and groups. The challenge for local participatory initiatives is to mediate competing claims through processes and strategies which are open, inclusive, democratic, egalitarian—in the sense that they recognize and appropriately compensate for power differentials—and are grounded in principles of social, rather than local, justice.

Conclusions

Before concluding we need to sound a few notes of caution. First, in the foregoing analysis of possible implications of recent trends, we should be careful not to get carried away with dystopian images. Dystopias are useful rhetorical devices with which to warn of dangers and pitfalls to avoid, but they do not, and are not intended to, reflect the present. We need to remain sensitive to the real tensions that exist between ideologies, policy discourses, and practices, as well as to the uneven development of these strategies and their problematic institutionalization. And yet, it has been the deliberate aim of this chapter to identify and accentuate the darker and more sombre aspects evident in unfolding developments. In this regard, the central warning is that in seeking to construct communities around crime we may be creating parochial and exclusive communities with intolerant values. Crime as an issue inherently bifurcates people, behaviours, and actions into the 'acceptable' and the 'unacceptable': the normal and the pathological. The notion of the criminal as 'other' lies at the heart of established criminological discourse. This is overlaid by the anxiety and strong emotions of fear, distress, and anger which crime and victimization engender. The meaning of 'community' may then become saturated with that which 'we' are not, as much as that which 'we' are or share in common. It is not hard to see how such a sense of 'us and them', particularly if constructed at a local geographical level, paves the way for those who have the resources to retreat behind 'gated communities'. Security, in such a context, can be identified with 'the degree of personal insulation from "unsavoury" groups and individuals' (Davis 1990: 224). As the market increasingly comes to dominate the capacity of groups and individuals to police and manage crime, security derives from wealth and the ability to find sanctuary in secure 'bubbles of governance' (Shearing 1995), private guards, new technologies, architectural designs, and defended spaces. As Bottoms and Wiles note:

The difficult question is whether these developments will continue to the point at which the city consists of defended locales, linked by protected routes, but with 'bad lands' elsewhere—the ultimate 'ghettoisation' of everyday life.

(1995: 36)

This 'neo-medieval' vision of the future may not be as far off as one might prefer to think. In and around many North American cities aspects of this vision are becoming essential and defining elements of everyday life (Davis 1990: chapter 4; 1992). Across such a fragmented social formation, I have argued, communities are less likely to be open, tolerant, and inclusive of values and differences, and more likely to be exclusive, parochial, and prejudiced. Cities like Los Angeles (Davis 1990) should act as a warning to British commentators, particularly to politicians who seem transfixed with looking to America for solutions to the crime problem, rather than seeking to avoid the chronic social breakdown which America's crime and inner-cities reflect. British cities are currently more culturally mixed and integrated than their American counterparts, but the question that needs to be asked is: what kind of city do we as a civilized nation want?

And yet, there are alternatives. Patterns of crime and victimization are the outcomes of conscious and unconscious political decisions by the public, criminal justice agencies, and government. These patterns are not immutable, as shown by crime displacement, but rather present alternative choices about where (spatially and socially) we, as a society, will tolerate the distribution of crime and thus about our own societal values. What is clear is that through much community-based crime prevention, whether by default or by design, we may be exacerbating the inequalities in the distribution of victimization by shifting some of it into less well protected and poorer areas, and by ignoring other forms of crime, i.e. domestic and corporate crime. The danger is that far from policy makers addressing these politically awkward issues, the growing concern for crime prevention and security consciousness will reinforce and exacerbate the inequalities in the distribution of victimization. What is clear is the enduring and growing potential within the wider polity 'for community safety to be diminished from a public [or social] good to a [local or] "club good" which, although remaining communal for its members, is not available to those who are excluded from membership' (Hope 1995b: 28–9).

The contested and uneven nature of the trends outlined should alert us to the need to engage in a progressive 'post social politics' (Shearing 1995: 2). This requires us to take seriously the changes in the local governance of crime which are happening around us and to appreciate the importance of the new 'partnerships' and community involvement. We need to acknowledge, therefore, that the sites of power are shifting and that important contemporary conversations and communications are occurring in novel and non-traditional settings. For, as Taylor has observed, 'these new conversations (over crime prevention, urban regeneration, and so on) are one of the main sites, or locales, for a very contemporary political struggle over notions of the public as well as private interest' (Taylor 1995a: 26). A politics of crime control which fails to acknowledge and address these issues will always be partial and limited. This presents a challenge to academics, policy makers, and citizens to think more politically and normatively than hitherto about the principles which should underpin the nature and form of 'partnerships' between communities and organizations, be they private, public or 'hybrid'. In the quest for a more socially just public sphere we need to be alert to the dangers of 'community' whilst acknowledging its potential. Strengthening communities is not always synonymous with the creation of social order and cohesion. An assertion of 'community' identity at a local level can be beautifully conciliatory, socially nuanced, and constructive but it can also be parochial, intolerant, oppressive, and unjust.

9
Towards Conclusions

In this book I have set out to map some of the dynamics of change and development in the local governance of crime. Around the conceptual trilogy of appeals to 'community', 'prevention', and 'partnerships' a new discourse has begun to emerge with important institutional effects. It has been argued that this shift of paradigm has problematized many traditional assumptions about crime and its control. In particular, it has raised fundamental questions regarding issues of organizational legitimacy and responsibility. The proliferation of 'partnerships', the actual involvement of communities in crime prevention, 'active citizenship', and other forms of 'government at a distance', have reconstituted relations across the public and private spheres. Intermediary structures have emerged which fuse and transcend, and at the same time pose new-found problematics upon, the relationship between the state, market, and civil society. These developments are embedded in, and have drawn sustenance from, neo-liberal ideology and associated political programmes. Further, they dovetail and connect with the wider growth of managerialism and the logics of the 'risk society'.

For over two hundred years, policing and crime control have represented the pre-eminent and central symbols of state sovereignty. However, the shifts outlined in this book delineate fundamental challenges to the capitalist state's claim to monopoly of public power and law. As we near the end of the twentieth century, the nation state's incapacity to maintain what, by its own standard, was one of its central functions—the maintenance of public law and order—has become increasingly transparent. Thus, the modern state has become confronted by its own limitations, even in this its last bastion of political power. These challenges have produced a volatile policy climate in which, as Garland has suggested, state sovereignty over crime is 'simultaneously denied and symbolically reasserted' (1996: 462). And yet, a central contention of this book (see Chapters 6 and 7) has been that in this context the management of the state in the public interest has become as indispensable as ever. The task of government is to confront the realities of governance and to use the state in its different forms as a 'power-container' in the interests of social justice.

As a result, I have argued that we are witnessing a redrawing of what constitutes the legitimate responsibilities of individuals, collectivities, and the state. 'Community' and 'partnerships' constitute the sites at which the rearticulation of new socio-political relationships is being played out and contested, and out of which new forms of local governance of crime are emerging. Politically, 'community' has been appropriated to fill the vacuum left by the redrawing of government responsibility for areas of crime control. It has been deployed as the central motif around which the public are to be mobilized to participate in crime prevention and to take on a greater share of responsibility for personal security and public safety. It has been my intention to highlight the broader aspects and possible ramifications of these trends. In so doing, I have sought to stress the ambiguous and contradictory nature of the combined forces and dynamics which underlie and are driving the trends outlined. This I have attempted to do, not in order to undermine their significance, but rather to stress their complex and nuanced essence.

The Centrality of Conflict

In both inter-organizational and community 'partnerships' the importance of conflict and difference have been examined and accentuated, with reference to the empirical research findings (in Chapters 4 and 5 respectively). Dominant strategies for managing conflict—through conflict avoidance, informalism, conceptual obfuscation, multiple aims, and an 'ideology of unity'—it has been argued, in the long-term, are ill conceived, counterproductive, and exclusive. They do not constitute the kind of terrain upon which stable and enduring trust relations can grow and be sustained. A culture of genuine cooperation and mutuality is not synonymous with conflict avoidance and an 'ideology of unity'. And yet, the recognition of conflict is not the same as the embracing of unbridled competition. Competitive individualism, or even competitive collectivism, can serve to exacerbate and undermine inter-organizational, intergroup, and intra-community activity and trust.

Some twenty years ago Nils Christie, in a seminal article, suggested that 'the goal for crime prevention might be to re-create social conditions which make the conflicts visible and thereafter manageable' (1977: 7). Today, this remains a poignant observation. The arguments in this book have sought to show that this insight is as valuable with regard to inter-organizational relations as it is for intra-community and intercommunity relations. Conflict and difference are fundamental aspects of social life, the mutual acceptance of which constitutes a more just premise from which to set out upon the quest for the conditions under which people will come together and find common purpose across sectional boundaries.

Consequently, I have sought to develop an approach which emphasizes the importance of diversity, disagreement and constructive conflict negotiation: one which exposes difference within the context of a common interest and public purpose without constructing, around the notion of 'community', a politics of identity which is exclusive. Hence, I have argued for a more openly accountable, inclusive, and socially just framework of local governance in the field of crime control, emphasizing the need for negotiation within a framework which mitigates differential power relations.

Local Governance

A qualified conceptualization of *local neo-corporatism* has been advanced (in Chapter 6) as offering a useful framework within which to make sense of the forms of 'government at a distance', 'regulated self-regulation', and 'private interest government' that 'partnerships' across the public-private threshold herald. Its analytic power lies in the questions that such a framework poses about the nature of social power relations pressing upon, and within, partnerships which draw together community groups, private business, voluntary sector, and state bodies. In so doing, neo-corporatist theory focuses attention upon the key issues of social exclusion, incorporation, and the dynamics of participation within asymmetries of power. Furthermore, neo-corporatist theory allows crucial space for tensions and contradictions within the unfolding shifts and tendencies of discourses and practices.

Hence, it has not been my intention to advance the argument that a coherent ideology of the local governance of crime through 'community partnership' is being successfully imposed upon unwitting communities, as 'cultural dupes', but rather that within the

dominant trends and strategies there are contradictions and ambiguities which expose weaknesses and which form the sites of resistance, all of which need to be better understood. There are clear
dangers of slipping all too readily into assumptions regarding the
effectivity of governmental strategies and techniques. I have sought
to emphasize the uneven development of these strategies and their
problematic institutionalization given potentially countervailing
institutional strategies and unintended consequences. For, appeals
to 'community' also connect with, and serve to advance, more
genuinely bottom-up community empowerment strategies in which
local people are able to obtain a more effective voice in their own
governance and forms of community safety. Given the reality of
crime for many people, constructive collective action can enable
them to create and sustain more secure environments in which to
live.

The arguments in this book, therefore, are not intended to suggest
that 'community', 'prevention', and 'partnerships' are inherently
'bad things', nor that they necessarily lead, in an inevitable way, to
specific consequences. Nor have I meant to imply that the fears and
concerns expressed in this book are inescapable, without producing
their own distortions, resistances, and alternatives. Rather, they
present fundamental questions about the nature of the social formation and social relations within it. As opposed to a rejection of
'partnerships' and 'community' in the prevention of crime, we need
to look to the conditions under which genuine forms of consultation, representation, and participation can occur side by side with
strategies for equalizing asymmetries of power and disadvantage.

Responsibility

Rather than reject the language of responsibility outright, and seek
to turn the clock back to a mythical age in which the central state
was perceived to be responsible for all crime control, we need to
problematize the conditions under which responsibility, either collective or individual, can be exercised and enhanced. We need to
develop a language which speaks of active citizenship, community
participation in public life, and the stimulation of ethical values as
necessary ingredients in a more socially just public polity. But such a
language should not see these as the antithesis of, in competition with, or instead of, 'public' provision. Rather, the state has a

fundamental role in seeking to empower and enable communities—particularly those most ravaged by the restructuring of British capitalism—to realize their potential and to integrate them within a wider social frame. Inward investment to combat structural inequalities and imbalances of power is a precondition for the performance and maximization of communal responsibility.

However, it needs to be recognized that this language of responsibility is a double-edged sword, susceptible to mistranslation (O'Malley 1994b). For, as I have noted, these 'responsibilization strategies' are core elements of the New Right agenda in calling for the dismantling of the welfare state because of its perceived perpetuation of a culture of dependency (Murray 1990). State dependency, so the New Right argues, undermines genuine responsibility (Davies 1987). There are dangers that the patronizing language of welfarism is replaced by the individualizing language of audit and accounting. The latter seductively replaces the 'client' with the 'sovereign consumer', but in the process deals a death blow to any notion of a 'public purpose' and the idea of security as anything more than a commodity: a 'club' good rather than a 'public' good. What is needed is an alternative discourse which seeks to press for the creation of conditions within which responsibility can be fully realized and extended, which does not fall into the rationalist embrace of neo-liberalism. And yet, such a discourse needs, simultaneously, to allow sufficient space for human agency and collective fulfilment within wider social constraints.

Towards an Understanding of 'Community'

As has become clear throughout this book (and discussed in detail in Chapter 5), the very elasticity of the term 'community' in part provides its appeal. Some commentators have suggested that this lack of clarity as to what community is, renders it a concept of doubtful utility (Stacey 1969: 134). One of the fundamental problems with 'community' as an open-textured concept is the way in which the normative and empirical understandings of the term collide and fuse. As we have seen, the term is overlaid with alluring connotations and resonances about its social value. Descriptions of communities carry with them heavy ideological baggage. 'Community' appears to offer an attractive means of (re)creating cohesion across a fragmented society. It is often assumed to be intrinsically linked to a positive relationship with crime prevention, such that 'more community' is believed to result in 'less crime'.

In much of the discussion of 'community', particularly within the communitarian literature, it is unclear to what extent 'community' constitutes an 'imagined' sense of something lost, an aspect of 'tradition'. Or alternatively, whether it constitutes a more progressive focus for building modern democratic institutions which seek to address the problems of social difference, cohesion, mutual empowerment, and differential power relations in an increasingly complex, differentiated, and individualized world. Around issues of crime prevention, I have tried to highlight the ways in which the former—the sense of something lost—may serve to undermine the latter—the progressive focus. Simultaneously, I have sought to identify defining aspects of the latter and preconditions for its realization.

And yet, whilst problematizing the term 'community', this contestability, far from undermining it, signifies its richness. Rather than being 'meaningless' (Halsey, cited in Crow and Allan 1994: 191), the term 'community' is *meaningful*, to the point of overflowing with meaning. This suggests a need to take the term seriously. Hence, instead of embarking upon a quest for an authoritative and 'closed' definition of 'community' and analogous social 'networks', I have sought to outline the diverse, fertile, and sometimes contradictory referents to which the term gives rise. I have tried to show that the notion of 'community' is a particularly salient one for people, policy makers, and researchers for a number of reasons. First, it represents a term of social organization which is meaningful to ordinary peoples' lives, and to their social existence, as well as commonly used in public discourse. It mediates between the personal and the institutional: between the private and the public worlds of actors. As Crow and Allan suggest, '[I]f it did not exist it would surely need to be invented . . . It does address an element or level of social experience which cannot be ignored or done away with.' (1994: 193). Secondly, the central thesis of this book has been that this (or some analogous) intermediary sphere—whether we call it a 'community', 'partnership', 'policy network', 'associative order', 'private interest government', or whatever—which transcends and blurs the familiar trilogy of 'state', 'market', and 'civil society', is growing both in its social role and significance. It is my contention, therefore, that in terms of the governance of the future, this field of inquiry will (or at least should) constitute a growing focus of analysis. Hence, academics and researchers will need to develop new and more sensitive conceptual tools. This book has attempted to sketch out some of the contours of such conceptual thinking and to identify some of the questions and problems for further investigation.

In the light of the previous arguments it is worthwhile briefly considering the outlines of an appropriate sociological frame of analysis which further specifies, without rigidifying, the core characteristics of 'community'. In line with my earlier arguments such a conceptual frame should be sufficiently expansive to incorporate the 'communities' of 'policy networks', 'partnerships', and other forms of social ordering. It should not, however, be so permissive as to mean everything to everyone. As a useful starting point, Clark defined the key characteristic of 'community' as being a 'sense of solidarity' and a 'sense of significance' (1973: 404). Whilst, as we saw in Chapter 5, community as a 'sense' is an important aspect both in the way in which it is deployed in policy discourse and in forming actual community boundaries, it is inadequate as a definition on its own. The structural and institutional aspects of 'community' require specification. Further, we need to locate these within a wider social context within which 'community' is constituted and changed. In other words, an open conceptualization of 'community' must seek to situate it within an understanding of the broader forces and dynamics which bring it into being, sustain, and challenge it.

In their book 'Habits of the Heart' Robert Bellah and colleagues (1985) usefully distinguish between 'lifestyle enclaves' and 'communities'. Lifestyle enclaves are formed by people who share some feature of private life, such as shared leisure activities, patterns of appearance, and consumption which serve to differentiate them from other lifestyles. 'They are not interdependent, do not act together politically, and do not share a history' (Bellah *et al.* 1985: 335). They are not yet 'communities', although they may be on the way to becoming ones. A 'community', on the other hand:

is a group of people who are socially interdependent, who participate together in discussion and decision making, and who share certain *practices* that both define the community and are nurtured by it . . . It almost always has a history and so is also a *community of memory*, defined in part by its past and its memory of its past.

(Bellah *et al.* 1985: 333, emphasis in original)

This is a useful distinction in that it commences from an empirical base and alerts us to the importance of history, the formation, and reaffirmation of community over time. It is in this history, preserved through memory, that the purpose, goals, and aspirations of a given community are inscribed. Interestingly, this suggests that the 'gated communities' built around security (considered in Chapter 8) may be closer to 'lifestyle enclaves' than genuine 'communities'. However, the importance of Bellah *et al.*'s distinction is to alert us to the possible ways in which 'security', for example, can act over time to constitute 'practices' and give rise to a 'memory', in this instance a memory of anxiety and danger. Practices and memory are constitutive of, and constituted by, each other. Importantly, 'memory' needs to be sustained over time for communities to endure. Here, therefore, lies a potential way into communities—to regulate them, or rather to encourage socially just practices—by confronting this 'memory' through a dialogue which seeks to inscribe into it the values of tolerance, openness, and reciprocity.

Further, this distinction forces us to go beyond simply the notion that 'community' is self-ascribed identity and requires us to begin to identify the characteristics of interdependencies and the practices to which they give rise. And yet, it is here that we need to go further than the definition offered by Bellah and colleagues. A key aspect of 'community' as a form of informal social control is its ability to transmit norms and regulate behaviour, in other words, to mould compliance.

Here we can gain insights from legal pluralists who have sought to identify and define normative orderings outside traditional legal apparatuses. To this end, Sally Falk Moore has suggested the appropriateness of a 'semi-autonomous social field' as the subject of inquiry:

[I]t can generate rules and customs and symbols internally, but . . . is also vulnerable to rules and decisions and other forces emanating from the larger world by which it is surrounded. The semi-autonomous social field has rule-making capacities, and the means to induce or coerce compliance; but it is simultaneously set in a larger social matrix which can, and does, affect and invade it, sometimes at the invitation of persons inside it, sometimes at its own insistence.

(1973: 720)

This adds an important dimension to the empirical study of communities, particularly within the context of their crime prevention potential. The notion of semi-autonomy highlights a number of salient factors. First, it identifies a community's rule making capacity, its ability to induce or press for compliance and conformity. Secondly, it focuses upon the relation between a social field and external regulation. No community is an island. Hence the importance of an understanding of the power relations which define the degree of autonomy and isolation, as against the power of external forces. This inter-relationship is a dynamic process. This further highlights the importance of both conflictual as well as consensual external relations, most particularly *vis à vis* central state norms and values. Thirdly, Moore's definition focuses attention upon the criteria, processes, and practices upon which belonging and membership are structured: the nature of the 'ties that bind'. Hence, it calls to attention the processes of boundary formation and maintenance. Fourthly, as with other legal pluralists (see Merry 1988), Moore is keen to emphasize the law-like qualities of the norms and practices generated within 'semi-autonomous social fields'. Fifthly, it highlights the fact that the effectivity of state norms and their capacity to mould behaviour within communities should not be taken for granted. Rather, Moore's concept is central to understanding the limits of regulation via 'state enforceable law' (1973: 720). Hence, 'social arrangements are often effectively stronger than ... new laws' (Moore 1973: 723). Sixthly, the bonds of 'semi-autonomous social fields' are not bounded by geography. A social field is not necessarily reducible to locality. It may be spatially dispersed. Finally, it highlights the fact that, simultaneously, individuals can be members of a plurality of communities with potentially divergent normative arrangements and claims on their members. Here again lies a potential source of normative conflict, the regulation of which is a defining attribute of community.

Importantly, therefore, the notion of semi-autonomy forces an interrogation of the relationships between insiders and outsiders, between one 'community' and the next. It also suggests the space for multiple membership within contemporary society. A 'community', be it grounded in locality, a common interest, or purpose, will not be the only point of social reference or identity for a person. Rather, people occupy multiple identities and are often members of different communities. An individual may be simultaneously a member of a local, familial, organizational, sectoral, cultural, ethnic, or religious community. However, what is important is the nature of the relationships between membership of different communities, how they fit together both for the individual and for the wider society. Unlike Etzioni's analogy of communities which fit together like 'Chinese nesting boxes' in which 'less encompassing communities . . . are nestled with more encompassing ones . . . which in turn are situated within still more encompassing communities' (1993: 32), we need to be aware of the fact that overlapping communities will not always be complementary, but may be in a tensed or antagonistic relationship. Here again, Moore's concept of 'semi-autonomy' is useful as it identifies the fact that 'rules, customs, and symbols' generated internally are 'vulnerable to rules and decisions' outside the orbit of that community. Rather, communities of all kinds (those based upon geography, interest, or identity) are frequently in competition for scarce economic resources and political power, as well as pursuing conflicting interests or promoting divergent values. The bonds of community will be more or less strong, and may differ as between the various communities to which one person belongs.

However, it is important to counter the slippery slope set by postmodernists who stress the phenomenon of 'multiple social identities' in the same breath as denying the concept of an 'essential' identity. This is because a problem arises when all 'identities', of whatever type or form:

are treated as of equal social validity, so that personal lifestyle preferences such as 'musical styles', physical attributes such as 'disability' and social products such as 'race' and 'class' are seen as being of the same moment . . . The result is that fundamental social relations such as racial oppression become reduced to lifestyle choices.

(Malik 1996: 9)

This often leads commentators to ignore the determining relations between the identity, or 'community', and the wider society within which it is set. By emphasizing and celebrating the relation between identity and choice, it reduces society to the outcome and aggregate of individual preferences and relationships. Finally, it fails to acknowledge that identity, like 'community', is not always freely chosen. It can be unwanted or unwarranted. It can be imposed, oppressive, and inescapable. Hence, following Moore's lead, we need to look to the conditions under which social fields and networks constrain and regulate boundaries and membership in a dynamic interaction with the wider social matrix in which they are set. We need to look to their rule making capacity which is socially situated and contained, most notably by relations of power. Identities will frequently be the product of such social networks, but an understanding of the former needs to be firmly located in an analysis of the latter.

Democratizing Partnerships and Communities

The source of friction within and between communities introduces an important dynamic of challenge and change which can be exploited for democratic ends. The potential for this arises through people's own multiple membership. If they are exposed to democratic processes as well as to the value of tolerance and the open negotiation of conflict, in different settings, in which these are inscribed into the 'rules of the game', it is anticipated that they will become institutionalized and 'normalized' within diverse communities. This will not just arise merely because individuals will leave undemocratic communities—using their so called 'right of exit'—preferring democratic ones (freedom of choice does not operate in such an unconstrained way), but rather, it will only arise through a process of continual challenge in which the external and internal forces are brought to bear upon the workings of communities. Multiple membership should be encouraged, not merely because it weakens the hold of any one community over its members, for it may not necessarily do so, but because it can encourage interaction and the spread of social and ethical values, both procedural and substantive, which help define, and encourage commitment to, the broader social body.

We should not assume, as do many communitarians and associationalists, that communities and associations are always happily embraced, chosen with pride, or even voluntarily entered into. Nor should we assume that they lack considerable suasive or coercive powers. Rather, we should assume the need for 'rules of the game' which allow difference and conflict to be expressed within processes of negotiation and the mediation of power differences. We need to build into the social fabric mechanisms which challenge and restrict the potential over-encroachment and abuse of such inherent capacities. These criteria are necessary principles for genuine community responsibilization.

Consequently, there is a pressing need for the democratization of partnerships and policy networks. Democratizing partnerships requires moving beyond traditional ideas about institutions of democracy and modes of participation. This necessitates imaginative thinking and experimentation which address two contemporary realities: first, the fact that the policy making processes are shifting and increasingly occurring in new networks outside the 'political sphere', shielded from any 'democratic gaze'; and secondly, the failure of traditional modes of representation to incorporate the interests of the politically marginalized. Some initial attempts to wrestle with these issues were outlined and critically reviewed in Chapter 7. This requires richer conceptions of democracy than hitherto institutionalized, which connect more directly to peoples' lived experiences and to the shifting forms of governance.

The Individual and the Community

Further, we need to acknowledge that the benefits of 'community' membership impose restraints upon 'voluntarism'—as negative freedom—which is taken as meaning that individuals are left alone by others unless, and until, they decide to 'get involved'. The simultaneous celebration of individualism and 'community', both of which underlie much of the contemporary appeal of 'community' and which I have sought to capture in the phrase 'collective individualism', embodies certain contradictions. 'Ontological individualism'—which suggests that we derive our sense of being and the 'truth of our condition', not from our social setting or our relationship to others, but from our isolated, atomistic, and inviolable selves—is out of sorts with 'community' membership. Voluntarism and autonomy need to be recognized as socially constructed and bounded; republican criminology's use of the concept of 'dominion' is pertinent here in highlighting freedom and liberty as both social and relational (Braithwaite and Pettit 1990). We become who we are through our relationships. Thus understood, dominion—or 'republican freedom'—is only experienced and enjoyed when we are living in a 'social world that provides you with an intersubjective set of assurances of liberty' (Braithwaite 1995: 279). Solidarity, reciprocity, trust, and shared commitment to the common good, therefore, are foundational aspects of such dominion.

The sacredness of the individual, his or her value, worth, and claims for respect, should not be confused with 'ontological individualism'. The 'self' and the 'social' are not locked into a zero sum relationship. Strong collectivities which respect difference and are bounded by notions of social justice can strengthen individual dominion. Hence, the quest for, and construction of, 'ideal' discursive communities (Benhabib 1992) need to start from an acceptance of procedural and substantive constraints as a condition for such dialogue to occur. This will need to include formal regulatory frameworks which empower, mediate, and govern informal activity.

Such democratic communities, subject to outside interruption, support, and challenge, can help empower people to regulate their own lives. They can encourage and inculcate pride in being law abiding and rights respecting. In addition, they can facilitate communal disapproval at violating these norms and processes of reintegrative shaming (Braithwaite 1995: 296). The arguments in this book are thus not *against*, nor wholly at odds with, greater 'community' involvement or the devolution of powers to relevant associations, networks, and groups. Rather, they have sought to identify some of the problematic concerns and implications of the construction of 'communities' and 'partnerships' around crime, as well as to set out the pre-eminent conditions upon which such a rearticulation could, or should, unfold. In so doing, the argument has been for an explicit concern with the ethical dimensions of political action, with normative reconstruction in both political and criminological theory, and which simultaneously engages with empirical trends.

Criteria for the evaluation of malign and benign tendencies within communities and private interest governments thus need to be further developed. We need to ask the question, what makes a 'community' or 'partnership' an 'ethical' one? Lines need to be drawn between forms of identity and difference which foster tolerance and democracy and those which serve to undermine them. This must involve commitments to a particular kind of process and the acceptance of certain 'ground rules' of incorporation and participation as the preconditions of democratic communication.

These 'rules of the game' should be as minimalist as possible, as suggested by Braithwaite and Pettit's principle of 'parsimony in any state invasion of dominion' as a fundamental element of justice (1990: 79). And yet, they should be sufficiently robust to protect minority interests and foster tolerance of 'otherness'. State intervention should be, in Braithwaite and Pettit's words, 'satiable' and 'stabilizing', that is, should not have an inbuilt tendency to increase state intervention, control, and punishment (1990:

chapter 5). However, those for whom 'community' is essentially an anti-statist concept need to confront the question, who or what will provide and secure the resources fundamental to allow 'communities' and 'partnerships' to maximize dominion and responsibility for their members' interests, their 'equality of liberty prospects'? For, if it is not the task and responsibility of an interventionist democratic state, then upon whose shoulders should such a burden fall? Advocating appeals to 'community' at a moment in history at which powerful neo-liberal political forces are seeking to dismantle the welfare state, requires a subtle and nuanced political response which accepts the contemporary limitations of state action but seeks to defend vigorous and responsible state action within a democratizing polity.

We need to know more about the way in which communities can be strong—both in the sense of being cohesive and providing for the interests of their members—without being exclusive or intolerant of other communities. How do governmental agencies and strategies foster cultures which appreciate the value of difference and which have the capacity to contain and manage conflict and diversity? How do public agencies connect with and support networks and communal orderings which transcend the public–private divide, whilst encouraging and facilitating socially just practices? In other words, what are the conditions for 'pluralism-within-unity', whereby various subcultures and social groups can find a legitimate place within an overarching and more encompassing whole, where citizens can negotiate social differences and co-exist in an organized and ordered civic polity.

Crime as the Focus for Rebuilding Communities

Crime constitutes a problematic focus for the construction of tolerant and open communities. Its tendency to categorize, differentiate, and bifurcate behaviour establishes a fertile but dangerous ground upon which 'defensive' communities can be constructed through reference to 'others'. In such a context, divisions between 'us' and 'them' and boundaries of belonging can be fuelled by ignorance and envy, as well as power and privilege. This is not to advocate a relativistic approach to the real harm and suffering caused by crime and criminality, nor to discount the very real fears and desires that feed social anxieties about crime and security. Furthermore, this should not be taken as promoting an abstention from confronting the vexed issues about the kinds of behaviours which should not be tolerated. Rather, the conditions for participation and also for exclusion, should remain as minimal and 'satiable' as possible, whilst the processes of reintegration should be as extensive and open as possible.

However, there are very real dangers that in the process of constructing 'community' around issues of crime and insecurity alone, we may encourage intolerant communities, whose cohesion is built upon its defensiveness. Moreover, whilst taking crime seriously we may over prioritize crime prevention as an end in itself. In this context, inequality and social disadvantage in their own right may become obscured. They may become viewed as something which constitutes a pressing social issue only when, and so far as, they lead to social disorder and crime, or at least the fear of crime. And yet, inequality not only influences the propensity to engage in crime but also compounds its effects.

A Public Polity

A politics in which the public good is merely the sum of individual market preferences can never tap the real empowerment potential of solidarity. Here, 'community' as a trope for 'collective individualism' merely represents a signifier which has been brought in to fill the vacuum left by the decline of the public sphere and the political exiling of 'society' to a conceptual limbo.[1] In this space vacated by society, 'the social' has returned in the specific and limited guise of 'the community' (Rose 1996).

This marketization of everyday life is symptomatic of a state and government driven by neo-liberal ideology, and yet confused by the confrontation with its own limitations. However, the irony is that this has left governments with little choice in the field of crime prevention and control, either to 'do nothing' and to leave individuals, organizations, and groups to cope with crime themselves, or to fall back on the traditional repressive apparatus. The former is a problematic strategy for governments to 'sell' to a public that expects agencies to 'do something', albeit the ground upon which responsibilization stands. The latter is the stuff of periodic punitive

---

[1] This was no more clearly expressed than in Mrs Thatcher's infamous declaration that 'there is no such thing as society' (1993: 626). For her the concept 'society' was little more than a ficton. In its place the world, she suggested, is made up only of individuals, families, and markets.

sound bites, if of little effective action. It is in this vacuum that appeals to 'community' have found a resonance. They appear to show agencies to be 'doing something'. In this sense they constitute a fundamental aspect of quests to address problems of legitimacy. And yet, legitimacy deficits and the ambiguities as to the state's role in the field of crime control and policing remain unresolved, but rather, are displaced and dispersed into new arenas.

The crime debate, particularly with regard to prevention, appears to have become wrapped up in technicist, administrative, and short-term thinking which has artificially severed it from broader concerns about the direction in which society is moving. Questions about the direction and methods of crime control and prevention are inherently political and not purely technical or administrative. Political choices exist, however, the crucial question is whether the political will exists to address these problems and to alter the course we appear to be following, almost like the blind driver of an out of control juggernaut.

The reinvigoration of a common interest, in the face of what Gitlin (1995) has provocatively described as 'the twilight of common dreams', requires the rearticulation of universalist categories, such as 'citizenship' and 'equal rights'. Moreover, this will necessitate the reintegration of the inner-city 'islands of neglect' into the wider social frame, and the rearticulation of the city with a public purpose. The future of the cosmopolitan and integrated city holds a particularly important and symbolic place in this regard. It is vital to refashion and recreate within and around cities communal places where people interact and communicate with each other, although in these public places 'ground rules' will need to be in place. Reconcentrating cities as varied and yet closely woven places with vibrant public spaces, remains a difficult but an important civic ideal to which greater political energies need turn.

Summary and Conclusions

In the foregoing discussions I have sought to highlight that current appeals to 'community' and 'partnerships' in crime control and prevention represent a significant shift in the governance of crime control, which require a more subtle understanding of wider social dynamics and their implications. Such an understanding demands a politics which takes account of the following:

1. Power differences both within and between communities need to be recognized and acknowledged in order not to compound existing social disadvantages and spatial polarization. This necessitates strategies and initiatives which address and seek to tackle differential power relations, as well as social and political exclusion.

2. In this, the language of responsibility should not be rejected but problematized. We need to examine the appropriate conditions under which the exercise of genuine responsibility can be fulfilled and enhanced, not merely by those with the financial ability to purchase 'security' and insulate themselves. In this the state has a crucial role as the promoter of a 'public interest'.

3. Hence, social institutions which mediate the impact of local or communal initiatives upon other areas and groups need to be established at different sectoral and spatial levels. Obvious spatial tiers include: the local, city, regional, and national levels. Here, the state has a fundamental empowering, mediatory, and regulatory role vis-à-vis communities, associations, and partnerships.

4. Resources from governmental and other agencies can contribute to the construction of community boundaries and the promotion of either competition or collaboration between different groups. Forms of competitive funding in which communities and groups are pitted against each other in the quest for scarce resources may serve to undermine the collaborative potential of communities and subsequently rigidify their boundaries, leaving them more, rather than less, exclusive and defensive.

5. Conflict avoidance, as a strategy for organizing partnerships and communities, does little to address the power differentials within and between agencies and groups. Silent consensus is not the expression of a healthy community. Argument and conflict about the meaning of values and goals and how they should be actualized are important aspects of a reflexive community. In such conditions, any consensus must be open, and subject, to period challenge and change over time.

6. Community partnerships need to ensure 'representativeness' of incorporated bodies and individuals. In addition, they need to be explicit and open about the grounds for, and claims of, representation.

7. Community partnerships need to develop structures and processes that enable full participation. Open and inclusive dialogue is a

fundamental aspect of 'ideal' discursive communities. However, as a condition for such dialogue to occur clear 'rules of the game' need to be set out. Dialogue needs to start from an acceptance of procedural and substantive constraints. This should embody aspects of 'formalism' which empower, mediate, and regulate 'informal' relations.

8. Multiple forms of accountability—informational, organizational, managerial, and political—are crucial to the open regulation of partnerships and policy networks, particularly given their inter-organizational location and the blurring of organizational boundaries which they foster.

9. In relation to crime control and prevention, democracy needs to be robust to secure pluralism and diversity by locating individual rights outside the reach of moral majorities.

10. A vision of democracy as an ongoing dialogue is an important premise. In such a vision, democracy is defined not in terms of popular majorities but in terms of the quality of decision making that arises out of the interaction between the governing agency and the intermediary representative bodies organizing the activity being governed. In this, the adequate flow of quality information, as a process of effective, two-way communication between the agencies and the public, is crucial.

11. The democratization of policy networks should be supplemented by new, multiple modes of reinvigorating democracy, which engage with recent socio-political shifts and trends in governance. This will require imaginative thinking and experimentation.

12. We need to develop forms of social cohesion which foster social solidarities whilst preserving a cosmopolitan acceptance of cultural difference. This requires a radically different conception of social order in which consideration is given to the conditions under which individuals or groups are prepared to co-operate with one another to reach common goals.

13. Crime alone may not be the most appropriate focus around which to organize open, tolerant, and inclusive communities. Rather, it is more likely to lead to greater defensiveness, exclusivity, and parochialism. The nurturing of tolerant communities, their institutions and structures, must be shaped around discussions and foci which are integrating rather than exclusive and bifurcating as is the case with 'crime'.

14. If 'community' is to have some normative or moral place in

politics then it needs to move beyond, and safeguard against, exclusive parochialism. Rigorous criteria for the evaluation between the malign, darker side of 'community' involvement and its more benign attributes need to be constructed. At the centre of such an analysis should be the extent to which the values of a given 'community' and its strategies for achieving them, accord with a vision of social justice and public good, so that it does not just have a responsibility to its own members but to a wider 'community of communities': *the social*.

15. Inculcating pride in communities alongside respect and tolerance for other, non-members can and should be encouraged around issues other than crime, narrowly understood. Prosocial patterns of behaviour in communities are more likely to be fostered around activities of care, nurturing, and mutuality. All of these may have consequences for crime prevention, but they should be accorded prominence for what they are, not what their consequences might be. For example, to turn the provision of high quality child care, education, or employment into issues, the importance of which is judged upon its (non)crimogenic implications, intrinsically is to devalue and distort it. For, as Tony Bottoms so aptly notes: 'At the end of the day, some things are more important than crime prevention' (1990: 19).

Appendix A
Research Case Studies

The research case studies, listed in alphabetical order, are briefly described below.

Community Crime Prevention Projects

Arlington Racial Harassment Monitoring Project

This was a racial harassment project in a Labour run London borough. The aims of the project were: to collate information on racial harassment within diverse public agencies, to raise the profile of racial harassment as a problem; and to develop and co-ordinate racial harassment policy. The project brought together senior personnel from various local authority departments, including housing and social services, the police and the probation service, as well as representatives of various ethnic minority groups. The project had a borough-wide focus and was staffed by a council administrator.

Churchway Anti-Crime Project

This project was part funded by a local Safer Cities initiative. It straddled two inner London boroughs (both Labour controlled). The project constituted one of the first joint initiatives between the two boroughs in the field of crime and its prevention. The history of relations between the two councils had involved little collaboration or mutual support. Consequently, the project was seen as an important step forward in establishing inter-borough working relations. The project brought together senior officers from both councils, alongside the police, probation service, community workers and community representatives. In part, the project sought to identify and raise the profile of the geographical areas as a political entity for the purpose of further funding, particularly from the Single Regeneration Budget. The project's main concerns were with co-ordinating policy and strategy in relation to the management and prevention of prostitution and drug related offences, for which the area had a well-known reputation. Addressing these issues, through high profile interventions, was seen as an important step in the economic regeneration of the area.

East Station Partnership

This project was aimed at crime prevention on a 'high crime' council estate not far from the Churchway area. The project was led by one of the councils involved in the Churchway project, an inner London (Labour controlled) local authority. The partnership also brought together representatives from the police and the local community. The council had developed a reputation in the 1980s as being an 'anti-police' authority. More recently, the council had attempted to shed this image by raising the profile of 'partnership' work with the police in particular.

Greengage Bicycle Theft Project

This project was a replication of a successful crime prevention initiative conducted in Amsterdam and funded by the Dutch Ministry of Justice. It was established in a reasonably affluent town in the London commuter belt. It was located in the county in the South East of England in which the survey of police and probation officers (reported in Chapter 4) was conducted. The aims of the project were: to address the problem of bicycle theft and to raise the profile, and promote the use, of bicycles as an alternative means of transport in the area. Second-hand bicycles (unclaimed from the police pound) were restored, painted a distinctive colour, and left at identified places for people to use. The project was established by key workers in the police, the local authority (a Conservative run borough council), and the probation service. The project gained significant financial support from private businesses. The council worker was a self-proclaimed cycling enthusiast and the project relied heavily upon the energy and enthusiasm of all three of the lead project workers. The project involved no direct community representation, but was considered by the workers as 'for' and 'in', even if not 'by', the 'community'.

Highfield Crime Prevention Group

This 'partnership' began as an initiative between the local council and the police to co-ordinate crime prevention throughout the borough. The Conservative controlled outer London authority set up a multi-agency working party to look at how it should address crime prevention in the light of the Morgan Report and associated government circulars. There had been no established history of council/police co-ordinated action. The former had taken the firm view that crime prevention was a police responsibility. Hence, the council were largely perceived to have been 'pushed' by central government into some action, rather than having 'jumped' into a partnership approach.

Illsworth Crime Prevention Project

This was an initiative focused upon an inner London (Labour controlled) local authority housing estate. A multi-agency group directed a number of front-line workers from the participating agencies. Incorporated agencies included the police, social services, neighbourhood officers, local authority representatives from the executive office, housing department, community safety unit, community workers, local community, and tenants association representatives. The aim was to reduce certain types of crime on the estate—most notably burglary and vandalism—through a multi-focused approach. For example, the police established a 'police surgery' on the estate to provide local people with a place to report crimes without having to go to the more remote local police station, the council neighbourhood officer successfully sought and attracted funds for a music rehearsal studio for the local community centre and the council also embarked upon architectural modifications and environmental design aimed at crime prevention.

Northley Multi-Agency Partnership

This project was a city-wide Safer Cities partnership, in the North of England, which brought together senior representatives from the police, probation service, the council, the health service, prominent interest groups, the voluntary and business sectors into a steering committee. Administered by a co-ordinator with limited secretarial support, and in line with similar schemes around the country (see Tilley 1993) the project had three years of government funding (approximately £100,000 each year) enabling a programme of small grants to be administered. The partnership aimed: to draw up a detailed crime and community profile of the city; to grant aid high profile and innovative community safety initiatives under the headings of 'fear of crime and victimisation', 'neighbourhood community safety', and 'young people and community safety'; to monitor and evaluate projects and disseminate good practice; and to develop an exit strategy which would extent the initial work of the project and link the community with the private sector.

Parkland Manors

This involved a series of related community crime prevention initiatives in a deprived area of a city in the North of England. The area straddled three different council wards. The initiatives drew upon city council and central government funding, paralleled by bottom-up attempts from within the community to establish their own residents' association in order to engage with public and private sector agencies, and to attract funding into the area. The area had a mixed and transient population with a high number of students attending the two local universities and other higher education colleges. There was a high level of local youth unemployment. The area was the site of minor street disturbances between local youths and the police. There was a particularly high burglary rate in the area, with an annual peak of recorded burglary in the months of September and October with the arrival (and return) of the student population as the principal victims. One of the central conflicts within the area revolved around the relations between the student population and the local residents, many of whom resented their apparent wealth, the attention that they received from certain local traders and publicans, and the disturbance (noise and litter) that they caused. The problem of private landlords buying up properties to rent to students further exacerbated relations.

South Ornley Burglary Project

This project was a joint police and local authority initiative aimed at giving free advice and assistance in upgrading the physical security of properties in an area of high burglary. The council was a Labour controlled London borough. The area was not exclusively council owned property but a mixture of forms of private tenure. The project involved the police, the local authority community safety officer, and community representatives working with private sector contractors. The initiative was in part a response to local residents lobbying the council and demanding that 'something be done' in the area. This lobbying was led by the local neighbourhood watch co-ordinator, who for some time had advocated council intervention. A number of other residents were unsupportive of the initiative, in the fear that it might attract unwanted and adverse publicity to the area. As a consequence, there was a particularly low take-up rate of the assistance offered by the scheme in the area.

Tenmouth Anti-Burglary Initiative

This project was a replication of the Home Office funded Kirkholt demonstration project (see Forrester *et al.* 1988; 1990). It aimed to reduce burglary through the systematic collection and collation of information (including data from interviews with offenders and victims); and to target repeat victims in the co-ordination of crime prevention. The project was established by the police and probation service. Both organizations seconded a full-time officer to the project during its two-year life span. The project had no obvious geographical boundaries, with a diverse ethnic population and housing tenure, and was spread over two police 'areas' of south and central Tenmouth which included eight local authority wards. The project was managed by a multi-agency committee incorporating senior police and probation officers, as well as representatives from Victim Support (the chair of the committee), the local authority, and a variety of 'community' groups. It was situated in a large commuter belt town, in the county in which the survey of police and probation officers (reported in Chapter 4) was conducted. The eventual aim of the project was that by the end of the secondment period it should be community 'owned'. The project report written at the end of the secondment period declared the aims to have been: 'To devise a joint plan between the statutory and voluntary agencies, commercial sector and the community towards frustrating the activities of burglars and the fear they provoke—and make it work!'

Westbridge Drug Project

This was a local authority led initiative which drew together senior personnel from the police, probation service, social services, the health authority, and the council (a Labour run London borough). The project was co-ordinated and administered from the council's crime prevention unit which, since the mid 1980s, had developed a history and reputation for innovative work with the police. The aim of the project was to develop, adopt, and co-ordinate an approach to drug abuse prevention, emphasizing the health and safety, as well as the law enforcement, aspects of regulation. This was to involve the prescription of 'clean' drugs to users. The initiative deliberately avoided direct 'community' representation, preferring to draw together local 'experts' with a 'community focus'.

Mediation Projects

Leighdale Victim/Offender Mediation Service

This was a county-wide victim/offender mediation scheme funded by the probation service (the same probation service as that funding the Oldcastle scheme). The service was initially set up by workers from a nearby, more established scheme to which it turned for training, expertise, and guidance in the early years. The service straddled a number of different organizational boundaries, in an area including one medium size city and a number of smaller, ex-industrial towns and villages. The advisory committee drew upon representatives of the police and Victim Support (in the two police divisions in the area), as well as local Justices of the Peace, Youth Justice workers, and senior probation managers. The scheme took referrals from a variety of agencies but primarily from the police, probation, and social services. It operated both pre- and post-sentence mediation. It claimed not to work to court deadlines, and this was borne out by the fact that most of the work occurred at the post-sentence stage. In relation to pre-sentence reports, mediators were willing to complete reports on the offender's progress which were submitted to the court for its consideration.

Northolt Community Mediation Service

This neighbourhood mediation scheme existed on low funding from charitable bodies and the local council, via the environment and housing departments. The unstable nature of funding meant that the scheme drifted from one financial uncertainty to the next. Consequently, much energy was put into the task of remaining solvent. The co-ordinator and volunteer mediators were overseen by a multi-agency management committee which drew together representatives from the police, probation service, social services, the local victim/offender mediation scheme, local community and ethnic groups. There was a high turnover of staff and management committee members. In addition to neighbourhood mediation the scheme sought to promote mediation in schools and 'elder mediation', between the elderly and those charged with caring for them.

Oldcastle Victim/Offender Mediation Scheme

This city-wide victim/offender mediation scheme was originally established, with multi-agency and Safer Cities Project funding, on two housing estates within the city. It was subsequently extended to cover the entire city and came to be funded entirely by the probation service upon the termination of Safer Cities funding. Initially, the scheme had sought to develop its own 'victim oriented' model of mediation, which was different from a nearby older and more established scheme in the same probation service. Over time and under pressure from probation service managers the scheme came more closely to resemble other schemes in the region including the Leighdale service. The multi-agency advisory committee was set up after the scheme initially survived without one. It incorporated key police officers, senior probation officers, representatives of voluntary organizations, advice agencies, and community groups. Unlike the Leighdale scheme it was initially unwilling to provide statements to the courts, but on the insistence of the probation management it changed its policy. However, the detail provided did not extend beyond a statement that the individual had been referred to the scheme or was undergoing mediation.

Appendix B

Survey of Mediation Schemes

Responses to the survey of mediation schemes in England were received from the following neighbourhood (N) and victim/offender (VO) mediation services. They are set out in alphabetical order.

Bolton Neighbour Dispute Service (N)
Bradford Community Mediation (N)
Bradford Victim/Offender Mediation Service (VO)
Bristol Mediation (N)
Cambridge and District Mediation (N)
Cleveland Mediation Project, UNITE (Uniting Neighbours in their Environment), Middlesbrough (N)
Coventry Reparation Scheme (VO)
Derby Mediation Service (N)
Dorset Community Mediation (N)
Islington Mediation Scheme (N)
Kingston Friends Workshop Group (N)
Kirklees Victim/Offender Mediation and Reparation Service (VO)
Lambeth Mediation Scheme (N)
Leeds Community Mediation Service (N)
Leeds Victim Offender Mediation and Reparation Service (VO)
Luton Mediation (N)
Milton Keynes Neighbour Dispute Mediation Service (N)
Newham Conflict and Change Project (N)
Northamptonshire Diversion Unit (VO)
Plymouth Mediation Service (VO and N)
Plymouth Victim Burglar Group (VO)
Reading Mediation Centre (N)
Sandwell Mediation Centre (VO and N)
Southwark Mediation Centre (N)
Walsall Mediation Scheme (N)
Wandsworth Independent Mediation Service (N)
Whitstable Mediation (N)
Wolverhampton Mediation Scheme (VO)
Wood End Community Safety Mediation Project, Coventry (N)
Worthing and District Mediation Service (N)

Bibliography

Abel, R. (1973) 'A Comparative Theory of Dispute Institutions in Society', *Law and Society Review*, 8, 217–347.

Abel, R. (ed.) (1982) *The Politics of Informal Justice, Vol. 1*, New York: Academic Press.

Abercrombie, N. (1991) 'The Privilege of the Producer', in R. Keat and N. Abercrombie (eds.) *Enterprise Culture*, London: Routledge, 171–85.

Adam Smith Institute (1984) *Justice Policy*, London: Adam Smith Institute.

Alder, C. and Wundersitz, J. (eds.) (1994) *Family Conferencing and Juvenile Justice: The Way Forward or Misplaced Optimism?*, Canberra: Australian Institute of Criminology.

Alderson, J. (1979) *Policing Freedom*, Plymouth: McDonald and Evans.

Anderson, B. (1983) *Imagined Communities: Reflections on the Origins and Spread of Nationalism*, London: Verso.

Anderson, M. (1989) *Policing the World: Interpol and the Politics of International Police Co-operation*, Oxford: Clarendon Press.

Anderson, M., den Boer, M., Cullen, P., Gilmore, W. C., Raab, C. D., and Walker, N. (1995) *Policing the European Union: Theory, Law and Practice*, Oxford: Clarendon Press.

Association of Chief Officers of Probation (1985) *ACOP Response to Safer Communities*, Wakefield: ACOP.

Association of Chief Officers of Probation (1988) *Crime Prevention and the Probation Service*, London: ACOP.

Association of Chief Police Officers (1990) *ACPO Strategic Policy Document: Setting the Standards for Policing: Meeting Community Expectations*, Report of an ACPO Working Party, London: ACPO.

Association of London Authorities (1994) *At A Premium*, London: ALA.

Association of Metropolitan Authorities (1990) *Crime Reduction—A Framework for the 1990s*, London: AMA.

Atkinson, J. M. (1982) 'Understanding Formality: The Categorization and Production of "Formal" Interaction', *British Journal of Sociology*, 3(1), 86–118.

Atkinson, M. M. and Coleman, W. D. (1992) 'Policy Networks, Communities and the Problems of Governance', *Governance*, 5(2), 154–80.

Audit Commission (1988) *The Competitive Council*, Management Paper 1, London: HMSO.

Audit Commission (1990) *Effective Policing: Performance Review in Police Forces*, Police Paper 8, London: HMSO.

Audit Commission (1991) *Pounds and Coppers: Financial Delegation in Police Forces*, Police Paper 10, London: HMSO.

Axelrod, R. (1984) *The Evolution of Cooperation*, New York: Basic Books.

Bader, V. (1995) 'Citizenship and Exclusion: Radical Democracy, Community, and Justice. Or What is Wrong with Communitarianism?', *Political Theory*, 23(2), 211–46.

Banton, M. (1974) 'The Definition of the Police Role', *New Community*, 3(3), 164–71.

Barclay, G. C. (1995) *The Criminal Justice System in England and Wales: 1995*, London: Home Office.

Barclay, P. (1995) *Joseph Rowntree Foundation Inquiry into Income and Wealth, Vol. 1*, York: Joseph Rowntree Foundation.

Barr, R. and Pease, K. (1990) 'Crime Placement, Displacement and Deflection', in M. Tonry and N. Morris (eds.) *Crime and Justice a Review of Research: Vol. 12*, Chicago: University of Chicago Press, 277–318.

Barry, A., Osborne, T., and Rose, N. (eds.) (1996) *Foucault and Political Reason*, London: University College London Press.

Batley, R. and Stocker, G. (eds.) (1991) *Local Government in Europe: Trends and Developments*, London: Macmillan.

Beck, U. (1992) *Risk Society: Towards a New Modernity*, London: Sage.

Beck, U., Giddens, A., and Lash, S. (eds.) (1994) *Reflexive Modernization: Politics, Tradition and Aesthetics in the Modern Social Order*, Cambridge: Polity Press.

Beetham, D. (1991) *The Legitimation of Power*, London: Macmillan.

Bell, C. and Newby, H. (1971) *Community Studies: An Introduction to the Sociology of Local Communities*, London: George Allen and Unwin.

Bell, D. (1993) *Communitarianism and Its Critics*, Oxford: Clarendon Press.

Bell, D. (1995) 'A Communitarian Critique of Authoritarianism', *Society*, 32, 38–44.

Bellah, R. N. (1986) 'Populism and Individualism', in H. C. Boyte and F. Reissman (eds.) *The New Populism: The Politics of Empowerment*, Philadelphia: Temple University Press.

Bellah, R. N., Madsen, R., Sullivan, W. M., Swidler, A., and Tipton, S. M. (1985) *Habits of the Heart: Individualism and Commitment in American Life*, Berkeley, California: University of California.

Benhabib, S. (1992) *Situating the Self: Gender, Community and Post-modernism in Contemporary Ethics*, Cambridge: Polity Press.

Bennett, T. (1990) *Evaluating Neighbourhood Watch*, Aldershot: Gower.

Bennett, T. (1991) 'The Effectiveness of a Police Initiated Fear Reducing Strategy', *British Journal of Criminology*, 31, 1–14.

Bennett, T. and Kemp, C. (1995) *An Evaluation of Area-Based Problem-Oriented Policing in Thames Valley Police Force Area*, Cambridge: Institute of Criminology.

Benson, J. K. (1982) 'A Framework for Policy Analysis', in D. L. Rogers and D. A. Whetten (eds.) *Interorganizational Coordination*, Ames: Iowa State University Press.

Blagg, H., Pearson, G., Sampson, A., Smith, D., and Stubbs, P. (1988) 'Inter-Agency Co-operation: Rhetoric and Reality', in T. Hope and M. Shaw (eds.) *Communities and Crime Reduction*, London: HMSO, 204–20.

Blagg, H. and Smith, D. (1989) *Crime, Penal Policy and Social Work*, Harlow: Longman.

Blair, T. (1996) *New Britain: My Vision of a Young Country*, London: Fourth Estate.

Blumstein, A. (1986) 'Coherence, Coordination and Integration in the Administration of Criminal Justice', in J. van Dijk *et al.* (eds.) *Criminal Law in Action: An Overview of Current Issues in Western Societies*, Arnhem: Gouda Quint, 247–58.

Blyth, E. and Milner, J. (1993) 'Exclusion from School: A First Step in Exclusion from Society?', *Children and Society*, 7(3), 255–68.

Bottoms, A. E. (1983) 'Neglected Features of Contemporary Penal Systems', in D. Garland and P. Young (eds.) *The Power to Punish*, London: Heinemann, 166–202.

Bottoms, A. E. (1990) 'Crime Prevention Facing the 1990s', *Policing and Society*, 1(1), 3–22.

Bottoms, A. E. (1994) 'Environmental Criminology', in M. Maguire *et al.* (eds.) *The Oxford Handbook of Criminology*, Oxford: Oxford University Press, 585–656.

Bottoms, A. E. (1995) 'The Philosophy and Politics of Punishment and Sentencing', in Clarkson, C. and Morgan, R. (eds.) *The Politics of Sentencing Reform*, Oxford: Clarendon Press, 17–49.

Bottoms, A. E. and Wiles, P. (1986) 'Housing Tenure and Residential Community Crime Careers in Britain', in A. J. Reiss and M. Tonry (eds.) *Communities and Crime: Crime and Justice a Review of Research, Vol. 8*, Chicago: University of Chicago Press, 101–62.

Bottoms, A. E. and Wiles, P. (1992) 'Explanations of Crime and Place', in D. J. Evans *et al.* (eds.) *Crime, Policing and Place: Essays in Environmental Criminology*, London: Routledge, 11–35.

Bottoms, A. E. and Wiles, P. (1995), 'Crime and Insecurity in the City', in C. Fijnaut *et al.* (eds.) *Changes in Society, Crime and Criminal Justice, Vol. 1, Crime and Insecurity in the City*, The Hague: Kluwer, 1–38.

Braithwaite, J. (1989a) 'The State of Criminology: Theoretical Decay or Renaissance?' *Australian and New Zealand Journal of Criminology*, 22, 129–35.

Braithwaite, J. (1989b) *Crime, Shame and Reintegration*, Cambridge: Cambridge University Press.

Braithwaite, J. (1993) 'Shame and Modernity', *British Journal of Criminology*, 33(1), 1–18.

Braithwaite, J. (1995) 'Inequality and Republican Criminology', in J. Hagan and R. D. Peterson (eds.), *Crime and Inequality*, Stanford: Stanford University Press, 277–305.

Braithwaite, J. and Daly, K. (1994) 'Masculinities, Violence and Communitarian Control', in T. Newburn and E. A. Stanko (eds.) *Just Boys Doing Business? Men, Masculinities and Crime*, London: Routledge, 189–213.

Braithwaite, J. and Mugford, S. (1994) 'Conditions of Successful Reintegration Ceremonies: Dealing with Juvenile Offenders', *British Journal of Criminology*, 34, 139–71.

Braithwaite, J. and Pettit, P. (1990) *Not Just Deserts: A Republican Theory of Criminal Justice*, Oxford: Oxford University Press.

Brake, M. and Hale, C. (1992) *Public Order and Private Lives*, London: Routledge.

Brantingham, P. J. and Faust, L. (1976) 'A Conceptual Model of Crime Prevention', *Crime and Delinquency*, 22, 284–96.

Brewer, J. and Styles, J. (eds.) (1980) *An Ungovernable People*, London: Hutchinson.

Bright, J. (1991) 'Crime Prevention: The British Experience', in K. Stenson and D. Cowell (eds.) *The Politics of Crime Control*, London: Sage, 62–86.

Bright, J. and Petterssen, G. (1984) *Improving Council House Estates*, London: NACRO.

Brittan, S. (1993) 'Social Tasks of Business', *Financial Times*, 2 September.

Broady, S. R. *The Effectiveness of Sentencing: A Review of the Literature*, Home Office Research Study No. 35, London: Home Office.

Brogden, M., Jefferson, T., and Walklate, S. (1988) *Introducing Policework*, London: Unwin Hyman.

Brownlee, I. D. (1994) 'Taking the Strait-Jacket Off: Persistence and the Distribution of Punishment in England and Wales, *Legal Studies*, 14(3), 295–312.

Bryant, M. (1989) *The Contribution of ACOP and Probation Services to Crime Prevention*, Wakefield: ACOP.

Buerger, M. E. (1994), 'A Tale of Two Targets: Limitations of Community Anticrime Actions', *Crime and Delinquency*, 40(3), 411–36.

Burchell, G., Gordon, C., and Miller, P. (eds.) (1992) *The Foucault Effect: Studies in Governmentality*, Hemel Hempstead; Harvester Wheatsheaf.

Burnside, J. and Baker, N. (eds.) (1994) *Relational Justice: Repairing the Breach*, Winchester: Waterside Press.

Butcher, H., Glen, A., Henderson, P., and Smith, J. (eds.) (1993) *Community and Public Policy*, London: Pluto.

Butler, A. J. P. (1996) 'Managing the Future: A Chief Constable's View', in F. Leishman *et al.* (eds.) *Core Issues in Policing*, London: Longman.

Butler-Sloss, E. (1988) *Report of the Inquiry into Child Abuse in Cleveland 1987*, London: HMSO.

Cain, M. (1988) 'Beyond Informal Justice', in R. Matthews (ed.) *Informal Justice?*, Sage: London, 51–86.

Campbell, B. (1993) *Goliath: Britain's Dangerous Places*, London: Methuen.

Campbell, B. (1994) 'The Underclass: Regressive Re-alignment', *Criminal Justice Matters*, 18, 18–19.

Campbell, D. (1996) ' "Citizen's Jury" Takes on Drugs', *The Guardian*, 18 April.

Cawson, A. (1982) *Corporatism and Welfare: Social Policy and State Intervention in Britain*, London: Heinemann.

Cawson, A. (1985) 'Introduction: Varieties of Corporatism', in Cawson, A. (ed.) *Organized Interests and the State: Studies in Meso-Corporatism*, London: Sage, 1–21.

Cawson, A. (1986) *Corporatism and Political Theory*, Oxford: Basil Blackwell.

Central Council of Probation Committees (1987) *Crime Prevention: A Role for Probation Committees*, London: CCPC.

Central Statistics Office (1995) *Social Trends*, London: HMSO.

Christie, N. (1977) 'Conflicts as Property', *British Journal of Criminology*, 17(1), 1–15.

Christie, N. (1993) *Crime Control as Industry*, London: Routledge.

Clark, D. B. (1973) 'The Concept of Community: a Re-examination', *Sociological Review*, 21(3), 397–416.

Clarke, R. V. (1980a) 'Situational Crime Prevention: Theory and Practice', *British Journal of Criminology*, 20(2), 136–45.

Clarke, R. V. (1980b) 'Opportunity Based Crime Rates', *British Journal of Criminology*, 24, 74–83.

Clarke, R. V. (1995), 'Situational Crime Prevention', in M. Tonry and D. Farrington, (eds.) *Building a Safer Society: Strategic Approaches to Crime Prevention—Crime and Justice a Review of Research*, Vol. 19, Chicago: University of Chicago Press, 91–150.

Clarke, R. V. and Hough, J. M. (1984) *Crime and Police Effectiveness*, Home Office Study No. 79, London: HMSO.

Clarke, R. V. and Mayhew, P. (eds.) (1980) *Designing Out Crime*, London: HMSO.

Cohen, S. (1979) 'The Punitive City: Notes on the Dispersal of Social Control', *Contemporary Crises*, 3, 339–63.

Cohen, S. (1985) *Visions of Social Control*, Cambridge: Polity Press.

Cohen, S. (1989) 'The Critical Discourse on "Social Control": Notes on the Concept as a Hammer', *International Journal of the Sociology of Law*, 17, 347–57.

Cohen, S. (1996) 'Crime and Politics: Spot the Difference', *British Journal of Sociology*, 47(1), 1–21.

Coleman, A. (1985) *Utopia on Trial*, London: Harry Shipman.

Commission on Social Justice (1994) *Social Justice: Strategies for National Renewal*, London: Vintage.

Condon, P. (1993) *Evidence to the House of Commons Home Affairs Committee*, 24 March, London: HMSO.

Cope, S., Leishman, F., and Starie, P. (1995) 'Hollowing-Out and Hiving-Off: Reinventing Policing in Britain, in J. Lovenduski and J. Stanyer (eds.) *Contemporary Political Studies 1995, Vol. 2*, Belfast: Political Studies Association.

Cornish, D. B. and Clarke, R. V. (1986) 'Situational Prevention, Displacement of Crime and Rational Choice Theory', in K. Heal and G. Laycock, (eds.) *Situational Crime Prevention: From Theory into Practice*, London: HMSO, 1–16.

Crawford, A. (1994a) 'The Partnership Approach: Corporatism at the Local Level?' *Social and Legal Studies*, 3(4), 497–519.'

Crawford, A. (1994b) 'Social Values and Managerial Goals: Police and Probation Officers' Experiences and Views of Inter-Agency Co-operation', *Policing and Society*, 4(4), 323–39.

Crawford, A. (1995) 'Appeals to Community and Crime Prevention', *Crime, Law and Social Change*, 22, 97–126.

Crawford, A. (1996a) 'The Spirit of Community: Rights, Responsibilities and the Communitarian Agenda', *Journal of Law and Society*, 23(2), 247–62.

Crawford, A. (1996b) 'Alternatives to Prosecution: Access to, or Exits from, Criminal Justice?', in R. Young and D. Wall (eds.) *Access to Criminal Justice: Legal Aid, Lawyers and the Defence of Liberty*, London: Blackstone Press, 313–44.

Crawford, A. (forthcoming) *Crime Prevention: Politics, Policies and Practices*, Harlow: Longman.

Crawford, A. and Jones, M. (1995) 'Inter-Agency Co-operation and Community-Based Crime Prevention: Some Reflections on the Work of Pearson and Colleagues', *British Journal of Criminology*, 35(1), 17–33.

Crawford, A. and Jones, M. (1996) 'Kirkholt Revisited: Some Reflections on the Transferability of Crime Prevention Initiatives', *Howard Journal*, 35(1), 21–39.

Crawford, A., Jones, T., Woodhouse, T., and Young, J. (1990) *The Second Islington Crime Survey*, Enfield: Centre for Criminology, Middlesex Polytechnic.

Critchley, T. A. (1978) *A History of Police in England and Wales*, London: Constable.

Crouch, C. (1983) 'Pluralism and the New Corporatism: A Rejoinder', *Political Studies*, 31(3), 452–60.

Crow, G. and Allan, G. (1994) *Community Life: An Introduction to Local Social Relations*, Hemel Hempstead: Harvester Wheatsheaf.

Currie, E. (1988) 'Two Visions of Community Crime Prevention', in T. Hope and M. Shaw (eds.) *Communities and Crime Reduction*, London: HMSO, 280–86.

Curtis, B. (1995) 'Taking the State Back Out: Rose and Miller on Political Power', *British Journal of Sociology*, 46, 577–89.

Dahrendorf, R. (1985) *Law and Order*, London: Stevens.

Daly, K. (1989) 'Criminal Justice Ideologies and Practices in Different Voices: Some Feminist Questions About Justice', *International Journal of the Sociology of Law*, 17, 1–18.

Danzig, R. (1973) 'Towards the Creation of a Complementary, Decentralized System of Criminal Justice', *Stanford Law Review*, 26, 1–54.

Davies, H. (1990) 'Effectiveness Through Delegation', *Policing*, 6(4), 596–606.

Davies, S. (1987) 'Towards the Remoralization of Society', in M. Loney (ed.) *The State or Market: Politics and Welfare in Contemporary Britain*, London: Sage, 172–88.

Davies, S. (1996) *Big Brother*, London: Macmillan.

Davis, G. (1992) *Making Amends*, London: Routledge.

Davis, G., Boucherat, J., and Watson, D. (1987) *A Preliminary Study of Victim Offender Mediation and Reparation Schemes in England and Wales*, Research and Planning Unit Paper, No. 42, London: Home Office.

Davis, G., Boucherat, J., and Watson, D. (1988) 'Reparation in the Service of Diversion: The Subordination of a Good Idea', *Howard Journal*, 27(2), 127–34.

Davis, G., Boucherat, J., and Watson, D. (1989) 'Pre-Court Decision-Making in Juvenile Justice', *British Journal of Criminology*, 29, 219–35.

Davis, M. (1990) *City of Quartz: Excavating the Future in Los Angeles*, London: Verso.

Davis, M. (1992) *Beyond Blade Runner: Urban Control the Ecology of Fear*, Westfield, NJ: Open Magazine Pamphlet Series.

Deakin, N. and Walsh, K. (1996) 'The Enabling State: The Role of Markets and Contracts', *Public Administration*, 74, 33–48.

Dennis, N. (1993) *Rising Crime and the Dismembered Family*, London: Institute for Economic Affairs.

Dennis, N. and Erdos, G. (1992) *Families Without Fatherhood*, London: Institute for Economic Affairs.

Department of the Environment (1994) *Planning Out Crime*, Circular 5/94, London: DoE.

Dixon, B. and Stanko, B. (1995) 'Sector Policing and Public Accountability', *Policing and Society*, 5, 171–83.

Donzelot, J. (1979) *Policing the Family*, London: Hutchinson.

Donzelot, J. (1991) 'The Mobilization of Society', in G. Burchell *et al.* (eds.) *The Foucault Effect: Studies in Governmentality*, Hemel Hempstead: Harvester Wheatsheaf, 169–79.

Douglas, M. (1986) *How Institutions Think*, Syracuse: Syracuse University Press.

Dowding, K. (1995) 'Model or Metaphor? A Critical Review of the Policy Network Approach', *Political Studies*, 43, 136–58.

Ehrlich, E. (1936), *Fundamental Principles of the Sociology of Law* (trans. W. Moll, first published 1913), Cambridge, Massachusetts: Harvard University Press.

Ekblom, P. (1992) 'The Safer Cities Programme Impact Evaluation: Problems and Progress', *Studies on Crime and Crime Prevention*, 1, 35–51.

Emsley, C. (1983) *Policing and Its Context 1750–1870*, London: Macmillan.

Emsley, C. (1991) *The English Police: A Political and Social History*, Hemel Hempstead: Harvester Wheatsheaf.

Emsley, C. (1995) 'Crime and Crime Control, c.1770–c.1945', in M. Maguire *et al.* (eds.) *The Oxford Handbook of Criminology*, Oxford: Oxford University Press, 149–82.

Ericson, R. (1994) 'The Division of Expert Knowledge in Policing and Security', *British Journal of Sociology*, 45(2), 149–75.

Ericson, R. (1996), 'The Risk Society', unpublished paper presented at the Australian and New Zealand Society of Criminology Conference, Victoria University of Wellington, 29 January–1 February 1996.

Etzioni, A. (1993) *The Spirit of Community*, New York: Simon Schuster.

Etzioni, A. (1995) 'The Attack on Community: The Grooved Debate', *Society*, 32 (5), 12–17.

Etzioni, A. (1996) 'The Responsive Community: A Communitarian Perspective', *American Sociological Review*, 61, 1–11.

European Commission (1994) *European Social Policy: A Way Forward for the Union*, Luxembourg: European Commission.

Evans, D. J., Fyfe, N. R., and Herbert, D. T. (eds.) (1992) *Crime, Policing and Place: Essays in Environmental Criminology*, London: Routledge.

Farrell, G. (1992) 'Multiple Victimisation: Its Extent and Significance', *International Review of Victimology*, 2(2), 85–102.

Farrell, G. (1995) 'Preventing Repeat Victimisation' in M. Tonry and D. Farrington (eds.) *Building a Safer Society: Strategic Approaches to Crime Prevention—Crime and Justice a Review of Research*, Vol. 19, Chicago: University of Chicago Press, 469–534.

Farrell, G. and Pease, K. (1993) *Once Bitten, Twice Bitten: Repeat Victimisation and Its Implications for Crime Prevention*, Crime Prevention Unit Paper No. 46, London: Home Office.

Farrell, M. (ed.) (1989) *Punishment for Profit?*, London: ISTD.

Faulkner, D. (1994) 'Relational Justice: A Dynamic for Reform', in Burnside and Baker (eds.) (1994), *Relational Justice: Repairing the Breach*, Winchester: Waterside Press, 159–74.

Feeley, M. and Simon, J. (1992) 'The New Penology: Notes on the Emerging Strategy of Corrections and Its Implications', *Criminology*, 30(4), 449–74.

Feeley, M. and Simon, J. (1994) 'Actuarial Justice: the Emerging New Criminal Law', in Nelken, D. (ed.) *The Futures of Criminology*, London: Sage, 173–201.

Fenwick, H. (1995) 'Rights of Victims in the Criminal Justice System: Rhetoric or Reality', *Criminal Law Review*, 843–53.

Fielding, N. (1984) *Probation Practice*, Aldershot: Gower.

Fielding, N. (1988) 'Socialisation of Recruits into the Police Role', in P. Southgate (ed.) *New Directions in Police Training*, London: HMSO, 58–73.

Fielding, N. (1995) *Community Policing*, Oxford: Clarendon Press.

Fielding, N. and Fielding, J. (1991) 'Police Attitudes to Crime and Punishment', *British Journal of Criminology*, 31(1), 39–53.

Fijnaut, C. (ed.) (1993) *The Internalization of Police Co-operation in Western Europe*, Deventer: Kluwer.

Fijnaut, C., Goethals, J., Peters, T., and Walgrave, L. (eds.) (1995) *Changes in Society, Crime and Criminal Justice, Vol. 1, Crime and Insecurity in the City*, The Hague: Kluwer.

Findlay, M. and Duff, P. (eds.) (1988) *The Jury Under Attack*, London: Butterworths.

Fine, B. (1984) *Democracy and the Rule of Law*, London: Pluto.

Fitzpatrick, P. (1992) 'The Impossibility of Popular Justice', *Social and Legal Studies*, 1(2), 199–215.

Forrester, D., Chatterton, M., and Pease, K. (1988) *The Kirkholt Burglary Prevention Project, Rochdale*, Crime Prevention Unit Paper 13, London: Home Office.

Forrester, D., Frenz, S., O'Connell, M., and Pease, K. (1990) *The Kirkholt Burglary Project: Phase II*, Crime Prevention Unit Paper No. 23, London: Home Office.

Foster, J. (1990) *Villains: Crime and Community in the Inner City*, London: Routledge.

Foster, J. (1995) 'Informal Social Control and Community Crime Prevention', *British Journal of Criminology*, 35(4), 563–83.

Foster, J, and Hope, T. (1993) *Housing, Community and Crime: The Impact of the Priority Estates Project*, Home Office Research Study 131, London: HMSO.

Foucault, M. (1977) *Discipline and Punish*, Harmondsworth: Penguin.

Foucault, M. (1979) *The History of Sexuality: An Introduction*, Harmondsworth: Penguin.

Foucault, M. (1991) 'Governmentality', in G. Burchell *et al.* (eds.) *The Foucault Effect: Studies in Governmentality*, Hemel Hempstead; Harvester Wheatsheaf, 87–104.

Frazer, E. and Lacey, N. (1993) *The Politics of Community: A Feminist Critique of the Liberal-Communitarian Debate*, Hemel Hempstead: Harvester Wheatsheaf.

Friedman, M. (1962) *Capitalism and Freedom*, Chicago: University of Chicago Press.

Friedmann, R. R. (1992) *Community Policing: Comparative Perspectives and Prospects*, Hemel Hempstead: Harvester Wheatsheaf.

Fyfe, N. R. (1992) 'Towards Locally Sensitive Policing? Politics, Participation and Power in Community/Police Consultation', in D. J. Evans *et al.* (eds) *Crime, Policing and Place: Essays in Environmental Criminology*, London: Routledge, 305–26.

Gallagher, J. (1995) 'Anti-Social Security', *New Statesman and Society*, 31 March.

Gamble, A. (1979) 'The Free Economy and the Strong State', *Socialist Register*, 1–25.

Gamble, A. (1986) 'The Political Economy of Freedom', in R. Levitas (ed.) *The Ideology of the New Right*, Cambridge: Polity Press, 25–54.

Garland, D. (1985) *Punishment and Welfare*, Aldershot: Gower.

Garland, D. (1990) *Punishment and Modern Society*, Oxford: Clarendon Press.

Garland, D. (1994) 'Of Crimes and Criminals: The Development of British Criminology', in M. Maguire *et al.* (eds.) *The Oxford Handbook of Criminology*, Oxford: Oxford University Press, 17–68.

Garland, D. (1996) 'The Limits of Sovereign State: Strategies of Crime Control in Contemporary Society', *British Journal of Criminology*, 35(4), 445–71.

Garland, D. and Young, P. (eds.) (1983) *The Power to Punish*, London: Heinemann.

Gatrell, V. A. C. (1996) 'Crime, Authority and the Policeman-State', in J. Muncie, E. McLaughlin, and M. Langan (eds.) *Criminological Perspectives: A Reader*, London: Sage, 383–91.

Genn, H. (1988) 'Multiple Victimisation', in M. Maguire and J. Pointing (eds.) *Victims of Crime: A New Deal?*, Milton Keynes: Open University Press, 90–100.

Geraghty, J. (1991) *Probation Practice in Crime Prevention*, Crime Prevention Unit Paper 24, London: Home Office.

Giddens, A. (1984) *The Constitution of Society*, Cambridge: Polity Press.

Giddens, A. (1985) *The Nation State and Violence*, Cambridge: Polity Press.

Giddens, A. (1990) *The Consequences of Modernity*, Cambridge: Polity Press.

Giddens, A. (1994) 'Living in a Post Traditional Society', in U. Beck *et al.* (eds.) *Reflexive Modernization: Politics, Tradition and Aesthetics in the Modern Social Order*, Cambridge: Polity Press, 56–109.

Gill, M. and Mawby, R. (1990a) *Volunteers in the Criminal Justice System*, Milton Keynes: Open University Press.

Gill, M. and Mawby, R. (1990b) *A Special Kind of Constable?*, Aldershot: Avebury.

Gilligan, C. (1982) *In a Different Voice*, Cambridge, Massachusetts: Harvard University Press.

Gilling, D. (1996) 'Crime Prevention', in T. May and A. A. Vass (eds.) *Working with Offenders: Issues, Contexts and Outcomes*, London: Sage, 222–41.

Gitlin, T. (1995) *The Twilight of Common Dreams*, H. Holt & Co: New York.

Gladstone, F. (1980) *Co-ordinating Crime Prevention Efforts*, London: HMSO.

Goldsmith, A. (1990) 'Taking Police Culture Seriously: Police Discretion and the Limits of Law', *Policing and Society*, 1(2), 91–114.

Goldstein, H. (1990) *Problem-Oriented Policing*, New York: McGraw Hill.

Gordon, P. (1987) 'Community Policing: Towards the Local Police State?', in P. Scraton (ed.) *Law, Order and the Authoritarian State*, Milton Keynes: Open University Press, 121–44.

Gray, J. (1993) *Beyond the New Right: Markets, Government and the Common Environment*, London: Routledge.

Gray, J. (1995), *Enlightenment's Wake: Politics and Culture at the Close of the Modern Age*, London: Routledge.

Grayson, D. (1994) 'Community Regeneration: Is It the Business of Business?' *Policy Studies*, 15(2), 37–51.

Greene, J. R. and Mastrofski, S. D. (eds.) (1988) *Community Policing: Rhetoric or Reality*, New York: Praeger.

Grönfors, M. (1989) 'Ideal and Reality in Community Mediation', in M. Wright and B. Galaway (eds.) *Mediation and Criminal Justice: Victims, Offenders and Community*, London: Sage, 140–51.

Habermas, J. (1976) *Legitimation Crisis*, London: Heinemann.

Habermas, J. (1989a) *The Structural Transformation of the Public Sphere*, Cambridge: Polity Press.

Habermas, J. (1989b) *The New Conservatism*, Cambridge: Polity Press.

Hakim, S. and Rengert, G. F. (1981) *Crime Spillover*, Beverley Hills, California: Sage.

Hall, S. (1979) *Drifting Into a Law and Order Society*, London: Cobden Trust.

Hanmer, J. and Maynard, M. (eds.) (1987) *Women, Violence and Social Control*, London: Macmillan.

Harden, I. (1988) 'Corporatism Without Labour: The British Version', in C. Graham and T. Prosser (eds.) *Waiving the Rules: The Constitution Under Thatcherism*, Milton Keynes: Open University Press, 36–55.

Hargreaves Heap, S., Hollis, M., Lyons, B., Sugden, R., and Weal, A. (eds.) (1992) *The Theory of Choice: A Critical Guide*, Oxford: Blackwell.

Harker, L. and Oppenheim, C. (1996) *Poverty: The Facts*, London: Child Poverty Action Group.

Harrington, C. B. (1993) 'Community Organizing Through Conflict Resolution', in S. E. Merry and N. Milner (eds.) *The Possibility of Popular Justice*, Michigan: University of Michigan Press, 401–33,

Harrington, C. B. and Merry, S. (1988) 'The Ideology of Community Mediation', *Law and Society Review*, 22(4), 709–35.

Harvey, L., Grimshaw, P., and Pease, K. (1989) 'Crime Prevention Delivery: The Work of Crime Prevention Officers', in R. Morgan and D. J. Smith (eds.) *Coming to Terms with Policing: Perspectives on Policy*, London: Routledge, 82–96.

Hay, C. (1995) 'Re-Stating the Problem of Regulation and Re-Regulating the Local State', *Economy and Society*, 24(3), 387–407.

Hay, D., Linebaugh, P., and Thompson, E. P. (1975) *Albion's Fatal Tree*, Harmondsworth: Penguin.

Hay, D. and Snyder, F. (eds.) (1989) *Policing and Prosecution in Britain 1750–1850*, Oxford: Clarendon Press.

Hayek, F. von (1944) *The Road to Serfdom*, London: Routledge and Kegan Paul.

Heal, K. (1988) 'Crime Prevention in Britain: From Start to Go', *Home Office Research and Planning Unit Research Bulletin No. 24*, London: Home Office.

Heal, K. (1992) 'Changing Perspectives on Crime Prevention: The Role of Information and Structure', in D. J. Evans *et al.* (eds.) *Crime, Policing and Place: Essays in Environmental Criminology*, London: Routledge, 257–71.

Heal, K. and Laycock, G. (eds.) (1986) *Situational Crime Prevention: From Theory into Practice*, London: HMSO.

Heidensohn, F. (1986) 'Models of Justice: Portia or Persephone? Some Thoughts on Equality, Fairness and Gender in the Field of Criminal Justice', *International Journal of the Sociology of Law*, 14, 287–98.

Heidensohn, F. (1992) *Women in Control?: Women in Law Enforcement*, Oxford: Oxford University Press.

Herrnstein, R. and Murry, C. (1994) *The Bell Curve*, New York: Free Press.

Hills, J. (1995) *Joseph Rowntree Foundation Inquiry into Income and Wealth, Volume 2*, York: Joseph Rowntree Foundation.

Hindness, B. (1991) 'Imaginary Presuppositions of Democracy', *Economy and Society*, 20(2), 173–95.

Hirst, J. (1995) 'A Sense of Community', *The Guardian*, Society Section, 9 August.

Hirst, P. (1994) *Associative Democracy: New Forms of Economic and Social Governance*, Cambridge: Polity Press.

Hirst, P. and Thompson, G. (1995) 'Globalisation and the Future of the Nation State', *Economy and Society*, 24(3), 408–42.

Hobbs, D. (1988) *Doing the Business*, Oxford: Oxford University Press.

Hobbs, D. (1994) 'A Bit of How's Your Father?' *Youth and Policy*, Winter/ Spring, 76–82.

Hobbs, D. (1995) *Dirty Business*, Oxford: Oxford University Press.

Hobsbawm, E. (1995) *Age of Extremes: The Short Twentieth Century, 1914–1991*, London: Abacus.

Holdaway, S. (1983) *Inside the British Police*, Oxford: Basil Blackwell.

Holdaway, S. (1986) 'Police and Social Work Relations—Problems and Possibilities', *British Journal of Social Work*, 16, 137–60.

Home Affairs Committee (1987) *Contract Provision of Prisons*, Fourth Report of the Home Affairs Committee, HC 291, London: HMSO.

Home Office (1965) *Report of the Committee on the Prevention and Detection of Crime*, London: Home Office.

Home Office (1984a) *Crime Prevention*, Circular 8/1984, London: Home Office.

Home Office (1984b) *Probation Service in England and Wales: Statement of National Objectives and Priorities*, London: HMSO.

Home Office (1985) *Arrangements for Local Consultation Between the Community and the Police Outside London*, Circular 2/1985, London: Home Office.

Home Office (1988a) *Crime Prevention Centre Handbook of Preventative Policing Skills*, Stafford: HOCPC.

Home Office (1988b) *Private Sector Involvement in the Remand System*, Cm 434, London: HMSO.

Home Office (1988c) *Application for Increases in Police Force Establishment*, Circular 106/1988, London: Home Office.

Home Office (1988d) *Punishment, Custody and the Community*, Cm 424, London: Home Office.

Home Office (1990a) *Partnership in Crime Prevention*, London: Home Office.

Home Office (1990b) *Crime Prevention—The Success of the Partnership Approach*, Circular 44/1990, London: Home Office.

Home Office (1990c) *Crime, Justice and Protecting the Public*, Cm 965, London: Home Office.

Home Office (1990d) *Supervision and Punishment in the Community*, Cm 966, London: Home Office.

Home Office (1990e) *Partnership in Dealing with Offenders in the Community*, London: Home Office.

Home Office (1991) *Practical Ways to Crack Crime*, 4th Edition (first published 1989), London: Home Office.

Home Office (1992a) *Three Year Plan for the Probation Service, 1993–96*, London: Home Office.

Home Office (1992b) *Partnership in Dealing with Offenders in the Community: A Decision Document*, London: Home Office.

Home Office (1992c) *Home Office Response to the Report 'Safer Communities—The Local Delivery of Crime Prevention Through the Partnership Approach'*, London: Home Office.

Home Office (1993a) *Crime Prevention Statement*, London: Home Office.

Home Office (1993b) *Police Reform: A Police Service for the Twenty-First Century*, Cm 2281, London: HMSO.

Home Office (1993c) *A Practical Guide to Crime Prevention for Local Partnerships*, London: Home Office.

Home Office (1994a) *Review of Police Core and Ancillary Tasks: Interim Report*, London: Home Office.

Home Office (1994b) *Home Office Research Findings*, Home Office Research and Statistics Department, No. 11, London: Home Office.

Home Office (1994c) *Partners Against Crime*, London: Home Office.

Home Office (1995a) *Closed Circuit Television Challenge Competition 1996/97*, London: Home Office.

Home Office (1995b) *Review of Police Core and Ancillary Tasks: Final Report*, London: Home Office.

Home Office (1996) *Protecting the Public*, Cm 3190, London: HMSO.

Hoogenboom, A. B. (1991) 'Grey Policing: a Theoretical Framework', *Policing and Society*, 2, 17–30.

Hope, T. (1985) *Implementing Crime Prevention Measures*, Home Office Research Study, No. 86, London: Home Office.

Hope, T. (1995a) 'Community Crime Prevention, in M. Tonry and D. Farrington (eds.) *Building a Safer Society: Strategic Approaches to Crime Prevention—Crime and Justice a Review of Research, Vol. 19*, Chicago: University of Chicago Press, 21–89.

Hope, T. (1995b) 'Community Safety and Inequality in England and Wales', unpublished paper presented to the 'Democracy and Justice' conference, Brunel University, 13–14 June.

Hope, T. and Foster, J. (1992) 'Conflicting Forces: Changing the Dynamics of Crime and Community on a "Problem" Estate', *British Journal of Criminology*, 32(4), 488–504.

Hope, T. and Murphy, D. J. I. (1983) 'Problems of Implementing Crime Prevention: The Experience of a Demonstration Project', *Howard Journal*, 22(1), 38–50.

Hope, T. and Shaw, M. (eds.) (1988a) *Communities and Crime Reduction*, London: HMSO.

Hope, T. and Shaw, M. (1988b) 'Community Approaches to Reducing Crime', in T. Hope and M. Shaw (eds.) *Communities and Crime Reduction*, London: HMSO, 1–28.

Hough, J. M. (1986) 'Victims of Violent Crime: Findings from the First British Crime Survey', in E. Fattah (ed.) *From Crime Policy to Victim Policy*, London: Macmillan, 117–32.

Hough, J. M. and Mayhew, P. (1983) *The British Crime Survey: First Report*, Home Office Research Study, No. 76, London: HMSO.

Howard, M. (1994) 'A Volunteer Army Awaiting the Call', *The Times*, 28 February.

Hudson, B. (1993) *Penal Policy and Social Justice*, London: Macmillan.

Hudson, J., Morris, A., Maxwell, G., and Galway, B. (eds.) (1996) *Family Group Conferences: Perspectives on Policy and Practice*, Annandale, NSW: Federation Press.

Hulsman, L. (1986) 'Critical Criminology and the Concept of Crime', *Contemporary Crises*, 10, 63–80.

Humphrey, C. (1994) 'Reflecting on Attempts to Develop a Financial Management Information System (FMIS) for the Probation Service in England and Wales: Some Observations on the Relationship Between the Claims of Accounting and its Practice', *Accounting, Organizations and Society*, 19(2), 147–78.

Humphrey, C., Miller, P., and Scapens, R. W. (1993) 'Accountability and Accountable Management in the UK Public Sector', *Accounting, Auditing and Accountability Journal*, 6(3), 7–29.

Hunt, A. (1981) 'Dichotomy and Contradiction in the Sociology of Law', *British Journal of Law and Society*, 8, 47–77.

Hunt, A. and Wickham, G. (1994) *Foucault and Law: Towards a Sociology of Law as Governance*, London: Pluto.

Hussain, S. (1988) *Neighbourhood Watch in England and Wales: A Locational Analysis*, Crime Prevention Unit Paper No. 12, London: Home Office.

Hutton, W. (1995) *The State We're In*, London: Jonathan Cape.

Ignatieff, M. (1981) 'State, Civil Society and Total Institutions: A Critique of Recent Social Histories of Punishment', in M. Tonry and N. Morris (eds.) *Crime and Justice: An Annual Review of Research, Vol. 3*, Chicago: University of Chicago Press, 153–91.

Ireland, P. (1995) 'Reflections on a Rampage Through the Barriers of Shame: Law, Community, and the New Conservatism', *Journal of Law and Society*, 22(2), 189–211.

Jacobs, J. (1961) *The Death and Life of Great American Cities*, New York: Vintage.

James, A. and Bottomley, A. K. (1994) 'Probation Partnership Revisited', *Howard Journal*, 33(2), 158–68.

Jeffers, S., Hoggett, P., and Harrison, L. (1996) 'Race, Ethnicity and Community in Three Localities', *New Community*, 22(1), 111–26.

Jefferson, T. and Grimshaw, R. (1984) *Controlling the Constable: Police Accountability in England and Wales*, London: Muller/Cobden Trust.

Jefferson, T., McLaughlin, E., and Robertson, L. (1988) 'Monitoring the Monitors: Accountability, Democracy and Policewatching in Britain', *Contemporary Crises*, 12, 91–106.

Jessop, B. (1993) 'Towards a Schumpeterian Workfare State? Preliminary Remarks on Post-Fordist Political Economy', *Studies in Political Economy*, 40, 7–39.

Jessop, B. (1995) 'The Regulation Approach, Governance and Post-Fordism: Alternative Perspectives on Economic and Political Change', *Economy and Society*, 24(3), 307–33.

Johnston, L. (1992) *The Rebirth of Private Policing*, London: Routledge.

Johnston, L. (1994a) 'Privatization: Threat or Opportunity?' *Policing*, 10(1), 14–22.

Johnston, L. (1994b) 'Privatization and Protection: Spatial and Sectoral Ideologies in British Policing and Crime Prevention', *Modern Law Review*, 56(6), 771–92.

Johnston, L. (1996) 'What is Vigilantism?', *British Journal of Criminology*, 36(2), 220–36.

Johnston, V., Shapland, J., and Wiles, P. (1993) *Developing Police Crime Prevention: Management and Organisational Change*, Crime Prevention Unit Paper, No. 41, London: Home Office.

Joint Consultative Committee (1990) *Operational Policing Review*, Surbiton, Surrey: Joint Consultative Committee.

Jones, C. (1993) 'Auditing Criminal Justice', *British Journal of Criminology*, 33(3), 187–202.

Jones, T., Maclean, B., and Young, J. (1989) *The Islington Crime Survey*, Aldershot: Gower.

Jones, T. and Newburn, T. (1995) 'How Big is the Private Security Sector?', *Policing and Society*, 5, 221–32.

Jones, T., Newburn, T., and Smith, D. (1994) *Democracy and Policing*, London: Policy Studies Institute.

Jones, T., Newburn, T., and Smith, D. (1996) 'Policing and the Idea of Democracy', *British Journal of Criminology*, 36(2), 182–98.

Jordan, B. and Arnold, J. (1995) 'Democracy and Criminal Justice', *Critical Social Policy*, 15(2), 170–82.

Jury, L. (1993) 'Vigilante Fear Over Street Patrols', *The Guardian*, 21 June.

Kaser, G. (1988) 'Value for Money Services in the Public Sector', *Capital and Class*, 36, 31–57.

Keat, R. (1991a) 'Introduction: Starship Britain or Universal Enterprise?'

in R. Keat and N. Abercrombie (eds.) *Enterprise Culture*, London: Routledge, 1–17.

Keat, R. (1991b), 'Consumer Sovereignty and the Integrity of Practices', in R. Keat and N. Abercrombie (eds.) *Enterprise Culture*, London: Routledge, 21–30.

Keat, R. and Abercrombie, N. (eds.) (1991) *Enterprise Culture*, London: Routledge.

Kelling, G. (1985) 'Order Maintenance: The Quality of Urban Life and Police: A Line of Argument', in W. Geller (ed.) *Police Leadership in America: Crisis and Opportunity*, New York: Praeger.

Kelling, G. (1987) 'Acquiring a Taste for Order: The Community and Police', *Crime and Delinquency*, 33(1), 90–102.

Kempson, E., Bryson, A., and Rowlingson, K. (1994) *Hard Times? How Poor Families Make Ends Meet*, London: Policy Studies Institute.

King, M. (1989) 'Social Crime Prevention à la Thatcher', *Howard Journal*, 28(4), 291–312.

Kinsey, R. (1985) *The Merseyside Crime and Police Surveys: Final Report*, Liverpool: Merseyside County Council.

Kinsey, R., Lea, J. and Young, J. (1986) *Losing the Fight Against Crime*, Oxford: Blackwell.

Labour Party (1987) *Protecting Our People: Labour's Policy on Crime Prevention*, London: Labour Party.

Labour Party (1994) *Partners Against Crime*, London: Labour Party.

Labour Party (1995a) *A Quiet Life: Tough Action on Criminal Neighbours*, London: Labour Party.

Labour Party (1995b) *Renewing Democracy, Rebuilding Communities*, London: Labour Party.

Lacey, N. (1994) 'Government as Manager, Citizen as Consumer: The Case of the Criminal Justice Act 1991', *Modern Law Review*, 57(4), 534–54.

Lacey, N. (1996) 'Community in Legal Theory: Idea, Ideal or Ideology?', *Studies in Law, Politics and Society*, 15, 105–46.

Lacey, N. and Zedner, L. (1995) 'Discourses of Community in Criminal Justice', *Journal of Law and Society*, 23(3), 301–25.

LaPrairie, C. (1995) 'Altering Course: New Directions in Criminal Justice', *Australian and New Zealand Journal of Criminology*, 78–99.

Lasch, C. (1980) *The Culture of Narcissism*, London: Sphere Books.

Lash, S. and Urry, J. (1994) *Economies of Sign and Space*, London: Sage.

Laycock, G. and Pease, K. (1985) 'Crime Prevention Within the Probation Service', *Probation Journal*, 32, 43–47.

Lazerges, C. (1995) 'De la Politique de Prévention de la Délinquance à la Politique de la Ville', in C. Fijnaut *et al.* (eds.) *Changes in Society, Crime and Criminal Justice, Vol. 1, Crime and Insecurity in the City*, The Hague: Kluwer, 213–49.

Lea, J. and Young, J. (1984) *What is to be Done About Law and Order?*, Middlesex: Penguin.

Leadbeater, C. (1996) *The Self-Policing Society*, London: Demos.

Leishman, F., Cope, S., and Starie, P. (1996) 'Reinventing and Restructuring: Towards a "New Policing Order" ', in F. Leishman *et al.* (eds.) *Core Issues in Policing*, London: Longman, 9–25.

Leishman, F., Loveday, B., and Savage, S. (eds.) (1996) *Core Issues in Policing*, London: Longman.

Leon, C. (1989) 'The Special Constabulary', *Policing*, 5(3), 265–86.

Levitas, R. (1986a) 'Introduction: Ideology and the New Right', in R. Levitas (ed.) *The Ideology of the New Right*, Cambridge: Polity Press, 1–24.

Levitas, R. (ed.) (1986b) *The Ideology of the New Right*, Cambridge: Polity Press.

Levitas, R. (1996) 'The Concept of Social Exclusion and the New Durkheimian Hegemony', *Critical Social Policy*, 16, 5–20.

Lewis, D. (1996) 'Free the Servants', *The Guardian*, 13 May.

Lewis, D. and Salem, G. (1986) *Fear of Crime: Incivility and the Production of a Social Problem*, New York: Transaction Books.

Liberal Democrats (1996) *Stronger Communities Safer Citizens: Proposals for Crime and Policing Policy in England and Wales*, Policy Paper 17, London: Liberal Democrats.

Liddle, A. M. and Bottoms, A. E. (1994) *The Five Towns Crime Prevention Initiative: Key Findings and Implications from a Retrospective Research Analysis*, London: Home Office.

Liddle, A. M. and Gelsthorpe, L. R. (1994a) *Inter-Agency Crime Prevention: Organizing Local Delivery*, Police Research Group, Crime Prevention Unit Series Paper 52, London: Home Office.

Liddle, A. M. and Gelsthorpe, L. R. (1994b) *Crime Prevention and Inter-Agency Co-operation*, Police Research Group, Crime Prevention Unit Series Paper 53, London: Home Office.

Lilly, J. R. and Knepper, P. (1992) 'The Corrections-Commercial Complex', *Prison Service Journal*, 87, 43–52.

Llewellyn, K. and Hoebel, A. (1941) *The Cheyenne Way*, Norman: University of Oklahoma Press.

Loader, I. (1994) 'Democracy, Justice and the Limits of Policing: Rethinking Police Accountability', *Social and Legal Studies*, 3(4), 521–44.

Loader, I. (1997) 'Private Security and the Demand for Protection in Contemporary Britain', *Policing and Society*, 7, 143–62.

Local Government Management Board (1996) *Survey of Community Safety Activities in Local Government in England and Wales*, Luton: LGMB.

Logan, C. (1990) *Private Prisons: Cons and Pros*, Oxford: Oxford University Press.

Loveday, B. (1995) 'Reforming the Police: From Local Service to State Police?', *Political Quarterly Review*, 66, 141–56.

Lowman, J. (1992) 'Street Prostitution Control: Some Canadian Reflections on the Finsbury Park Experience', *British Journal of Criminology*, 32(1), 1–17.

Lowman, J., Menzies, R., and Palys, T. S. (eds.) (1987) *Transcarceration: Essays in the Sociology of Social Control*, Aldershot: Gower.

Lukes, S. (1974) *Power: A Radical View*, London: Macmillan.

Lukes, S. (1977) *Essays in Social Theory*, London: Macmillan.

Lustgarten, L. (1986) *The Governance of the Police*, London: Sweet and Maxwell.

Macaulay, S. (1986) 'Private Government', in L. Lipson and S. Wheeler (eds.) *Law and the Social Sciences*, New York: Russell Sage Foundation, 445–518.

Mabbott, J. (1993) 'The Role of Community Involvement', *Police Studies*, 14(2), 27–35.

Maguire, M. and Corbett, C. (1987) *The Effects of Crime and the Work of Victim Support Schemes*, Aldershot: Gower.

Maguire, M. and Pointing, J. (eds.) (1988) *Victims of Crime: A New Deal?* Milton Keynes: Open University Press.

Maguire, M., Morgan, R., and Reiner, R. (eds.) (1994) *The Oxford Handbook of Criminology*, Oxford: Oxford University Press.

Mair, G. and Nee, C. (1990) *Electronic Monitoring: the Trials and their Results*, Home Office Research Study No. 120, London: Home Office.

Malik, K. (1994) 'Creating a Sense of Us and Them', *The Independent*, 8 August.

Malik, K. (1995) 'Same Old Hate in the New Byword for Bigotry', *The Guardian*, 12 August.

Malik, K. (1996) 'Universalism and Difference: Race and the Postmodernists', *Race & Class*, 37(3), 1–17.

Mandelson, P. and Liddle, R. (1996) *The Blair Revolution: Can Blair Deliver?* London: Faber.

Manning, P. (1977) *Police Work*, Cambridge, Massachusetts: MIT Press.

Marsh, D. and Rhodes, R. (eds.) (1992a) *Policy Networks in British Government*, Oxford: Clarendon Press.

Marsh, D. and Rhodes, R. (1992b) 'Policy Communities and Issue Networks: Beyond Typologies', in D. Marsh and R. Rhodes (eds.) *Policy Networks in British Government*, Oxford: Clarendon Press, 249–68.

Marshall, T. and Merry, S. (1990) *Crime and Accountability: Victim/Offender Mediation in Practice*, London: HMSO.

Marx, G. T. (1989) 'Commentary: Some Trends and Issues in Citizen Involvement in the Law Enforcement Process', *Crime and Delinquency*, 35(3), 500–19.

Mathieson, T. (1983) 'The Future of Control Systems—The Case of Norway', in D. Garland and P. Young (eds.) *The Power to Punish*, London: Heinemann, 130–45.

Matthews, R. (1987) 'Decarceration and Social Control: Fantasies and Realities', *International Journal of the Sociology of Law*, 15, 39–60.

Matthews, R. (ed.) (1988) *Informal Justice?*, London: Sage.

Matthews, R. (ed.) (1989) *Privatizing Criminal Justice*, London: Sage.

Matthews, R. (1992a) 'Replacing Broken Windows: Crime, Incivilities and Urban Change', in R. Matthews and J. Young (eds.) *Issues in Realist Criminology*, London: Sage, 19–50.

Matthews, R. (1992b) 'Regulating Street Prostitution and Kerb-Crawling: A Reply to John Lowman', *British Journal of Criminology*, 32(1), 18–22.

Matthews, R. and Young, J. (eds.) (1992) *Issues in Realist Criminology*, London: Sage.

May, T. (1991) 'Under Siege: The Probation Service in a Changing Environment', in R. Reiner and M. Cross (eds.) *Beyond Law and Order: Criminal Justice Policy and Politics in the 1990s*, Basingstoke: Macmillan, 158–85.

Mayhew, H. (1861) *London Labour and the London Poor, Vol. 1*, London: Griffin, Bohn & Co.

Mayhew, P., Clarke, R. V., Sturman, A., and Hough, M. (1976) *Crime as Opportunity*, London: HMSO.

McConville, M. and Shepard, D. (1992) *Watching Police Watching Communities*, London: Routledge.

McCrystal, C. (1993) 'Heroes and Villains', *The Independent on Sunday*, 11 July.

McCrystal, C. (1995) 'Private Lives', *The Independent on Sunday*, 11 June.

McDonald, D. C. (1994) 'Public Imprisonment by Private Means: The Re-emergence of Private Prisons and Jails in the United States, the United Kingdom and Australia', *British Journal of Criminology*, 34, 29–48.

McLaughlin, E. (1994) *Community, Policing and Accountability*, Aldershot: Avebury.

McLaughlin, E. and Muncie, J. (1994) 'Managing the Criminal Justice System', in J. Clarke, A. Cochrane and E. McLaughlin (eds.) *Managing Social Policy*, London: Sage, 115–40.

McLaughlin, E. and Murji, K. (1995) 'The End of Public Policing? Police Reform and "the New Managerialism" ', in L. Noaks *et al.* (eds.) *Contemporary Issues in Criminology*, Cardiff: University of Wales Press, 110–27.

McMahon, M. (1990) 'Net-Widening: Vagaries in the Use of a Concept', *British Journal of Criminology*, 30(2), 121–49.

McMullan, J. L. (1987) 'Policing the Criminal Underworld: State Power and Decentralised Social Control in London, 1550–1700', in J. Lowman *et al.* (eds.) *Transcarceration: Essays in the Sociology of Social Control*, Aldershot: Gower, 119–38.

McWilliam, W. (1990) 'Probation Practice and the Management Ideal', *Probation Journal*, 37(2), 60–7.

McWilliams, W. (1992) 'The Rise and Development of Management Thought in the English Probation System', in R. Statham and P. Whitehead (eds.) *Managing the Probation Service: Issues for the 1990s*, Harlow: Longman.

Mediation UK (1995) *Newsletter*, 11, 2, Spring.

Mendus, S. (1989) *Toleration and the Limits of Liberalism*, Basingstoke: Macmillan.

Merry, S. E. (1981) *Urban Danger: Life in a Neighbourhood of Strangers*, Philadelphia: Temple University Press.

Merry, S. E. (1982) 'Defining "Success" in the Neighbourhood Justice Movement', in R. Tomasic and M. Feeley (eds.) *Neighbourhood Justice: An Assessment of an Emerging Idea*, New York: Longman, 172–92.

Merry, S. E. (1988) 'Legal Pluralism', *Law and Society Review*, 22(5), 869–96.

Merry, S. E. and Milner, N. (eds.) (1993) *The Possibility of Popular Justice*, Michigan: University of Michigan Press.

Miller, P. and O'Leary, T. (1994) 'Governing the Calculable Person', in A. G. Hopwood and P. Miller (eds.) *Accounting as Social and Institutional Practice*, Cambridge: Cambridge University Press, 98–115.

Miller, P. and Rose, N. (1991) 'Programming the Poor: Poverty, Calculation and Expertise', in J. Lehto (ed.) *Deprivation, Social Welfare and Expertise*, Research Report, No. 7, Helsinki: National Agency for Welfare and Health.

Miller, P. and Rose, N. (1995), 'Political Thought and the Limits of Orthodoxy: A Response to Curtis', *British Journal of Sociology*, 46(4), 590–7.

Milne, K. (1995) 'Doing it for Real', *New Statesman and Society*, 3 March, 22–3.

Milne, K. (1996) 'Citizens' Juries are an Attractive, Democratic Idea. But Will Anyone Let Them Decide the Really Big Questions?', *New Statesman and Society*, 30 August, 8–9.

Moore, S. F. (1973) 'Law and Social Change: The Semi-Autonomous Social Field as an Appropriate Subject of Study', *Law and Society Review*, 7, 719–46.

Morgan, J. (1991) *Safer Communities: The Local Delivery of Crime Prevention Through the Partnership Approach*, Standing Conference on Crime Prevention, London: Home Office.

Morgan, P. (1985) *Modelling the Criminal Justice System*, Home Office Planning Unit Paper No. 35, London: Home Office.

Morgan, R. (1989) 'Policing By Consent: Legitimating the Doctrine', in R. Morgan and D. J. Smith (eds.) *Coming to Terms with Policing: Perspectives on Policy*, London: Routledge, 217–34.

Morgan, R. and Smith D. J. (eds.) (1989) *Coming to Terms with Policing: Perspectives on Policy*, London: Routledge.

Morgan, R., Maxwell, G., and Robertson, J. P. (1993) 'Giving Victims a Voice: A New Zealand Experiment', *Howard Journal*, 32(4), 304–21.

Morris, P. and Heal, K. (1981) *Crime Control and the Public*, Home Office Research Study, No. 67, London: HMSO.

Mouffe, C. (1993) *The Return of the Political*, London: Verso.

Moxon, D. (ed.) (1985) *Managing Criminal Justice: A Collection of Papers*, London: HMSO.

Mudd, J. (1984) *Neighbourhood Services*, New Haven: Yale University Press.

Mulgan, G. (1993) *The Power of the Boot: Democratic Dismissal, Competition and Contestability Among the Quangos*, Demos Working Paper, London: Demos.

Murray, C. (1990) *The Emerging British Underclass*, London: Institute for Economic Affairs.

Murray, C. (1994) *Underclass: The Crisis Deepens*, London: Institute for Economic Affairs.

Murray, C. (1995) 'The Next British Revolution', *The Public Interest*, 108, Winter, 3–29.

National Association for the Care and Resettlement of Offenders (1995) *Crime and Social Policy, Report of the Crime and Social Policy Committee*, London: NACRO.

National Association for the Care and Resettlement of Offenders (1989) *Crime Prevention and Community Safety: A Practical Guide for Local Authorities*, London: NACRO.

National Association of Probation Officers (1984) *Draft Policy Statement: Crime Prevention and Reduction Strategies*, London: NAPO.

National Audit Office (1992) *Reducing Crime in London: A Study of the Partnership and Other Methods Used by Five Metropolitan Police Divisions*, London: HMSO.

National Crime Prevention Council (1994) *The Problem of Crime: Proceedings of the Workshop on Community Safety and Crime Prevention*, Ottawa, Ontario: NCPC.

Neill, R. (1994) *Crime Prevention Strategies: The New Zealand Model*, Wellington: Department of Justice.

Nelken, D. (1985) 'Community Involvement in Crime Control', *Current Legal Problems*, 38, 239–67.

Nellis, M. (1995a) 'Probation Values for the 1990s', *Howard Journal*, 34(1), 19–44.

Nellis, M. (1995b) 'Probation Partnerships, Voluntary Action and Community Justice', *Social Policy and Administration*, 29, 91–109.

Newburn, T. and Stanko, E. A. (eds.) (1994) *Just Boys Doing Business? Men, Masculinities and Crime*, London: Routledge.

Newman, O. (1972) *Defensible Space: People and Design in the Violent City*, London: Architectural Press.

Noaks, L., Levi, M., and Maguire, M. (eds.) (1995) *Contemporary Issues in Criminology*, Cardiff; University of Wales Press.

Norton, A. (1994) *International Handbook of Local and Regional Government: A Comparative Analysis of Advanced Democracies*, Aldershot: Edward Elgar.

Offe, C. (1984) *Contradictions of the Welfare State*, London: Hutchinson.

O'Kane, M. (1994) 'Cruising, Abusing or on the Game', *The Guardian*, 23 July.

O'Malley, P. (1992) 'Risk, Power and Crime Prevention', *Economy and Society*, 21(3), 252–75.

O'Malley, P. (1994a) 'Neo-Liberal Crime Control', in D. Chappell and P. Wilson (eds.) *The Australian Criminal Justice System: The Mid 1990s*, Sydney: Butterworths, 283–98.

O'Malley, P. (1994b) 'Responsibility for Crime Prevention: A Response to Adam Sutton', *Australian and New Zealand Journal of Criminology*, 27, 21–4.

O'Malley, P. (1996) 'Indigenous Governance', *Economy and Society*, 25(3), 310–26.

O'Malley, P. and Palmer, D. (1996) 'Post-Keynesian Policing', *Economy and Society*, 25(2), 137–55.

O'Malley, P. and Sutton, A. (eds.) (1996) *Crime Prevention in Australia— Current Issues and Contemporary Problems*, Sydney: The Federation Press.

Ortet-Fabregat, G. and Perez, J. (1992) 'An Assessment of the Attitudes Towards Crime Among Professionals in the Criminal Justice System', *British Journal of Criminology*, 32(2), 193–207.

Osborn, S. and Bright, J. (1989) *Crime Prevention and Community Safety*, London: NACRO.

Osborne, D. and Gaebler, T. (1992) *Reinventing Government: How the Entrepreneurial Spirit is Transforming the Public Sector*, Reading, Massachusetts: Addison-Wesley.

Panitch, L. (1986) *Working Class Politics in Crisis: Essays on Labour and the State*, London: Verso.

Patten, J. (1988) 'Introduction', in T. Hope and M. Shaw (eds.) *Communities and Crime Reduction*, London: HMSO, v–vi.

Pearson, G. (1983) *Hooligan: A History of Respectable Fears*, London: Macmillan.

Pearson, G., Blagg, H., Smith, D., Sampson, A., and Stubbs, P. (1992) 'Crime, Community and Conflict: The Multi-Agency Approach', in Downes, D. (ed.) *Unravelling Criminal Justice*, London: Macmillan, 46–72.

Pease, K. (1994), 'Crime Prevention', in M. Maguire *et al.* (eds.) *The Oxford Handbook of Criminology*, Oxford: Oxford University Press, 659–703.

Peters, A. A. G. (1986) 'Main Currents in Criminal Law Theory', in J. van Dijk *et al.* (eds.) *Criminal Law in Action: An Overview of Current Issues in Western Societies*, Arnhem: Gowda Quint, 19–36.

Philips, D. (1980) ' "A New Engine of Power and Authority": The Institutionalisation of Law-Enforcement in England 1780–1830', in V. A. C. Gatrell, G. Parker, and B. Lenman (eds.) *Crime and the Law: The Social History of Crime in Western Europe Since 1500*, London: Europa, 155–89.

Philips, D. (1989) 'Good Men to Associate and Bad Men to Conspire: Associations for the Prosecution of Felons in England, 1760–1860', in D. Hay and F. Snyder (eds.) *Policing and Prosecution in Britain 1750–1850*, Oxford: Clarendon Press, 113–70.

Philips, A. (1994) 'Pluralism, Solidarity, and Change', in J. Weeks (ed.) *The Lesser Evil and the Greater Good: The Theory and Politics of Social Diversity*, London: Rivers Oram, 235–52.

Pinker, R. (1995) 'Golden Ages and Welfare Alchemists', *Social Policy and Administration*, 29, 78–90.

Pliatzky, L. (1992) 'Quangos and Agencies', *Public Administration*, 70, 555–63.

Plummer, J. (1994) *The Governance Gap: Quangos and Accountability*, York: Joseph Rowntree Foundation.

Pollard, C. (1996) 'Public Safety, Accountability and the Courts, *Criminal Law Review*, 152–61.

Poulantzas, N. (1978) *State, Power, Socialism*, London: Verso.

Powell, W. W. (1991) 'Neither Market Nor Hierarchy: Network Forms of Organization', in G. Thompson *et al.* (eds.) *Markets, Hierarchies and Networks*, London: Sage, 265–76.

Power, A. (1984) *Local Housing Management: A Priority Estates Project Survey*, London: DoE.

Power, A. and Tunstall, R. (1995) *Swimming Against the Tide: Polarization or Progress on 20 Unpopular Council Estates, 1980–1995*, York: Joseph Rowntree Foundation.

Pratt, J. (1989) 'Corporatism: The Third Model of Juvenile Justice', *British Journal of Criminology*, 29, 236–54.

Pyle, D. J. (1995) *Cutting the Costs of Crime*, London: Institute for Economic Affairs.

Quill, D. and Wynne, J. (eds.) (1993) *Victim & Offender Mediation Handbook*, Leeds: Save the Children/West Yorkshire Probation Service.

Raine, J. W. and Willson, M. (1993) *Managing Criminal Justice*, London: Harvester Wheatsheaf.

Rallings, C., Temple, M., and Thrasher, M. (1994) *Community Identity and Participation in Local Democracy*, London: Commission for Local Democracy.

Reiner R. (1991) *Chief Constables*, Oxford: Oxford University Press.

Reiner, R. (1992a) 'Policing a Postmodern Society', *Modern Law Review*, 55(6), 761–81.

Reiner, R. (1992b) *The Politics of the Police* (2nd edition), Hemel Hempstead: Harvester Wheatsheaf.

Reiner, R. (1992c) 'Fin de Siècle Blues: The Police Face the Millennium', *Political Quarterly Review*, 63(1), 37–49.

Reiner, R. (1993) 'Police Accountability: Principles, Patterns and Practices', in R. Reiner and S. Spencer (eds.) *Accountable Policing: Effectiveness, Empowerment and Equity*, London: Institute for Public Policy Research, 1–23.

Reiner, R. and Cross, M. (1991a) 'Beyond Law and Order: Crime and Criminology into the 1990s', in R. Reiner and M. Cross (eds.) *Beyond Law and Order: Criminal Justice Policy and Politics in the 1990s*, Basingstoke: Macmillan, 1–17.

Reiner, R. and Cross, M. (1991b) *Beyond Law and Order; Criminal Justice Policy and Politics in the 1990s*, Basingstoke: Macmillan.

Reiner, R. and Spencer, S. (1993a) 'Conclusions and Recommendations', in R. Reiner and S. Spencer (eds.) *Accountable Policing: Effectiveness, Empowerment and Equity*, London: Institute for Public Police Research, 172–91.

Reiner, R. and Spencer, S. (eds.) (1993b) *Accountable Policing: Effectiveness, Empowerment and Equity*, London: Institute for Public Policy Research.

Reiss, A. J. (1986) 'Why are Communities Important in Understanding Crime?', in A. J. Reiss and M. Tonry (eds.) *Communities and Crime: Crime and Justice a Review of Research, Vol. 8*, Chicago: University of Chicago Press, 1–33.

Reiss, A. J. and Tonry, M. (eds.) (1986) *Communities and Crime: Crime and Justice a Review of Research, Vol. 8*, Chicago: University of Chicago Press.

Rhodes, R. A. W. (1981) *Control and Power in Central-Local Relations*, Farnborough: Gower.

Rhodes, R. A. W. (1985) 'Corporatism, Pay Negotiations and Central Government', *Public Administration*, 63, 287–307.

Rhodes, R. A. W. (1991) 'Policy Networks and Sub-central Government', in G. Thompson *et al.* (eds.) *Markets, Hierarchies and Networks*, London: Sage, 203–14.

Rhodes, R. A. W. (1994) 'The Hollowing Out of the State: The Changing Nature of the Public Service in Britain', *Political Quarterly Review*, 65, 137–51.

Rhodes, R. A. W. (1995) *The New Governance: Governing Without Government*, ESRC State of Britain Seminar II, Swindon: ESRC.

Rhodes, R. A. W. and Marsh, D. (1992) 'Policy Networks in British Politics: A Critique of Existing Approaches', in D. Marsh and R. A. W. Rhodes (eds.) *Policy Networks in British Government*, Oxford; Clarendon Press, 1–26.

Robertson, R. (1995) 'Globalization: Time–Space and Homogeneity and Heterogeneity', in M. Featherstone, S. Lash, and R. Robertson (eds.) *Global Modernities*, London: Sage, 25–44.

Robins, D. (1992) *Tarnished Visions: Crime and Conflict in the Inner City*, Oxford: Oxford University Press.

Rock, P. (1990) *Helping Victims of Crime: The Home Office and the Rise of Victim Support in England and Wales*, Oxford: Oxford University Press.

Rose, N. (1992) 'Governing the Enterprising Self', in P. Heelas and P. Morris (eds.) *The Values of the Enterprise Culture: The Moral Debate*, London: Routledge, 141–64.

Rose, N. (1994) 'Expertise and the Government of Conduct', *Studies in Law, Politics and Society*, 14, 359–97.

Rose, N. (1996) ' "The Death of the Social?": Refiguring the Territory of Government', *Economy and Society*, 25(3), 327–56.

Rose, N. and Miller, P. (1992) 'Political Power Beyond the State: Problematics of Government', *British Journal of Sociology*, 43(2), 173–205.

Rosenbaum, D. P. (1987) 'The Theory and Research Behind Neighbourhood Watch: Is It a Fear and Crime Reduction Strategy', *Crime and Delinquency*, 33(1), 103–35.

Rosenbaum, D. P. (1988a) 'A Critical Eye on Neighbourhood Watch: Does it Reduce Crime and Fear?', in T. Hope and M. Shaw (eds.) *Communities and Crime Reduction*, London: HMSO, 126–45.

Rosenbaum, D. P. (1988b) 'Community Crime Prevention: A Review and Synthesis of the Literature', *Justice Quarterly*, 5(3), 323–93.

Rosenbaum, D. P. (ed.) (1994) *The Challenge of Community Policing: Testing the Promises*, London: Sage.

Roskill (1986) *Report of the Department Committee on Fraud Trials*, London: HMSO.

Russell, D. E. H. (1982) *Rape in Marriage*, New York: Macmillan.

Rutherford, A. (1993) *Criminal Justice and the Pursuit of Decency*, Oxford: Oxford University Press.

Ryan, M. and Ward, T. (1989) *Privatization and the Penal System*, Milton Keynes: Open University Press.

Safe Neighbourhoods Unit (1993) *Crime Prevention on Council Estates*, Department of the Environment, London: HMSO.

Said, E. W. (1988) 'Michael Walzer's "Exodus and Revolution": A Canaanite Reading', in E. W. Said and C. Hitchens (eds.) *Blaming the Victims: Spurious Scholarship and the Palestinian Question*, London: Verso, 161–78.

Sampson, A., Stubbs, P., Smith, D., Pearson, G., and Blagg, H. (1988) 'Crime, Localities and the Multi-Agency Approach', *British Journal of Criminology*, 28, 473–93.

Sampson, A. and Smith, D. (1992) 'Probation and Community Crime Prevention', *Howard Journal*, 31(2), 105–19.

Sampson, A., Smith, D., Pearson, G., Blagg, H., and Stubbs, P. (1991) 'Gender Issues in Inter-Agency Relations: Police, Probation and Social Services', in P. Abbott and C. Wallace (eds.) *Gender, Power and Sexuality*, Basingstoke: Macmillan, 114–32.

Santos, B. de Sousa (1982) 'Law and Community: The Changing Nature of State Power in Late Capitalism', in R. Abel (ed.) *The Politics of Informal Justice, Vol. 1*, New York: Academic Press, 249–66.

Santos, B. de Sousa (1992) 'State, Law and the Community in the World System', *Social and Legal Studies*, 1(2), 131–42.

Sarat, A. (1988) 'The New Formalism in Disputing and Dispute Processing', *Law and Society Review*, 21, 695–715.

Scarman, L. (1981) *The Brixton Disorders, 10–12 April 1981: Report of an Inquiry*, London: HMSO.

Schmitter, P. C. (1974) 'Still the Century of Corporatism?', *Review of Politics*, 36, 85–131.

Schmitter, P. (1985) 'Neo-Corporatism and the State', in W. P. Grant (ed.) *The Political Economy of Corporatism*, Basingstoke: Macmillan, 32–62.

Schmitter, P. (1989) 'Corporatism is Dead! Long Live Corporatism', *Government and Opposition*, 24(1), 54–73.

Scraton, P. (1985) *The State of the Police*, London: Pluto.

Selznick, P. (1995) *Moral Commonwealth: Social Theory and the Promise of Community*, Berkley, California: University of California Press.

Shapiro, M. (1981) *Courts: a Comparative and Political Analysis*, Chicago: University of Chicago Press.

Shapland, J. and Vagg, J. (1988) *Policing By the Public*, London: Routledge.

Shearing, C. (1992) 'The Relation Between Public and Private Policing', in M. Tonry and N. Morris (eds.) *Crime and Justice: A Review of Research: Vol. 15*, Chicago: University of Chicago Press, 399–434.

Shearing, C. (1995) 'Governing Diversity: Explorations in Policing', un-published paper presented to the Socio-Legal Studies Association Conference, University of Leeds, 27–29 March.

Shearing, C. (1996) 'Public and Private Policing', in W. Saulsbury, J. Mott, and T. Newburn (eds.) *Themes in Contemporary Policing*, Plymouth: Latimer Trend & Co, 83–95.

Shearing, C., Farnell, M., and Stenning, P. (1980) *Contract Security in Ontario*, Toronto: University of Toronto Press.

Shearing, C. and Stenning, P. (1981) 'Modern Private Security its Growth and Implications', in M. Tonry and N. Morris (eds.) *Crime and Justice: An Annual Review of Research, Vol. 3*, Chicago: University of Chicago Press, 193–245.

Shearing, C. and Stenning, P. (1983) 'Private Security Implications for Social Control', *Social Problems*, 30(5), 493–506.

Shearing, C. and Stenning, P. (1984) 'From Panopticon to Disney World: The Development of Discipline', in A. Doob and E. Greenspan (eds.) *Perspectives in Criminal Law*, Aurora: Canada Law Book, 335–49.

Shearing, C. and Stenning, P. (1987) 'Reframing Policing', in C. Shearing and P. Stenning (eds.) *Private Policing*, London: Sage, 9–18.

Sheehy, P. (1993) *Inquiry into Police Responsibilities & Rewards*, London: HMSO.

Sheptycki, J. W. E. (1995) 'Transnational Policing and the Making of a Postmodern State', *British Journal of Criminology*, 35(4), 613–35.

Sherman, L. W., Gartin, P. R., and Buerger, M. E. (1989) 'Hot Spots of Predatory Crime: Routine Activities and the Criminology of Place', *Criminology*, 27(1), 27–55,

Shonholtz, R. (1987) 'The Citizens' Role in Justice: Building a Primary Justice and Prevention System at the Neighbourhood Level', *Annals of the American Academy of Political Science*, 494, 42–52.

Silbey, S. and Merry, S. (1986) 'Mediator Settlement Strategies', *Law and Policy*, 8, 7–32.

Simey, M. (1988) *Democracy Rediscovered: A Study in Police Accountability*, London: Pluto Press.

Simon, J. (1987) 'The Emergence of a Risk Society: Insurance, Law and the State', *Socialist Review*, 95, 61–89.

Simon, J. (1988) 'The Ideological Effects of Actuarial Practices', *Law and Society Review*, 22, 772–800.

Skelcher, C. and Stewart, J. (1993) *The Appointed Government of London: A Study for the Association of London Authorities*, Birmingham: INLO-GOV.

Skogan, W. (1988) 'Community Organisations and Crime', in N. Morris and M. Tonry (eds.) *Crime and Justice: An Annual Review of Research*, Chicago: Chicago University Press, 39–78.

Skogan, W. (1990a) *Disorder and Decline*, New York: Free Press.

Skogan, W. (1990b) *The Police and Public in England and Wales: A British Crime Survey Report*, London: HMSO.

Skolnick, J. (1966) *Justice Without Trial*, New York: Wiley.

Smith, D., Paylor, I., and Mitchell, P. (1993) 'Partnerships Between the Independent Sector and the Probation Service', *Howard Journal*, 32(1), 25–39.

Smith, S. (1986) *Crime, Space and Society*, Cambridge: Cambridge University Press.

Snyder, F. (1981) 'Anthropology, Dispute Processes and Law: A Critical Introduction', *British Journal of Law and Society*, 8(2), 141–80.

South, N. (1988) *Policing for Profit*, London: Sage.

South, N. (1995) 'Privatizing Policing in the European Market', *European Sociological Review*, 10(3), 219–33.

Southgate, P., Bucke, T., and Byron, C. (1995) *The Parish Special Constables Scheme*, Home Office Research Study, No. 143, London: Home Office.

Sparks, J. R. (1992a) *Television and the Drama of Crime*, Milton Keynes: Open University Press.

Sparks, J. R. (1992b) 'Reason and Unreason in "Left Realism": Some Problems in the Constitution of the Fear of Crime', in R. Matthews and J. Young (eds.) *Issues in Realist Criminology*, London: Sage, 119–35.

Sparks, J. R. (1994) 'Can Prisons be Legitimate? Penal Politics, Privatization and the Timeliness of an Old Idea', *British Journal of Criminology*, 34, 14–28.

Sparks, J. R. and Bottoms, A. E. (1995) 'Legitimacy and Order in Prisons', *British Journal of Sociology*, 46(1), 45–62.

Sparks. R. (1981a), 'Survey of Victimisation', in M. Tonry and N. Morris (eds.) *Crime and Justice: An Annual Review of Research*, Vol. 3, Chicago: University of Chicago Press, 1–60.

Sparks, R. (1981b) 'Multiple Victimisation: Evidence, Theory and Future Research', *Journal of Criminal Law and Criminology*, 72, 762–78.

Spencer, S. (1985a) *Called to Account: The Case for Police Accountability in England and Wales*, London: National Council for Civil Liberties.

Spencer, S. (1985b) 'The Eclipse of the Police Authority', in B. Fine and R. Millar (eds.) *Policing the Miners' Strike*, London: Lawrence & Wishart, 34–53.

Spitzer, S. (1983) 'The Rationalization of Crime Control in Capitalist Society', in S. Cohen and A. Scull (eds.) *Social Control and the State*, Oxford: Blackwell, 312–33.

Spitzer, S. (1987) 'Security and Control in Capitalist Societies: The Fetishism of Security and the Secret Thereof', in J. Lowman *et al.* (eds.) *Transcarceration: Essays in the Sociology of Social Control*, Aldershot: Gower, 43–58.

Squires, J. (1994) 'Ordering the City: Public Spaces and Political

Participation', in J. Weeks (ed.) *The Lesser Evil and the Greater Good: The Theory and Politics of Social Diversity*, London: Rivers Oram, 79–99.

Stacey, M. (1969) 'The Myth of Community Studies', *British Journal of Sociology*, 20(2), 134–47,

Stanko, E. A. (1990a) 'When Precaution is Normal: A Feminist Critique of Prevention', in L. Gelsthorpe and A. Morris (eds.) *Feminist Perspectives in Criminology*, Milton Keynes: Open University Press, 173–83.

Stanko, E. A. (1990b) *Everyday Violence*, London: Pandora.

Statham, R. and Whitehead, P. (eds.) (1992) *Managing the Probation Service: Issues for the 1990s*, Harlow: Longman.

Steedman, C. (1984) *Policing the Victorian Community: The Formation of English Provincial Police Forces, 1956–80*, London: Routledge.

Steenhuis, D. W. (1986) 'Coherence and Coordination in the Administration of Criminal Justice', in J. van Dijk *et al.* (eds.) *Criminal Law in Action: An Overview of Current Issues in Western Societies*, Arnhem: Gouda Quint, 229–46.

Stenson, K. (1993) 'Community Policing as a Governmental Technology', *Economy and Society*, 22(3), 373–99.

Stenson, K. and Cowell, D. (eds.) (1991) *The Politics of Crime Control*, London: Sage.

Stewart, J. (1996) 'Innovation in Democratic Practice in Local Government', *Policy and Politics*, 24(1), 29–41.

Stewart, J., Kendall, E., and Coote, A. (1994) *Citizens' Juries*, London: IPPR.

Stewart, J. and Walsh, K. (1992) 'Change in the Management of Public Services', *Public Administration*, 70, 499–518.

Storch, R. D. (1975) ' "The Plague of Blue Locusts": Police Reform and Popular Resistance in Northern England, 1840–57', *International Review of Social History*, 20, 61–90.

Storch, R. D. (1976) 'The Police as Domestic Missionary: Urban Discipline and Popular Culture in Northern England, 1850–80', *Journal of Social History*, 9, 481–509.

Strang, H. (1995) 'Replacing Courts with Conferences', *Policing*, 11(3), 212–20.

Stratta, E. (1990) 'A Lack of Consultation', *Policing*, 6(3), 523–49.

Straw, J. (1995a) 'Streets Free of Fear', *The Independent*, 7 September.

Straw, J. (1995b) 'Put the Heart Back into Communities', *The Times*, 8 November.

Straw, J. (1996) 'I Have a Dream—and I Don't Want it Mugged', *The Guardian*, 8 June.

Streeck, W. and Schmitter, P. (1985) *Private Interest Government*, London: Sage.

Tame, C. (1991) 'Freedom, Responsibility and Justice: The Criminology of the New Right', in K. Stenson and D. Cowell (eds.) *The Politics of Crime Control*, London: Sage, 127–145.

Taylor, I. (1981) *Law and Order: Arguments for Socialism*, London: Macmillan.

Taylor, I. (1992) 'Left Realism and the Free market Experiment in Britain', in J. Young and R. Matthews (eds.) *Rethinking Criminology: The Realist Debate*, London: Sage, 95–122.

Taylor, I. (1995a) 'Critical Criminology and the Free Market', in L. Noaks *et al.* (eds.) *Contemporary Issues in Criminology*, Cardiff: University of Wales Press, 400–28.

Taylor, I. (1995b) 'Justice, Social Anxiety and Place: The Condition of England', unpublished paper presented to the 'Democracy and Justice' conference, Brunel University, 13–14 June.

Taylor, I. (1995c) 'Private Homes and Public Others: An Analysis of Talk about Crime in Suburban South Manchester in the Mid-1990s' *British Journal of Criminology*, 35(2), 263–85.

Taylor, I. (1996) 'Fear of Crime, Urban Fortunes and Suburban Social Movements: Some Reflections from Manchester', *Sociology*, 30(2), 317–37.

Taylor, I. , Evans, K., and Fraser, P. (1996) *A Tale of Two Cities: Global Change, Local Feeling and Everyday Life in the North of England, A Study of Manchester and Sheffield*, London: Routledge.

Taylor-Gooby, P. (1994) 'Welfare Outside of the State', in R. Jowell, J. Curtice, L. Brook, and D. Ahrendt (eds.), *British Social Attitudes, the 11th Report*, Aldershot: Dartmouth, 27–35.

Thatcher, M. (1993) *The Downing Street Years*, London: Harper Collins.

Therborn, G. (1985) *Why Some People are More Unemployed Than Others*, London: Verso.

Thompson, E. P. (1977) *Whigs and Hunters*, Harmondsworth: Penguin.

Thompson, G., Frances, J., Levačić, R., and Mitchell, J. (eds.) (1991) *Markets, Hierarchies and Networks*, London: Sage.

Tilley, N. (1992) *Safer Cities and Community Safety Strategies*, Crime Prevention Unit Paper 38, London: Home Office.

Tilley, N. (1993) 'Crime Prevention and the Safer Cities Story', *Howard Journal*, 32(1), 40–57.

Tonry, M. and Farrington, D. (eds.) (1995) *Building a Safer Society: Strategic Approaches to Crime Prevention—Crime and Justice a Review of Research, Vol. 19*, Chicago: University of Chicago Press.

Tonry, M. and Morris, N. (eds.) (1981) *Crime and Justice: An Annual Review of Research, Vol. 3*, Chicago: University of Chicago Press.

Travis, A. (1995), 'Howard Faces Grilling in Commons', *The Guardian*, 19 October.

Trickett, A., Osborn, D. K., Seymour, J., and Pease, K. (1992) 'What is

Different About High Crime Areas?', *British Journal of Criminology*, 32(1), 81–9.

Trickett, A., Ellingworth, D., Farrell, G., and Pease, K. (1995) 'Crime Victimisation in the Eighties: Changes in Area and Regional Inequality', *British Journal of Criminology*, 35(3), 343–59.

Tuck, M. (1988), 'Crime Prevention: A Shift in Concept', *Home Office Research and Planning Unit Research Bulletin, No. 24*, London: Home Office.

Tuck, M. (1991) 'Community and the Criminal Justice System', *Policy Studies*, 12(3), 22–37.

United Nations (1991) *Eighth United Nations Congress on the Prevention of Crime and the Treatment of Offenders*, Havana, 27 August–7 September 1990, New York: United Nations Secretariat.

van den Haag, E. (1975) *Punishing Criminals: Concerning a Very Old and Painful Question*, London: University Press of America.

van den Haag, E. (1985) *Deterring Potential Criminals*, London: Social Affairs Unit.

van Dijk, J. (1995) 'In Search of Synergy: Coalition-Building Against Crime in the Netherlands', *Security Journal*, 6, 7–11.

van Dijk, J., Haffmans, C., Ruter, F., and Schutte, J. (eds.) (1986) *Criminal Law in Action: An Overview of Current Issues in Western Societies*, Arnhem: Gouda Quint.

Walker, N. (1993) 'The International Dimension', in R. Reiner and S. Spencer (eds.) *Accountable Policing: Effectiveness, Empowerment and Equity*, London: Institute for Public Policy Research, 113–71.

Walklate, S. (1991) 'Victims, Crime Prevention and Social Control', in R. Reiner and M. Cross (eds.) *Beyond Law and Order: Criminal Justice Policy and Politics in the 1990s*, Basingstoke: Macmillan, 202–22.

Walklate, S. (1995) *Gender and Crime*, Hemel Hempstead: Harvester Wheatsheaf.

Wall, D. (1994) 'The Ideology of Internal Recruitment: The Selection of Chief Constables and Changes within the Tripartite Arrangement', *British Journal of Criminology*, 34, 322–38.

Walzer, M. (1983) *Spheres of Justice*, New York: Basic Books.

Walzer, M. (1990) 'The Communitarian Critique of Liberalism, *Political Theory*, 18, 6–23.

Walzer, M. (1993) 'Exclusion, Injustice, and the Democratic State, *Dissent*, Winter, 55–64.

Weale, S. (1993) 'DIY Justice Raises Community Spirit', *The Guardian*, 10 August.

Weale, S. (1995) 'Price of Fame Proves too High for Lumb Lane', *The Guardian*, 27 May.

Weatheritt, M. (1983) 'Community Policing: Does it Work and How Do

We Know? A Review of Research', in T. Bennett (ed.) *The Future of Policing*, Cropwood Papers, 15, Cambridge: Institute of Criminology.

Weatheritt, M. (1986) *Innovations in Policing*, London: Croom Helm.

Weatheritt, M. (1993a) 'Community Policing', in H. Butcher, A. Glen, P. Henderson and J. Smith (eds.) *Community and Public Policy*, London: Pluto, 124–38.

Weatheritt, M. (1993b) 'Measuring Police Performance: Accounting or Accountability', in R. Reiner and S. Spencer (eds.) *Accountable Policing: Effectiveness, Empowerment and Equity*, London: Institute for Public Policy Research, 24–54.

Weber, M. (1966) *On Law and Economy in Society*, M. Rheinstein (ed.), Cambridge, Massachusetts: Harvard University Press.

Webster, C. (1994) *Youth Crime, Victimisation and Racial Harassment: The Keighley Crime Survey*, Ilkley: Centre for Research in Applied Community Studies, Bradford and Ilkley Community College.

Weeks, J. (ed.) (1994) *The Lesser Evil and the Greater Good: The Theory and Politics of Social Diversity*, London: Rivers Oram.

Weiner, J. M. (1990) *Reconstructing the Criminal: Culture, Law and Policy in England, 1830–1914*, Cambridge: Cambridge University Press.

Whitaker, G. P. (1980) 'Coproduction: Citizen Participation in Service Delivery', *Public Administration Review*, 40(3), 240–6.

Wieviorka, M. (1995) *The Arena of Racism*, London: Sage.

Wikström, P-O. H. (1991) *Urban Crime, Criminals and Victims: The Swedish Experience in an Anglo-American Comparative Perspective*, New York: Springer-Verlag.

Wiles, P. (1992), 'Ghettoization in Europe', *European Journal on Criminal Policy and Criminal Research*, 1(1), 52–69.

Willemse, H. (1994) 'Developments in Dutch Crime Prevention', *Crime Prevention Studies*, 2, 33–47.

Willetts, D. (1992) *Modern Conservatism*, London: Penguin.

Williams, F. and Pillinger, J. (1996) 'New Thinking on Social Policy Research into Inequality, Poverty and Social Exclusion', in J. Millar and J. Bradshaw (eds.) *Social Welfare Systems; Towards a Research Agenda*, Bath: Centre for the Analysis of Social Policy/ESRC, 1–32.

Williams, J., Dunning, S., and Murphy, P. (1988) 'Professional Football and Crowd Violence in England: The Case for a Community Approach', in T. Hope and M. Shaw (eds.) *Communities and Crime Reduction*, London: HMSO, 164–79.

Williams, J. and Taylor, R. (1994) 'Boys Keep Swinging: Masculinity and Football Culture in England', in T. Newburn and E. A. Stanko (eds.) *Just Boys Doing Business? Men, Masculinities and Crime*, London: Routledge, 214–33.

Wilmott, P. (ed.) (1987) *Policing and the Community*, London: Policy Studies Institute.

Wilson, J. Q. and Kelling, G. (1982) 'Broken Windows: The Police and Neighbourhood Safety', *The Atlantic Monthly*, March, 29–37.

Wilson, J. Q. and Kelling, G. (1989) 'Making Neighbourhoods Safe', *The Atlantic Monthly*, February, 46–52.

Woolf, H. and Tumim, S. (1991) *Prison Disturbances April 1990: Report of an Inquiry*, Cm 1456, London: HMSO.

Wright, M. (1991) *Justice for Victims and Offenders*, Milton Keynes: Open University Press.

Wright, M. and Galaway, B. (eds.) (1989) *Mediation and Criminal Justice: Victims, Offenders and Community*, London: Sage.

Yllö, K. and Bograd, M. (eds.) (1988) *Feminist Perspectives on Wife Abuse*, Beverly Hills, California: Sage.

Yngvesson, B. (1993) 'Local People, Local Problems, and Neighbourhood Justice: The Discourse of "Community" in San Francisco Community Boards', in S. E. Merry and N. Milner (eds.) *The Possibility of Popular Justice*, Michigan: University of Michigan Press, 379–400.

Young, J. (1986) 'The Failure of Criminology', in R. Matthews and J. Young (eds.) *Confronting Crime*, London: Sage, 4–30.

Young, J. (1988) 'Risk of Crime and Fear of Crime: A Realistic Critique of Survey-Based Assumptions', in M. Maguire and J. Pointing (eds.) *Victims of Crime: A New Deal?*, Milton Keynes: Open University Press, 164–76.

Young, J. (1991) 'Left Realism and the Priorities of Crime Control', in K. Stenson and D. Cowell (eds.) *The Politics of Crime Control*, London: Sage, 146–60.

Young, J. (1992) 'Ten Points of Realism', in J. Young and R. Matthews (eds.) *Rethinking Criminology: The Realist Debate*, London: Sage, 24–68.

Young, J. and Matthews, R. (eds.) (1992) *Rethinking Criminology: The Realist Debate*, London: Sage.

Young, P. (1987) *The Prison Cell*, London: Adam Smith Institute.

Yuval-Davis, N. (1992) 'Women and Citizens', in A. Ward, J. Gregory, and N. Yuval-Davis (eds.) *Women and Citizenship in Europe*, Stoke: Trentham Books.

Zedner, L. (1994) 'Reparation and Retribution: Are they Reconcilable?', *Modern Law Review*, 57, 228–50.

Zehr, H. (1990) *Changing Lenses: A New Focus For Criminal Justice*, London: Metanoia.

Zhang, S. X. (1995) 'Measuring Shame in an Ethnic Context', *British Journal of Criminology*, 35(2), 248–62.

Index

Note 'fn' denotes that entry appears in the footnotes.